Music's Making

Music's Making

The Poetry of Music, the Music of Poetry

MICHAEL CHERLIN

Published by State University of New York Press, Albany

© 2024 State University of New York

All rights reserved

Printed in the United States of America

No part of this book may be used or reproduced in any manner whatsoever without written permission. No part of this book may be stored in a retrieval system or transmitted in any form or by any means including electronic, electrostatic, magnetic tape, mechanical, photocopying, recording, or otherwise without the prior permission in writing of the publisher.

Links to third-party websites are provided as a convenience and for informational purposes only. They do not constitute an endorsement or an approval of any of the products, services, or opinions of the organization, companies, or individuals. SUNY Press bears no responsibility for the accuracy, legality, or content of a URL, the external website, or for that of subsequent websites.

For information, contact State University of New York Press, Albany, NY
www.sunypress.edu

Library of Congress Cataloging-in-Publication Data

Name: Cherlin, Michael, author.
Title: Music's making : the poetry of music, the music of poetry / Michael Cherlin.
Description: Albany : State University of New York Press, [2024]. | Includes bibliographical references and index.
Identifiers: LCCN 2023055104 | ISBN 9781438498454 (hardcover : alk. paper) | ISBN 9781438498478 (ebook)
Subjects: LCSH: Music—Philosophy and aesthetics. | Music and philosophy. | Music and literature. | Music theory—Philosophy. | Music—Religious aspects—Judaism.
Classification: LCC ML3845 .C449 2024 | DDC 780.1—dc23/eng/20231213
LC record available at https://lccn.loc.gov/2023055104

10 9 8 7 6 5 4 3 2 1

For my teachers

It cannot be received at second hand. Truly speaking, it is not instruction, but provocation, that I can receive from another soul.

—Ralph Waldo Emerson, "The Divinity School Address"

Rabbi Akiva says: *Sing every day, sing every day.*

—Sanhedrin 99b

Contents

Foreword   ix
   Phil Ford

Preface   xv

Introduction: Remembering David Benjamin Lewin   1

Part I

1. Music as Fiction   9

2. That Which Emerges out of Itself, That Which Is Created   13

3. Moving toward *Middle Voice*   25

4. Liminal Space   37

5. An Ethics of Intersubjectivity   47

6. Character, Canon, and Poetic Influence   65

Part II

7. Phrase as Musical Event, Wave as Musical Metaphor, and the Silence of Musical Space   113

8. Metric, Ametric, Fractured Meter, and a Sea of Silence   147

9. Smooth Space, Striated Space: Nomadic Space, Agrarian Space   177

10. What Repetition Can Do: Time's Arrows   197

11. The Horizontal and the Vertical: Worldly and Spiritual   217

Notes   243

Bibliography   267

Index   275

Foreword

Everythingology

PHIL FORD

Michael Cherlin has forgotten more about music, music theory, poetry, fiction, literary theory, philosophy, and religion than I (and probably you) will ever learn. You might say that *Music's Making: The Poetry of Music, the Music of Poetry* is a crystallization of that great learning, but that would put too much emphasis on the thinginess of this book, and of thinking itself. For thinking is not merely a means to the end of its "products"— books and essays and whatnot. In Michael's case, at least, thinking is a practice just as meditation is a practice, autotelic and self-justifying, that leaves traces of itself in tangible objects while transcending them. This book is the sediment of a lifetime's practice of aesthetic and philosophical contemplation.

Music's Making is therefore "theoretical" in the sense that a work by Slavoj Žižek is: one reads it to arrive at a certain way of looking at things, peculiar to the author but generalizable to far-flung disciplines and literatures. The point of coherence around which such works are formed is, ultimately, the writer himself, not his subject matter. But this kind of self-assertion will come off as presumptuous to a certain sort of academic critic: what's so special about *your* point of view?

In this situation, the imperializing and oracular tone customary to high-end cultural theory can prove useful. Cultural theory has always been a performance art, and successful acts of cultural theory call for an egomaniacal performance style of pretended omniscience and bullying obscurity delivered *de haut en bas* in a stream of totalizing statements. Without such a performance, we would see that it's just someone making it all up. Not that there's anything wrong with making it all up: that's what artists do, after all. But we are unwilling to concede to scholars the prerogatives of art unless they act the part. The voice of this book is gentle, humble, and good-humored, and without the usual displays of artistic temperament to cue them, readers might miss what Michael is up to.

This is what I think he is up to. He is sharing his practice with us, inviting us to follow the movements of his mind across artworks and ideas so that we may arrive not at products of thought, but at events of thinking, namely our own. The field on which such events are constituted is the domain of *everythingology*.

In the Platform Sutra, Huineng wrote, "originally, there is not one single thing." He is speaking of the cosmos as a whole, but he was not speaking as scientific moderns would about the universe. He is not saying, "first there was nothing and then there was a Big Bang, which produced matter and forces." For Chan (Zen) Buddhists like Huineng, as for Jewish Kabbalists, the mysterious emergence of Something out of Nothing, the Manifest from the Unmanifest, is happening at every moment. Everything is just as you see it—different kinds of things, the chair you're in, the trees outside, you and the people around you—and also, in that very moment, everything is quite other, identities and particularities gone, lost in their interdependency.

We might guess that "not one single thing" means nothing, but taken from another angle it means *everything*. A cosmos in which there is not one single thing is a cosmos that is itself the thing, indivisible.[1] When we come to see our world under the aspect of "not one single thing"—no boundaries or distinctions, no differentiation of things into their specialized categories—the world stands before us radically unified. Whether that unity be resolved in One or Nothing is a matter of dispute. But either way, mystical and esoteric writing is devoted to understanding the world in that other aspect, which Duns Scotus called the *Unus Mundus*. And because the *Unus Mundus* is also the very world you see right now, esoteric thinking always finds its way back to the everyday world of chairs and trees and people. And yet in their journey from here to there and back to here again (always understanding that, in some paradoxical way, there *is* here), esoteric thinkers return to the everyday world to find it transformed.

Esoteric thinking takes the shape of its activity: a series of travels out and back again. Thus the esoteric habit of conceiving of philosophy not as a collection of things (thinkers, texts, ideas) but as a practice. A cosmos of "not one single thing" is the kind of idea that entails action on the part of the reader, as Pierre Hadot suggests ancient philosophy demanded of its practitioners. It is not the kind of idea that sits inert on the page, awaiting the reader to inscribe it in some book of memory and carry it away with them for future use. As Thelonious Monk once said to Steve Lacy, "you've got to dig it to <u>dig</u> it, you dig?"

So dig:

> A theory of music is a theory of life in that the experiential flow of living is a concomitant of the experiential flow of music as is the experiential flow of music a concomitant of the experiential flow of life. Scholars may debate whether music is a branch of bio-chemistry or bio-chemistry is a branch of music. Scholars of religion may place both, music and bio-chemistry into the sphere of religious studies. Good cooks may insist that all three, music, bio-chemistry, and religious studies, are subsumed under the heading of food understood as life sustaining.

This is an "unattributed note on an index card" with which Michael begins the second half of this book, and it is as good an example as any of this book's distinctly esoteric style of thought.

To dig this note I have to get involved with it; I have to do something. So I begin my activity by considering the opening sentence: "A theory of music is a theory of life in that the experiential flow of living is a concomitant of the experiential flow of music as is the experiential flow of music a concomitant of the experiential flow of life." My mind is invited to compare the experiential flows of music and life (an intriguing notion right there) but also to reason from that comparison the possibility that music theory could also be life theory—a kind of everythingology.

Everythingology is my made-up word for the impossible subject of esoteric styles of thinking: everything in a world for which there is not one single thing. Everythingology is a slippery and elusive discipline. It embraces all that life embraces—music, food, religion, and so on—yet it finds that such elements constantly swap places with one another in their support of the whole, each taking turns to claim mastery of the others. Thus do the next three sentences of the unattributed note ramble through a few combinatorial possibilities: music as biochemistry, biochemistry as music, religion as the sum of both, and then cooking as the sum of all—after all, even a theologian has to eat. But if this meditation had continued (here and elsewhere we are tacitly invited to continue it ourselves, pursuing our practice), we could have pointed out that even cooks have to dance, and so we find our way back to music. Round and round they go, the procession of arts and their -ologies, their divisions generating the heat of contention that fuels mainstream intellectual life. But the esoteric thinker perceives that the domain of everythingology they circle is one in which all human thought, feeling, and expression resolve into a great wholeness in whose unity apparent divisions shape-shift and even dissolve.

How can human beings find their way in such a domain? Not through the specialized mental habits of the academy, but through an intuitive leap into a wholeness that comprises both self and other. Here we see the significance Michael's notion of the "middle voice," a mode of grammar whereby subject and object are fused and, in this book, a musical and existential principle as well.

There is an insight at the heart of *Music's Making* about music as a representation of the fundamental mystery of life. No, not a representation of it but an instance of it, something consubstantial with life itself. The middle voice is a way of figuring music heard from the standpoint of that mystery. Put differently, *Music's Making* articulates a nondual theory of music listening. If I say that I am listening to a piece of music, that is a dualistic (and thoroughly natural) way for me to think about it. "I," a subject, am listening to "music," an object, something set against me. Yet the middle-voiced music listening that Michael theorizes constitutes an intimacy where such firm positions melt away. The occultist Robert Anton Wilson described this nondual state by saying that in it, "mind and its contents are functionally identical": "If I am so fortunate as to be listening to the Hammerklavier sonata, the only correct answer, if you ask me suddenly, 'Who are you?' would be to hum the Hammerklavier. For, with music of that quality, one is hypnotized into rapt attention: there is no division between 'me' and 'my experience.'"

Wilson's voice reaches us from an unknown land, which is, again, the domain of everythingology. His notions are strange to us, yet they fascinate, drawing us into that zone, which, like the Zone in Tarkovsky's *Stalker*, is a weird and miraculous territory that we never enter the same way twice. So again, how do we get there? The same way you get to Carnegie Hall: practice. Your practice starts now, with this book. Who knows what put it in your hands, but whatever it is, take it as the intervention of some benevolent spirit—perhaps the same spirit that gently herded me into Michael's 1993 seminar on Brahms's chamber music, where I met both my future wife and my future *Doktorvater*. (A good day's work for that spirit, I can tell you.) Thirty years on, I am sometimes tempted to congratulate myself on having attained a certain originality of thought . . . but then I read *Music's Making* and realize that all the best things in my bag I got out of his.

Preface

Practice, Practice, Practice

There is an old joke where a tourist in New York City asks a stranger, "How do I get to Carnegie Hall?" The stranger replies: "Practice." Thanks to the efforts of Isaac Stern and others, Carnegie Hall is still there, and one still has to practice to get there.

Humans, evidently, aren't the only ones who practice music. Carl Safina, who writes engagingly about the songs of birds and the songs of whales, provides us with a thought that will get us going.

> Earning control over sound requires practice for babies, for musicians, and for birds, too. The incentive for practicing over and over again is that, as with a child or a musician getting it right, birds' brains give them satisfying does of dopamine and natural opioids when they do. The neurotransmitter dopamine is involved in both human speech and birdsong. Dopamine is both an enabler and a motivator. In songbirds, singing causes the brain to release dopamine. People who lose the neurons that make dopamine are referred to as having Parkinson's disease, and Parkinsonian patients who receive high-dose dopamine-replacement therapy occasionally develop compulsive humming and singing . . . And because dopamine is a kind of "feel good" chemical, we can answer the age-old question of whether birds sing because they are happy. Simply, birds are happy because they sing, *and* they sing because they are happy.[2]

Musical practice is verbal and substantive alike, a verb hiding behind a noun, a noun covering its verbal coming-into-being. Musical practice in all of its senses is a summoning of the past into the ongoing of a present. Calling to mind the ram's horn's call at Rosh Hashanah, Roseanna Warren writes, "To practice for tomorrow means letting the past surge through."[3] Within a musical work, within a musical practice, within the practicing that leads to musical expression, it is always this way: music is a means of letting the past surge through.

Music in its infinitely varied forms plays an essential role in most cultures; it is integral to our ways of self-defining, integral to our customs and our faiths. Grace Schulman captures this sense in her poem "Songs of My Fathers." " 'What is the faith?' I asked my grandmother, / . . . / 'It is tenacity. The will to live. To sing.' "[4] Among its many qualities, music is a constituent of our well-being, a stimulant to biochemical processes necessary to our mental and emotional health. And to make music requires practice. Hearing music well also requires practice, and both the well-practiced musician and the well-practiced listener, often one and the same, evolve through effort and grace over time. The practice of music is not isolated from our other human qualities and aspirations, the cognitive and emotional constituents of our being. A book about music, that is only about music, misses the point, unless we mean "only about music" to encompass just about anything we can think of. Phil Ford, in his preface to *Music's Making*, writes that the book invites "the possibility that music theory could also be life theory—a kind of everythingology." So be it.

In Prospect, In Retrospect

What kind of book would I like mine to be? Before retiring from academia in the spring of 2016, I spent nearly forty years studying and teaching various aspects of music theory. Like analytic philosophy, most scholarly publication in the field of music theory is read only by specialists in the field, a field that like others in the academy is subdivided into highly technical subspecialties so that a very few, even among music theorists, can or do read widely across the field's subdisciplines. Without special training, a high percentage of the work in music theory cannot be read by performing musicians, let alone the musical audiences. Advanced music theory isn't quantum mechanics, but for most listeners it might as well be.

Now, there is nothing intrinsically wrong with specialists writing for specialists. On the contrary, highly technical research that is meant to be read by a limited audience is as important in the humanities as it is in the sciences. Moreover, if one works in a research institution, highly technical research is required if one is to advance in the field. And after all, one has to make a living. There is a place for highly technical speculative work in the academy. But that's not the kind of book I would like mine to be.

And while it might be nice to write the "Harry Potter" of music scholarship, movie rights and all, so that in my final years I'd be rolling in cash, that's not in the cards either. Lite entertainment too has its place in the world, and pulling it off successfully is more difficult than many of those who do "serious work" might suppose. It's just that that's not the kind of book I'd like mine to be.

I would like my book to be personal, an individual human voice speaking to other individuals in a shared language that both opens up and closes in our worlds. Words that point to music are one way of saying (or being) about yet another way of saying (or being). When meaningful, the ebb and flow of words or music leave a trace that touches us and by that touch changes our way of being in the world, what we make of it, how we're made by it.

Publishers typically ask prospective authors to describe the proposed book's significance to the field. The query had me stumped as I questioned myself, just what is "the field." The title, *Music's Making: The Poetry of Music, the Music of Poetry*, is a good indication, so far as it goes. The book, to a large extent, is about what we might characterize as the musical aspects of poetry as they interact with the poetic aspects of music, as such bridging literary theory and music theory. But one of the book's central perspectives claims "music as fiction." Like our other modes of fiction, music is among the ways through which we know and shape ourselves through our responses to and interactions with other selves. Our responses to and interactions with other selves brings me to a consideration of ethics. What we might call "the ethics of music making" is also part of what the book is about.

Music, along with theater and literature more generally, more than unfolding in passing time (the clock time of a musical or theatrical performance, the time it takes to read and absorb a novel or a poem), actively shapes our sense of time and space. A significant concomitant of that shaping is the role of memory: remembering where we've been in the context of a song or poem, remembering how that song or poem remembers and transfigures other songs or poems; musical memory in that evanescent moment of the present is cultural memory and personal memory, and that too is what *Music's Making* is about.

Both of my previous books—*Schoenberg's Musical Imagination* (Cambridge University Press, 2007) and *Varieties of Musical Irony* (Cambridge University Press, 2017)—approached their topics from a broad-based humanistic perspective. In both, as much as possible, I tried to avoid the highly specialized language typical of advanced works in music theory. Nonetheless, both assumed a fairly good command of music-theoretical constructs; both included extensive, graphic musical examples; and both included technical analyses of the studied musical compositions. The present book, much more so than its predecessors, is broadly humanistic in its scope and references. It draws extensively on work done in philosophy and literary criticism, and only secondarily (yet still substantially) on the scholarship of musicologists and music theorists. The poetry referenced in the book's title includes the poetry of scripture, and although I am ecumenical in that regard, that I come out of a Jewish heritage will be evident to anyone reading the book. Jewish studies, the imaginative stories of the Hebrew Bible, and the radically transformative receptions of those stories in Kabbalah and Rabbinic traditions complement and augment the other sources for the book's central ideas.

Naturally, I hope that musicians and scholars of music will find the book of interest. Yet the intended reader is not necessarily versed in the ongoing discussions in musicology or music theory. The book might be described as being written for the curious intellectual—someone who reads widely in the humanities, someone who has more than a passing interest in literature as well as the other arts, someone who is an open-minded listener interested in a wide range of musical experiences.

The book is without notated musical examples, and I have tried to avoid technical language as much as possible throughout. Those modest technical terms that I use are explained either within the primary text or in an endnote. All of the musical works that I discuss are easily available through YouTube or various music streaming services. Just as a book of literary criticism expects the reader to have read or be about to read the literature being discussed, this book implicitly asks the reader to listen along with me. For musicians, or anyone highly literate in the world of music, much of the music will already be familiar. Hardly anyone, if anyone, will be familiar with all of the music, and so gaining that familiarity (an open-ended process in any case) will be part of experiencing the book.

Without doubt, the biggest departure from my previous publications, in books and in journals, is the highly personal nature of this book. As pre-publication readers have noticed, *Music's Making* is part memoir (and part everything else). At more than one point in the book, I cite Emerson's observation: "The deeper [the scholar] dives into his privatest, secretest presentiment, to his wonder he finds, this is the most acceptable, most public, and universally true. The people delight in it; the better part of every man feels, This is my music; this is myself."[5] The personal asides that weave through the book's texture are always meant in that spirit.

Like any responsible scholar, in preparing this book, I have read (and listened) as widely and deeply as my capacity will allow. Like almost any book, this one reflects the extended moment of its creation. Another extended moment might have resulted in another range of values and attributions. Point in case: the vast majority of philosophical writings cited and developed in *Music's Making* are European (Husserl, Heidegger, Merleau-Ponty, Levinas, and Deleuze, to name those most prevalent). All of these are here for good reasons, guiding and goading me toward the imaginative space that fills this volume. Yet I might have developed similar if not identical ideas about middle voice, ethics of responsibility, emergence, transformation, and many of the other concerns of this book, drawing on the rich traditions of American philosophy (John Dewey, Alfred North Whitehead, Josiah Royce, Susanne Langer, Nelson Goodman, Richard Rorty, and others). My reader will misunderstand me if it's understood, by implication, that the absence of this tradition indicates their irrelevance. Another book might have ignored the Europeans and magnified and developed the American tradition. It is just so with the music and poetry that I draw upon throughout. As with the philosophical traditions, these are the music and poetry that guided and goaded me. Yet other poets and other music might have filled this book, and I would welcome other books that would augment, or perhaps challenge, what I have written, drawing on alternative traditions, alternative musics and poetries.

This last point, that I value and welcome other perspectives, other life experiences different from and even at odds with my own, needs emphasis. This book, despite the diverse sources and voices within its purview, remains Eurocentric and moreover dominated by the voices of white males (although in some circles, Jews don't qualify: who's white depends on your politics). Seventy-six years old, as I write, I am the child of immigrants whose world was largely shaped by Yiddish culture, which is to say a culture that fused European values with those derived from Judaism in diaspora. To pretend otherwise would be dishonest. I write about the world I know best. It's not that I am without experience in music not adequately addressed. At one point in the book, I reflect on my experience playing saxophone in a soul music group based in Brooklyn, New York, for more than four years, from 1969 through 1972. I cherish that experience and still love many of the songs that we played regularly, but I cannot claim expertise in the scholarship the addresses that music and its times. During the early part of that same period, I studied tenor saxophone with Joe Henderson, an African American who was one of the most celebrated tenor sax players of his generation. During those years, I was immersed in the New York jazz scene, lucky enough to see performances by Miles Davis, John Coltrane, Sonny Rollins, Thelonious Monk, Charlie Mingus, Ornette Coleman, and many other leading jazz performers of those times. I make reference to some of that music in the book, but I cannot claim to be a scholar of the formidable literature devoted to jazz, both technical and concerned with its societal aspects. It is for this reason that these musical traditions, while mentioned in passing, are not given the same focus as the scholarship, music, and poetry that are predominant. The same could be said about many other musical and poetic traditions.

I can only reflect on my times, my experience, well aware of my own limitations, not the least of which is imposed by a sense of running out of time, well aware that "we strut and fret our hour upon the stage and then are no more." Although in Shakespeare's case, as is true for many others, the words and deeds linger on. Why else write a book at my age?

We change, and the words and deeds we leave behind change without our leave. It would be a mistake to assume that Monday's declaration still holds on Tuesday, and an equal mistake to assert otherwise. Human lives are inconclusive; our books too.

I hope I do not misstate in saying that "objectivity" is an intrinsic and emphatic value of mathematics and mathematically-based science. The main streams of music theory, at least during my lifetime, have been informed by such objectivity, whether through mimicking physical science or otherwise.

In objective prose, the personal "I" has little to no place. To the degree that scholarship on music, or the other arts, shares the assumptions of math-based science, the personal "I" is inappropriate, banished from academic publications. The author's voice pretends to vanish, hiding behind the objectivity of the prose (it's there all along, anyway). In any case, that is not the kind of book I want this to be. There is a place for detached, disinterested scholarship, but this is not that place.

For most readers, I assume, the alternative to objectivity is subjectivity; in our case, a subjective account of musical experience. This book challenges that assumption, exploring a *middle voice*. It argues that dividing the world into subjects and objects is not suitable toward our ends.

Synopsis: Guide through the Labyrinth

A reader of the manuscript that became this book suggested that an overview of the whole would be helpful, a guided tour of what to expect. Other readers, like myself, generally prefer to see where a book is taking us as we get there. Readers of the latter disposition often skip the part of the introduction that outlines the chapters to come. We might liken the two sorts of readers to two kinds of persons visiting a museum for the first time. There are those who prefer proceeding with a map in hand, a pathway to guide them through the labyrinth of rooms, a guide toward finding, for example, an anticipated portrait by Rembrandt. An alternative is to wander haphazardly or at least without a floorplan before us, so that the portrait by Rembrandt, as we happen upon it, may take us by surprise. The latter sort of reader might want to skip or skim through the guide that follows. But here it is for those who like to see where they are going.

Music's Making comprises two large parts; in the story that I tell, they function much like separate books of a larger novel. The first book develops global attitudes toward music: emergence out of self, hearing *through*, middle-voice, liminal space, an ethics of intersubjectivity, character, and canon among them. The second book, to a large degree, might be characterized as a book in search of metaphors, figurative language toward understanding music's endlessly variegated shapings of time-space.

I begin with a homage to David Benjamin Lewin. Here, I summarize some of Lewin's most central ideas about music, ideas principally expressed through mathematical modeling, ideas that *Music's Making* will reformulate into poetic terms. Two ideas that are implicit, although not explicit, in Lewin's theoretical writings are developed extensively in this book, "middle voice" and liminal space (both to be described in what follows). At the outset of this study, I thought of middle voice and liminal space as two discrete, fully separate topics. As my work has evolved, more and more I have come to realize that limen and middle voice are intimately related, perhaps two approaches toward the same end. As the book progresses, Lewin's voice recedes to the background and reemerges time and again as his work intersects with and informs the varied topics that comprise the whole.

The second section of the first half is titled "Music as Fiction." Fictions are the stories that shape us as individuals, as members of a social or ethnic group, as instances of a common humanity, and as creatures who inhabit a planet shared with other creatures in an all-encompassing environment. "Music as Fiction" places music within this universal need, mutually shaped by us and shaping us, interacting with our other modes of self-creation, but not reducible to those other modes.

"That Which Emerges out of Itself, That Which is Created" follows. The idea of emergence out of self is exemplified through the creation story in the *Bṛhadāranyaka Upanishad*. The idea of creation out of some primordial stuff is exemplified through the two creation stories in the Hebrew Bible: the six days of creation preceded by the primordial *tohu-va-bohu*, and the shaping of Adam out of clay. Neoplatonism provides a second example of creation as emergence, one that impacted religious experience through the Medieval period and beyond, and that lies at the basis of the Schenkerian concept of tonal harmony as developed in the early twentieth century. Neoplatonic thought is among the ideas that stimulate that varied body of Jewish speculation known as Kabbalah, and the Kabbalistic image of the *sefirot*, the ten points of emanation from Divinity, becomes the locus for three models of human seeing and knowing: following, mirroring, and seeing/knowing "through." We close our consideration of emergence versus creation with an extended excursus on the juxtaposition of "high and low" in Jewish thought, including a somewhat more extended consideration of the music of Gustav Mahler.

The principal focus of the next major section of *Music's Making* is the concept of "middle voice" as developed in the discourse of philosophical phenomenology. As a grammatical construct, middle voice is found in a number of languages including Sanskrit and ancient Greek. Middle-voiced verbs work in ways similar to reflexive verbs in English and other languages. I give the common example, "I wash myself," where agent (doing the washing) and patient (receiving the washing) are one and the same. I introduce the section with an apposite passage from Jacques Derrida and then trace the development of middle voice as well as a cluster of related topics through the writings of Edmund Husserl, Maurice Merleau-Ponty, and Don Ihde. The section closes with a discussion of Martin Heidegger's concept of *Gelassenheit*, a state of serenity or equanimity, a *releasement* that entails letting go of willfulness, allowing one to step outside the subject/object dichotomy.

The subversion of subject/object opposition is a global concern of *Music's Making*. Phil Ford, in his review of the manuscript for SUNY Press, accurately described this aspect of middle voice as the "axial idea" of *Music's Making*. I prompt the reader in that direction from time to time as the book progresses, but even where not explicit, the middle-voiced experience of making and perceiving music is meant to inform the whole of *Music's Making*.

More so than any other philosopher considered, the writings of Emmanuel Levinas have had a profound influence on the ways I think about music. Levinas is especially important in providing an ethics that subsumes my middle-voiced approach, placing it into an all-embracing metaphysics. Liminal states of experience are central to Levinas's philosophy, and before going on to an exposition of Levinas's thought I devote a section of the book to an exploration of liminal time-space.

Our exploration of liminal space opens with Paul Valéry's remarkable aphorism: "A poem: a long-drawn hesitation between sound and sense." Liminal space is the space of thresholds, all that is in between settled states and places of being. When the unsettledness of an in-between is dilated, the effect can be uncanny, states of being studied in the early twentieth century by Sigmund Freud, and states of being inhabited in the stories of Franz Kafka and in the music of Arnold Schoenberg. In studying liminality, I draw upon literary theory, poetry, and music.

The thought of Emmanuel Levinas is given extended treatment. For Levinas, responsibility to the other, always understood as another human being, is foundational and paramount. Against the grain of Western metaphysics, Levinas places this responsibility as existentially prior to Being, more fundamental than ontology. Levinas abhorred all totalizing thought, emphasizing the open-ended relationship of each unique human to each unique other. For Levinas, it is just this ability to respond to another that allows us, each of us as individuals, to avoid a deadening self-totalization. Along similar lines, Levinas lauds the ongoing quality of diachrony and disparages the totalizing quality of synchrony. We subsequently return to these concerns in another guise in the context of our discussion of rhetorical tropes within the writings of Harold Bloom and John Hollander. What we have characterized as liminal space, threshold experiences, gains new perspectives in Levinas's thought. Levinas's idiosyncratic idea of "proximity" is a remarkable case in point, where "proximity," fundamental to any ongoing human relationship, "is not a state, a repose, but a restlessness . . . outside of the place of rest . . . proximity does not congeal into a structure." In opening Levinas's thought to the makings of music, I expand his notion of engagement with the other to include ways of "saying" that are non-verbal, music and the visual arts included.

The final extended section of the first half of *Music's Making* is devoted to the thought of Harold Bloom. Like David Lewin, Bloom has had a profound influence on my scholarship, second to none. Unlike Lewin, who was my dissertation advisor and beloved mentor through the early stages of my academic career, my relationship with Bloom was primarily through his publications. I met Bloom in person only once, a meeting that I describe in this book. And yet my relationship with Bloom was highly personal, and it wounds me greatly to know that the fashions of academia, albeit with many exceptions, disparage Bloom. Well-meaning readers have warned me to keep Bloom out of this book. But this book would not be without Bloom's looming presence.

I've read Bloom's writings over many years, and that which I valued most changed over time as the years passed: the vast erudition; the audacity of thought; his sensitivity to the ways scholarly books, poems, and novels respond to one another; and finally, most valued of all, the singular human voice that I came to know through his writings. The very personal voice of my book is in large part inspired by that quality in Bloom's writings.

The larger section on Bloom is titled "Character, Canon, and Poetic Influence." I address each of these topics in turn, considering literature and music in each case. The final part of this section studies the historical usages and then Bloom's adaptation of the rhetorical trope named metalepsis (or transumption). Here I am informed by John Hollander's book *The Figure of Echo* as well as by Bloom's extensive writings on the topic. I then go on to suggest ways to think about metalepsis in musical contexts.

Three broad topics inform the first part of the second book of *Music's Making*: phrase as musical event, wave as musical metaphor, and the silence of musical space. In discussing musical phrases, I draw parallels between syntax in language and syntax in music (with or without words). As a constituent of phase, musical intervals are considered in their two fundamental senses: distance traversed and time elapsed. Also within the purview of musical phrase, we discuss the most basic phrase shapes in Western music, along with the role of meter in forming those shapes.

After briefly considering "wave" in its literal sense, the metaphor of wave in poetry and music is unpacked at length. Drawing on the work of Angus Fletcher, we consider Walt Whitman's innovative use of wave formations in shaping his poetic visions, his poetic songs. Continuing, we explore the co-determinants of wave, energy and impedance, wave as metered and nonmetered, and we then broach the topic of silence perceived in metric time-space versus silence perceived in nonmetered time-space. This brings us to an extended discussion of wave imagery in two of John Ashbery's poems as well as in an essay by Brian Ferneyhough where Ashbery's images are applied directly to musical thought.

Having briefly broached the topic of silence, we go on to a more extended consideration of the role of silence in poetry and music. Topics include the poetic caesura and its musical analogues, *abruptio*, breaking off an anticipated continuity of flow, as well as more subtle pauses, so important in articulating syntax in poetry and music. Music that emerges out of silence is exemplified in the Ninth Symphonies of Beethoven and Mahler. Music that fades into silence is explored in a number of works, both popular and classical, including Brahms's Third Symphony, works by the Second Viennese (Schoenberg, Berg, and Webern), and Mahler's *Das Lied von der Erde*.

In what follows, we continue and expand upon our previous considerations of meter and silence. I begin with a comparison of metered poetry with metered music, instances of regular flow and instances of a variegated flow, through both subtleties of pacing and elasticity of phrase shapes, rubato, and syncopation.

Drawing upon a variety of musical works, I next consider a distinction between ametric poetry and music and "fractured" meter, where the former is devoid of a metric framework and the latter employs quickly changing metric groupings so that no single overriding meter is projected or perceived. As we turn to the music of Anton Webern, the interaction of fractured meter with silence moves center stage. From here we segue to an extended consideration of sound and image emerging from "a sea of silence" and the blankness of negative space.

In this context, we consider the remarkable uses of ellipses in Walt Whitman's original version of the poem later titled "Song of Myself," following this with some readings from the Hebrew Bible where sound and image surrounded by silence and blankness are palpable. Morton Feldman's composition *Rothko Chapel* provides the occasion for an extended glimpse into sound and image emerging out of silence and blankness as the composer discovers musical means for expressing the painterly, spiritual values of Mark Rothko. James Dillon's work for string quartet and orchestra, *The Gates*, continues our exploration of sound and silence along with the veiled echoes of earlier voices, musical, poetic, and spiritual, that inform Dillon's composition. I close this section of *Music's Making* with a brief evocation of "black fire, white fire," reversing the imagery of biblical commentary where letters of black fire are written on a surface of white fire to become the image of the sounds of white fire emerging out of the black fire of silence.

Drawing principally on the writings of Pierre Boulez, Gilles Deleuze, and Félix Guattari, the next large section of *Music's Making* develops global metaphors for our experience of time and space. Here, time and space are most basically bifurcated into two fundamental types: smooth and striated in Boulez; nomadic and agrarian (among their many names) in Deleuze and Guattari. Most simply put, nomadic space is inhabited without clear boundaries and without subdivisions while agrarian space divides the whole into delineated parts. Moreover, nomadic space is nonhierarchical while agrarian space invokes hierarchies. Of particular interest are the ways the two types of time-space interact, in music as in virtually all of our life experiences. Metaphors spun off from the basic division of temporal and spatial experience that are especially suggestive in our contexts are those based on fabric: pressed felt, woven cloth, and patchwork quilt. To these I add the metaphor of an errant thread. Related to the errant thread is Deleuze's characterization of a demonic leaping over boundaries, a violation of the distinctive separations of agrarian space, like finding some alfalfa in the wheat field. We explore the dialectic of smooth and striated space through examples from Debussy, Schoenberg, and Mahler, as well as in the Beatles song "All You Need Is Love."

We close the section on varieties of time-space by noting that the cluster of names associated with each basic type, nomadic-smooth-demonic-fluid-nonhierarchical contrasted with agrarian-striated-delimited-settled-hierarchical, is itself nonhierarchical in that no name intrinsically subordinates the others. At this point we return to the ten *sefirot* of Kabbalah, first introduced early on in the first half of *Music's Making*. In this context, I quote Arthur Green: "it is most useful to think of the *sefirot* not as some sort of cosmic "entities," but as *clusters of symbolic associations*, the mention of any of which (whether in daily life, in speech, or in a text) automatically brings to mind all the others as well." The same holds true for music, where each singularity is a multiplicity as well.

The next principal section of the book explores the extremely variegated roles of musical repetition, subsequently introducing and developing the idea of "temporal vectors." We begin with a quick glimpse at the role of repetition in the opening of the Rodgers and Hammerstein song "Oh What a Beautiful Morning" and then move on to a more elaborate consideration of repetition at the outset of Debussy's *Prélude à l'Après-midi d'un faune*. Drawing on the writings of Susanne Langer and Camile Paglia, we consider different models for linear time versus cyclical time, suggesting that in music and poetry we experience a dialectic between the two. Gilles Deleuze's book *Différence et repetition* provides the locus for an extended exploration of repetition's qualities. At end, I recommend a Janus-faced approach toward understanding the elusive role of repetition, parallel to Arthur Green's translation of the Hebrew tetragrammaton יהוה YHWH as "Is-Was-Will Be," incorporating and fusing now-past-future time. With this trifold concept of time in mind, passages from two of Shakespeare's tragedies, *Macbeth* and *Hamlet*, provide an opening toward a discussion of temporal vectors, energized flows that point toward a past, a future, or hover in a dilated now-time. We return to the theoretical writings of David Lewin within this context, also recalling various other topics broached earlier and now reconsidered in the light of our augmented discussion of repetition. Our treatment of repetition closes by asking the question as to why some works (poems, novels, music, paintings) seem to augment through multiple encounters (readings, hearings, viewings) while others diminish. I provide two tentative answers to my query, a heightened sense of contingency (an awareness of roads not taken) and a complexity of design or affect more deeply perceived through multiple encounters with the work.

The final section of *Music's Making* is to some extent a gathering of ideas that have free-floated through the earlier part of the book. In doing so it brings us full force into music's spirituality, a topic foreshadowed but not of central focus in earlier discussions. I begin with an extended discussion of the terms "horizontal" and "vertical" along with a host of associated words to include vertex, vortex, whirlpool, and whirlwind. Forces in dynamic interaction, the horizontal gathers into the vertical while the vertical spreads out to become horizontal. We draw parallels between the metaphoric extensions of horizontal and vertical with Clifford Geertz's distinction between *thick* and *thin* descriptions and then return to the writings of Merleau-Ponty, where vertical conceptions of the world form a unified field perceived all at once while horizontal thought spreads out over time and divides into constituents. This brings us to a consideration of Anthony Steinbock's book *Phenomenology and Mysticism: The Verticality of Religious Experience*. Drawing on writings of three mystics,

Jewish, Catholic, and Sufi, Steinbock explores "vertical" experiences "that take us beyond ourselves." Love is the characteristic that unifies all three visionaries, but sound and music per se are integral to their experiences. The ideas we associated with the thought of Emmanuel Levinas also return, resonating with Steinbock's observations. Our earlier discussion of phenomenology emphasized experience, including musical experience, as bodily. We now complement that one-sided apprehension, describing a dynamic circuit between music as embodied and music as disembodied, where the health of the body is coefficient with the health of the spirit.

The correlations between physical health and mental health are explored through a consideration of work songs, drawing on Ted Gioia's scholarship. Two more terms are explored as we approach the end our journey, grace and eros. Both terms reflect on earlier discussions, and both develop those discussions in new ways. I end the book with a coda, and as with musical codas the coda to *Music's Making* is a reflection back on the sojourn that has comprised the book.

Closing Our Opening and Some Expressions of Gratitude

This book announces itself as "Music's Making." And so all of the fields of inquiry that I bring into it—chiefly poetry, philosophy, religious studies, literary criticism and theory, and, to a lesser degree, theater and dance—are there as complements and augmentations of the way I experience music and understand music's making. A different book using a very similar cluster of references, a similar bibliography, might easily be titled *The Poetics of Poetry*, *Fiction's Making*, or any number of alternatives. Yet, simply put, here all roads lead to music. The same roads, with adjustments in direction, might have led to poetry, philosophy, contemplation of the Divine, or how to make friends . . . well, maybe not.

And now to thank some friends. Paul Wilson, Béla Bartók scholar and friend since graduate school days, read the first draft of *Music's Makings* as it emerged. Paul's gracious counsel saved me from the excesses of myself time and time again. Poet and distinguished translator of poetry Peter Cole read a large portion of the text, including my observations on Kabbalah and my reminiscences of Harold Bloom. Peter's insights and encouragements are greatly appreciated. Tiffany Skidmore read the manuscript and offered thoughtful critique and gracious support. Paul Benjamin

Cherlin recommended some key readings in phenomenology, invaluable in helping to develop my ideas concerning middle voice. Sumanth Gopinath and Matthew Rahaim suggested important readings in music theory, musicology, and ethnomusicology. I am grateful for the thoughtful support of Richard Carlin, senior acquisitions editor for music for SUNY Press, and for the good work done by the staff of SUNY Press in preparing this volume. And I am grateful to the three anonymous readers for the press whose critical comments have helped me to make the book a better one. Special thanks are due to Phil Ford for his gracious preface.

This book is dedicated to my teachers. My love for them has augmented over the years, knowing that without their guidance and encouragement I would not be. As always, my wife and dearest friend, Rose Papagno Cherlin, was a patient sounding board as I struggled through the good work of making a book.

Introduction

Remembering David Benjamin Lewin

In 1987 David Benjamin Lewin published what was to become a classic in music-theoretical literature of the late twentieth century: *Generalized Musical Intervals and Transformations*, hereafter GMIT.[6] Immediately following the completion of his book manuscript, seemingly in a single burst of energy, the residue of having completed the book, Lewin wrote a separate, lengthy article, "Music Theory, Phenomenology, and Modes of Perception."[7] At the time, at least to me, the article didn't seem to engage the ideas presented in the book. It seemed just another burst of creativity from Lewin's fertile and quick-grasping mind.

Lewin passed away in 2003, and it's too late now to ask him if he thought of the phenomenology article at least in part as providing another perspective on the matters discussed in GMIT. It took me a long time to see a connection; others may have been more perspicacious, but I now understand that the book and article are more related than they first appeared to be.

Lewin, who has been described as the most gifted and influential music theorist of his generation, was dauntingly intelligent, fluent in at least a half-dozen languages, conversant in I don't know how many more, widely read, a brilliant pianist, and a Harvard-educated mathematician. He was also a great wit.

Lewin was my dissertation advisor, my topic being Arnold Schoenberg's opera *Moses und Aron*. Prior to my study, Lewin had published a remarkable essay on the opera that remains one of the most insightful discussions of Schoenberg's work to date. Like me, Lewin was a baseball fan. Within the essay on *Moses und Aron*, Lewin describes the crux of the opera by analogy with a triple play in baseball: God to Moses, Moses to Aron, Aron to Volk Israel. The triple play breaks down between Moses and Aron. It's not so much that Aron drops the ball, it's simply that Moses's throw cannot be caught: Aron's formidable skill with language cannot but betray the ineffable vision of Moses. In conversation about the essay, Lewin told me that he had been advised that the baseball reference was inappropriate and that he should remove it from the essay. I'm glad that he didn't, and I suspect that most readers would agree.

At Yale, at least in those days, as a graduate student, one had to pass a preliminary exam prior to the approval of one's dissertation topic. Mine was to be a study of Schoenberg's opera, a work based on Schoenberg's twelve-tone method. I had discussed the topic with Lewin, and he was enthusiastic. My ability to study the work wasn't challenged by Lewin, but I hadn't taken a course specifically devoted to twelve-tone theory, and this became a point of contention at the preliminary exam. At the end of the session, it was determined that I would survey some of the key documents in twelve-tone theory, Lewin's and Milton Babbitt's essays among them, and that I would write a written report on my findings; only then would I be given permission to proceed with the dissertation. In coming to that determination, things got a bit contentious, as they will in such circumstances. In truth, I felt a bit beleaguered. As we were leaving the room, Lewin sidled up next to me, saying in the sing-song of Sprechstimme, "Cherlin ist ein guter Mensch, ein guter Mensch."

Readers who know Alban Berg's opera *Wozzeck* will recognize the source. Early on in the opera, the much-beleaguered Wozzeck is harangued by both his captain and by his doctor. At one point, just after the doctor has lectured poor Wozzeck with dire predictions about his health, the captain imagines the mourners weeping at Wozzeck's funeral. "Aber sie werden sagen: 'Er war ein guter Mensch, ein guter Mensch'" ("But they will say: 'he was a good man, a good man'"). Lewin knew that, beyond the reference to the opera, the word "Mensch" would have a special resonance for me, the child of Yiddish-speaking parents.

∼

David Lewin was one of the two greatest teachers that I have encountered; the other being Harold Bloom. (In naming my teachers, I omit my mother and father only in that their impact is unfathomable, far beyond my capacity to assess.)

GMIT, at least in large part, reads like a mathematics textbook: definitions, theorems, proofs, functions and formulas. Like Milton Babbitt, Robert Morris, and some few others that I have known, David Lewin's mathematical formulations seamlessly connected with his musical intuitions. Both the mathematical underpinnings of Lewin's approach, as well as the direct application of his ideas toward the analysis of musical structures and transformations, have been well and even brilliantly addressed by the next generation of theorists.[8] Although I probably have spent more time and effort on reading GMIT than any other book of music theory, the essays of Milton Babbitt taking second place, its mathematical approach has never become second nature for me. Nonetheless, the big global concerns of the book, aside from how they give rise to its technical machinery, should be of concern to anyone who thinks or writes about music.

GMIT is divided into two halves. The first half, subdivided into "Generalized Interval Systems" and "Generalized Set Theory," imagines music in objectified space, as though projected on a Cartesian grid. Common-practice music notation can be understood more or less in this way: time is plotted on the horizontal, pitch on the vertical. Placed in objective space, we can measure musical intervals within a sound-object (chord, motif, melody, etc.) or between objects. In a similar way, we can tabulate ordinal permutations (e.g., C-D-E-F permuted to C-E-D-F), or the augmentation or diminution of temporal intervals measuring elapsed time from one object to another. We can invoke equivalences, like octave equivalence, or set-type equivalences (collections of musical objects, e.g., pitches, that share the same catalogue of intervals, however those intervals are defined), and we can invoke congruences (as when the duration of some object, motive, melody, whatever, is the same as the duration of another).

The second half of the book, titled "Transformation Graphs and Networks," considers ways to think about the ways a musical shape (motive, melody, whatever) can be morphed into a subsequent shape. "Given locations s and t in our space, this attitude does not ask for some observed measure of extension between reified 'points'; rather it asks: 'If I am *at* s and wish to get to t, what characteristic gesture . . . should I perform in order to arrive there?' "[9] To use a homey analogy, the first, intervallic approach asks, "what is the distance and time it takes to get from my study to the kitchen?" while the second, transformational approach asks, "what do I have to do to get from my study to the kitchen?" The first objectifies space and time, while the second is gestural and experiential.

In what follows I modify Lewin's description just a bit, hopefully shedding light on its parallels with other creative thought while still keeping to the spirit of what Lewin intended. Instead of saying "how do I get from s to t?" I want to ask how I can imagine t so that it seems to emerge out of s, or, alternatively, what potential in s allows or causes it to transform into t. Moreover, while recognizing the power and utility of quantification, I am content to leave mathematical formulations to those better qualified than myself, and instead look to ways that prose and poetry have expressed these same qualities in disciplines other than music, as well as in descriptions of music.

One more thought on GMIT before going on: if we read Lewin's transformations as resulting from the application of the various functions as it were *from the outside*, then the transformational model slips back into a Cartesian grid, just what Lewin wanted to avoid. If the internal pressures of the events generate their emergent transformations, and the listener or interpreter perceptually participates in that experience, as it were *from the inside*, then we escape projection from without. In the first model, a subject (the theorist or whomever) considers and interprets an object (the musical score or the acoustic event in a musical performance). The second model, to the extent that it succeeds, eradicates subject/object opposition. Something happens, and then something else happens as a result of the first thing that happened. Music imagined this way emerges out of itself, and the listener or interpreter is a participant, not an external observer. Agent—that which does the action—and patient—that which undergoes the action—are one and the same. Put another way, Lewin's models are successful to the degree to which we hear *through* the transformations. Hearing *through*, generalized to knowing *through*, is a major theme of the present book.

Lewin's phenomenology article touches on a good number of topics. Perhaps better than any other single publication, "Music Theory, Phenomenology, and Modes of Perception" gives us a window onto the capacious and singular human being whom I knew as David Lewin.[10] The article's principal model for a phenomenology of music, applied to a Schubert song, imagines a moving time cursor that hovers over each subsequent musical event.[11] Each event either confirms or denies what was anticipated given a previous event (I expect X to happen here and it does or does not). Each event is understood in its own light (here's what seems to be happening right now). And each event projects or anticipates a subsequent event or events that in turn will either be confirmed or denied. In this sense, what defines a musical object/event is not a singular thing (the acoustic event), but rather something that takes on multiple aspects as we move through experiential musical time-space. Moreover, the subject, performer or listener, and the multivalent object/event are fully interactive: as we interpret and reinterpret, the separation of subject and object becomes diffused. To be sure, the listener and performer have separate tasks, but it's not the case that listeners are passive while performers are active. Both tasks are interactive. As such, Lewin's phenomenological model does some of the same work that his transformational model did in GMIT.

Before proceeding to the main body of this book, I want to mention two other aspects of Lewin's work, one that anticipates developments in GMIT and another that is seemingly independent, although that independence may be an assumption worth questioning. To get at the first body of work, we can contrast generic ways of describing musical relationships with context-sensitive ways. For example, transposition-by-some-interval is generic, what Lewin calls a *canonical operation*. Transposition by some interval, let's say by a perfect fifth, can potentially be applied to any passage or song or, for that matter, to an entire composition. Transposition by a fifth globally moves all the musical matter up or down a fifth; it doesn't matter what that matter is. Now, if the passage or song or motif is internally rich in perfect fifths, as in the sequence C-G-D-A, then transposition by fifth will move multiple pitches onto their fifth-related notes, in this case three of four (transposition up a fifth moves C-G-D-A to G-D-A-E or transposition down a fifth moves C-G-D-A to F-C-G-D). "Transposition by a perfect fifth" doesn't capture the salient quality of preserving three of the four pitches in musical event. For the sake of comparison, let's posit another four-note motif, this one fully chromatic: C-C♯-D-D♯. If we transpose by a fifth, no notes are held in common, but if we transpose up or down a semitone once again, three of the four notes are held in common. As with transposition by a fifth in the previous example, here transposition by a semitone doesn't capture the salient quality of "transposition that preserves three pitches." But, more importantly, if the motif in fifths and the motif in semitones are interrelated compositionally through transpositions that preserve three of the four pitches, then naming the transformation accordingly better captures what's at stake, while the canonical operations do not. Both the generic and the context-sensitive ways of thinking have their place, but if we are trying to capture a sense of something emerging from something, then the salience of particulars matters most. Lewin's work on context-sensitive operations predates GMIT, and much of GMIT comprises defining context-sensitive transformations.

A second area of Lewin's work that is important to the main body of this book comprises his many essays on music with text.[12] I was lucky enough to attend Lewin's seminar on this topic at Yale during the academic year 1979–1980. Lewin was a sensitive reader of poetry, and he was particularly astute in his understanding of the ways that music and poetry can mutually shape one another. The particulars of his analyses of texted music comprise some of the most engaging, insightful, and compelling essays on texted music that I have encountered. However, it wasn't the particulars that I learned from Lewin in studying texted music that mattered most: it was opening of possibilities, possibilities that I pursued during my career as an active teacher, and possibilities that I pursue in this book.

Part I

1

Music as Fiction

The Online Etymology Dictionary is a useful resource from which I cut and pasted the following: "early 15c., *ficcioun*, 'that which is invented or imagined in the mind,' from Old French *ficcion* 'dissimulation, ruse; invention, fabrication' (13c.) and directly from Latin *fictionem* (nominative *fictio*), 'a fashioning or feigning,' noun of action from past participle stem of *fingere*, 'to shape, form, devise, feign,' originally 'to knead, form out of clay,' from PIE root *dheigh- 'to form, build.'"[1] The noun *fiction* hides a verbal form, an active shaping or feigning. Let's concentrate on the active shaping aspect of the word first, and then turn to feigning or dissimulation, where fiction might be contrasted with truth, although we will see in the end that the relationships between "truth" and "fiction" are more subtle than the simple dichotomy might suggest.

    Among the root meanings of fiction is the shaping of clay, or the kneading of dough. In the Hebrew Bible, God shapes Adam out of the earth, *Adama* in Hebrew. Adam is our fiction of the first man. God is the proto-artist, shaping the cosmos and all that is in it out of the mysterious תהו ובהו (*tohu-va-bohu*), Hebrew words whose original meaning is obscure, translated as "without form and void" in the King James Bible. Was the stuff there beforehand, and only later shaped by God, or did God create the stuff out of nothing and then shape it? The Rabbis and Church Fathers have argued the case, sometimes vehemently. Our latest versions include the big bang theories of speculative physics. Even with a big bang, we can ask the question, from whence and where?

    Writers, poets, playwrights, novelists, journalists, and others create their poetry and prose out of words, most of which are already there—

although William Shakespeare, no ordinary writer, is credited with inventing some 1,700 words. Some writers want their language to be transparent, so that we hardly notice that it's there. Such use of language tells its story while minimally drawing attention to itself. Other writers want us to notice the active shaping through language, the sound and sense of the words, the plays of meaning, the rhythms of sound and sense, the order of presentation, things implied but not literally said, allusions to other words and other stories, and all the like. The front page of the *New York Times* generally aspires toward transparency, although literary flair will occasionally make a showing. The prose in a good novel, let's say by William Faulkner or Toni Morrison, will call attention to itself while telling its story at the same time. Faulkner, Morrison, and other great novelists expect their careful readers to notice the active shaping, the art of making fiction. Taken to an extreme, in extended passages in James Joyce's *Finnegan's Wake*, for example, it is the very opacity of language that reflects back on itself. To be worthy of the name, poetic language always calls attention to itself, whether it tells a story, captures a mood, gives shape to a perception, or whatever.

The great American poet Wallace Stevens wrote of "supreme fictions." "What makes the poet the potent figure that he is, or was, or ought to be, is that he creates the world to which we turn incessantly and without knowing it and that he gives to life the supreme fictions without which we are unable to conceive of it."[2] He said, "The final belief is to believe in a fiction, which you know to be a fiction, there being nothing else. The exquisite truth is to know that it is a fiction and that you believe in it willingly."[3] The truth of fictions comes out of our human needs. Stevens also wrote, "Reality is a cliché from which we escape by metaphor."[4]

We tell stories because storytelling is a basic human need. While language acquisition may not be as exclusively human as we once thought it was, it is fundamental to our humanity. Our mother tongues, no matter what they are, are basic to our orientation to the world. And yet I believe it is a mistake to make language the exclusive means through which we tell our stories and through which we know ourselves and our world. The seeing eye also creates its own fictions of seeing, and the great visual artists help us to see the world afresh.[5] As with the seeing eye, the hearing ear, which is the hearing mind, participates in the active shaping of our worlds. When we trivialize seeing or hearing, we diminish our own humanity.

Music too is among the necessary fictions that we need to be fully human. Musicians create their fictions out of air, as Shakespeare's Prospero would have put it, "out of thin air." The bride and groom walk down the aisle accompanied by celebratory music. The music shapes the experience; it measures the pace of their steps; it adds splendor, dignity, and joy to the occasion. Words cannot substitute for the music. The regal personages of times past had brass instruments announce their most important appearances. The music expressed authority and power, setting the regal person apart from the ordinary person. Words cannot substitute. Or, to take an example from film, Darth Vader, revealed as Anakin Skywalker, removes his mask, and the harp tenderly plays the musical motive that had been in the ominous horns and trombones before. The transformation of Darth Vader, archfiend, into Anakin Skywalker, resurrected Jedi knight, takes place through the musical transformation. Words cannot substitute for the music.

Sometimes, like everyday use of language, the music seems virtually transparent. It accompanies our trips to the supermarket, elevator rides, and the like. Musicians often find this kind of music to be irritating; I hesitate even to use the term music. And yet it is a kind of music, and while it may be an irritant to me, I recognize that for some, or many, it is an enhancement. And, to be honest, once in a while I hear a song that pleases as I stroll through the vegetable isle. Yet I will insist that the music that matters most calls attention to itself in ways that the language of a poet or strong novelist draws attention to itself.

Music actively shapes our place within and our orientation toward the world. Grounded music, whether through a drone or through an intermittently recurrent tonic, grounds our experience so that we can travel through the mind's inner ear and find our way back home. The *inevitability* of the closing tonic in Bach brings us to our final resting place. It is essential to his worldview. It expresses his religious faith and his sense of the order of the cosmos. The *inescapability* of the final tonic in Schubert is essential to *his* worldview, a very different world from that Bach once knew. Schubert's tonic often expresses tragically that which cannot be avoided. The *unattainability* of a closing tonic for post-tonal Schoenberg is expressive of his worldview, where ending in perfection can no longer express an honest fiction.

Fictions are active *shapings*, but they are also active *feignings*. Make believe, so that we can believe. I believe in the magic space of the proscenium. We read a poem or a novel, we watch a play or a film, to enter into its magic space. I believe that art allows an augmentation of belief, a dilation of our visible sphere and audible space, a way of self-knowing and self-making that increases our humanity, our understanding of self and others.[6]

The idea of something being "true" can be quite useful. I don't touch the fire because it will burn. That is a truth that I learned sometime long ago, beyond my recollecting. Literally and metaphorically, it is a sure guide through life. There are many other useful truths. When I hear a competent improviser or the work of an accomplished composer, creating music that is vivid and compelling, bringing to my imagination something that was not there before, and thereby augmenting my sense of self, I hear an honesty, a truthfulness in the music. When an improviser or composer strings along a chain of clichés, music that sounds stale, even on first hearing (which isn't first hearing, after all), that strikes me as false, a bad kind of feigning, a misrepresentation or at least a poor representation of what I call art.

But there is another kind of feigning, that is the necessary counterpart to the active making that is fiction. The musician, on the opera stage or the concert stage, plays a role. For me, the idea that the performer's job is only to serve the composer is nonsense. We can only serve the composer by collaborating with him or her (and the audience as well, even if you the performer are alone and the only audience). Jingles, and wallpaper music aside, the musical artist best serves the composer by making the song not quite his or her own, but a shared experience. The interpretive artist takes on a role, alone, with another, or within an ensemble, and she feigns a new persona on the spot. This is the acting that turns an actor into Hamlet or Ophelia, not just someone playing Hamlet or Ophelia. This is the playing that embodies and vivifies a musical work, rather than simply reciting it, playing the notes. This is the feigning that is the most honest truth.

2

That Which Emerges out of Itself, That Which Is Created

> But now, O Lord, thou art our father; we are the clay, and thou our potter; and we are all the work of thy hand.
>
> —Isaiah (KJV) 64:8

Let us begin by comparing two stories about the creation of the world. In the first story the world emerges out of itself. In the second, actually two variations on the theme, the world is made out of the stuff evidently antecedent to its making.

The creation story in the *Bṛhadāraṇyaka Upanishad* was written somewhere around 700 BCE.[1] There, in the beginning the world was just a single body, shaped like a man. He found no pleasure and wanted a companion. So he divided his body into two, giving rise to a husband and wife. He copulates with his wife and the human race begins. She, overcome by his amorous appetite, decides to hide from him and transforms herself into a cow. He sniffs out her ploy, he becomes a bull, they copulate, and cattle come into being. This pattern of mutual transformation, female then male, continues as the female changes to mare, he to stallion, she to jenny, he to jackass, on and on. "In this way he created every male and female pair that exists, down to the very ants."[2]

In this story the world is created by a (infinite?) series of self-transformations, preceded by a bifurcation that is the first transformation. Keep the general principle, and change all of the particulars, and we have a way of thinking that would be comfortable with twenty-first century thought in biology or physics, epidemiology, or environmentalism: natural processes transform nature from within. The *me* who was a boy and the *me* now a seventy-six-year-old man have transformed over time, out of myself. If something is missing from this ancient story, it is the sense of an environment of interacting forces and interacting beings. The story of boy become man becomes a poor fiction if boy-man is taken out of his context of being, let's call it nature. Nature in this sense is all-inclusive, even beyond our knowing; it includes you, who reads this page, and me, who strikes the keyboard signaling the computer to make electronic words on a screen, later to be printed and distributed. And, as recent events have begun to make horribly clear, neither you nor I, nor our species, nor the species comprising the environment within which we live, can survive if we neglect our co-relations in the world, air, oceans, and land.

The Hebrew Bible tells two creation stories, back-to-back, in Genesis. In the first, Genesis 1, God creates the heaven and earth out of the unformed, watery void. God's רוח (*ruach*)—translated variably as breath, spirit, wind—sweeps over the water, and God says, "Let there be light." Each God-day adds a new aspect to the Creation, making every living creature and then man in His image on the sixth day, and on the seventh day He rests. While one can read this first part of Genesis as a version of the world coming out of itself, the plain and simple reading imagines God, the Maker, as taking the primordial stuff and making the world out of it. Where the primordial stuff comes from, we are not told. God's mode of fashioning is not labored; it is by fiat. He says, "Let there be light," and there *was* and *still is* light. Yet whatever the means, this creation is a making.

The second Creation story, which follows immediately in Genesis 2, is more explicit in its sense of making. Here God forms man, אדם (*adam*), out of אדמה (*adama*), the dust of the earth. He then blows the breath of life into the nostrils of His clay creature, later removing a rib and fashioning the first woman. The man later (Genesis, 3.20) names his wife חוה (*Havvah*, Eve in English) "life-giver," "for she became the mother of all the living."[3] In Genesis 2, God is the Divine worker with clay who instead of making pots shapes the first of mankind. Our images of God as the Divine architect, as in William Blake's famous drawing of God with compass, are variants of this theme, where God as Creator is God as Maker. By this way of imagining, the human made in God's image is *homo faber*.

As noted, in comparing the story from the Upanishad to that in the Hebrew Bible, we find two prototypical ways of understanding creation: creation either comes out of itself or creation happens through the shaping of some preexisting stuff. In the first story-type, agent and patient—that which precipitates change and that which undergoes change—are merged: just as from the caterpillar the chrysalis, from the chrysalis the butterfly. In the second, the agent makes something out of the stuff used in the making: the carpenter builds a house out of wood, the potter shapes clay into a pot, the poet, as a wordsmith, shapes words into poems. Both ways of experiencing music are useful. Making music out of preexisting material is more predominant in discourse about music. In much of what follows, I explore the model of creation as coming out of itself. One can argue that music actually emerges out of itself or that music can create the *illusion* that it emerges out of itself. On this matter, I am indifferent. Whether or not music truly comes out of itself, as nature seems to do, is less important than the ability to apprehend *as though* the generative force is intrinsic to the sound-shapes we hear. After all, I've claimed that music is among our necessary fictions.

Dividing the world into subjects and objects, agents and patients, is so ingrained in our thought that it takes effort to think outside of what's become our second nature. But stories of how things emerge out of themselves have also been part of the human imagination for a very long time. Neoplatonism and its many offshoots should be counted as chief among those ways, at least in Western civilization. Emerging in the second century CE, gaining prominence through the writings of Plotinus (ca. 204–271 CE), later Proclus (412–485 CE), and numerous others, in the Medieval period Neoplatonism became integrated into various aspects of Jewish, Christian, and Muslim thought, especially into those ways of being-in-the-world that we collect under the umbrella of mysticism, Kabbalah and Sufi mysticism included. Neoplatonism is a vast and difficult topic: anyone who has tried to read Plotinus or Proclus will readily agree. However, a cartoon version of Neoplatonism is quite simple to formulate: all being emanates out of the source of Divine Being in gradations that lessen in their participation in the Divine source as they move down the chain of emanations.[4] In twentieth-century music theory, the work of Heinrich Schenker is an example of a distant relative of Neoplatonism.

The theories of Heinrich Schenker (1868–1935) and its offshoots began to dominate the way tonal harmony was taught in American colleges, universities, and conservatories somewhere in the 1970s. Ways of understanding harmony derived from Schenker continue to be an important constituent of higher education training in the analysis of tonal music in the United States to this day.

The Schenkerian theorist posits the prototypical key-defining move of tonic-dominant-tonic as generated out of the tonic itself, the single tone that engenders all others to which all others are subordinate, Schenker's musical substitute for Divinity. From this prototype, what Schenker calls the *Ursatz* (typically translated as "source-shape"), the deep "background," the composition generates multiple layers, typically divided into "middle ground" and "foreground," reaching into the surface of the fully manifest work.

Schenker's adaptation of Neoplatonism almost certainly came by way of Jewish thought, either mystical or Talmudic. Music theorists John Rahn and Wayne Alpern have recognized this.[5] At least some of the descriptions within Neoplatonic thought posit a two-way relationship: down from the Divine source and up, from the bottom as it were, toward that Divine source.[6] I think of a Schenker graph in a similar way: as we move from foreground through middle ground, toward background, the hierarchy of harmonic relationships simplifies until we arrive at the singular tonic the controls the whole. Or we can move the other way: the tonic generates its triad, which generates its dominant, so on and so forth until Beethoven's Ninth Symphony emerges!

Paul Ricoeur makes a related observation in the context of discussing *practices* (extended in meaning to include virtually any field of human activity). "The practical field is not constituted from the ground up, starting from the simplest and moving to more elaborate constructions; rather it is formed in accordance with a twofold movement of ascending complexification starting from basic actions and from practices, and of descending specification starting from the vague and mobile horizon of ideals and projects in light of which a human life apprehends itself in its oneness."[7] This same principle is at the heart of the so-called hermeneutical circle, where part and whole form a dialectical circuit, each informing the other, so that smallest details are understood in their global contexts, just as global concerns, structures, and the like are created out of their constituent details.

The expansions of harmonic context are a brilliant aspect of Schenkerian theory, as are its ways of understanding compositional unity. That something can mean something now and then something else later is not part of the Schenkerian vision of a musical world. All meaning is stable, and no level of reality (foreground, middle ground, background) can contradict another. The Schenkerian approach offers unity at the price of contingency, where meaning changes as the music emerges.

We have seen that this quality of instability of meaning as a concomitant of emergence is a quality David Lewin focused on in his article on musical phenomenology. It is also a quality often found in poetry. Prose can sometimes do what a poem does almost always, or almost

That Which Emerges out of Itself, That Which Is Created | 17

always tries to do; its meaning emerging slowly, as though reluctant to be revealed, emerges as what begins as if in darkness, or in half-light, moves into clarity, a clarity that can continue to brighten over time. Music too can share this quality, moving from puzzlement to revelation. In music without words, revision of boundaries (the sense of an ending) is often an analogue to revision of meaning in poetry.

To extend the metaphor, emergence from half-light to full light of day might also entail revision in the sense that what was perceived as so-and-so is re-perceived as thus-and-such. Poetic enjambment entailing *contre-rejet* (opposed-rejection) involves just such a revision.[8]

Emily Dickinson's poem "A Bird, came down the Walk -" contains a passage that underwent three telling revisions. Helen Vendler's commentary on the poem provides all three versions.[9]

1. He stirred his velvet head like one in danger, cautious. I offered him a Crumb

2. He stirred his Velvet Head like One in danger, Cautious, I offered him a Crumb

3. He stirred his Velvet Head. Like on in danger, Cautious, I offered him a Crumb

Here is the passage in the context of the final version of the poem (I give the final line of the third stanza and the first two lines of the fourth, out of five stanzas in total):

He stirred his Velvet Head.—

Like one in danger, Cautious,
I offered him a Crumb,

In her revisions, Dickinson shifted the noun to which the adjective "cautious" applies from the bird to the poet who watches and attempts to feed the bird. And yet, in the final version, as I read it, the "one in danger, Cautious," as the third stanza opens, seems still to refer to the bird. The second line of the stanza works as a *contre-rejet*, where "I offered him a Crumb" now assigns "I" as subject, the one who is "like one in danger." The rejected first meaning remains, not so much erased, but changed by a shifting perspective. Like in a Hegelian *Aufhebung*, the dialectical negation retains the trace of that which is negated.

18 | Music's Making

Seeing Through, Hearing Through: An Image from Kabbalah

While "seeing through" might imply translucence, what might it mean "to hear through?" If we take "seeing through" as a metaphor for "knowing through" or "understanding through," the visual metaphor suggests a way to interpret the metaphor for the knowing that is hearing. I turn to yet another creation story aided by a remarkable graphic spun out of Jewish Kabbalah.

Kabbalah and its offshoots comprise a large, complex, and diverse body of work, within which various descriptions of the *sefirot*, God's emanations, play a key role.[10] There are ten *sefirot* whose names vary according to their source. The graphic below, derived from Castilian Kabbalah of the late thirteenth century, is taken from the diagram of the *Ten Sefirot* in the Pritzker Edition of the Zohar.[11] Variations of this graphic are commonplace in discussions of Kabbalah.

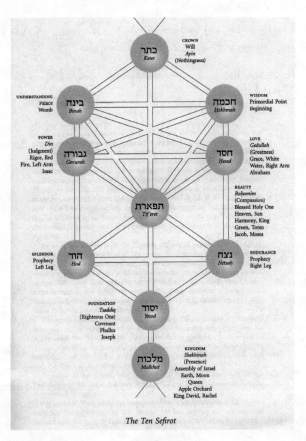

The Ten Sefirot

The image is an abstraction based on the human form (man made in God's image). It combines male and female aspects of Divinity. Within our immediate context, there is no need to go into the meanings and manifestations of the various *sefirot*. Instead, I want to focus on one aspect of its design: what is understood as the right side (*Hokhmah, Hesed, Netsah*) is on the right, and so the left side (*Binah, Gevurah, Hod*) is on the left. Now, if we were gazing on the Divine emanations, as it were face to face, the right side would be on our left, and the left side would be on our right. Evidently, one does not gaze at the *sefirot* head-on.

I can think of three options for making sense of this reversal. First, we might think we are viewing the image from behind. That way, the right would be on our right, and left on our left. There is a passage in the Hebrew Bible that might suggest such a reading, Exodus 33.18–23. In the passage, Moses speaks with God.

> He said, "Oh, let me behold your Presence!" And He answered, "I will make all my goodness pass before you, and I will proclaim before you the name LORD, and I will grant the grace that I grant and the compassion that I show. But," He said, "you cannot see My face, for man may not see Me and live." And the LORD said, "See, there is a place near Me. Station yourself on the rock and, as My Presence passes by, I will put you in a cleft of the rock and shield you with My hand until I have passed by. Then I will take My hand away and you will see My back; but My face must not be seen."[12]

This seeing-from-behind becomes recurrent in Kabbalistic experience of the final *sefirah*, the *Shekhinah*.[13] Seeing-from-behind might imply a partial vision, or a seeing that implies following the leader who shows the way. In all of the arts, as elsewhere in human creativity, visionaries, prophets of one sort or another, lead the way. Seeing from behind, we follow the leader, hopefully adding something of value of our own.

Following in addition to being led along has another attribute as in following along, where we attend to the flow of experience as it unfolds. This sort of following, a close attentiveness to all things, is a concomitant of wisdom.

A second option would be to think that the image is a reflection, as in a mirror. In a mirror image my left hand reaches out to touch my left, and my right to touch my right. Mirror imagery is basic to human understanding; we "reflect" on matters that concern us.[14] Arthur Green's

Introduction to the *Zohar* includes a description of the second and third *sefirot* where mirror imagery is central.

> But Ḥokhmah, meaning "wisdom," is also the primordial *teaching*, the inner mind of God . . . As Ḥokhmah emerges, it brings forth its own mate, called *Binah*, "understanding" or "contemplation." Ḥokhmah is described as a point of light that seeks out a grand mirrored palace of reflection. The light seen back and forth in those countless mirrored surfaces is all one light, but infinitely transformed and magnified in the reflective process. Ḥokhmah and *Binah* are two that are inseparably linked to one another; either is inconceivable to us without the other. Ḥokhmah is too fine and subtle to be detected without its reflections or reverberations in *Binah*. The mirrored halls of *Binah* would be unknowable without the light of Ḥokhmah.[15]

"To see through a glass darkly" (Corinthians 13:12) is familiar through Christian scripture. Mirrored reflections are quite common in music. For example, a major triad (e.g., ascending C-E-G) has been historically understood (among other formulations) as the mirror image of a minor triad (descending C-A♭-F).

(In the major triad, starting on C, we ascend four semitones to E (a major third) and then ascend another three semitones to G (a minor third). In the minor triad, we mirror the ascent with an equal descent, placing C at the center of our mirror, descending four semitones to A♭ (a major third) and then another three semitones to F (a minor third).)

Mirroring of melodic lines is common in many musical practices. Moreover, metaphoric reflection is as important in perceiving music as it is in other aspects of our cognitive and emotional lives. To reflect on divinity is no trivial matter. Seeing the *sefirot* as mirroring ourselves is clearly a powerful way to understand the image. And yet there is a third option that I believe is more powerful yet: instead of gazing on the *sifirot*, we gaze *through* them.

By perceiving the image this way, rather than a reflection, the image depicts an outward flow, emanations through which Divinity is manifest in the universe. In this model, the mystery and power of Being are broken into facets and forces through which divinity emanates. If we hold onto the lucent metaphor for knowing, this sort of knowing requires translucence. Rather than reflecting back, the *sefirot* are an active force through which we see and through which all there is comes into being. Seeing-through is a synecdoche for being-through, and through seeing-through the *sefirot* we participate or even merge with creation itself. While creation as emanation is fully manifest in the *Bṛhadāraṇyaka Upanishad*, the transformational process that gives rise to the diversity of beings is not described as an active force through which each individual being participates in creation. In seeing-through, hearing-through, and being-through the sefirot the precipitant dynamics of creation are concomitantly participant dynamics of creation.

We find a passing reference of "seeing through" in Martin Heidegger's "The Teacher Meets the Tower Warden at the Door of the Tower Stairway," the second of Heidegger's "Country Path Conversations."[16] The warden of the tower is evidently a sage, although not explicitly named as such, what in Yiddish we'd call a *tsadik*, although Heidegger would have, no doubt, been uncomfortable with the reference to Yiddish culture. The teacher in the dialogue has come to visit the warden "to solve the [nature of the] wondrous." A little way into the dialogue, the teacher mentions a picture he has seen in the tower that he leaves somewhat reluctantly to join the warden in conversation on the country path. The warden tells the teacher that they are going to meet "the guest" who gave him the picture, but that the teacher will be disappointed if he thinks the guest will be able to solve just what makes the picture wondrous. He then goes on to say that the guest will surely have an "acquaintanceship in relation to the picture." After the teacher notes the "careful manner" of the warden's speech, the warden replies: "This is necessary; for we must distinguish whether we mean acquaintanceship *of* [*von*] the picture or acquaintanceship *through* [*durch*] the picture.[17]

In a gazing at a painting, let's say a Cezanne (to get an image in mind), we can be sensitive to the play of shapes and colors, proportions, and, of course, representations of someone or something outside the painting, such as "a painting of a house" or "a painting of a field." By gazing *through* the painting, we learn, at least to a degree, to see through Cezanne's eyes. Gazing through does not eliminate any of the observations of gazing at, but it conditions far more: the way we see a house, the way we see a field, the ways we observe the play of light and forms. Hearing through music, though not normally involving houses and fields, has analogous implications. Having heard a musical theme, and then another, we can hear the second through our experience of the first, or in anticipation of the second theme we can hear the first as a foreshadowing of what is to come. Or hearing through a particular composition might provide a model for the workings of human consciousness and human emotions; through the music's self-reflecting we gain an understanding of our self-reflecting. Through the music's sojourn, we recognize our own sojourn.[18]

One revisionary aspect of Kabbalah, perhaps its most powerful revision in transforming our understanding of Torah, is the shift from making and shaping to emanation, where the universe emerges out of unfathomable divinity. In modern physics, this emergence is "naturalized" into a big bang. From whence?

The great Andalusian-Jewish poet Shelomo Ibn Gabirol (1021/22–c. 1057/58) was in some ways a precursor of Kabbalistic thought.[19] Here is a fragment from Ibn Gabirol's "Kingdom's Crown" in Peter Cole's translation.

> You are wise,
> and your wisdom gave rise to an endless desire
>   in the world as within an artist or worker—
>
> to bring out the stream of existence from Nothing,
>   like light flowing from sight's extension—
>
> drawing from the source of that light without vessel,
> giving it shape without tools,
>   hewing and carving,
>   refining and making it pure:[20]

In the passage, God is primarily depicted as maker, although one who shapes without tools, yet still "hewing and carving, / refining and making it pure." The wisdom of God as maker "gave rise to an endless desire / in the world as within an artist or worker." And yet there is a hint that all this making comes out of an underlying emanation. Bringing out "the stream of existence from Nothing, / like light flowing from sight's extension."

∽

Excursus: High and Low

One of my favorite stories out of Jewish mystical thought is that of Enoch, a cobbler who becomes transformed into the highest of the Archangels, Metatron. According to Gershom Scholem, the story comes out of thirteenth-century German Hasidism.[21] I cannot speak with any authority on the social status of cobblers in thirteenth-century Germany, but it's a fair assumption that thirteenth-century shoemaking wasn't a lofty profession. To this day, to do something "like a shoemaker" is a pejorative (my apologies to shoemakers everywhere).

Whether derived from Neoplatonism or from some other source, Jewish mysticism posits multiple "worlds," where the world of our physical realities is only one manifestation, the lowest, of a more encompassing universe. According to the story, as he worked each day at his awl stitching the upper leather to the sole, Enoch meditated on bringing together all the higher worlds with all the lower worlds. In later Kabbalah this would be understood as תיקון עולם (tikkun olam), "repair of the world." Repairing shoes takes on a universal meaning.

As in my reading of the Kabbalah's image of the sefirot, where the image implies a seeing-through that is a being-through, the story of the cobbler become Archangel entails a transformation brought about by seeing through the sewing of upper leather to sole.

The quality of bringing together that which is most lofty with that which is most mundane seems to be baked into the Jewish imagination. The Yiddish language, which evolves out of German Judaism in roughly the same period as the story Enoch-as-cobbler-become-Metatron, had a remarkable florescence in the late nineteenth and early twentieth centuries. Yiddish is replete with juxtapositions of just this sort.[22] As an example, one of many, I take a passage from Sholem Aleichem's טביה דער מילכיקער (Tevye der milkhiker, Tevye the Dairyman). In the lead-up to the passage, Tevye, a poor man, has chanced upon two women lost in the woods. Going out of his way, but hoping for something good to come out of it, he takes the women home. As it turns out, the women belong to a class far above Tevye's in wealth and creature comforts. Tevye is famished, and he looks longingly as an abundance of rich foods are brought out for the women. Soon after, he is invited to eat as well. This sets off Tevye's comparison of God with man. "He sits above, and we, mankind, sit below. We toil, we drag logs—one has a choice? As the Gemorah says: in a place where there are no men—a herring is a fish." The final phrase rhymes in the Yiddish original: "במקום שאין איש—איז א הערינג פיש (B'makom she-ein ish—iz a hering fish)."[23]

The seeming non sequitur, Tevye's rhyming of ish, Hebrew for man, with fish, Yiddish for fish, is taken from a Yiddish proverb that in turn is based on one of Hillel's sayings in Pirkei Avot (Sayings of the Fathers):

"In a place where there is no man, strive to be a man." In the Yiddish saying, Hillel's aphorism is transformed into "in a place where there is no man, a herring is also a fish."

The Yiddish substitutes the second part of the saying with the poor person's fish, herring, making musical (non)sense through a homey metaphor. If you want a fish dinner and cannot afford a finer fish, a herring will have to do. If you are looking for a worthy man and there's no one else around, I, like a herring among fishes, will have to do. If I am to share a meal with you, a gentleman, I guess that I, a poor man, will have to do.[24]

Spanning the late nineteenth and early twentieth centuries, Gustav Mahler's music shares the juxtaposition of low and high that we find in the Enoch story and in Sholem Aleichem. I surmise that Mahler's juxtapositions of the banal with the lofty, all on the way to the sublime, are manifestations of his suppressed Yiddishkayt.[25]

Throughout his mature years, Mahler insisted that he was German and that his music was German music. Methinks he doth protest too much. Mahler's orchestration alone betrays the cosmopolitan Jew; although Mahler learned much from the very German voice of Richard Wagner, his orchestration is not Wagnerian. He may have insisted that he was German, but to the trained ear the music doesn't sound German, not Wagnerian, not Brahmsian, not Beethovenian. At the very least, Mahler's orchestra incorporates lessons he learned from the French, Berlioz and onward, and from Italians as well, for example, Rossini's brilliant use of woodwinds. The anti-Semites recognized this foreign element in Mahler's music, as did Theodor Adorno. "A foreigner speaks music fluently, but as if with an accent. This was registered [i.e., recognized] by reactionary zealots; it was studiously ignored by the Schoenberg school, by way of protest, whereas it is only in the moment of inauthenticity, which unmasks the lie of authenticity, that Mahler has his truth . . . it [musical language] is seen from outside."[26] The "accent" is elsewhere identified as "jargon," code word for Yiddish. Both anti-Semite and Jew alike would recognize the repressed mother tongue of European Jews, a mother tongue that had become an embarrassment for those who wanted to be part of the Western culture that rejected and disparaged Jew as Other.

3

Moving Toward *Middle Voice*

Effacement of Subject-Object Oppositions in Philosophical Phenomenology

The effacement or overcoming of subject/object oppositions runs like a thread though the branch of philosophy named phenomenology: Husserl, Heidegger, Merleau-Ponty, and others. The dissolution of the gap and opposition between subject and object can be expressed as being *middle voiced*. A middle-voiced verb is neither passive, receiving the action, nor active, the cause or agent. Instead, in middle voice agent and patient are one and the same. Sanskrit and ancient Greek have middle-voiced constructs; English and most modern European languages do not. However, we can approximate middle voice with reflexive verbs. A common example in English: "I wash myself," where I do the washing and receive the washing.

Middle voice as I understand it and espouse it here is the juncture of what I bring to experience with what I receive from experience. There is no pure subject, nor is there a pure object; each is complicit in the other. They meet in the middle.[1]

What the composer brings to the music, what the performer brings, and what I, the listener, bring are all mutually codependent. That which I learn about the music, through reading commentaries by the composer, performer, or musical scholar, to the degree that that learning is integrated into my hearing of the music, becomes part and parcel of the music, not auxiliary, not addendum, but integral to it. When my hearing is aware of a musical lineage, echoes of musical precursors, foreshadowings of musical consequents, that too is, or has become, integral to the music.

In this sense, a musical work, or a musical performance, is not a static singularity. A musical work, a musical performance, is always a work in progress. All such comingling of musical meaning is an inflection of a middle-voiced experience.

In his preface to *The Middle Voice of Ecological Conscience*, John Llewelyn cites a passage from Jacques Derrida's *Margins of Philosophy*.[2] Derrida's thought was informed by many sources, including the tradition of phenomenology ranging from Husserl to Levinas.[3] As I read Derrida, his vast erudition sometimes comes off as embodying a wise guy more than a wisdom seeker, the smart guy in the class who has a chip on his shoulder. Yet the passage Llewelyn cites is exemplary in revealing the centrality of middle voice in the traditions of thought that Derrida continued, one to be further continued in Llewelyn's "ecological conscience." In the passage, Derrida explicates his concept of *différance*.

> In a conceptuality adhering to classical strictures *différance* would be said to designate a constitutive, productive, and originary causality, the process of scission and division which would produce or constitute different things or differences. But, because it brings us close to the infinitive and active kernel of *différer*, *différance* (with an *a*) neutralizes what the infinitive denotes as simply active . . . We must consider that in the usage of our language the ending *-ance* remains undecided *between* the active and the passive. And we will see why that which lets itself be designated *différance* is neither simply active nor simply passive, announcing or rather recalling something like the middle voice, saying an operation that is not an operation, an operation that cannot be conceived either as passion or as the action of a subject on an object, or on the basis of the categories of agent or patient, neither on the basis of nor moving toward any of these *terms*. For the middle voice, a certain intransitivity, may be what philosophy, at its outset, distributed into an active and passive voice, thereby constituting itself by means of this repression.[4]

Simply put, *différance* is Derrida's term for the creative principle through which new modes of being and meaning emerge. While he invokes "originary causality," which would be something like Aristotle's *first cause*, the subsequent invocation of middle voice negates the active-passive process denoted by cause and effect. As such, Derrida's *différance* is a variation on the theme of coming-out-of-itself that we have explored in the story from the Upanishads and through the image taken from Kabbalah. Derrida closes his paragraph with a broad (grandly hyperbolic, we might say) claim: that the history of philosophy based on active and passive constructs is itself a repression of the middle voice, which I paraphrase as repression of creation coming out of itself. With this in mind, we can move on to some of Derrida's precursors.

Edmund Husserl

Edmund Husserl (1859–1938), generally recognized as the founder of modern phenomenology, had his career tragically curtailed by the rise of Nazi Germany, his former student Martin Heidegger fully complicit. Like Heidegger, Husserl's ideas evolved over the course of his career, and the difficulties of sorting out his various positions over time were compounded by Nazi suppression of his work during the Third Reich. Dan Zahavi's 2003 study *Husserl's Phenomenology* provides a useful and lucid overview of Husserl's work, including material that became available only after the philosopher's death.[5] In what follows I draw principally on Zahavi's exposition of Husserl's work, fully cognizant that contending schools of thought disagree as to Husserl's positions on some of the key ideas.

A cluster of Husserl's ideas is apposite to our concerns. Early on, Husserl suggested that "linguistic meaning is rooted in prelinguistic and prepredicative encounter with the world," thus challenging the assumption that all meaning is linguistic in nature.[6] While the shaping force of language is profound, the assumption that all meaning is language based must strike anyone who works with nonverbal media as absurd. Something experienced as having meaning can take on its meaning in many ways, emotional as well as cognitive, nonverbal as well as verbal. A meaningful glance need not be reduced to a verbal description of that glance, even though language, especially in the hands of an accomplished writer, is amazingly adept at describing meaningful glances.

While granting a "prelinguistic and prepredicative encounter with the world," the mutuality of sound and sense can either involve language or not. A musical commonplace might clarify. In modal and tonal music, we can define a musical phrase as that which is terminated by some sort of cadence, a harmonic-melodic event that works approximately like the punctuation mark that signifies the end of a written sentence. Having expressed a musical thought, we cadence, then breathe. Recognition of the musical scheme can be apprehended intuitively and without verbalization. On the other hand, verbal description might be useful toward helping the listener attend to and interpret the musical scheme. Presumably, that's why people like me write books about music. Because sound and sense, verbal and otherwise, have been interacting from time immemorial, the question of whether the words shape the music or the music shapes the words remains unresolvedly open-ended. There is a mutuality between language and music, each emerging out of the other. One can imagine a threshold, with two-way traffic, where voice changes from sound to sense and sense to sound.

The poet Amy Clampitt imagines just such a threshold in her poem "Syrinx." The poem is composed of two eighteen-line stanzas followed by a three-line envoy. I give fragments of the second stanza.

> Syntax comes last, there can be
> no doubt of it:
> . . .
> is, in extremity, first to
> be jettisoned:
> . . .
> breaking free . . .
> . . .
> [of the] husk of the particular, rises
> past saying anything, any
> more than the wind in
> the trees, waves breaking,
> or Homer's gibbering
> *Thespesiae iachē*[7]

We are lucky to have a remarkable review of Clampitt's book, her last, written by John Hollander, a scholar-poet who was well up to the task. Worth reading in whole, I quote only Hollander's description of the transliterated words of Homer. "Homer's words ("unearthly wail") describe the cries uttered by the souls as they crowd around Odysseus in the land of the dead. We are left with a contingent eloquence just this side of silence."[8] The two-way transit that Clampitt describes moves from pure sound to syntax ("syntax comes last") and then in the embodied voice of singer, "breaking free . . . of the husk of the particular," saying, once again, as the wind says, as the waves say, "a contingent eloquence just this side of silence."

Middle voice, as we have characterized it, is an alternative to the dyadic opposition of subject and object; another approach toward the same end is captured in the term *intersubjectivity*. The constitutive role of subjectivity has evidently been a vexing issue for interpreters of Husserl's work, with some readers accusing his phenomenology of tending toward solipsism. Zehavi characterizes Husserl's final position as entailing a threefold structure, *subjectivity-intersubjectivity-world*.[9] In interacting with the world, our individual and unique subjective experience is shaped by (and shapes) the subjective experience of other persons (or more generally other beings). Zehavi quotes *Zur Phänomenologie der Intersubjektivität II*: "Ontologically speaking, every appearance that I have is from the very beginning a part of an open, endless, but not explicitly realized, totality of possible appearances of the same, and the subjectivity belonging to this appearance is open intersubjectivity."[10] In the case of language acquisition and use, intersubjectivity is an obvious necessity. However, it's not just knowing through language, but all knowing, all experience, that is inextricably linked with intersubjectivity. Moreover, experience is bodily where "the body is a condition of the possibility for the perception of and interaction with spatial objects . . . and that every worldly experience is mediated and made possible by our embodiment."[11]

Just so, hearing music and making music in all of its guises can be understood as embodiment of the threefold *subjectivity-intersubjectivity-world*. And as we shall see, the a priori intersubjectivity of being takes on profound ethical dimensions in the writings of Emmanuel Levinas.

Maurice Merleau-Ponty

In his preface to Merleau-Ponty's *Phenomenology of Perception*, Taylor Carman writes: "Interior and exterior, mental and physical, subjective and objective—these notions are too crude and misleading to capture the phenomenon. Perception is both intentional and bodily, both sensory and motor, and so neither merely subject nor objective, inner nor outer, spiritual nor mechanical. The middle ground between such categories is thus not just their middle, but indeed their *ground*, for it is what they depend on and presuppose."[12] Merleau-Ponty addresses this very issue by rejecting the comparison of our perceptions to a searchlight by which we can orient ourselves toward anything, since it "takes for granted the given objects upon which intelligence projects its light."[13] He continues by positing an "intentional arc." "[T]he life of consciousness—epistemic life, the life of desire, or perceptual life—is underpinned by an 'intentional arc' that projects around us our past, our future, our human milieu, our physical situation, our ideological situation, and our moral situation, or rather, that ensures that we are situated with all of these relationships."[14] This unity of perception is later applied toward literature and music, as well as the more fundamental experience of being human.

> A novel, a poem, a painting, and a piece of music are individuals, that is, beings in which the expression cannot be distinguished from the expressed, whose sense is only accessible through direct contact, and who send forth their signification without ever leaving their temporal and spatial place. It is in this sense that our body is comparable to the work of art. It is a knot of living significations and not the law of a certain number of covariant terms.[15]

Merleau-Ponty picks up this thread some fifty pages later. "The experience of one's own body, then, is opposed to the reflective movement that disentangles the object from the subject and the subject from the object, and that only gives us thought about the body or the body as an idea, and not the experience of the body or the body in reality."[16] What is true of our relationship to a work of art, or our own bodies, generalizes into our relationship to the world that surrounds us: "we must no longer conceive of perception as a constitution of the real object, but rather our inherence in things."[17] Perception is just that kind of act where there can be no question of separating the act itself and the term upon which it bears.[18]

Merleau-Ponty sums up his discussion of passivity and activity within the larger section of his work devoted to temporality with a lovely poetic image: "we are the sudden upsurge of time." "We are not, in some incomprehensible way, an activity tied to a passivity, a machine surmounted by a will, or a perception surmounted by a judgment; rather, we are entirely active and entirely passive because we are the sudden upsurge of time."[19] In the terms we have developed and will continue to develop, "entirely active and entirely passive" entail a middle-voiced experience. Merleau-Ponty's "sudden upsurge" might be understood as a gathering of horizontal experience into a transformative verticality. We will return to consider this aspect of Merleau-Ponty's work as this book approaches its conclusion.

Don Ihde

Don Ihde, building on the work of Husserl, Heidegger, Merleau-Ponty, and others, wrote a book that is highly cogent in our context, *Listening and Voice: A Phenomenology of Sound*.[20] The bodily immersion, so important to Merleau-Ponty's thinking, is invoked in Ihde's description of hearing a Beethoven symphony within a concert hall setting. "The music is even so *penetrating* that my whole body reverberates, and I may find myself absorbed to such a degree that the usual distinction between the sense of inner and outer is virtually obliterated."[21] Ihde's description, a dissolution of subject/object oppositions, is congruent with what we might call the *listener's sublime*, where hearing and the hearer merge into a unity of experience.

Later in the book, in a chapter titled "The Center of Language," Ihde brings up another point, also important to our present context. "My experiential listening stands in the near distance of language which is at one and the same time *the other speaking* in his voice. *I hear what he is saying*, and in this listening we are both presented with the penetrating presence of voiced language which is 'between' and 'in' both of us."[22] Playing music, especially chamber music, brings this kind of interaction to a height rarely achieved in any other kind of human endeavor. The long-lived genre of the classical string quartet, vital from Haydn's day to our own both in the world of musical composition and in the correlative world of musical performance, is to my mind an apex of subtle and complex human interaction. The best-performing string quartets make vivid the "between" and "in" each of the four players. In the world of jazz performance, the closest that I have encountered to this chamber music ideal was in the ensembles led by Miles Davis, especially in the late 1960s into the early 1970s. More than simply "playing together," the members of Davis's groups interacted with an extraordinarily subtle give and take. We also see this kind of flowing, heightened human interaction in ensemble acting, dancing, and sometimes in team sports.

Before moving on to a consideration of an aspect of Heidegger's work, I would like to consider one final passage from Don Ihde's *Listening and Voice*. "To listen is to be dramatically engaged in a bodily listening which 'participates' in the movement of the music . . . In concentrated listening its enchantment plays upon the full range of self-presence and calls upon one to *dance*."[23] Ihde goes on to say that this impulse to dance need not be literal. It includes the dance one feels internally while sitting still in the concert hall. While I recognize the kind of internal dancing that Ihde invokes, I also recognize that some music is more dancy than others.

At some point while I was his student, David Lewin, comically serious as he would be from time to time, spoke of two kinds of composers: dancers and singers. Handel was a dancer, Bach a singer. Mozart was a singer, Beethoven a dancer. Of course, we know that Mozart was also a dancer: his dances sing. While Beethoven could also sing: sometimes his music seems to chant without a bit of dancing to be heard. Both Wagner and Brahms were primarily singers, as was Schoenberg. Stravinsky was in essence a dancer. In the soul music of my youth, James Brown was a dancer who sang, Otis Redding a singer who danced. The Beatles were all singers, even the pitch-challenged Ringo. Michael Jackson was a perfect synthesis; although he started off as a wonderfully gifted boy singer, as he matured the dancing and singing seemed inseparable. Mick Jagger is an odd one: without the traditional skills of a dancer and without the traditional skills of a singer, he has been one of the most enduring and talented entertainers of the rock 'n' roll era.

The bodily physicality of music encompasses much more than we think of as literal or figurative dance. For the instrumentalist, the instrument is an extension of the body. Somewhere, I can't recall where, I've read that each of our ten fingers is like a brain unto itself. In *Musicking Bodies*, Matthew Rahaim relates an experience in his apprenticeship toward learning to sing Indian classical music.

> One of the first obstacles I myself faced in learning to sing raga music was my fixation on discrete notes and my inability to apprehend melodic trajectories. I was singing stiffly, rendering one note after another. My teacher, Vikas Kashalkar, insisted again and again that I needed to "connect the notes." I struggled for months with my eyes closed, but it wasn't until I opened

my eyes and noticed his hands moving while he sang that I understood that these curves were also manifest in a gesture as he sang.[24]

∽

Excursus: A Personal Memoir and Musings on Body and Voice in Music

The first period of my own musical life was as a clarinetist, including three years of playing in army bands during the Viet Nam War. Although I had played some saxophone, before the army and in the army bands, the clarinet was my musical home during those years. In a time of personal crisis, the years immediately following the army years, I turned from the clarinet, performing within the tradition of classical music and its more popular offshoots, to a period where the tenor saxophone was my principal instrument. As a saxophonist I performed in two musical worlds: for nearly five years I played in a soul music band, based in Brooklyn, New York, performing songs by James Brown, Otis Redding, Percy Sledge, Wilson Pickett, and others of that genre and period. At the same time, for a shorter period, I was a member of a "free jazz" ensemble, getting some good press but not too much further before the ensemble dissolved. The transition from making music off of the printed page on a clarinet to never seeing notation at all, mentally or optically, was certainly not automatic, but eventually, in its very different way, the saxophone became just as much, if not more, of a musical home as the clarinet had been before. In both "homes," the physical and musical were comfortably inseparable. Of course, countless hours in the practice room preceded this state of being; for most musicians, the "getting to know you" stage of musical apprenticeship is long and arduous. Yet the sense of home that I've described is one that I share with any musician.

With wind instruments, breathing and playing are concomitants. For players of string instruments, the bow is an extension of the right arm down to the fingertips. For the trombonist, the left arm and slide are continuous. And, of course, for the singer, her body is the instrument. For some singers, who self-accompany, voice and instrument seem to be extensions of one another.

I vividly hear this sense of unity in some early Delta blues. Blind Willie Johnson's recording of "Dark Was the Night, Cold Was the Ground" is remarkable in this respect. If you don't know the song, take a listen on

YouTube. You'll recognize instantly what I mean. The guitar doesn't so much accompany the voice as the two are inseparable aspects of the same thing. Jimi Hendrix also participates in this tradition; I'd be hard-pressed to say whether his voice is an extension of his guitar or his guitar an extension of his voice. Franz Schubert, I imagine, accompanying himself on piano or guitar, must have had this sensibility. The most satisfying performances of voice accompanied by piano, or larger ensemble, approach the condition of chamber music, but this is rare. It requires not only that the pianist breathe with the singer, but that the two engage in a kind of musical embrace where each inflection, each motion is mutual. The same problem occurs when a soloist is accompanied by an orchestra. Perhaps the high cost of rehearsals precludes achieving the intimacy of chamber music, but the ideal of a concerto performance requires that the soloist and orchestral players really listen to and respond to one another. When this happens, then both mutually affect one another. Then the real magic happens.

Martin Heidegger's Country Path Conversations

Heidegger's *Sein und Zeit* (*Being and Time*) is regarded by many scholars as one of the most important philosophical writings of the twentieth century. The book was dedicated in 1926 to Heidegger's teacher Edmund Husserl. With the rise of Adolf Hitler, Heidegger would betray Husserl, the Jew. I must admit to a deep distrust of any philosopher who could call for deference to the will of the Führer in 1933–1934, no matter that he later changed his mind. Suffice it to say that *Being and Time* is a landmark study in ontology, philosophy of being, where middle voice is posited as proper to the original sense of "phenomenon."[25] "The Greek expression φαινόμενον [*phenomenon*] . . . is derived from the verb φαίνεσθαι [*phainesthai*], which signifies 'to show itself' . . . φαίνεσθαι [*phaínesthai*] itself is a *middle-voiced* form which comes from φαίνω [*phaínō*]—to bring to the light of day, to put in the light."[26] In our context, rather than attempting an exposition of Heidegger's phenomenology, I turn to the philosopher's late work and his evolving concept of will, the faculty of choice, intention, or purpose. Heidegger changed his mind over time with regard to "will," at times ambivalent, at times celebrating willfulness, and in his late work recoiling against his former self, as his concept of *Gelassenheit*, a letting go of willfulness, most fully emerges.[27] Moving outside the philosophical subtleties of *Gelassenheit*, we might say that the Beatles, in their song "Let It Be," are advocates of late-Heideggerian philosophy. *Gelassenheit* plays a key role in Heidegger's late work, *Country Path Conversations*, a brief consideration of which follows.[28]

Country Path Conversations, in its first and principal section, is set up as a conversation among three people, a scientist, a scholar (evidently a historian or historiographer), and a *Weise*, translated as a guide, but also meaning a wise one. The German is replete with plays on words, a quality nicely captured and annotated by its translator into English, Bret W. Davis. Reading like a parody of the Platonic dialogues, the "conversation" can be alternatingly maddening, mystifying, and even hilarious as it hems and haws its way toward an adequate understanding of *Gelassenheit*, serenity, calm, equanimity, among its normative translations into English. It is this sense of wandering that I find most appealing in *Country Path Conversations*, where there is no direct path toward revelation (or call it truth), yet where an unanticipated clearing (*Lichtung*) might appear, just around the bend. In this sense, Heidegger's truth seeker is like Spenser's errant knights.

Heidegger takes the term *Gelassenheit* from the thirteenth-century Christian mystic Meister Eckhart. In Eckhart, *Gelassenheit* denotes a renunciation of self-will, giving up one's motivations to the will of God.[29] In Heidegger, *Gelassenheit*, translated as *releasement*, denotes not the-will-not-to-will but rather a letting go of the will altogether. This letting go entails a kind of stepping outside the subject/object dichotomy: "Then releasement lies—if we may still speak of a lying here—outside the distinction between activity and passivity."[30] The other key term in Heidegger's conversation is *die Gegnet*, translated as the open-region of being. *Gelassenheit* brings us toward this open-region releasing us from subject/object horizons of knowing.

Bringing Heidegger's heavenly concept down to earth, is it too far-fetched to think of Heidegger's *Gelassenheit* as a lofty variant of what athletes call "being in the zone"? There too, a heightened awareness enhances a way of being in the world. Might it be that a kind of automatic pilot takes over, where the individual is fully in harmony with and fully interactive with the flow of their environment? Musicians and actors too know something like this—the magic in a concert hall, the magic of theater.

Another way to read *Country Path Conversations*, not exclusive of the first, is to place foremost its play on words, German and Greek. Here is a passage that Bret Davis gives in translation as well as in the original German prose. The words in square brackets are included in Davis's translation. "The drink [*Trank*] abides in the whole gathering involved in the event of drinking [*Getränk*]. This gathering is the belonging-together in the event of drinking of what is offered and received as drinkable. The whole gathering of the drink [*Getränk*] consists of the drink offered [*Trank*] and the drink received [*Trunk*]" (*Das Getränk nennt das Zusammengehören des tränkenden Trinkbaren und des trinkbaren Getrunkenen des Trinkens. Das Getränk ist Trank und Trunk*).[31] The philosophical point is that the concept "drink" combines linguistic function as a noun and as a verb; just so, *being* is both substantive and verbal (beings, and being). Davis's translation shows good taste by modifying the German into decent English prose. In literal translation it might read something like this: "Beverage names the belonging together of the potable which is drunk and the potability entailed in the drinking of the drink. The beverage is the drink and the act of drinking." Perhaps the proliferation of t's and k's in the German mimics the clink of glasses. Although perhaps one has had a few too many clinks. I recall writing my dissertation under the tutelage of David Lewin and his negative responses to any alliteration in my prose, with marginal comments like "Donald Duck?" "Porky Pig?" What might Lewin have made of this? *Trank* and *Trunk*, clanging like drank and drunk, seem better placed in a *Katzenjammer Kids* cartoon strip than a work of philosophy. Perhaps Heidegger's comical use of language is intentional.

Whatever may be the case, from the perspective of a play on language, the point is well taken: the play of language itself reveals and invents meaning. Sonic transformations, of the kinds exploited by poets, give rise to multiple metaleptic series (e.g., *trinkbaren . . . Getrunkenen . . . Trinkens . . . Getränk . . . Trank . . . Trunk*), transforming meaning, opening to discovery of that which was concealed. Read this way, *Country Path Conversations* is an argument for the importance of playing with words. In both readings, the metaphysics of letting go or the play of language, the emergent process is paramount.

The next major figure in phenomenological thought that I want to consider in the contexts of *Music's Making* is Emmanuel Levinas. However, before turning to Levinas, we will make a major detour to follow some of the paths of liminal time-space. As we shall subsequently see, liminal space will play a significant role in Levinas's thought.

4

Liminal Space

In what may be the most perceptive aphorism on poetic meaning that I have encountered, Paul Valéry observes: "A poem: a long-drawn hesitation between sound and sense."[1] Valéry's "long-drawn hesitation" is an example of what this study calls liminal space.

The principal literary theorist of liminal spaces was the late Angus Fletcher. In *The Prophetic Moment*, his 1971 study of Spenser's *Fairy Queen*, Fletcher posits three types of time-space: the temple, the labyrinth, and the threshold. These same spaces are further explored in *Colors of the Mind*, where Fletcher uses the terms "threshold" and "liminal" interchangeably. In Spenser, the labyrinth is "the wandring wood, this *Errours* den," a space of wandering and error, likened to a malevolent maze.[2] The time of wandering in the labyrinth is roughly historical time.[3] In contrast, the temple is a sacred space, set apart, where time stands still. "The liminal crossing between these two "spaces" marks the moment of prophetic vision in which the poet sees life from the joint perspective of passing and immutability."[4] I find a related sentiment expressed by the poet Charles Wright: "A door opens, a door closes, all doors are holy."[5]

Liminal space is Janus-faced, and Fletcher reminds us that the Romans "consecrated a god of the gates, Janus, whose bifrontal face looked opposite ways, in and out of the city, blessing or cursing the passer in his entrance to or exit from the city."[6] Just so, musical passages can be anticipatory or reflective, and they can also look both ways, forward to some time and space yet to be entered and back to a time and space already experienced.

Liminal space, the space of a threshold, is an in-between space, neither here nor there. Dawn and dusk are liminal, the thresholds between day and night. And so is that state at the moment of awakening when sleep still holds its loosened grasp, or its inverse, when the sensations and perceptions of waking life loosen their grip. Liminal spaces, elusive to description, are the mainstay of all creativity.

Harold Bloom was fond of quoting a passage from Ralph Waldo Emerson's essay "Self-Reliance": "Life only avails, not the having lived. Power ceases in the instant of repose; it resides in the moment of transition from a past to a new state, in the shooting of the gulf, in the darting to an aim."[7] For writers of poetry or prose, the "shooting of the gulf," what Bloom called "poetic crossings," is manifest by the move from one mode of figuration to another; it can coincide with the emergence of a new, significant, creative writer, or with the emergence of a new phase in the life-work of such a writer.[8] Of course, there are direct analogues for the creative musician or any other creative thinker.

Liminal experience is a heightened awareness of transition; taken to an extreme, all experience is liminal. Angus Fletcher cites Michel de Montaigne's essay "Repentence." "I do not portray being, I portray passing . . . stability itself is a more languid motion."[9] Be that as it may, most intensely felt liminal experiences are fleeting: evanescent, they elude our grasp. Wallace Stevens captures this sense of the liminal in his poem "The Auroras of Autumn," where Stevens imagines the aurora borealis, the northern lights, as a serpent flickering in the sky.[10]

> This is where the serpent lives, the bodiless.
> His head is air. Beneath his tip at night
> Eyes open and fix on us in every sky.
> . . .
> This is form gulping after formlessness,
> Skin flashing to wished-for disappearances
> And the serpent body flashing without the skin.

Stevens says that "this is form gulping after formlessness," and the meaning is as unstable as the images that provoke it. Form swallows the unformed, forming form itself. Form chases formlessness, finding its culmination therein. The liminal is the in-between of form and no form.

Harold Bloom, always appreciative of the work of Angus Fletcher, adds additional insights into Fletcher's triad, labyrinth, temple, threshold. "Ambivalently the labyrinth can image panic or delight in wandering. Between labyrinth and temple, image of centrality, intervenes a threshold, almost identical to the questing poet–hero."[11] The questing poet–hero is the Romantic poet, exploring unfathomable inwardness, always on the verge, and so dilating liminal space.

In Bloom's estimation, John Ashbery was the preeminent American poet as we crossed the millennium into the twenty-first century. He writes that "Ashbery is always on a threshold, poised between a labyrinthine Eros and a templar Thanatos. Perilous beauty is his reader's reward."[12]

John Ashbery's poem "Words to That Effect" includes the following:

. . . . The days
scudded past like tumbleweed, slow then fast,
then slow again. . . .
You remember how still it was then,
a season putting its arms into a coat and staying unwrapped
for a long, a little time.[13]

Self-contradiction is a mode of evanescence in that our moods are fleeting.

When liminal space is dilated, so that we hover for a moment in the in-between, *das Zwischen* in German, it can take on a strangeness that we call the uncanny, *das Unheimliche*. The poets and composers who bring us into Romanticism explore this dilated liminal space. I think of Franz Schubert's setting of Heinrich Heine's "Ihr Bild" with its uncanny wavering between dream and awakening, or his setting of Goethe's "Erlkönig" wavering between normal waking consciousness and hallucination, between life and death.

Evocations of the uncanny in Mozart, among many others, anticipate such developments in musical Romanticism. The central chapter of Scott Burnham's *Mozart's Grace* studies Mozart's uncanny thresholds. "Mozart often stages the uncanny threshold of another dimension, whether deeply interior or incipiently transcendent, by composing passages the seem to rise above the discourse of their surroundings."[14] Burnham includes a discussion of the scene in *Don Giovanni* where the Don mortally wounds the Commendatore: a hushed, hovering texture expresses the Commendatore's liminal state, the threshold between life and death.[15]

At another point, Burnham discusses a passage in Mozart's G minor symphony where the previous chromatic bassline is slowed down to three times its original duration (eights moving to dotted quarters) and transferred to become the highest voice, hovering over a tonic pedal tone. "The music brushes a threshold, the path to its appointed cadence merging for a one moment with a path from some other time, some other space."[16]

There is a long, not so long, trajectory (a long, a little time) between the early Romantics and the first generation of the twentieth century. A generation after Brahms, we associate the uncanny in music with Arnold Schoenberg, and the uncanny in literature with Franz Kafka. Our major theorist of the uncanny, also from that generation, is Sigmund Freud. In Kafka's "The Metamorphosis," Gregor Samsa awakens to find himself in the body of a larger-than-life cockroach. But his mental habits remain those of a human being—he worries about missing the train and being late for work. In another of Kafka's stories, "The Hunter Gracchus," the story's protagonist finds himself suspended between life and death, a boat carrying his funeral bier from port to port without ever coming to a final rest. Schoenberg's *Erwartung* and *Die Glückliche Hand*, among his many works that open liminal space, are extended expressions of the liminal as uncanny.

If we take Schubert and Schoenberg to be our musical bookends, ignoring for now the ongoing exploration of the liminal as uncanny in composers like Brian Ferneyhough and Helmut Lachenmann, then Brahms, rather than as the culmination of a musical practice, as Heinrich Schenker and his followers would have it, appears as *das Zwischen*. How we define or experience the liminal depends to a great degree on how we frame our definition or frame our experience.

Conceptions of liminal space in music can vary from something not literally stated as an acoustic event, an in-between that's heard through its omission, to something extended through a large expanse of time and space. Horizons are liminal, and to the extent that a sense of horizon is evoked by the music, a sense of the liminal can be pervasive.

Of particular interest in music are those evanescent liminal spaces that are mental constructs, not acoustic events. For example, in a standard musical keyboard, A♯ and B♭ involve striking the same key, but in tonal music a notated B♭ has different implications from a notated A♯. Consider the chords C-E-G-B♭ and C-E-G-A♯, a dominant seventh chord and an augmented sixth chord, respectively. As acoustic events, the two are exactly the same, but in tonal practice the two have opposed implications. B♭, in this context a flatted seventh, normally resolves downward to A (or A♭); A♯, in this context an augmented sixth, normally resolves upward to B. Although the two sonorities (and hand gestures on the keyboard) are identical, in context they imply differing expectations of what will come next. If we enter the chord hearing "dominant seventh" (expecting resolution to an F major or F minor chord) and exit hearing "augmented sixth" (resolving to a B chord, normally the dominant of E), the liminal space connecting/separating the two is a mental construct, a reevaluation of where we've been in light of where we've gone. The juncture of implication/affirmation-denial in Lewin's phenomenology is just such a liminal space.

In a through-composed, multi-movement work that is unified overall by transformations of a single source idea, as in Beethoven's Fifth Symphony, the space in between movements can be heard as liminal, thresholds between one type of figuration and another.

∽

Personal Excursus

In music and literature, theater and life, the shading between labyrinth and liminal can be vague and difficult to define. An example from my musical past: after three years of playing clarinet in army bands during the Viet Nam war, I returned to my parental home for a short period. It was late 1968. Exiting the army was a joyous occasion, one of only a few times in my life where I literally felt like I was walking on air. Maybe it was the change from combat boots to sneakers. But a personal and musical crisis soon ensued. I felt cut adrift, and the music and instrument that had been central to my self-identity felt sullied, prostituted by being complicit in a war that I could not support, a war that was still ongoing. I seriously considered giving up music altogether, but I couldn't let go. The solution, temporary in the greater scheme of things, was to abandon the clarinet and classical music, move into the Brooklyn borough of New York City, and redefine myself as a tenor saxophonist, complete with a revered image of John Coltrane on the wall of my room. Was the time between army and Brooklyn liminal, or was it a wandering in the labyrinth? With the hindsight of more than fifty years, the episode seems more liminal than labyrinthine. Yet at the time of drift, being lost in life's labyrinth would have seemed more to the point. So with labyrinth and liminal it can be a matter of perspective.

∽

Having developed a sense of liminal space, we can return to Angus Fletcher's triad, labyrinth-temple-threshold, to briefly consider his other terms. If we expand the Spenserian labyrinth, where wandering is error, to a more positive sense of wandering or drifting, as in so many passages in Debussy, we can conceptualize musical labyrinths without any overlay of error or despair. And like lifetime passages, musical labyrinths can be reenvisioned, heard another way, as liminal spaces, in Debussy time-spaces in-between passages that settle into harmonic clarity.

The timelessness of "the temple" is more difficult to imagine in musical terms. After all, time in music cannot stop. Even in silence, time passes. Fletcher's discussion of rhetorical tropes as they align with the three time-spaces can help. Fletcher sets up the discussion of tropes with a cautionary note. "In the modern era, when not only music but all the arts have tried to hold their balance while experiencing the loss of tonal center, poets and novelists have testified to the complete loss of cadence within the figurative structures provided by traditional poetics. Atonalism and even aleatory procedures are natural, in an era such as ours. But before its radical breakdowns had occurred, poets could still employ the ancient figurative structures, by bending them."[17] I am not convinced that the ancient figurative structures can't be further bent, yet Fletcher's admonition is a necessary caution against trying to fit newly emerging thought into old, established categories. When one's sense of "what music is" is hardened by one's musical experiences, rather than being opened to new possibilities, then hearing is filtered through hard-wired perceptual modes that will not allow admission of the new. This kind of cognitive and emotional blockage is particularly commonplace in shutting down our ability to hear music that doesn't fit our preconceptions of what music is.

Fletcher's cautionary tale is followed directly by his affiliation of the three time-spaces with three rhetorical tropes.[18] Timeless temple space is associated with hypotactic structures (where the components are linked and subordinated to the encompassing space, here the temple) and with the part/whole relations denoted by the trope *synecdoche*. Blake's "to see the world in a grain of sand" is synecdochic. The labyrinth is paratactic (events are set side by side without causative or subordinating relations). Its trope is the metonym, here denoting association by contiguity. "The throne" is metonymic for "the king." The threshold is associated with metaphor, the trope that allows us to see (hear) something through our understanding of something else. We recall our discussion of Kabbalah and the imagery of seeing/hearing/being *through*. As such, metaphor creates new meaning by merging things that were separate and apart before metaphor united them.

Returning to our quandary as to what "temple space" might mean in music, we can reflect that part-whole relations, like events nested within and subordinated to a larger encompassing event, are perceived as it were by stepping outside the flow of time. This imaginary is a time-space where we dwell within. In common musical parlance, a theme-area, as opposed to an introduction, transition, or interlude, is a place where we settle in. Something like "temple space" (without its sacred connotations) is experienced. In the classical canon, such "temple space" is more typical of Schubert than Beethoven; in Schubert we often seem to hover within a thematic area, whereas in Beethoven the onrush of incessant becoming, where about-to-be supersedes here-and-now, is more typical. In popular music, prolonged steady-states, like the circular-motion vamping at the end of songs, might be thought of as "temple space."

In poetry we have the useful distinction between dramatic and lyric. Dramatic poetry moves through its images as a story unfolds. Lyric poetry hovers in a relatively timeless mode, singing about being in love or feeling despair, a state of being rather than a sequence of events. Music too can be dramatic or lyric. The hovering of lyric music uses the flow of time to capture a sense of timelessness. In sonata forms, the lyric second theme can provide respite from the onrush of a dramatic first theme.

We return to things concerning liminal space by considering what Thomas Weiskel named "the Liminal Sublime," the topic of the final chapter of his book, *The Romantic Sublime*.[19] Weiskel cites the famous passage in William Wordsworth's "Prelude," where the poet describes "spots of time," privileged moments of experience.

> There are in our existence spots of time,
> That with distinct pre-eminence retain
> A renovating virtue, whence, depressed
> By false opinion and contentious thought,
> Or aught of heavier or more deadly weight,
> In trivial occupations, and the round
> Of ordinary intercourse, our minds
> Are nourished and invisibly repaired;
> A virtue, by which pleasure is enhanced,
> That penetrates, enables us to mount,
> When high, more high, and lifts us up when fallen.
> This efficacious spirit chiefly lurks
> Among those passages of life that give

> Profoundest knowledge to what point, and how,
> The mind is lord and master—outward sense
> The obedient servant of her will.[20]

Weiskel perceptively notes that the "efficacious spirit . . . lurks," as though it were some subterranean force hidden from conscious thought. " 'Passages' [as in passages of life] refers presumably to events that involved a passing from one state to another and also to the passing back and through of retrospection . . . Such passages "give" knowledge but conceal the efficacious spirit; at the very least this spirit, lying as it were in ambush, is to be distinguished from knowledge of the mind's sovereignty."[21] "Spots of time" work in two ways. The liminal, subsurface "efficacious spirit" is not the result of knowledge; it is the cause that underlies our ways of being and knowing in the world. In this guise, the spots of time remain unconscious; they lurk among those passages of life. But the spots of time can also be recalled or reconstructed through retrospection, a type of experience not captured in the quoted passage, but clear elsewhere in Wordsworth's poetry. In this latter guise, a vivid memory of the source of the "efficacious spirit" is conditioned by the life experiences (passages) that connect and separate the memory from its source. In this sense, the subterranean force rises to the surface, the shaping of our experiences that had remained unconscious becomes conscious, though modified through the passing of time.

I find both aspects of Wordsworth's spots of time apposite toward understanding music, especially in large-scale works of the nineteenth and early twentieth centuries. A privileged event, for example a principal musical theme, can seem to be worked out, become absent from the musical surface, and then reappear as a modified memory of its inception, with the effect of having worked subsurface all along. Later, we will understand Brahms's Third Symphony as exemplifying this very property. Music can also involve disturbing events that submerge only to return to the musical surface as painful memories. Rather than Wordsworth's efficacious spirit, we find emotional dissonance, a disequilibrium that has not been properly resolved.

The spots of time, at least in the passage from Wordsworth's "Prelude," are positive, life enhancing, "efficacious spirits." Sigmund Freud's concept of repression explores the dark side of a similar if not the same effect. There a repressed event operates subsurface, in the unconscious, only later to manifest consciously as the return of the repressed. Freud's concept of *Nachträglichkeit* is a darkening of Wordsworth's spots of time. In *Nachträglichkeit*, literally translated as *belatedness*, a repressed memory becomes traumatic only in retrospect. The source event might hardly be noticed at the time of its occurrence; it becomes recalled and traumatic in light of later developments. The fate motive in Arnold Schoenberg's *Pelleas und Melisande* works precisely in this manner.[22]

Continuing to cite Wordsworth, Weiskel further develops spots of time as liminal space with examples that seem tailored to exemplify Freud's *Nachträglichkeit*, only with healing rather than wounding power. At one point in the "Prelude," the young Wordsworth is returning home for a Christmas visit. Unbeknownst to young Wordsworth, his father is terminally ill and will die before the holiday is over. The poet describes the place where he awaits transport to home.

> . . . 'twas a day
> Tempestuous, dark, and wild, and on the grass
> I sate half-sheltered by a naked wall;
> Upon my right hand couched a single sheep,
> Upon my left a blasted hawthorn stood;[23]

After the death of his father, the images take on an unanticipated significance.

> And, afterwards, the wind and sleety rain,
> And all the business of the elements,
> The single sheep, and the one blasted tree,
> And the bleak music from the old stone wall,
> The noise of wood and water, and the mist
> That on the line of each of those two roads
> Advanced in such indisputable shapes;
> All these were kindred spectacles and sounds
> To which I oft repaired, and then would drink,
> As at a fountain.[24]

Weiskel describes the effect of the initial imagery as a liminal threshold, using the vocabulary of semiotics, as signifiers awaiting their signified, signs of something not yet understood, and so not yet articulated by the poet: a premonition not yet recognized as such, and without the sense of what it is a premonition of. Music too can have these sorts of premonitions, only to be known as such in retrospect. For example, the opening motto of Beethoven's Fifth Symphony arguably goes on to generate the entire symphony. Only once the entire journey is over can we appreciate the meaning of its opening gesture, though its urgency might indicate that it has lots to say. The opening motto of Brahms's Third Symphony provides another vivid example. Later, we will explore, to the same effect, the implications of the "breaking of a wave" in the poetry of John Ashbery and in the music and writings of Brian Ferneyhough.

5

An Ethics of Intersubjectivity

Emmanuel Levinas and Responsibility to the Other Human Being: הנני (hineni)

My treatment of Emmanuel Levinas is more expansive than that of his precursors in philosophical phenomenology. The reason for this is simple: reading Levinas has had a fundamental impact on my approach toward studying and teaching music. In what follows, I am careful to represent Levinas's thought as accurately as I can, that is to say, I do not consciously misrepresent his ideas. Yet, as will become clear, my adaptation of Levinas's ethics is not about following the master to the letter of the law. I am not shy to resist his dicta when I don't find them helpful given the aspirations of this book. Talmudic Judaism, so important in Levinas's thought, places the divergent opinions of great rabbis side by side. Readers must sort through those opinions and come to their own conclusions. I read Levinas in that spirit.

Ethan Kleinberg, in *Emmanuel Levinas's Talmudic Turn*, imagines Levinas's thought as comprising a three-strand braid: Western philosophy, French Enlightenment universalism, and Lithuanian Talmudic tradition.[1] In Kleinberg's chronicle of Levinas's early life, we learn that Levinas's parents had intended a secular education for their son, principally based in the Russian language. As a youngster, Levinas read widely in Russian literature, including Gogol, Pushkin, Dostoyevsky, and Tolstoy. Events in Europe, World War I, and the Russian Revolution forced a change of plans, and in 1920 Levinas began studies in German literature. Moving to Strasburg in 1923, Levinas's studies in philosophy began in earnest.[2]

During his time in Strasburg, Levinas was influenced by the universalism of French Enlightenment thought, the second of Kleinberg's three braids. It was also during this time that Levinas first read Husserl, beginning his studies in phenomenology.[3] "For Levinas, phenomenology was the possibility of moving beyond the systematic organization of knowledge under the rubric of reason to the interrogation of the dynamic act of knowing and the mechanism of its origin. In this way it moved past the subject-object split by emphasizing consciousness at the locus of the relationship between the subject and the object."[4] Levinas's "Talmudic turn" came far later, only after World War II, when Levinas had settled in Paris. During this time, Levinas met and subsequently studied with an elusive, enigmatic person who went by the name of Shushani (also spelled Chouchani), a mysterious figure of whom little is known, but who was revered as a master of Talmudic thought by those who knew him.[5]

Lithuanian Talmudic Judaism (the Mitnageddic tradition) was opposed both to the more Westernized, liberalizing reforms centered in Germany (known as Haskalah), as well as to the mystical, ecstatic Hasidic movement prevalent in Poland and the East. In reading Levinas, whether his more philosophical writings, his Talmudic commentaries, or his ideas about education in general, I find it helpful to keep in mind Kleinberg's threefold braid: Western philosophy, Enlightenment universalism, and Lithuanian Talmudic Judaism.[6]

The most striking and most basic aspect of Levinas's transformation of Western philosophy is his placement of responsibility to the other (always understood as another human being) as antecedent to and more fundamental than Being (*Sein* in Heidegger) or beings (*Seinendes*). The concomitants of this assertion are multiple. First and foremost, both ontology, theory of being, and phenomenology, theory of perception, are superseded by the ethics of responsibility to the other, or, as Levinas sometimes says, responsibility to one's neighbor. Each human is understood as unique, and one's responsibility to the other is always singular, where each unique individual is called upon, as an individual, to be responsible for their neighbor, who is likewise a unique individual. My responsibility is to You. Moreover, the only way to break up, break into, or break open one's radical subjectivity, one's closed and totalizing world, is through one's encounter with the other. Later we will see, in contrast, that Harold Bloom's understanding of Shakespeare's characters centers predominantly on self-overhearing, where the self itself becomes the other.

Levinas does not explicitly characterize this encounter with the other as middle voiced. Instead, he asserts a deeper subjectivity. Yet this deeper subjectivity entails departure from subject-object relations; to my mind it is commensurate with what we have been calling middle voice. "The Other does not affect us as what must be surmounted, enveloped, dominated, but as other, independent of us . . . It is this way of welcoming an absolute existent that we discover in justice and injustice . . . [welcoming the Other] expresses a simultaneity of activity and passivity which places the relation with the other outside of the dichotomies valid for things: the a priori and the a posteriori, activity and passivity."[7] It is this very core of Levinas's thought, one's responsibility toward the other, that I would place as central in my relationship toward all aspects of humanity, including art, for art is human utterance. In studying a musical score, or performing a musical work, I would claim, I develop and augment my individual and unique experience through knowing another, or others, each equally individual and unique. The balance of individuality and mutuality lies at the heart of human being, and within the worlds of music making, it is the highly individuated that I value most—those rare musicians who sound only like themselves, but who simultaneously are members of a larger community, a larger tradition from which they spring, which they expand, transform, and extend.

While Levinas restricts his idea of responsibility to the other to a human being whom I approach "face to face," I see no reason to limit this responsibility to persons. And while Levinas asserts that language is my gateway toward the other, "saying" as he likes to say, I would include all forms of human utterance, the painter's brush strokes, the actor's gestures, the musician's shaping of sound. And beyond the purview of this book, I would argue that the ethics of responsibility cannot be limited to human interaction, for human interaction takes place in a larger world, it dilates to include anything that I might approach, the flowers in my garden, the water I drink, the air I breathe, the art I make. As we stand on the brink of environmental disaster, this universal responsibility toward the other gains an urgency perhaps unsurpassed in human history. And yet to apply Levinas's core idea to all aspects of being is to contradict much of what Levinas says. And so, before modifying Levinas toward addressing the concerns of this book, let's try to get a better sense of what he says.

Scholarly consensus places two of Levinas's numerous publications as the most comprehensive statements of his mature thought: *Totality and*

Infinity (*Totalité et Infini*), first published in 1961, and *Otherwise than Being, or Beyond Essence* (*Autrement qu'être*), first published in 1974. The "totality" of *Totality and Infinity* refers principally to the totalizing impact of subjective experience, where objects are brought into subjective life, becoming part of the "same." Levinas, a survivor of the Holocaust, argues against totalizations of every sort, and though the totalitarian government that he survived isn't mentioned explicitly, any sensitive reader will recognize the trauma that informs Levinas's antipathy toward totalizing thought.[8] In contrast, "infinity" is that which is opened through responding to the other, the neighbor, whose radical otherness (their subjective experience) breaks open my subjectivity.

The principal themes of *Totality and Infinity* are expanded and somewhat modified in *Otherwise than Being*, where the "otherwise" is basically equivalent to the "infinity" of the earlier book. The word "essence" in the book's subtitle, *Beyond Essence*, denotes Being, roughly equivalent to Heidegger's *Sein*.[9] Both books, to a significant degree, are critiques of Levinas's precursors, Husserl and, more pointedly, Heidegger. But to see Levinas's thought simply as a critique of earlier phenomenology is far too reductive. In a broader sense, Levinas takes on the whole of Western philosophy, going back to the pre-Socratics, and continuing until his own time. The key toward understanding Levinas's radical departure from Western metaphysics, where metaphysics *is* ontology, is through recognizing the profound influence of Jewish scripture and rabbinical commentary on that scripture on Levinas's thought.

Throughout his writings, Levinas refers to one's encounter with the other as being "face-to-face." The biblical resonances of this formulation are inescapable. In Genesis 32:25, Jacob encounters "a man," whom some interpret as the Angel of Death, with whom he wrestles through the night. At the break of dawn Jacob receives the blessing, his name now "Israel, for you have striven with beings divine and human, and have prevailed." And "Jacob named the place Peniel, meaning, 'I have seen a divine being face to face, yet my life has been preserved.'" In Exodus 33.11, we read that "The Lord would speak to Moses face to face, as one man speaks to another."[10]

Rabbi Hillel (110 BCE–10 CE) is among the most revered teachers in Jewish tradition. Learned commentaries on Levinas, including the scholarship of Edith Wyschogrod, Ephraim Meir, and Hillary Putnam, have emphasized the impact of Hillel's most well-known formulations on *Totality and Infinity* in particular. Hillel's three questions, *Perkei Avot* (*Sayings of the Fathers*) 1:14, are implicit, yet central to Levinas: "If I am not for myself, who is for me? And when I am for myself, what am I? And if not now, when?" Even more pervasive in its impact is Hillel's "golden rule": "That which is hateful to you, do not do to your fellow. That is the whole Torah; the rest is the explanation; go and learn."[11]

Another aspect of Levinas's thought with deep connections to Jewish tradition is his insistence on the uniqueness and irreplaceability of each human. Catherine Chalier, in her essay "Levinas and the Talmud," writes that

> the style of the Talmudic tractates—often sharp and passionate discussions, opinions always expressed in the names of their authors—incites us to claim that "real thought is not," as Plato would have it, "the silent dialogue of the soul with itself" but rather "a discussion between thinkers." Thinkers who keep their own names for "the totality of the true is made up of multiple persons: the uniqueness of each way of hearing bearing the secret of the text."[12]

Yet, if I were to reduce Levinas's ethical metaphysics to one word, it would be the Hebrew הנני (*hineni*). Translated as "Here I am" in the Jewish Publication Society edition of the *Tanakh*, הנני (*hineni*), among its multiple instances in the Hebrew Bible, is Abraham's response to God's calling in Genesis 22. For Levinas, הנני (*hineni*) and its various French equivalents, including *moi, c'est moi*, summarize one's responsibility to the other, an obligation that precedes any understanding of the command of the calling.[13]

For Levinas, the "here I am" of הנני (*hineni*) is in response to a moral imperative. Concerning "the antecedence of responsibility and obedience with respect to the order received," Levinas says, "It is as though the first movement of responsibility could not consist in awaiting nor even in welcoming the order (which would still be a quasi-activity), but consists in obeying this order before it is formulated."[14] Seemingly nonsense on the face of it, the "order" that one neither awaits nor welcomes is an imperative, for Levinas, more fundamental than being. It is obvious that the idea of obeying prior to understanding the command takes on dark meaning in a totalizing context, including the hideous problems we face in America and in the world today. For Levinas, as in the Jewish tradition more generally, הנני is restricted to its positive implications, the human responsibility toward each individual other, the human responsibility to God. In Levinas, responsibility to another human being is tantamount to responsibility to God.

In words evocative of Franz Kafka's *Der Process* (*The Trial*), Levinas says:

> Responsibility for another is not an accident that happens to a subject, but precedes essence in it, has not awaited freedom, in which a commitment to another would have been made. I have not done anything and I have always been under accusation—persecuted . . . The word *I* means *here I am*, answering for everything and everyone . . . I am summoned as someone irreplaceable. I exist through the other and for the other, but without this being alienation: I am inspired.[15]

"I have not done anything and I have always been under accusation—persecuted . . . I am inspired": trauma and calling are inseparable. And then, on the next page, "Outside of any mysticism, in this respiration, the possibility of every sacrifice for the other, activity and passivity coincide." As we have already noted, in statements like this, where activity and passivity coincide, Levinas approaches what we have called middle voice.

Elsewhere, Levinas invokes the term "glory," one of many formulations where responsibility toward the other is tantamount to religiosity. "Glory is but the other face of the passivity of the subject. Substituting itself for the other . . . inspired by the other, I, the same, am torn up from my beginning in myself, my equality with myself. The glory of the infinite is glorified in this responsibility . . . 'here I am.' The saying prior to anything said bears witness to glory."[16] As already mentioned, for Levinas, "saying" is restricted to language, for Levinas I can only say with words. My relationship with the other, through which I am augmented, is based on language, "primordially enacted as conversation (*discours*), where the same . . . as a particular existent unique and autochthonous, leaves itself."[17]

> Truth arises where a being separated from the other is not engulfed in him, but speaks to him.[18]

> The manifestation of the face is already discourse. . . . He at each instant undoes the form he presents.[19]

> . . . to face the Other, in a veritable conversation. Then this being is nowise an object, is outside of all emprise. This disengagement from all objectivity means, positively, this being's presentation in the face, his *expression*, his language.[20]

In all of these formulations, the other is a living presence, my neighbor. I would extend this. For example, when I study or perform a score by Mozart, to choose a composer with whom I've had a relationship for well over sixty years, his living presence is revivified, and I address him, reach out to him, through my interaction with the music that he has prepared for me. It is always this way, music, literature, sculpture, painting; these are not things, objects for me to manipulate or master. Each is an aspect of an other's humanity to which I am called on to respond. Of course, the responsibility runs both ways: the artist, sculptor, musician, is responsible toward me too. Each is a "me" unto his- or herself.

Levinas has a special admiration for his teachers, as do I. But as with all responsibility to the other, he seems to limit teaching to use of language. "Teaching is a discourse in which the master can bring to the student what the student does not yet know. It does not operate as maieutics, but continues the placing in me of the idea of infinity. The idea of infinity implies a soul capable of containing more than it can draw from itself."[21] The maieutics that Levinas refers to is Socratic intellectual midwifery, where the teacher draws out of the student what is already latent within. As with all genuine human relations in Levinas's understanding, what the teacher brings to the student is something new, not something already there. This ability to teach and learn is open-ended, infinite in Levinas's vocabulary. With all this I heartily agree. But learning can be visual too, and it can be aural beyond words. Implicit in, but concordant with, other aspects of Levinas's teaching is the idea that the teacher responds to and respects the unique individuality of the student, as the student responds to and respects the unique individuality of the teacher. There are teachers of musical performance whom I have known who want the student to play the music like they do. In my estimation, and in agreement with Levinas, my best teachers developed in me a better sense of whom I might be. David Lewin was such a teacher for me, and I've heard the same from his other students as well.

Two aspects of music making that are easily overlooked and often explicitly avoided in technical descriptions of music are its sensory and emotional impact, both of which are inextricably linked with the bodily aspects of making and hearing music. In his introduction to *The Cambridge Companion to Levinas,* Simon Critchley writes that Heidegger's investigation into the meaning of Being "does not presuppose a merely intellectual attitude, but rather the rich variety of intentional life—emotional and practical as well as theoretical."[22] Critchley goes on to point out that in spite of their many differences, this comprises a fundamental agreement between Levinas and Heidegger. Both are critical of what they perceive to be the intellectualism of Husserl's phenomenology. For Levinas, "the upsurge of the self" begins in enjoyment, where happiness belongs to axiology, a theory of values, rather than ontology, a theory of being.[23]

> We live from "good soup," air, light, spectacles, work. Ideas, sleep, etc . . . These are not objects of representations.[24]

> In the paradisal enjoyment, timeless and carefree, the distinction between activity and passivity is undone in agreeableness [agrément].[25]

> It is vulnerability, enjoyment and suffering, whose status is not reducible to the fact of being put before a spectator subject.[26]

> Satisfaction satisfies itself with satisfaction. Life enjoys its very life . . . There is enjoying of enjoyment before any reflection, but enjoyment does not turn toward enjoyment as sight turns toward the seen.[27]

While clearly appreciative of sensory and emotional constituents of lived experience, Levinas was highly conflicted when it came to his assessments of art. Observations that in one passage seem to place great human value on the arts, music included, in other places view the arts with great distrust. One factor, perhaps, is Levinas's antithetical relationship to Heidegger, who reserves high praise for the poetry of Hölderlin. I hold Hölderlin in similar esteem while also recognizing that a survivor of the Holocaust might well have developed deep doubts about the high art of which the Germans were so proud. Yet Levinas doesn't seem to recognize that the very psalms and writings of the prophets that he so admires are poetry too. Sung poetry!

At one point in *Totality and Infinity*, Levinas contrasts "discourse," by which he means "saying" to the other, with poetry, or at least a certain kind of poetry. Using a Nietzschean vocabulary, mockingly, he writes as though poetry is a noxious intoxicant, a "beguiling rhythm" whereby, in a Dionysian mode, the artist *becomes* a work of art. To this he opposes "the language that at each instant dispels the charm of rhythm and prevents the initiative from becoming a role. Discourse is rupture and commencement, breaking of rhythm which enraptures and transports the interlocutors—prose."[28] In my experience, the poet, a poet who has honed the craft of poetry through deep reading, whose every word is thoughtfully chosen and carefully placed, is better at "saying" (with words) than just about anybody else. As Harold Bloom recognized, and as Paul Wilson has reminded me, this philosophical distrust of poetry is an ancient quarrel, as least as old as Plato's battle with Homer. Levinas, wary of false ecstasies, harmful intoxicants, throws out the baby with the bathwater!

In a discussion of art within *Otherwise than Being*, Levinas seems to veer between cautiousness and exuberance. The prose quoted below, like much in Levinas, is difficult to unpack.

> Art is the pre-eminent exhibition in which the said is reduced to a pure theme, to absolute exposition, even to shamelessness capable of holding all looks for which it is exclusively destined. The said is reduced to the Beautiful, which supports Western ontology. Through art essence and temporality begin to respond with poetry or song. And the search for new forms, from which all art lives, keeps awake everywhere the verbs that are on the verge of lapsing into substantives. In painting, red reddens and green greens, forms are produced as contours and vacate their vacuity as forms. In music sounds resound; in poems vocables, material of the said, no longer yield before what they evoke, but sing with their evocative powers and their diverse ways to evoke, their etymologies; in Paul Valéry's *Eupalinos* architecture makes buildings sing. Poetry is productive of song, of resonance and sonority, which are the verbalness of verbs or essence.[29]

The opening salvo asserts that art, pure theme, exemplifies what he elsewhere calls structuration. The totalizing of "said" and "synchrony" as opposed to "saying's" response to the other. "The said reduced to the Beautiful" might charitably be paraphrased by one of the criteria that Wallace Stevens formulates in "Notes Toward a Supreme Fiction," that "it must please." But then Levinas places this quality "Beauty" within the purview of his bugbear "Western ontology," beings totalized within being. It's difficult to read these first two sentences as anything more than a lukewarm response to art. There seems to be a shift as I read on. Essence, we recall as Levinas's term for Being (Heidegger's *Sein*), and time, being's mode of being, respond with poetry or song. Is this response a good thing? It would seem so because in the following sentence Levinas writes, insightfully, that "the search for new forms, from which all art lives, keeps awake everywhere the verbs that are on the verge of lapsing into substantives." In Levinas's theory of language, the verb is capable of "saying" while the noun hardens reality into the "said." From this perspective, one I share, art is precious indeed. Art vacates the vacuity of forms. A lovely thought! Not filling the form, but emptying out its emptiness! We recall Wallace Stevens' "form gulping after formlessness."

The most difficult word to make sense of in this passage is Levinas's use of the word "etymologies." As I read the passage, etymology works as a metaphor for the resonance of musical sound, or poetic vocable, with an ever-deepening sense of self, just as an awareness of the etymology of words adds depth to their meanings. But he says they—sounds, vocables—*do not yield* to their etymologies. They evoke but do not yield, for the work of art is capable of opening new meaning, whereas their a priori etymologies are a closed list. As Levinas says of painting, "red reddens and green greens," expanding the palette of what red and green might mean. The word "etymologies" is followed immediately by a remarkable endnote that reads: "And that no doubt is what Paul Valéry was thinking of when he named poetry a hesitation between sound and meaning."[30] In language we have already developed, that "hesitation" is a liminal space, where we hover in between sound and meaning. Such liminal spaces already have been suggested in *Totality and Infinity* by the enigmatic "dead time": "being between two times . . . the very rupture that creation operates in being."[31] This enigmatic in-between, unsettled, emergent, is the gateway to the infinite.

The end of the passage quoted above makes reference to a prose dialogue by Paul Valéry, *Eupalinos, or the Architect*, a strange and wonderful work. Valéry's dialogue takes place between two interlocutors, Socrates and Phaedrus, both borrowed from Plato's *Phaedrus*. Here the interlocutors have already died, and we hear the voices of their shades in the afterlife. As the title indicates, much of the dialogue refers to the architect Eupalinos, and it is Phaedrus who tells Socrates about Eupalinos's views on the craft and aesthetics of architecture. Much of Phaedrus's telling is his remembered conversations with Eupalinos, set as direct quotes. At one point Phaedrus remembers Eupalinos saying, "Tell me (since you are so sensible to the effects of architecture), have you not noticed, in walking about this city, that among the buildings with which it is peopled, certain are *mute*; others *speak*; and others, finally—and they are the most rare—*sing*?"[32] We recall Eduard Hanslick's claim that among the arts, music is most kindred to architecture, architecture that moves. Hanslick's famous dictum is preceded by Fredrick van Schelling, who writes in his *Philosophy of Art* that "architecture, as the music of the plastic arts, thus necessarily follows arithmetical relationships. Since it is music in space, however, in a sense, solidified music."[33] Valéry's Eupalinos turns the tables; the rarest of architecture sings. For Levinas, this ability to sing is a transitive saying, more like a verb than a noun, not hardened into a nominative said.

On the very next page after the passage that we have just focused on, Levinas mentions an actual musical work. The mention of an actual musical work must happen elsewhere in Levinas, but where I cannot recall. The musical example is Iannis Xenakis's "Nomos Alpha for Unaccompanied Cello," a work that uses what is sometimes called "extended techniques."[34] Levinas says that Xenakis "bends the quality of the notes emitted into adverbs." What a clever way of saying that the musical work modifies (as adverb) what it is to be (a verb) a cello.[35]

Gerald L. Bruns, in his essay "The Concepts of Art and Poetry in Emmanuel Levinas's Writings," discusses art as a modality of transcendence, where art is "no longer an object for us, but a thing in itself, a pure exteriority. Basically, art is ecstasy . . . or exteriority temporally as an interruption of being: the *entre-temps*." The idea that art takes us out of normal experiential time rings true for me, especially in the temporal arts of theater, film, and music. As the quote makes clear, "pure exteriority" is not equivalent to objectivity. Rather this exteriority is the sense of being taken out of oneself: intimate contact with another. This *entre-temps* might be described as a dilated liminal space.[36]

Later in the same essay, Bruns cites a passage where Levinas's deeply conflicted feelings about art once again come to the fore. Art "brings the irresponsibility that charms as a lightness and grace. It frees. To make or to appreciate a novel and a picture is to no longer have to conceive, is to renounce the effort of science, philosophy, and action. Do not speak, do not reflect, admire in silence and peace—such are the counsels of wisdom before the beautiful . . . There is something wicked and egoist and cowardly in artistic enjoyment. There are times when one can be ashamed of it, as of feasting during a plague."[37] Or, I suppose, fiddling while Rome burns.

The kind of passivity that admires in silence and peace is at odds with my own experiences of art, and it is certainly not a quality shared by art's practitioners. Here I speculate: once again in Levinas's prose I hear the trauma of the Holocaust. I imagine the inspired listeners, Berlin 1944, hearing Wilhelm Furtwängler's magnificent performances of Beethoven, while Levinas's teachers, friends, and family are being exterminated. And then I understand that there are times when "one can be ashamed."

Levinas's review of Michael Leiris's book *Biffures*, "The Transcendence of Words," raises a number of interesting issues regarding both literary prose and painting. In that context, Levinas contrasts seeing with hearing. Seeing, he writes, "is being in a world that is completely *here*, and self-sufficient." In contrast,

> There is in fact in sound—and in consciousness understood as hearing—a shattering of the always complete world of vision and art [presumably visual art]. Sound is all repercussion, outburst, scandal. While in vision a form espouses a content and soothes it, sound is like the sensible quality overflowing its limits, the incapacity of form to hold its content—a true rent in the fabric of the world—that by which the world that is *here* prolongs a dimension inconvertible into vision. It is thus that the sound is symbol *par excellence*—a reaching beyond the given . . . To really hear a sound is to hear a word. Pure sound is the word.[38]

I am not convinced that vision is necessarily or essentially totalizing. Visual art has the capacity to augment my sense of seeing, running contrary to "a complete world of vision." To look at a Rembrandt portrait is to know that painting goes beyond form, soothing though it may be.

Even more striking is Levinas's incredibly reductive characterization "to hear a sound is to hear a word. Pure sound is the word." Pure sound may be characterized as the word in poetry, although Valéry's hesitation between sound and meaning gets deeper into the core of poetry, but the sound of birds singing, or the sound of a string quartet, is not reducible to words; there, sound is pure song. On the other hand, Levinas's assertion that sound overflows its limits, "the incapacity of form to hold its content," strikes me a very insightful. A reduction of bird song or music to form or function misses this point.

In the opening essay of *Difficult Freedom*, "Ethics and Spirit," Levinas once again articulates his conflicted view of art.[39] After a consideration of violence, "in which one acts as if one were alone to act," followed by a contrasting consideration of "the face" of the other, where "The banal fact of conversation, in one sense, quits the order of violence. This banal fact is the marvel of marvels," he goes on to say, "Things *give*, they do not offer a face. They are beings without a face. Perhaps art seeks to give a face to things, and in this its greatness and its deceit simultaneously reside."[40] Conversation can entail deceit, and so can art. Conversation can be "face-to-face," and I would argue, so can art. Levinas's refusal to recognize art, music included, as human utterance, with or without words, is his blind spot, his inability to hear.

Levinas makes a startling observation about creativity in his essay "Temptation of Temptation," a reading of the Talmud Tractate *Shabbath*, 88a–88b, published in *Nine Talmudic Readings*.[41] The epigraph that opens the essay cites a fragment from Exodus 19:17: "And they stopped at the foot of the mountain . . ." More to the point, however, is Exodus 24:7, which I cite using Everett Fox's translation.

> Then he [Moshe] took the account of the covenant
> and read it in the ears of the people.
> They said:
> All that YHWH has spoken, we will do and we will harken!

In the Hebrew *we will do and we will harken* is expressed by two words נעשה ונשמע (*na'ahseh v'nishma*). Rabbinical commentary notes that doing and hearing are here reversed from their normal cognitive order (normally we hear and then do, rather than do and then hear), although many translations read *v'nishma* figuratively to mean obey. (The most central Hebrew prayer opens with the words *Shema Yisrael* [Hear, Oh Israel], derived from the same root word.)

We get a similar reversal in Psalm 103:20. Most translations do not bring this out, but rabbinical commentary associates the Psalm passage with the passage from Exodus. Here is the translation given in Emmanuel Levinas, *Nine Talmudic Readings* (31): "Bless the Lord, Oh, His angels, you mighty ones who do His word, harkening to the voice of His word." The words for "do" and "harken," עשי (*osei*) and לשמע (*li'shmoah*(in the Psalm, are derived from the same root words as in the passage from Exodus. The rabbis who correlate the two passages argue that in *doing and then hearing* the Israelites take on the mode of the angels. Levinas cites and discusses this and then goes on: "one accepts the Torah before one knows it. This shocks logic and can pass for blind faith or the naivete of childish trust, yet it is what underlies any inspired act, even artistic, for the act only brings out the form in which it only now recognizes its model, never glimpsed before."[42]

To *bring out the form in which it only now recognizes its model, never glimpsed before*: a wonderful way of describing the creative act. In Hebrew scripture, God, above all, creates and then sees that it is good. There are times when an author, or composer, or an artist or creative thinker of any stripe, has a breakthrough, something that with hard work can be prepared for, but that willful intention cannot achieve. Call it inspiration, drawing on the unconscious mind, one's daemon superseding one's normal abilities, in any model we may choose, in each case "the act only brings out the form in which it only now recognizes its model, never glimpsed before." We have earlier discussed the word הנני (hineni), the "I am here" that obeys before understanding the command. To do and then harken is a variant on הנני.

To *bring out the form in which it only now recognizes its model, never glimpsed before* is also related to what Percy Shelley called "unpremeditated art." Here is the opening stanza of Shelley's "To a Skylark."

> Hail to thee, blithe Spirit!
> Bird thou never wert,
> That from Heaven, or near it,
> Pourest thy full heart
> In profuse strains of unpremeditated art.

Since Shelley's time, we have learned that the singing of birds is premeditated, for they too learn the art of song. Even so, Shelley gets at something wonderfully apt toward recognizing authenticity in music and in the music of poetry: that it seems to flow naturally, as though unpremeditated. And I am convinced that in the rarest of cases it is just so, as natural as breathing.

We have already discussed several instances of "hesitation," *entretemps*, what we have called liminal space. To close this segment on Levinas's thought, we now turn to further developments of thresholds. In the context of distinguishing between "saying," which actively engages the other, and "said," in which saying hardens into what he calls (totalizing) thematization or structuration, Levinas writes the following: "The plot of the saying that is absorbed in the said is not exhausted in this manifestation. It imprints its trace in the thematization itself, which hesitates between, on the one hand, structuration, order of a configuration of entities . . . and on the other hand, the order of non-nominalized apophansis of the other."[43] The word *apophansis* is borrowed from the Greek, denoting a categorical statement, what in Levinas's context is equivalent to an attribution, only here non-nominative, and so not hardening into a structure. The "trace" that hesitates between structuration and engagement with the other is a liminal time-space. We recall that the phrase "hesitates between" associates with Levinas's citation of Paul Valéry some seven pages earlier in the book to the effect that poetry hesitates between sound and meaning, another liminal space.[44] Here Levinas says that when saying hardens into said, all is not lost. A trace remains. We might say that despite the setback, the opening that closes, something is gained. I hope that I do not do too much violence to Levinas's idea by saying that in the history of any art, music certainly included, the most conspicuous openings, hesitations in liminal space, leave their trace so that others may also find their gateway, an opening toward infinity.

Another enigmatic liminal space is denoted by Levinas's use of the word "proximity," a key term in Levinas's understanding of one's relation to the other. "Proximity is not a state, a repose, but a restlessness, null site, outside of the place of rest . . . Never close enough, proximity does not congeal into a structure save when represented in the demand for justice as reversable, and reverts into a simple relation . . . This surplus or this lack throws me outside the objectivity characteristic of relations."[45] By "null site," Levinas intends some-non-thing outside of the totalizing structures of being. The sentence that begins "Never close enough" requires some unpacking. Earlier on in *Otherwise than Being* (and elsewhere), Levinas idiosyncratically develops the terms synchronic and diachronic.[46] For Levinas, synchronic time is totalizing, as are the constituents of synchronic language, all there at once, as in a closed system. Levinas's diachronic time transcends the synchronicity of being, it breaks open synchronicity; diachrony is operative in one's response to the other. Levinas states this idea succinctly within Part II of *Of God Who Comes to Mind* where he writes, "The proximity of the neighbor remains a dia-chronic break, or a resistance of time to the synthesis of simultaneity."[47]

Levinas's spelling, "dia-chronic," separates the prefix "dia," derived from the Greek δια, denoting "through," or "across," from "chronic," derived from the Greek χρόνος, "time." In Levinas's usage, "saying" is diachronic, non-totalizing, while the "said" is synchronic. The idea of justice, which is invoked in the cited passage, also needs explanation. Justice for Levinas requires a "third party," a person outside the individual and unique me-you dyad that is central to Levinas's metaphysics. Although not as explicitly defined as the relationship between plaintiff and defendant, as viewed from the outside by a judge, the parallels are evident. Justice for

Levinas is synchronic;[48] it exists within a system. The judge sees me-you as reversable, two instances of "you," each of whom knows herself or himself as "me," reversable as innocent/guilty or justified/not justified, in a relationship where responsibility is mutual. For Levinas, the diachrony of one's responsibility to the other in antecedent to the synchronicity of justice.

Like "trace," which hesitates between totalizing structuration and engaging the other, and like Valéry's concept of poetry, where we hesitate between sound and meaning, proximity is a liminal term, where one and the other are close, "never close enough," because always each remains distinctive and unique.[49] As with so many of Levinas's terms, proximity can be adapted toward understanding one's relation to a work of art. In most musical experiences, sustained proximity in Levinas's sense is mutually dependent on three factors: the work must have depth so that it can continue to reveal itself over time; the musical performers must have sufficient acuity of interpretive skills so that they can plumb that depth; the listener must have sufficient imagination, a cognitive and emotional depth, to sustain a relationship with the interpreted work. The poem or composition that can keep on unfolding meaning, even after a lifetime of reading or hearing, is one where proximity is sustained. Picking up one of the principal threads of this study, we might say that "this surplus or lack" that "throws me outside of the objectivity characteristic of relations" is middle-voiced.

Before closing our discussion of Levinas's thought, I want to turn to a couple of points made near the end of Hillary Putnam's essay "Levinas and Judaism." Putnam is critical of the asymmetrical extreme to which Levinas describes one's obligation to the other: "the 'asymmetry' of the ethical relationship need not be carried as far as Levinas carries it."[50] It seems to me that Putnam is right about this. In many passages, Levinas's formulations, such as "tearing the bread out of one's mouth," read as self-mortification. Putnam also addresses Levinas's critique of Martin Buber. Buber, antecedent to Levinas, had centered his ethics on an "I-Thou" relationship whose prototype was each person's relationship with God. "Thou" is a term of intimacy, at odds with Levinas's radical otherness of the other. One of Levinas's terms that I find more mystifying than revealing is his coinage "illeity." Alphonso Lingis, in his translator's introduction to *Otherwise Than Being*, describes illeity as "the movement of infinition, Levinas names God."[51] Near the beginning of *Otherwise Than Being*, Levinas writes: "Illeity lies outside the 'thou' and the thematization of objects.⁵² Evidently, Levinas does not feel that I-thou captures the diachrony and spirituality espoused in his obligation to the other. In contrast, Putnam argues that Levinas's ethics is one-sided, restrictive in what might comprise a relationship and not open to alternatives.

> It is Aristotle who taught us that to love others one must be able to love oneself. The thought seems utterly alien to Levinas. I also described Levinas's ethics as "one-sided." It is because it is one-sided that, I think, Levinas's relation to Buber is fundamentally a competitive one. Rather than seeing Buber as someone who identified a different "I-Thou" relation from Levinas's, someone who identified a different *sine qua non* of the "true life," Levinas must see Buber as someone who (had insights to be sure, but) got it wrong. But the ethical life has more than one *sine qua non*.⁵³

To amplify Putnam's important point, we can say that not all relationships are the same. I return to this idea later in thinking about what a musical canon might entail.

6

Character, Canon, and Poetic Influence

The Poetics of Harold Bloom

For a short while in the 1980s, the writings of Harold Bloom were a hot topic among academics, music theorists included. Then, for many, like the bell-bottomed trousers in the changing styles of clothing, Bloom was discarded as no longer relevant. My own experience was otherwise. Like David Lewin, whose model showed me the way if not the method of being a music scholar, Bloom continued to profoundly shape my world. And though Bloom mentioned music only rarely, he deeply influenced how I thought about music.

To say something about Harold Bloom that no one can contest, I might be reduced to saying that he wrote a lot. When you write a lot, those who admire your work have lots to choose from, and those readers who find that your work rubs them the wrong way will likewise have lots to complain about. Critics of this master critic have found much to dislike, while Bloom's most dedicated readers found him to be the most inspired and inspiring literary critic of his generation.

As advocate for a literary canon, Bloom was and is lauded for his unsurpassed capacity to assess, integrate, and evaluate a vast literature, ancient, contemporary, and seemingly all in between. Others find the very idea of a canon oppressive, attacking Bloom for sins of omission and for the high and mighty tone of his assessments. Bloom could count among his most ardent admirers many of the most accomplished poets, novelists, and scholars of his day, as well as what he liked to call common readers, those who read for the pleasure of reading. Yet legions resented his formulation of a "school of resentment," what one of my friends and colleagues characterized as a "cheap shot." Some found his writings on religion inspiring, even liberating; others said he would be damned to hell. Somewhere, Bloom with zestful exuberance quotes a speech from former governor of the great state of Texas, who said that "If English was good enough for Jesus, it's good enough for me." He angered "observant" Jews by insisting on naming God "Yahweh," a transliteration of יהוה, the tetragrammaton never pronounced in Jewish tradition, even in the most fervent prayer. And he pissed off Christians by insisting that we have no direct quotes from Jesus: this based on the simple fact that Jesus spoke Aramaic and Hebrew, while the earliest Christian Bible is written in Greek. I find Bloom, in his inspired passages, and there are so very many of them, to be among the very best writers of prose I have encountered. Yet not everyone seems to agree. Well, no one can please everyone. Take a breath and someone will complain that you're using up all of the oxygen. A mighty champion for those he loved, Bloom could also be cruel. "He was a man, take him for all in all, I shall not look upon his like again."

I first encountered Harold Bloom while reading David V. Erdman's edition of the poetry and prose of William Blake. Bloom had written the extensive commentary published in minuscule print in the back of the book. The year was 1967, and my day job at the time was playing clarinet in one of the two US Army bands in Fort Dix, New Jersey. Alice Klein had given me the book as a present. I was young and naive about scholarship and a great many other things, but I still remember being blown away by Bloom's erudition. I wondered, who is this guy? It was the learnedness of Harold Bloom that first attracted me to his work.

Decades later, I and so many of my colleagues became immersed in the flurry of books Bloom wrote, starting with *The Anxiety of Influence*: revisionary ratios, kabbalistic mysticism, Freudian defense mechanisms, and a strangeness of visionary synthesis that astounded. There was plenty of erudition there, but it was the audacity of thought and prose that enraptured me and so many others. In a review of Angus Fletcher's work, published in 1971, Bloom refers to Fletcher as a "terminological buccaneer," an epithet well-put and highly appropriate. Yet Bloom must also have been describing himself. Beyond the erudition, it was the audacity of thought of Bloom's synthetic imagination and the pizzazz of his prose that now drew me to his work.

And then there is the Bloom who had read so many, many books and could tell us about them, Bloom's presence always vivid in the telling. Although I was no child prodigy, far from it, I had developed a love of poetry and literature more generally as a teenager, some years before encountering Bloom. Yet he opened worlds for me, as he must have for so many others. One aspect of reading that I vaguely recognized before reading Bloom became vivid after being immersed in his writings: that in a scholar's library the books speak to and through one another. These days, retired from teaching and tucked away in a corner of Chandler, Arizona, my library buzzes with conversations and arguments, citings and slightings. No one taught me more than Bloom about how the books to talk to one another. Musical compositions and musical performances also speak (or sing) to on another, and one doesn't necessarily need a literary critic to recognize that. Yet, for me, Bloom conditioned and augmented an awareness of the cross-singing of generations within any composition or performance.

Yet, more than any of these attributes, more than the specifics of any of Bloom's critical assertions, as the years went on it was the individual person I heard in Bloom's so-human voice that I most came to admire. Here was a scholar, foibles and grandeur, who was fully human. In Bloom, the reader chants like the cantors of his Yiddish childhood. The reader and the poem enter into an intimate and knowing relationship, like a prayer. And even when he was cranky, you knew that it was only because he cared so deeply. Look no further than the erudite and disarming headnotes in his two poetry anthologies, *The Best Poems in the English Language* and *Till I End My Song: A Gathering of Last Poems*, and you'll see something other than the usual, objective facts. There is a magic there, the magic of human presence.

More so than prose, apart from prose that verges on poetry, reading poetry, like playing music, is performative. Reading poetry is concomitant with recognizing subtleties of inflection, pace and pause, assonance and consonance. Bloom was fond of calling poetry "cognitive music," perhaps hearing Valéry's hesitation between sound and meaning in the background of his thought. But instrumental music too is cognitive music. Cognizing Mozart, for example in one of his late string quintets, vies with cognizing just about anything I can think of. But cognition and sound (if music is reduced to sound), while necessary, are not sufficient. Character and emotional tone are required as well. Bloom knew this, and his concept of music in poetry and prose, though rarely articulated, has this resonance. John Hollander, remarkable poet and scholar, Bloom's close friend for many years, was highly sensitive to the music of poetry, and he wrote about it explicitly and astutely. Throughout the nearly thirty years that I taught a course on "music and text" at the University of Minnesota, Hollander's handbook *Rhyme's Reason* was required reading. In contrast, Bloom was rarely explicit in mentioning the musical elements in poetry, yet somehow the music was conveyed.

Bloom's last works became an ever-augmenting weave of self-reflection and autobiography with musings on the poetry and novels that haunted him night and day. Bloom had an enormous influence on my own writing. This book exemplifies that.

∼

Personal Excursus

I got to meet Harold Bloom in person only once, in December 2013. Although I had spent four years at Yale as a graduate student, 1978–1982, a time when Bloom was very much a presence at Yale, that was a time when my wife Rose and I were fully consumed with graduate studies and raising our two sons, Joseph Jacob and Paul Benjamin, both born while we were at Yale. I became fully immersed in Bloom's writings only after moving to the State University of New York at Stony Brook, my first teaching job. By the time my book on Arnold Schoenberg, *Schoenberg's Musical Imagination*, was published in 2007, reading Bloom had been a consuming passion for more than two decades. As was the influence of David Lewin, the influence of Harold Bloom was pervasive and basic to the book. David had already passed away. It took me more than four years to summon the courage to send a copy of the book to Harold. Bloom wrote to me with kind words soon after receiving the book, inviting me to visit if I ever came back to Yale. That was December 2011. It took two more years before Rose and I were able to make the trip. I quote Rose's email to me, written later that same day.

> Today we drove to New Haven, CT, to visit Professor Bloom and his wife Jeanne. We were invited for tea at 4pm. The visit lasted a mere 50 minutes since we found Harold in poor health, recovering from an illness that had him in two hospitals for 11 days. He looked weak, tired, and thin.
> He called us children, beautiful children, signed two books for Michael, and gave Michael one dedicated to him [a

Festschrift written in celebration of Bloom's 80th birthday]. He made three telephone calls trying to make some connections for Michael, one to Peter Cole, with whom Michael spoke briefly. We left soon after. Harold was very tired, but gracious, as was Jeanne. Phone numbers and addresses were exchanged. We were invited to visit again in New Haven or NY. WOW! A beautiful man.

Shortly after arriving, I noticed sitting among the books scattered about on Bloom's table a new book by the poet and distinguished translator of poetry, Peter Cole. I had previously been reading and admiring some of Cole's work, and reacted with surprise, "ah, a new book by Peter Cole." Almost instantly, Bloom was on the phone calling John T. Irwin, brilliant scholar of Hart Crane's poetry, who under the pseudonym of John Bricuth had published two wonderful, zany books of comic poetry, *Just Let Me Say This about That*, and *As Long as it's Big: A Narrative Poem*. Irwin, working for Johns Hopkins University Press, was looking for someone to review Cole's new book, and Bloom recommended me for the job. Not long afterwards, sad to say, Irwin had a devastating stroke and he soon passed away. Before his passing, Irwin and I had had a lively email correspondence, including a commission to review Cole's book with its Bloom-influenced title, *The Invention of Influence*. Peter Cole, to this day, remains a treasured email friend. The kindness shown to me by Bloom must have been matched by who knows how many other kindnesses to others.

Never Resting Mind

The Anatomy of Influence: Literature as a Way of Life, published in 2011, was intended, among other things, to be Bloom's final statement on literary influence. To go back and revisit the astounding cluster of books that Bloom wrote on literary influence, starting with *The Anxiety of Influence* and continuing through *A Map of Misreading, Poetry and Repression, Kabbalah and Criticism, Agon*, and *Ruin the Sacred Truths*, to name only the most central of Bloom's incessant brooding on the topic, would entail being mired in a range of references that would edge out all of the other concerns of this book. Bloom's not quite final words on literary influence will suffice: "I define influence simply as *literary love, tempered by defense.* The defenses vary from poet to poet. But the overwhelming presence of love is vital to understanding how great literature works."[1] Anyone who was blessed to grow up in a loving home, as I did, and who remembers their adolescence and young adulthood, as I do, and who went through a prolonged period of trying to shape one's own sense of self, as I did, should recognize love tempered by defense. Transfer this from persons to works, add vast experience in reading and brooding on what has been read, and you get Bloom's theory of influence. For a musician of my background and tastes, this includes recognizing that Beethoven became Beethoven, in part, because he could never out-Mozart Mozart. Whether or not Beethoven was cognizant of anxiety, and my guess is that he wasn't, his defense, embodied in the works not the person, was against a lesser replication of what came before. In Beethoven's extraordinary case, the move from his middle works into his late period was a self-overcoming, a defense against his former self. And all of this is complicated by Beethoven's relation to J. S. Bach. Bach's fugues shadowed generations of composers. To my mind, after Bach, only Beethoven took the fugue and made it fully his own. He did this by radically reimagining what a fugue could be. To do this, he had to ward off the majesty of Bach's fugues, so that he could achieve the majesty of Beethoven's.

Bloom's earliest scholarship focused on the English Romantics, Wordsworth, Byron, Shelley, Keats, and their astounding precursor William Blake. But Bloom's enormous appetite and capacity for reading had enormous range, and it is a mistake to circumscribe his areas of interest. If we divide his universe of reading into galaxies, one of those galaxies to which he gave special attention was American literature. By his later years, he judged Walt Whitman to be the greatest writer of the Western Hemisphere. Highly appreciative of earlier generations of American poets and novelists, Emily Dickinson, Nathaniel Hawthorne, Herman Melville, and others, Bloom also wrote brilliantly on a host of his American contemporaries. In Bloom's American pantheon, Ralph Waldo Emerson had a special place. *The Anatomy of Influence* includes an extended treatment of Emerson, much of it apposite toward music's makings, to which I now turn.

Ralph Waldo Emerson was for Bloom the "begetter of much (if not most) of American literature and thought." Yet Bloom's Emerson is hard to hold onto. He quotes Henry James Sr., "O you man without a handle," and then goes on say, "Try to grasp the American prophet and Proteus slips away."[2]

> He defined freedom as wildness, and his never-resting mind is always at a crossing, shooting a gulf, and darting to a new aim. You can read Waldo by ambushing him, but generally he has gone forward when you make your move . . .
>
> His discontinuous rhetoric is designed to break down conventional responses, as any original religious discourse has to do . . .
>
> Emerson's spirit is agonistic, and he wants you to wrestle with him, a frustrating demand on the reader because Waldo is too slippery to hold.[3]

Levinas and Emerson are two very different personalities, with two very different life experiences, but both have in common an antipathy to all totalizing thought. The Emerson that is too slippery to hold onto is an Emerson who resists totalizing.

Contrasting his reading of Emerson with that of David Bromwich, Bloom writes, "Though Bromwich sees that Self-Reliance can be read as a religious term, he seems to prefer a social interpretation of it. But I follow Emerson in insisting that it is a religious naming . . . . This relies upon Emerson's invention of what could be called a purely daemonic American unconscious."[4] In his preferring individualized religious meaning over social meaning, I read Bloom not as negating social meaning, but rather as finding a center of balance in the individual (poem, person) as they relate to another individual, or composite figure (poem, poems, poet, poets). There are writers who place each individual human as a center, generating society outward, and there are writers who place society at the center, moving from the collective toward individuals. William Faulkner and Toni Morrison strike me as writers who move from individuals toward society, while John Steinbeck and Masha Gessen (to choose a non-fiction writer) strike me as writers who move from more encompassing social issues toward individuals.[5] We can value both approaches.

We recall Bloom's earlier comment that Emerson's "discontinuous rhetoric is designed to break down conventional responses, as any original religious discourse has to do." Emersonian religiosity is an ethics-informed creativity, and the poets, Shakespeare above all others, were recognized as its prophets. A striking passage from Bloom's *Ruin the Sacred Truths* is apposite toward recognizing Bloom's understanding of religiosity.

> The scandal is the stubborn resistance of imaginative literature to the categories of sacred and secular. If you wish, you can

insist that all literature is secular, or, should you desire it so, then all strong poetry is sacred. What I find incoherent is the judgement that some authentic literary art is more sacred or more secular than some other. Poetry and belief wander about, together and apart, in a cosmological emptiness marked by the limits of truth and of meaning.[6]

Bloom was fond of quoting the startling final sentence of Percy Shelley's extraordinary essay "A Defense of Poetry": "Poets are the unacknowledged legislators of the World." Shelley, I assume, at least in large part, was referring to the poets who composed scripture; presented as the voice of God, these poets are indeed the unacknowledged legislators of the world. In judging Emersonian self-reliance as religious, Bloom reads him as an American prophet, recognizing the Emersonian quest for transcendence, a reaching beyond quotidian experience. Along similar lines, near the opening of his 2015 book *The Daemon Knows: Literary Greatness and the American Sublime*, Bloom explains the criteria in his choice of the twelve authors whose works he will discuss: "these writers represent our incessant effort to transcend the human without forsaking humanism."[7]

In a passage from Emerson's "Self-Reliance" quoted by Bloom, the New England prophet gives the names Spontaneity and Instinct, and then Intuition, to the force Bloom calls "daemonic." "The inquiry leads us to that source, at once the essence of genius, of virtue, and of life, which we call Spontaneity or Instinct. We denote this primary wisdom as Intuition, whilst all later teachings are tuitions. In that deep force, the last fact behind which analysis cannot go, all things find their common origin."[8] Emerson's "intuition," translated into Bloom's "daemon," is kindred to Levinas's (and Talmudic) reversal of hear and obey: to *bring out the form in which it only now recognizes its model, never glimpsed before.* That "deep force," called religious, though highly personal, is also social. I once again recall Levinas, where responsibility to the other is the gateway to augmenting one's sense of self. For Levinas, this is a calling that can be named religion, with the self, responsible to the other, at its core: Hillel's "If I am not for myself, who will be. If I am only for myself, what am I?"

I might say, for example, that my love of Beethoven's music is centered on the individuality of whichever of his works I am attending. And that work is unique, an individual, irreplaceable human utterance. And yet any given work is poorly understood, if understood at all, outside of the tradition that nurtured it as well as the tradition that springs from knowing that work. In the varied worlds of music making, placing the collective above the individual might entail the "best practices" of developing orchestral players, where sticking out will get you fired. And yet I always hope there is room for *some* personality, at least within solo passages, to hear the voice of an individual playing the flute, or violin, or whatever, not just the sound of an instrument. An orchestral conductor without personality, where technique supplants an individual voice, is, in my experience, hardly worth listening to (jingles and other purely "functional" music aside, where the generic is the point). I am so biased in my views of musical composition that I find it difficult to even articulate what it might mean to place social needs at the center of creativity, unless we mean something like the views of art in Nazi Germany or Soviet Russia.

One of the themes of this book is that creativity, while immersed in tradition, is dependent on developing an ever-deepening sense of the uniqueness of one's self. Bloom warns that "Founding another academic industry upon Emerson betrays him, since self-union is not a social enterprise."[9] University instruction too often, alas, squelches individual thought. And yet the paradox that needs to be recalled is found in Emerson's "The American Scholar." "The deeper [the scholar] dives into his privatest, secretest presentiment, to his wonder he finds, this is the most acceptable, most public, and universally true. The people delight in it; the better part of every man feels, This is my music; this is myself."[10] I recall being at one of those dreadful faculty retreats years ago, where one of my colleagues opined that our primary obligation as teachers was to the students. Already irritated just by being there, I ruffled some feathers, and was surely misunderstood, in responding that the teacher's primary obligation was to self-nurturing through deep learning: that only then can one be responsible toward one's students. I firmly believe that "teaching colleges" that place method over discipline-based substance go about teaching teachers the wrong way. The teachers we love the most, at least in my experience, are those who bring to us their deep love and understanding of whatever it is that they teach.

This is not to say that an artist might not respond and respond powerfully to social needs. Many of our greatest writers, as with artists in any medium, do just that. But, to my mind, that is not what makes them great writers, musicians, painters, whatever. Bloom addresses this aspect of Toni Morrison's work in *Novelists and Novels: A Collection of Critical Essays.*[11] "No contemporary novelist of anything like Toni Morrison's eminence is so insistent that she desires political interpretation by her exegetes . . . If the United States achieves a larger measure of social justice in a generation or so, then Morrison yet may be esteemed more for her narrative art, invention, and style than for her exemplary political correctness."[12] In Bloom's view, one that I share, Morrison could so powerfully redress social injustice in her novels *because* she was a strong writer, because she was a master of her craft, because she could create vital characters, because she could shape the English language with a level of achievement few others could attain. For some readers, such an assertion over-aestheticizes Morrison's writing. For some readers, Morrison is most essentially a political writer (and so I've been told, with a voice of authority). As with the novels of Charles Dickens, social justice is never far from Morrison's literary imagination. Still, to call her a great writer sounds good to me, while to call her a great political theorist, or something of the sort, seems odd beyond belief.

In my teen years into my early twenties, John Coltrane was an enormous presence in American music. The dignity and power of this American original, beyond the presence of his music, taught many white Americans to better attend to African American contributions to our greater society. It was the dignity and power of his music that spoke.

In *The Anatomy of Influence*, Bloom writes: "I do not believe that poetry has anything to do with cultural politics. I ask of a poem three things: aesthetic splendor, cognitive power, and wisdom."[13] Bloom can be inflammatory in his insistence that poetry has nothing to do with cultural politics. Of course, it can have lots to do with cultural politics, and, incendiary rhetoric aside, Bloom must have recognized this. Yet, if I understand him correctly, the larger point is that one's stand on cultural politics, however it's evaluated, is not the criterion on which poetic (or musical) imagination is to be judged.

Character: Persons and Personality

Bloom assessed Shakespeare the greatest of writers, in large part because of the hundreds of characters he so vividly created. Bloom opens *Shakespeare: The Invention of the Human* with a marvelous note "To the Reader." Here is its first paragraph and just a bit more.

> Literary character before Shakespeare is relatively unchanging; women and men are represented as aging and dying, but not as

changing because their relationship to themselves, rather than to the gods or God, has changed. In Shakespeare, characters develop rather than unfold, and they develop because they reconceive themselves. Sometimes this comes about because they *overhear* themselves talking, whether to themselves or to others. Self-hearing is their royal road to individuation, and no other writer, before or since Shakespeare, has accomplished so well the virtual miracle of creating utterly different yet self-consistent voices for his more than one hundred major characters and many hundreds of highly distinctive minor personages.

The more one reads and ponders the plays of Shakespeare, the more one realizes that the accurate stance toward them is one of awe. How he was possible, I cannot know, and after two decades of teaching little else, I find the enigma insoluble.[14]

Bloom also recognized Charles Dickens, a novelist of the first rank, as the inventor of a rich abundance of characters. And there are many others who do likewise in Bloom's pantheon. Yet no one matches Shakespeare's ability to create persons. As to range of characters in music, we have no Shakespeare. In my experience, the closest we come is Mozart, especially in the extraordinary operas with libretti by Lorenzo Da Ponte. It's not that Mozart is comparable to Shakespeare in number of vivid characters, not nearly so, but Mozart's best characters are as fully human as those created by Shakespeare. In *Le nozze di Figaro* alone, Susana, Figaro, the Count and Countess, and Cherubino are fully human. And, as in Shakespeare, the lesser characters, Doctor Bartolo, Mercellina, Don Curzio, Basilio, and Antonio, are all wonderfully etched. Da Ponte gave these characters their words, and the words are wonderfully wrought and clearly important, but it is the music that gives these characters character. Within the Italian opera tradition, Giuseppe Verdi, nearly the match of Mozart in this capacity, is also the inventor of many vital characters. Yet even Mozart and Verdi combined cannot vie with Shakespeare when it comes to inventing the range of persons that we find in the histories, tragedies, and comedies of this supreme master.

But the musical invention of character is not limited to opera, characters set on a stage, where the characters express their humanity through a fusion of words-sounds and nonverbal sounds. Instrumental music too has the potential of expressing a strong sense of character or interacting characters. Mozart's music, for example, almost always has the potential to project a strong sense of character, whether the music is theatrical or not. Of course, whether that potential is achieved depends on the collaboration of performer and composer and audience to take it all in. Closer to our own time, much of Elliott Carter's music develops multiple musical characters in coordination and conflict with one another. Sensitive performances will recognize and manifest this.

One common musical technique, especially prevalent in chamber music, is for one voice to imitate another. So, for example, the second violin might play something, which is then mimicked by the first violin, perhaps an octave higher. Normally, the responding voice will inflect the musical phrase so as to closely match its antecedent. An alternative would be to insist on restating the phrase with a different emphasis. We might call this the "'you say tom-ay-to and I say to-mah-to' effect," drawing on George and Ira Gershwin for our newfound technical vocabulary. Elliott Carter's *String Quartet No. 2* makes a version of this technique thematic by giving each instrument its own vocabulary of musical intervals and its own personal characteristics.[15] Within the literature of music theory, two closely related approaches have been developed to address at least some aspects of what I've called character: musical *semiotics* and musical *topics*.[16]

The idea of sign and signified is easily understood: the stop sign signifies that I must stop. Musical semiotics understands musical ideas as signs that point toward their meanings; for example, a downward gesture might signify a sigh. Musical topics, referred to by Leonard Ratner as "a thesaurus of characteristic figures," also signify "extra-musical" associations.[17] A dance topic, for example, might associate with a certain subgroup within a larger society. Mozart uses this technique masterfully in *Don Giovanni*.[18]

The posthumous publication of Wye Allanbrook, *The Secular Commedia: Comic Mimesis in Late Eighteenth-Century Music*, comprises a sustained and well-developed argument for the centrality of topic theory in the study and performance of eighteenth-century opera buffa.[19] Building on the work of historical precursors, including Leonard Ratner and Raymond Monelle, Allanbrook's concept of musical topics entails an expansive notion of mimesis to include what I would distinguish as metonymic thought (association by contiguity), as well as musical character.

> Opera buffa articulated an entire social cosmos, highborn to lowly, and its emphasis was comparative: on the *ēthē* [character]

rather than *pathē* [emotions or passions], on character-signaling behavior rather than on the discursive expression of the passions.[20]

The new, communally defined *mimēmata* [mimetic imitation] came embedded in this more inclusive social world; they were connected with class and associated with social institutions—the church, the court, the theater, and the dance hall. They suggest movement from a notion of emotions that seize us momentarily (*pathē*) to one of habits which are natively disposed (*ēthē*)—the difference between passions and character states.[21]

As useful as they might be, to study music through semiotics or topics, at least to my mind, implies objectification, this despite the inclusion of "character" in Allanbrook's expansive concept of topics. Thinking (creating, performing, and hearing) of musical *character* not as an objective category (topic) but as a vivifying life-force allows for a fusion of agent/patient: one who acts and is acted upon, one who remains constant or one who changes over time. Moreover, to my mind, middle-voiced character is a far more inclusive way of speaking about music than signs and topics. In any case, character or personality cannot be realized by just playing the notes or singing the song. The performer has to meet the composer halfway. Of course, the same hold true of Shakespeare's characters, where actor or reader plays the role of performer.

In these days of YouTube, something I like to do from time to time is to listen to multiple, different recordings of a "tin pan alley" standard, where each singer brings his or her unique voice to the music. Sometimes a single performance will emerge as a favorite, but better yet is when multiple voices vie for and achieve an excellence that disallows a single favorite.

In my years as a teacher, I attended literally hundreds of student recitals. Understandably, student performances will vary in excellence; any teacher worthy of the name looks for a spark that can be fanned into a flame. What I came to miss most in so many of those performances was a strong sense of the music's character, what I'd now call a strongly presented middle voice where performer and composer collaborate. Character is not in the score; no matter how carefully annotated, the score can only point out a direction. The performer then must embody and achieve a musical character that the direction suggests. When the performer is blessed with a strong sense of self, including the courage to contradict teachers when they stifle that sense of self, character will emerge simply because it cannot be squelched.

Most pop performers, even the most memorable, have a single persona, personality, character. Although, tempered by the mood of the song, Dean Martin, a wonderful crooner, always sounds like Dean Martin. Name changed, the same might be said about many, even most pop artists (generic performers aside, where character is supplanted by lack of character). One stunning exception to this rule is Bob Dylan. Through the 1960s into the 1970s and 1980s, Dylan, a musical chameleon, kept changing his voice and his musical persona. I remember those years, waiting to hear what Dylan would next become. The Beatles, a veritable music variety show, also could take on radically different characters, but one always recognized the Beatles behind the mask. The great composers in the classical tradition(s) were capable of creating many different sorts of personae, explicit in music for the theater, implicit in instrumental music. Like a capable actor, the capable performer of music shapes the sounds, giving them a personality that is co-invented in collaboration with the composer.

Returning to Bloom's appreciation of Shakespeare's characters, we can add, as Bloom was well aware, that the great roles call for great actors, each of whom brings a different personality to the role. There is no single Hamlet, just the many brought to life by the actors who portray him. Bloom judged the character of Falstaff, along with Hamlet, as Shakespeare's greatest creations. But Bloom's Falstaff is not the coward, liar, and buffoon evident to most readers of Shakespeare.

> I recall the greatest Falstaff I shall ever see, Ralph Richardson in New York City in 1946, playing so marvelously that he eclipsed Laurence Olivier as Hotspur in *Part I* and as Shallow in *Part II*. I was a child of sixteen, and in two successive evenings I received the most profound Shakespearean education ever made available to me. Richardson was a revelation. His Falstaff was no mere glutton, boozer, scoundrel, but the greatest wit and dryly comic intelligence ever staged. Indeed this Falstaff was the Socrates of Eastcheap, rueful wisdom itself.[22]

Along similar lines, I recall several years ago being treated to Mark Rylance's performance of Shakespeare's Richard III. I had read the play multiple times and had seen at least one other performance. I thought I knew the character of Richard. Rylance's sour-comic portrayal of Richard III taught me otherwise. The actor or musician is most memorable when they can combine a strong sense of character with a strong sense of surprise, a strangeness that we would not know without them.

Also, along similar lines, I remember as a teenager hearing, for the first time, Glenn Gould's first recording of Bach's *Goldberg Variations*. It was like hearing Bach for the first time. It was almost like hearing the piano for the first time. What Gould brought to the Goldberg Variations, and to virtually all of the Bach that he recorded, was a new sense of the music's character. To give one more example, my two favorite recordings of Beethoven's Archduke Trio are the Rubinstein, Heifetz, and Feuermann recording of September 1941, and the Cortot, Thibaud, and Casals recording of November and December 1928. I knew the recording by Rubinstein et al., as a teenager, and for decades it was for me *the* standard that other performances had to live up to. It was many decades later that I first heard the earlier recording by Cortot et al., a revelatory experience. Utterly different in temperament, I now treasure both versions. The sense of musical character is strong in both, utterly different is each, and yet each is as compelling as the other. Or, for an example from popular music, there is Bob Dylan's song "All Along the Watchtower," so powerfully rendered in recordings by the composer and by Jimi Hendrix. Radically different, each strongly projects the unique personality of the singer, and I'd be loathe to choose between them for musical excellence.

Bloom's interest in character and characters correlates significantly with his ideas about human agency. The question as to whether humans create language or language creates humans lies at the heart of Bloom's disagreement with deconstruction as in the writings of Paul de Man, Jacques Derrida, and others. In sorting out this issue, I have found Peter de Bolla's *Harold Bloom: Towards Historical Rhetorics* to be of great help. In *A Map of Misreading*, Bloom characterizes Derrida's "Sublime trope" "[Where] we are told that 'there is no psyche without text,' an assertion that goes beyond Derrida's precursor, Lacan, in his grand trope that the structure of the unconscious is linguistic."[23] For the deconstructionists, in using language, it would seem, the human is kindred to the Sorcerer's Apprentice: he invokes the magic that he then cannot control; on the contrary, it controls him. De Bolla writes that "The major objection Bloom raises concerns what he takes to be the dehumanizing power of a theory based on the exigencies of language."[24] He goes on to quote a passage from *Agon* that I give in part. "That *language* itself *knows* anything is a considerable trope, reflecting a currently fashionable shibboleth, Franco-Heideggerian and monolithic, that is another usurpation, language-as-Demiurge replacing the self-as-Abyss or even the self-as-Jehovah . . . I think it is at best gorgeous nonsense . . . and this just has no relevance in our perpetually Emersonian America."[25] If we are to think of music along deconstructive lines, asserting that music is created by the vicissitudes of prior music, human agency is voided out of the picture. The assumptions and assertions of this book say that music's making is human, although the birds and whales and the wind and rain too have their say.

Canon

> Although canons, like all lists, have a tendency to be inclusive rather than exclusive, we have now reached a point at which a lifetime's reading and rereading can scarcely take one through the Western Canon. Indeed, it is now virtually impossible to master the Western Canon. Not only would it mean absorbing over three thousand books, many, if not most, marked by authentic cognitive and imaginative difficulties, but the relations between these books grow more rather than less vexed as our perspectives lengthen. There are also vast complexities and contradictions that constitute the essence of the Western Canon, which is anything but a unity or stable structure. *No one has the authority to tell us what the Western Canon is, certainly not from about 1800 to the present day. It is not, cannot be, precisely the list I give, or that anyone else might give. If it were, that would make the list a mere fetish, just another commodity.*
>
> —*The Western Canon*, 37[26]

The idea of a canon, literary, musical, painterly, or otherwise, is as vexing a problem as any that this book might confront, given that this book's aspirations fall short of ending hatred, stopping poverty, healing the ill, or cleaning the planet, problems that make my worries over canonicity paltry indeed. It seems to me, that if we are to make distinctions among competence and incompetence or between excellence and mediocrity, then some sort of canon making is inevitable. To speak of "worlds of music making," as I do, is to recognize that musical creativity is not limited to any one tradition or to any one type of musical competence. Aside from the ability to place sounds in time, the competent player in a string quartet has nothing in common with the competent rapper (unless the rapper also performs in a string quartet, or the string quartet player can rap). And while "sounds placed in time" might be a good global definition for almost any music, even when chance is involved, such defining doesn't get us very far.

Staying within the worlds of music making, we can make a distinction between musical practices and musical works, understanding that *works* always subsist in practices, while practices do not necessarily give rise to highly individuated works. Chanting of the Latin Mass was a musical practice in Catholic churches, while works, musically notated compositions, that set the Mass emerged from out of that practice. Written language allowed Homer's *Iliad* and *Odyssey* to solidify into works, somewhere around the eighth century BCE. Sophisticated musical notation evolved nearly two thousand years later. Prior to recordings only developed in the past hundred years and a bit more, notation was the only way to preserve those manifestations of practice we call works. When a later-day composer sets the Mass, like Bach in his B minor Mass, or Beethoven in his *Missa Solemnis*, that composition emerges out of prior compositional practices, which is to say that it emerges out of a composer's reception of works that are its precursors. The works whose relevance endures do so because later creativity comes out of confronting them. The works that matter to the creators of new works are most properly understood as canonical. The key idea in understanding what it means to be canonical is through understanding that a work that endures over multiple generations accrues power over time.

To be canonical entails more than competence, even more than excellence. Canonical art, art that reaches across generations, is art that takes on multiple meanings across time. The power of a Beethoven string quartet might be heard in any good performance of the work. But that is to greatly underestimate that power. Beethoven, in radically transforming the idea of what a string quartet might be, furthered what he inherited in the already extraordinary quartets of Haydn and Mozart to give rise to a lineage in music that endures to this day. Beethoven's children include Schubert, Brahms, Schoenberg, Crawford-Seeger, Carter, Ligeti, Nono, Ferneyhough, and Dillon. Recently, I'm told, a music scholar equated Beethoven's achievement with someone winning a Grammy Award. My response is that in roughly two hundred years we will be able to assess the validity of that judgment. If the Grammy awardee sustains and augments his or her power over a few centuries, influencing excellences in music yet to come, I will gladly grant the sound judgment of that scholar. None of us will be around to see, but it's not a good bet.

In discussing character, I have mentioned the strangeness of remarkable interpretations of dramatic roles and musical performances. Francis Bacon, in his essay "Of Beauty," first published in 1597, writes: "There is no excellent beauty that hath not some strangeness in the proportion."[27] Martin Heidegger, in the dialogue named "The Teacher Meets the Tower Warden at the Door to the Toward Stairway," has the teacher say: "why should we not hold fast to the wondrous in order to fathom it and thereby appropriate it?" The warden, evidently a sage who is the teacher's guide, replies: "Because prior to that [wonder], the strange is there for us to find."[28] In our discussion of Levinas, it was the radical otherness of the other that requires our response. In contrast to Buber's I-Thou relation, which emphasizes intimacy, Levinas's formulation of mutual responsibility emphasizes the strangeness of the other. Bloom recognizes strangeness as a criterion for canonical status in his book *The Western Canon*.

> I have tried to confront greatness directly: to ask what makes the author and the works canonical. The answer, more often than not, has turned out to be strangeness, a mode of originality that either cannot be assimilated, or that so assimilates us that we cease to see it as strange.[29]
>
> Dante is the largest example of the first possibility, and Shakespeare, the overwhelming example of the second.[30]

Reading Dante, in the original Italian or in translation, is indeed a journey into the strangeness of that great poet's imagination. There are other poets who can transform words into hallucinatory visual imagery; in my experience, none is better at this than Dante. The beauty of the music of Dante's Italian is simply stunning, the creation of poetic form is unsurpassed, and the sheer audacity of the poem with its canonization of Beatrice as saint placed highly in the heavenly choirs of Paradise cannot be overestimated, but it is the vividness and strangeness of vision that haunts the reader. This vividness accompanies us through the journey, from the horrific images of the *Inferno* to the sublime strangeness of *Paradiso*.

Bloom's claim about Shakespeare's imagination, one that so assimilates us that we cease to see it as strange, is largely based on that characteristic of persons as created by Shakespeare who learn to think and to change largely by overhearing themselves. Bloom makes the claim that Freud's model of human thought is more based on Shakespeare than the Viennese doctor was willing to admit. Freud placed his fount of influence at a comfortable distance by naming the Oedipal complex after the character in Sophocles. Bloom claimed that the complex might more accurately be named the Hamlet complex. Here is Bloom writing in *The Western Canon* about both Freud and the philosopher Ludwig Wittgenstein: "Wittgenstein, who resented Freud, nevertheless resembles Freud in his suspicious and defensive reaction to Shakespeare, who is an affront to the philosopher as he is to the psychoanalyst. There is no cognitive originality in the whole history of philosophy comparable to Shakespeare's, and it is both ironic and fascinating to overhear Wittgenstein puzzling out whether there is an authentic difference between the Shakespearean representation of thinking and thinking itself."[31] It is this claim, hyperbolic or not, that informs the subtitle of Bloom's book on Shakespeare: *The Invention of the Human*.

Bloom tells the story of rereading John Milton's *Paradise Lost*, willfully trying to recapture a strangeness that attenuated over time. Elsewhere, Bloom writes about his first confrontation with the work, which he memorized so that he could walk around the Bronx apartment of his childhood with his eyes closed, chanting the poem, trying to imagine what it was like for the blind Milton to conceive it. Perhaps it was something like that early engagement with the work that Bloom attempted much later in life. "[I attempted to] start all over with the poem: to read it as though I had never read it before, indeed as no one had ever read it before me. To do so meant dismissing a library of criticism from my head, which was virtually impossible. Still, I tried . . . And while I read, until I fell asleep in the middle of the night, the poem's initial familiarity began to dissolve."[32] I have written elsewhere that Bloom's two possibilities can be applied to music as well: a strangeness that cannot be assimilated and a strangeness that so assimilates us that we cease to see it as strange.[33] I surmise that the strangeness of Schoenberg's *Erwartung* or *Die Glückliche Hand* or *Pierrot Lunaire* will always be strange, a strangeness that will not be attenuated over time. In contrast, I think we've mostly lost the ability to recognize the utter strangeness of Mozart's Apollonian perfections.

∾

PERSONAL EXCURSUS

Years ago, I had an experience curiously parallel to Bloom's story about reading and rereading Milton. I played, or tried to play, Mozart's Clarinet

Concerto for the first time at the age of thirteen or fourteen. I had had very little exposure to classical music by that time, and I remember recognizing something wonderfully strange in the curves of Mozart's lines. I have never lost my love of Mozart, but the sense of strangeness attenuated over time. Years later, having completed my three years in the US Army and another four years playing in bands in New York City and studying tenor saxophone with the remarkable jazz saxophonist Joe Henderson, I became a belated undergraduate at Rutgers University from 1975 to 1978, having flunked out of that same institution in 1965 a full decade earlier. I was dedicated and determined enough to do well the second time around, and for my final year I was named a Henry Rutgers Scholar, with an allotted twelve university credits distributed over the 1977–1978 academic year. In the fall, under the tutelage of Robert Moevs, a gifted composer and teacher, I studied as many contemporary string quartets as I could manage while composing a string quartet of my own, my third attempt at the genre. The quartet was finished by the spring, and it was time to copy out the parts while turning to a new project, suggested by my principal mentor while at Rutgers, Martin Picker. Picker, a distinguished scholar of music in the Renaissance, also had a particular appreciation of contemporary art music. He suggested that I write an extended paper on the music of Elliott Carter. I became immersed in Carter's music, which had baffled me prior to that engagement, even though I'd been listening to contemporary music since my teen years. Martin Picker passed away a few years ago; I remain thankful to him to this day for his teaching, and especially for insisting that I tackle Carter's music, which still engages me. At one point late in the spring semester, not having played or listened to any music older than the twentieth century for quite some time, I decided to try my hands at some Mozart. Unlike Bloom's willful attempt at rehearing Milton, my experience was not willed, and certainly not anticipated. Mozart sounded simply wonderful (not in my performance, but as I imagined it might be) but also weird! Even more intensely than my initial contact with this wonderful music, I recognized its utter strangeness.

One can only imagine how strange the last quartets of Beethoven's music have seemed to his contemporaries. A good performance, even today, can bring out the strangeness of his musical imagination. Among our contemporaries in art music, Helmut Lachenmann strikes me as one whose strangeness is likely to remain over time. Bob Dylan is a strangeness that we've become accustomed to and no longer likely to notice. At least for some of us, the strangeness of Jimi Hendrix is not likely to go away anytime soon.

Performers of music can intensify or attenuate strangeness in music. Although I recognized the particular genius of Chopin, the incredible grace of his musical lines, the rightness of his left-hand punctuations as the bass dips down, I never thought of the music as strange until hearing some of Alfred Cortot's extraordinary recorded performances of the 1920s. If you think you know Chopin but haven't heard Cortot's Chopin, give it a listen. You might be surprised!

In considering questions of social justice and art, I have already quoted a short passage from *The Anatomy of Influence*. I return to that passage here. "I do not believe that poetry has anything to do with cultural politics. I ask of a poem three things: aesthetic splendor, cognitive power, and wisdom."[34] Placing the negation of cultural politics aside, let's consider the three positive criteria: aesthetic splendor, cognitive power, and wisdom.

We might think of aesthetic splendor and cognitive power as coefficients. Aesthetic value can be something we intuit immediately, a beauty that hits us at first glance, at first hearing. Or it can be a beauty that we recognize only after significant effort. Bloom's word "splendor" indicates a bright shining; if the shining is bright enough, it can approach a blinding intensity, like gazing at the sun. Works that overwhelm us at first can have this blinding intensity, so blinding that we cannot see or hear their beauty. In such cases, only the hard work of getting to know the work sufficiently can overcome that blindness so that the splendor instead of blinding enlightens. To experience this is to experience an aesthetic splendor that gives light to a kind of beauty that we have not known before.

Cognitive power is richness and depth of thought. Power, from the Latin *posse* "to be able," might substitute for Bloom's earlier formulation of a capable imagination. But power also denotes an ongoing potency; in the canon it denotes a force that endures across generations. When Shelley characterized poets as "the unacknowledged legislators of the World," he recognized their hidden power, a power antecedent to the power struggles of religious orthodoxies. Music scholarship, at least in my generation, has tended to focus on the cognitive side, embarrassed by any talk of beauty. Yet few, if any, first come to love music because it makes them think. A natural musician is normally swept away by music's beauty first (and by a biochemical reaction to that beauty) and only later recognizes music's rich cognitive content. For most casual listeners, it might not ever occur that music has cognitive power. Human intelligence takes on many guises, and one kind of knowing doesn't necessarily entail another kind. Great performers have great intelligence as performers. Great composers have intelligence as composers. Which comes first, aesthetic splendor or cognitive power? Chickens and eggs.

Bloom's third criterion for canonicity is wisdom. With perhaps the exceptions of places of worship, it's not much in fashion to speak of wisdom these days. Too bad. The biblical wisdom writings were pragmatic guides to living; Facebook, not so much. But the Hebrew Bible had a more inclusive sense of wisdom than we normally include in the word today. There was the wisdom of the psalms and prophets, to be sure, but there was also the wisdom of the hands of the craftsperson. Move a thousand or so years later and we might think of Michelangelo's great wisdom, the high craft that sculpted David, Moses, the Pieta. All instrumental musicians must develop wisdom of the hands. Composers develop the wisdom of their craft. Listeners develop the wisdom of attentive listening. The best listeners develop the wisdom of an openness to musical experience, the ability to hear in ways they've never heard before, the ability to distinguish authentic creativity as opposed to a cliché-ridden same-old.

To deny wisdom of the canonical is to deny the wisdom of our mothers and fathers. And the coefficient of wisdom is love.

How might we define a greater wisdom in musical composition, or in musical performance? Here's an attempt: a composer or performer who can recognize and absorb the best of what came before, where "best" is an excellence that is self-empowering, ward off being cowed by that prior magnificence, and transform that which he or she has learned from into something new, expanding the universe of the possible, to create something likewise personal and enduring. That is the wisdom of Mozart, Beethoven, Brahms, Mahler, Schoenberg, Debussy, Ravel. In the lineage of jazz performance, that is the wisdom of Louis Armstrong, Ella Fitzgerald, Miles Davis, John Coltrane. In rock music, that is the wisdom of the Beatles, the Rolling Stones, Bob Dylan, Jimi Hendrix, Otis Redding. Since rap has endured for a half century, I am sure that it has or will develop its own canon as well; I'm not sufficiently versed in that genre to suggest candidates, but I suspect it will be (or already is) constituted by those rappers who bring strangeness, cognitive power, aesthetic splendor, and wisdom to their craft. In positing these multiple versions of canonicity, there are several caveats to keep in mind, and contrasting what a literary canon might mean with what a musical canon might entail will help to sort out the issues involved.

In the world of literature, the huge variety of human languages is an impediment not easily overcome. Translations help enormously, but they cannot ever capture the music of the original, for every language has a music, and that music has many variations; at best translators create a new music in the language of translation. Translating poetry, Valéry's art of hesitating between sound and meaning requires that the original music is translated into a subsequent music. Translating the meaning and music of poetry must be among the most difficult literary practices we have. Our best translators do amazing work, sometimes matching or even surpassing the musicality of the original while holding onto meaning at the same time. At best, translations provide a variant of Bloom's "the meaning of a poem is another poem."

The time-worn assertion that music is the universal language can be more misleading than helpful. If by "universal language" we mean that humans (and others) share a capacity, even a need, to express ourselves musically, one way or another, then music's universality should be granted. As I've said at the outset, music is one of our necessary fictions. If, on the other hand, we imply that music is a kind of universal translator, then the claim is dubious at best. That the music that's meaningful to me might not be meaningful to you seems obvious enough.[35]

True, I can listen to Tchaikovsky without learning Russian, or Bartók without learning Hungarian, or Takemitsu without learning Japanese. This is undoubtably a great advantage of the musical art. I won't hear the nuances that a native or specialist in Russian or Hungarian or Japanese cultural might recognize, yet I won't be lost at sea as I would be by staring at Tolstoy or Imre Kertész or Takuboku Ishikawa in their original languages. If I was a better learner, I might try to take on those languages, but any one of them would be a daunting task; all three, and a hundred or so others, would be so far out of my ken that it's not worth considering.

On the other hand, listening with any acuity requires a familiarity with the musical practice and musical works that form music's rich and varied traditions. Knowing rap music doesn't help much when it comes to listening to late Beethoven. And my love of late Beethoven doesn't give me a leg up in understanding the lineages and transformations inherent in rap artistry.

Far, far more difficult to overcome, really impossible, is the difference between reading and music making, whether from the performer's perspective or that of the composer. To read, the reader needs a book (or magazine, newspaper, computer image, etc.). With notable exceptions, such as reading in a place of worship, reading is a solitary practice. The closest analogue in music making is singing by oneself, or playing a musical instrument, alone.

The training of musicians in an age of multiculturalism is far more complicated than the training of readers, problems of language competency aside. And training as a musician is far more restrictive than the choices available to a listener in this day of instant access to recordings. As a listener with access to Spotify or Apple Music, I might start my musical day with Louis Armstrong, move on to Puccini's *Madama Butterfly*, sample a bit of Rogers and Hammerstein's *Oklahoma*, move on to some throat singing by Tibetan monks, and end the day with a recorded performance of *Pharmakeia* by James Dillon. The next day might start with Willie Nelson . . . you get the picture. As a listener I can move through all of these musical practices, perhaps not with the same acuity for each, but without being totally at a loss for any. This is perfectly analogous to what might fill my day as a reader, at least with the help of translations. I could range through centuries and diverse literary practices, if not with relative ease, then with the tools available to at least begin to comprehend. Not so for the performing musician. Each musical practice, each body of musical works, requires different training, different competency. The long, laborious apprenticeship required to play string quartets has little to no overlap with the long, laborious apprenticeship required to play Indian classical music, and neither will help me much if I want to sing in Chinese opera, *Xiqu*. Learning Hebrew cantillation won't help much, maybe a little, if I want to try *cante flamenco*. Learning to play or sing Country and Western music doesn't prepare one to rap, although the idea of rapping cowboys is less far-fetched than might first be imagined. I love the singing of Dinah Washington, and I love the singing of Maria Callas, but I'd not be interested in hearing Dinah Washington sing the role of Gilda in Giuseppe Verdi's *Rigoletto*, nor would I want to hear Callas sing the Rodgers and Hart song "Manhattan."

Even if a musician learns to perform in multiple traditions, the performance is highly unlikely to be an authentic representation of any. Maybe that's the best we can do if we want our musicians to be multiculturalists: a new international music might be something other than any particular culture's music. Something might be gained. Much will be lost.

Which is not to say that vital new music cannot emerge from the rubbing together of two or more diverse cultures. For decades, the Great

American Songbook was dominated by Jewish American songwriters and lyricists, immigrants or the children of immigrants: George and Ira Gershwin, Irving Berlin, Harold Arlen, Rodgers and Hart, Rodgers and Hammerstein, and Lerner and Loewe, to name just some of the most distinguished. During those same decades, many, arguably most, of the memorable renditions of those songs were sung or instrumentally performed and recorded by African Americans: Louis Armstrong, Billie Holiday, Ella Fitzgerald, Dinah Washington, Johnny Hartman, Lena Horne, Miles Davis, and John Coltrane, to name just some of the most distinguished. This collaboration between cultures was uniquely American, but it wasn't initiated by a college curriculum or government program.

I take two more remarkable examples of music emerging out of cultural fusion (and conflict) from María Rosa Menocal's *Shards of Love: Exile and the Origins of the Lyric*: the verse/song form known as *muwashshaḥāt* and the tradition of the troubadours, the latter of extraordinary importance in the emergence of lyric poetry in the West.

Emerging in the eleventh century, the *muwashshaḥāt* comprise an Arabic genre of poetry/song that resulted from a fusion of at least three cultures. "The *muwashshaḥāt* invent new Romance and Arabic and Hebrew poetics in one swoop, all in the same poem: strophes both defined and differentiated by rhyme schemes; in contrast, in the classical languages—Arabic, Hebrew, Latin alike—this was unheard of. Within these poems, which are in fact songs and are best referred to in that way—this is the crucial issue to which I will return repeatedly—we hear a calliope of languages and voices."[36] Later in the same book, Menocal cites Gershom Scholem's *Origins of the Kabbalah*. I give only a portion of the cited text. "Provence, and especially Languedoc, was the seat of a developed courtly and feudal culture. An intimate contact was established there . . . between Islamic culture penetrating from Spain and North Africa and the culture and chivalry of the Christian Middle Ages. There, during this same period, the poetry of the troubadours reached its peak. *But beyond that, southern France was an area particularly characterized by strong religious tension unparalleled in other lands of Christian culture.*"[37] After quoting the passage from Scholem, much more extended than the portion I give, Menocal provides commentary on Scholem's text.

> His description, with swift and sure lines, sets out a remarkably volatile and unconventional, almost forgotten, world in which the troubadours flourished and died . . . the fortunes of the Cathars . . . the rise of a different phenomenon, the

> Jewish Kabbalah . . . reading Scholem, we realize with some force that *languedoc* . . . bred multiple lyric forms. A whole host of movements inimical to the grand narrative [of Christian hegemony] flourished: from the Kabbalah to *canso*, from *muwashshaḥāt* to the Gnostic prayers, and back again, all in impossibly confusing eddies.[38]

The meeting of significant cultural differences can generate an energy of spirit, a heightened awareness of otherness; if that energy is directed in a positive way, affirming new creativity will naturally emerge. Negative energy, which is conflict, can also generative creativity but of opposing aesthetics, cognitive claims, and ideas of wisdom. Creativity that comes out of extreme conflict comes with the cost of extreme human suffering. Extraordinary beauty can be found in songs responding to the slavery of Africans in America. I treasure the post-Holocaust poems of Jacob Glatshteyn and others, and I am greatly moved by Luigi Nono's *Il canto sospeso*, but wish that the need for them never came to be.

As I write, many academics are concerned about a perceived hegemony of Western civilization in colleges and universities. Music education is no exception. I have made it clear, I hope, that I value many different musical traditions; if I were more learned, I would integrate more than I am able to within this book. But I have also asserted that canons are made out of works, and while these works always grow out of practices, the two are not equivalent. Practice, tradition by another name, is collective, while works are either created by an individual or, as in the case of cinema or ensemble performance, an individuated group of persons.[39] Traditions are made out of constituent individuals, but unless their names, their works, are written down or otherwise memorialized, those individuals become anonymously absorbed into those traditions. I have also asserted, following Bloom and others, that canonical works gain strength across generations; I gave Beethoven's string quartets as an example. Sophisticated music notation was invented in the West, notation capable of notating many voices singing or playing simultaneously. Music notation is antecedent to recordings by some thousand years; works within the Western canon, however selected, have had time to develop their lineages.

Notated music, while not intrinsically superior to non-notated music, does have the advantage of enduring across time, but it also has the advantage, in the case of well-composed music, of creating large-scale forms with a potential for development simply not available otherwise.

Like a well-written novel, large-scale composition can invent characters (in the inclusive sense that we have considered) that develop and change over time, characters that remember and change through remembering. Moreover, with the invention of polyphony, many voices, many characters, can be combined simultaneously, whether in concord or in conflict. In this the composer has the advantage over the novelist. Even the playwright, who can have multiple actors speaking simultaneously, cannot compete with the composer in this regard. All of this brings us back to the concerns of educating musicians in our multicultural world.

The problems of what shall comprise musicianship in a multicultural age are compounded by the problems of creating and sustaining musical ensembles, especially large ensembles like the modern orchestra. To be sure, publishing and distributing books requires a fairly complex and costly apparatus, but this is nowhere near as complex and costly as sustaining a modern symphony orchestra or an opera company that includes such an orchestra and much more as well. In the world of orchestral music, depending on the work, a performance requires paying somewhere between forty and eighty musicians, sometimes fewer, sometimes more. And while a musical performance can be recorded and distributed, in this sense like film, recordings are not the same experience as attending a live performance; in this sense music is just like theater. And behind the immediately visible costs of paying forty to eighty highly skilled musicians, there is the infrastructure of music students and teachers, only some small subset of whom can hope to be employed by a symphony orchestra. The tradition of Western art music is a glorious one. Yet I fear that it might not be sustainable in a society that ceases to value that tradition. As Bloom fears, the study of canonical literature might shrink to the size of classics departments in our universities, where a select few can learn to read what has been elbowed out of the general curriculum. In the case of music, a model like that is simply not viable. I can offer no solution to this quandary.

Further Instances of Liminal Spaces in Bloom's Writings

Bloom's penultimate book, *Possessed by Memory*, is in large part a place where Bloom revisits the poems that continued to haunt his final years. With some exceptions, the book is arranged chronologically, moving toward Bloom's contemporaries in its final chapters. Personal reminiscence is woven throughout, and this is intensified as Bloom remembers dear friends who have passed on. "When I read my departed friends, I have an uncanny sensation that they are in the room."[40]

The second chapter in the book is titled "The Poetry of Kabbalah," and it is in that context that Bloom discusses Peter Cole's poem "The Reluctant Kabbalist's Sonnet."

The Reluctant Kabbalist's Sonnet[41]

"It is known that 'desire' is, numerologically . . . 'the essence of speech.'"

—Avraham Abulafia, *The Treasures of the Hidden Eden*

It's hard to explain   What was inside came
through what had been between, although it seems
that what had been within remained the same
Is that so hard to explain   It took some time
which was in passing made distinctly strange
As though the world without had been rearranged,
forcing us to change: what was beyond
suddenly lying within, and what had lain
deep inside—now . . . apparently gone
Words are seeds, like tastes on another's tongue
Which *doesn't* explain—how what's inside comes
through what is always in between, that seam
of being   For what's within, within remains,
as though it had slipped   across the lips of a dream[42]

Bloom's chapter gives its examples of poetry from Kabbalah in translations taken from Cole's *The Poetry of Kabbalah*.[43] His discussion of "The Reluctant Kabbalist's Sonnet," placed before the translations out of Kabbalah, is a break in the roughly chronological design of the book.

Prior to citing and discussing Cole's poem, Bloom provides a quick overview of Kabbalah and some of its central texts. A brief discussion of the ten sefirot, using the same image that I have considered earlier in this study, emphasizes the interplay between sefirah that are gendered female on the left, those gendered male on the right, and those along the central column that combine male and female aspects of divinity.[44] Citing Moshe

Idel's *Kabbalah and Eros*, Bloom remarks that in kabbalistic tradition marital intercourse is regarded as redemptive, "both of individuals and of the cosmos."[45] It is with this background that Bloom introduces Cole's "The Reluctant Kabbalist's Sonnet."

Bloom reads the poem as a representation of "conjugal coupling," emphasizing the wit and sense of play inherent in the sonnet. But it would be a mistake to take conjugal coupling as being reduceable to a merely physical act. Read another way, Cole's poem is an exploration of liminal space, very close to the concept of "proximity" that we have found in Levinas. The opening epigraph, citing Avraham Abulafia's use of gematria to associate speech and desire, might appear to be consonant with Levinas's privileging of speech, but when poets speak their speech is a kind of music. In reading Cole's poem, I had originally contrasted speech with music, rather than recognizing, as I should have, that poets' words morph back into the music that use and abuse had hidden over time. I had the good fortune of discussing this point with Peter Cole in an email correspondence. He wrote: "For me speech is a kind of music—it's the melodic, textural, rhythmic, material aspect of speech that I am always trying to bring out, in different ways and to different degrees, so that it points to something more."[46] To amplify his point and its connection to the epigraph by Abulafia that opens the poem, Cole brought to my attention a passage written by Amnon Shiloah in "The Symbolism of Music in the Kabbalistic Tradition."

> In his *Gan Na'ul* (Closed Garden) [Abulafia] writes: "Know thou that the combination of letters can be compared to the listening to music, for the ear hears and the sounds are combined in accordance with the (required) form of a melody, or the syllables (of speech). The proof can be found in the combination formed by the kinnor and nevel (biblical terms for instruments designating two types of lyres) whose associated voices cause the listener's ear to perceive a variety of emotional meanings. And the strings touched by the right and left hand bring through their vibration sweet sensation to the ear. And from the ear this sensation travels to the heart, and from the heart to the spleen, and enjoyment is continually renewed through the recurrence of tunes. It is impossible to produce such delight except through the combination of sounds, and the same is true of the combination of letters" . . . Thus we

> learn that the combination of letters creates enjoyment in the soul just as musical harmony does, because of the unveiling of secrets confined in such combinations.[47]

The blank space in the first line of Cole's poem, between "explain" and "What," is a poetic caesura that literalizes "what was inside came through what had been between," where the gap inside the poetic line is the in-between that we go through. As the poem progresses through its second gap, in line four, the liminal blank is dilated, "it took some time." And in that passing, it is "as though the world without had been rearranged." The "that" that had remained the same, is "now . . . apparently gone." The "self" changes and augments through knowing the other, whether that knowing is in the biblical sense or otherwise. Yet the central mystery of the poem remains: though words are seeds, this "*doesn't* explain—how what's inside comes through what is always in between."

In understanding Cole's kabbalistic crossings of the blank in-between, I also recall one of Bloom's many broodings on Ralph Waldo Emerson, the essay "Emerson: Power at the Crossing."[48] There, as elsewhere, Bloom cites Emerson's "Self-Reliance." I have cited this passage earlier; here it is again. "Life only avails, not the having lived. Power ceases in the instant of repose; it resides in the moment of transition from a past to a new state, in the shooting of a gulf, in the darting to an aim."[49] In music, just as in poetry, just as in life, this shooting of a gulf, this transition from a past to a new state is hard to explain.

Bloom's final book, *Take Arms Against a Sea of Troubles*, parts of which were written just days before he passed, approaches the liminal time-spaces of in-between through several perspectives. The first draws upon Hebrew grammar and the stem formation called *Niphal*. In Hebrew grammar, stem formation indicates the kind of verbal action (simple, stative, causative, etc.) as well as the voice of the verb (active, passive, reflexive, etc.). In biblical Hebrew, the *Niphal* stem can express either a passive or reflexive voice, but it can also express middle voice among its modes of action.[50]

> Agata Bielik-Robson, Polish-English authority on modern Jewish studies, in her response to my book *Possessed by Memory* (2019), perceived my reliance on the dialectical position of the Hebrew stem called *Niphal*, which founds the paradigmatic

> Jewish wisdom, explained in my paraphrase of Rabbi Tarphon: "We are not required to complete the work, but neither are we free to desist from it." *Niphal*, the transitive mode of in-between, perfectly defines the role of the particular ring in the "chain of tradition," granted a middle voice between activity and passivity, "doing and suffering," but also—perhaps most importantly—between mortality and immortality.
>
> . . . My sense of *Niphal* is precisely the refusal to think about this in the simplistic terms of either/or. *Niphal* can be active doing or passive suffering. Yet the word is ambiguous: Does it tell us that doing and suffering are one and the same?[51]

The answer to Bloom's question, at least in the contexts explored in this book, is yes, which is to say that it's middle voiced.

Also in *Take Arms Against a Sea of Troubles*, Bloom discusses liminal space in two of Wallace Stevens poems, "Credences of Summer" and "Of Mere Being." "Of Mere Being," Bloom reflects, "No single reading of it is possible. Yet I hear an augury of transcendence as though a doorway is about to open and a new threshold appear on the verge to the unapparent."[52] Later in the book we read, "If achieved love is templar, then the perplexing road to get there will be labyrinthine, and pragmatically most of our erotic relationships will take place on the threshold between assurance and perplexity."[53] And later yet, Bloom picks up this thread in a discussion of "spiritual gates" in the Hart Crane poem "Emblems of Conduct." "In Angus Fletcher's formulation, Hart Crane is lost in the labyrinth and must find spiritual gates to reach the temple."[54] The spiritual gates are the openings that we have seen described in other terms and other ways by Heidegger and Levinas.

As with the continuing influence of Ralph Waldo Emerson, the ideas of Sigmund Freud haunted Bloom through all his mature life. *Take Arms Against a Sea of Troubles* includes Bloom's final thoughts on the Viennese master, a striking discussion of what Bloom terms "frontier concepts." Frontier concepts comprise an augmentation of what we, following Angus Fletcher, have been calling liminal space. I quote only part of Bloom's longer discussion.

> But what exactly is the Freudian drive, if it is a bodily demand that makes every mental response inadequate? . . . I go back to Freud's

own authority, in the *New Introductory Lectures:* . . . "Drives are mythical entities, magnificent in their indefiniteness." "Magnificent in their indefiniteness" is a marvelous formula, and not so humorous as it sounds. We are incessantly pushed and pressured by a shadowy splendor, which we recognize only through the tensions supposedly caused by its force. Aside from these tensions, all that we know about the drive is its non-location. It is neither in the body nor in the mind, but on the frontier between outward and inward. Yet that beautifully locates our tensions, which are neither bodily nor psychic but hovering on or near those ghostly demarcations, as our circumference flows in or out.

. . .

Few questions of spiritual or intellectual history are as vexed as the Jewishness of Freud. It mystified Freud, more than he knew, and we go on weakly misreading it.

. . .

Jewish dualism is neither the split between body and soul, nor the abyss between subject and object. Rather it is the ceaseless agon within the self not only against all outward injustice but also against what might be called the injustice of outwardness or, more simply, the way things are.

. . .

Like the Freudian concept of the drive, the notion of the bodily ego seems to lie precisely upon the frontier between the mental and the physical. . . . Freud implies that the drives and the bodily ego alike are constructed ambivalently—that is to say, from their origins they are dualistic. In both, the borders between the psychical and the somatic are forever in dispute.[55]

The split between body and soul is Cartesian and also Christian; the split between subject and object is Kantian, and built into our grammars of subject and object. To recognize that "the borders between the psychical and the somatic are forever in dispute" is to recognize that all perception, music certainly included, takes place in an in-between. Is music, among our necessary fictions, a response to the injustice of outwardness, the way things are? For me, the answer is "yes," but only in part. Music is also a celebration of the way things are, as are all of the arts.

Poetics of Influence:
Bloom's Tropes of Limitation and Tropes of Representation

Taking in and expelling or flowing out are the most basic of human biological, apperceptive, and social dualities. Our hearts, with or without our knowing, take blood in and pump blood out. Our lungs do the same for air. Our sexuality is expressed in rhythms of taking in and giving out. And, of course, we eat and excrete. Cognitive taking in is apprehension, while giving out is expression. We form social groups through inclusion and exclusion. And all human commerce is a balance of output and intake. On the cosmic level, super novae and black holes are extreme examples of efflux and influx.

In terms of bodily gesture, raising one's arms while placing one's hands palms-out signifies "stop" or "keep away." Placing one's palms facing inward, with an inward bend of the fingers, signifies a beckoning, "come closer." In music too, the rhythms of expressing outward and breathing inward are basic, yet subtle and hard to perceive, harder to describe. Some thirty years ago I became fascinated by this very problem, convinced that one could find gestures of inward and outward flow in music. After pursuing the problem for a while, I gave up, having found my analyses to be hopelessly idiosyncratic: I faltered in finding objective criteria. Then, a few years ago, I watched some films of the esteemed orchestral conductor Carlos Kleiber. Kleiber's use of hand gestures seemed uncannily to match my own sense of outward and inward flow in the music. Clearly, here was something that needed further exploration.

The move from outward to inward is a turning of direction. Our word "trope" comes to us from the Greek τρόπος (trópos), in its verbal form τρέπειν (trépein) "to turn." In language, a trope turns one meaning into another. We can imagine "sunshine" and "a person beloved" as utterly unrelated, that is, until some proto-poet uttered, in some proto-language, "you are my sunshine." And the world has never been the same. We trivialize trope by its commonplace definition, turning literal meaning into figurative meaning, only in that most meaning in language that we take to be literal began as figurative. The concept is further trivialized by our current use of the word "spin." In language, trope is the means through which new meaning emerges.

Trope as turning is echoed in English through words such as heliotropic (as in plants that turn toward the sun) and tropics (as in the Tropics of Capricorn and Cancer, imaginary lines where the sun seems to turn in its course). In mathematics and physics we have the word "isotropy," a technical term with a wide range of applications. We also have the word "apotropaic," something, a talisman or a saying, that turns away evil, such as "God forbid." The Yiddish "קיין עין־הרע" (*keinehora*), "no evil eye," is an apotropaic saying common among Yiddish speakers, a saying that I heard my mother speak throughout the years of my childhood. In Greek myth, three sisters are imagined as spinning, measuring, and cutting the threads of life. The third sister, the one who cuts the thread, is named Atropos; she is the one who cannot be turned away. Of the many, many things that music can do, warding off evil is among them. Am I whistling in the dark?

Personal Excursus

My mom was the youngest child of three who survived. Her parents and siblings were born in Europe in a shtetl in the Eastern Austro-Hungarian Empire (now part of Poland). Mom, born in Manhattan, grew up on the Lower East Side of New York, later moving to the Bronx. The language in their home was Yiddish. Dad was born in Vilna, speaking Yiddish in his childhood home as well. When I was a child, English was the primary language spoken in the home, but as I recognized in retrospect, it was clearly a Yiddish-inflected English. Dad, a Lithuanian Jew, was proudly averse to superstition, "bubbe-meise" (grandmas' tales), as he called it. In contrast, mom was very superstitious and full of the wisdom of simple folk. Growing up, I heard mom say "keinehora" (pronounced "kinehura") whenever she talked about family. I had no idea what "keinehora" meant. I thought it was simply an interjection, like "to be sure." Later in life, mom counseled me "be a mensch." The attitude toward music and life that this book proposes is better captured in those simple words than any others I can think of. Mom passed nearly fifty years ago; though I've often failed, I'm still trying to be a mensch, kinehura.

We've gone far afield, but I haven't forgotten Harold Bloom. For Bloom, the strong poet is the inventor of new modes of figuration, and the influence of one poem on another can be understood through the history of tropes. From *The Anxiety of Influence* (1973) to *The Anatomy of Influence* (2012) and on into his final works, Bloom brooded over poetic influence more than any other of his myriad of scholarly concerns. In doing so, Bloom idiosyncratically divided rhetorical tropes into two types: tropes of limitation and tropes of representation or restitution. (In *Kabbalah and Criticism*, Bloom clarifies his use of the word *representation*, saying that representation comes to us from Old French, where it meant bringing something absent into presence.)[56] In their various and distinctive ways, tropes of limitation cast out, while tropes of representation or restitution take in or heal what was broken asunder, a kind of bringing together. The poem self-limits by creating a figurative boundary; we might say (figuratively!), "keep out, I need to create or consolidate my own space." The poem self-represents by opening up the (figurative) gates and taking in; "I augment myself through incorporating something not there before."

Bloom's "dialectics of revisionism" take place between limitation and representation among three pairs of rhetorical tropes: irony ↔ synecdoche, metonymy ↔ hyperbole, metaphor ↔ metalepsis. Thus, irony separates while synecdoche brings together. On a higher level in Bloom's schema, with changes in modes of figuration, metonymy and hyperbole work analogously; and, on the highest level, the work of limitation and representation is done by the pair of metaphor and metalepsis (also named transumption). Understanding how each individual trope works is extremely useful in understanding how language works, and each can be applied, with appropriate modifications, toward understanding music. Yet I, and I suspect most readers, find it difficult to apply Bloom's six-trope sequence *as sequence* applied toward reading, let alone music.[57]

Late in life, Bloom recognized this in print. "My esoteric six-fold does have a way of showing up in a fair number of ambitious poems in the Romantic tradition, but, like all exegetical instruments, it is subject to abuse, and I have ceased to recommend it to my students or to anyone else. I regard it now as a purely personal dialectical dance, part of the Kabbalah of Harold Bloom."[58] For Bloom, poetic meaning, at least in terms of influence, does not take place within a poem, but only *between* poems. As such, we might consider Bloom's entire project of revisionary ratios and their concomitants as an exploration of liminal space.

David Lewin, in "Music Theory, Phenomenology, and Modes of Perception," either purposely or inadvertently misreads Bloom. In Lewin's understanding, "another poem," which he extends toward musical composition, is one that comes afterward, not the one that came before.[59] Time's arrow works both ways. We value most those works that call for a response and those that adequately respond. On this, I'm sure, David and Harold would have most certainly agreed.

Metalepsis in Harold Bloom and John Hollander

Bloom's crowning trope, metalepsis, has fascinating implications for musical thought, and we turn to that trope now. Bloom described the poet-scholar John Hollander as his closest friend over many decades. As with Angus Fletcher, the mutuality of influence between Hollander and Bloom is sometimes difficult to unravel. In 1981, Hollander published *The Figure of Echo: A Mode of Allusion in Milton and After*. Hollander's book contains a final chapter titled "Echo Metaleptic," followed by an appendix, "The Trope of Transumption," the latter evidently being the first thoroughgoing history of the term transumption, the Latinate version of the Greek metalepsis. Published some eight years after *The Anxiety of Influence*, the initiatory salvo of Bloom's sixfold trope and associated revisionary ratios, Hollander's treatment of metalepsis/transumption, at least in part, is a filling out and filling in of Bloom's loftiest of tropes, one that historically had been rarely named, and when named, confusingly defined. Reading Hollander will help us to better understand Bloom's revision of metalepsis, the final trope of restitution, the trope of an ever-early self-begetting.

We encountered an evaluation of diachrony over synchrony within our discussion of Levinas. The twin terms are complemented and augmented in Hollander and Bloom. Indeed, Bloom's entire enterprise with regard to rhetorical tropes might be understood as a quest toward developing a diachronic rather than synchronic theory of tropes. Hollander writes, "It is even more inevitable that the trope of echo should come to stand for crucial questions about poetic language itself . . . It is even more inevitable that the delay between prior voice and responding echo in acoustical actuality should become in naturalized romantic mythology a trope of diachrony, of the distance between prior and successive poems."[60] Hollander discusses a spectrum from direct quotation to allusion to echo as a metaphor for allusion that "does not depend on conscious intention." "The reader of texts, in order to overhear echoes, must have some kind of access to an earlier voice, and to its cave of resonant signification, analogous to that of the author of the later text."[61] This is just so with music. My experience, over a lifetime of making and studying music, is that this sense of hearing echoes of earlier and later composers or performers in any musical score or performance has augmented over time. Perhaps it need not be added that this phenomenon extends to all human experience. As we grow old, the echoes of our past loves, sorrows, and all in between, resonate more and more deeply.

Hollander opens his chapter "Echo Metaleptic" with the following:

> Implicit in the previous discussions has been the treatment of allusive echo, leading from poem to poem, as being itself a trope of the later text. But rhetoric, like many theories of signification, is a synchronic study; what we seem to have been considering is a sort of diachronic figure.
>
> . . .
>
> In short, we deal with diachronic trope all the time, and yet we have no name for it as a class. An echo of the kind we have been considering may occur in a figure in a poem, and it may echo the language of a figure in a previous one. But the echoing itself makes a figure, and the interpretive or revisionary power which raises the echo even louder than the original voice is that of a trope of diachrony.
>
> I propose that we apply the name of the classical rhetorician's trope of *transumption* (or *metalepsis*, in its Greek form) to these diachronic, allusive figures. Quintilian identified transumption as a movement from one trope to another, which operates through one or more middle terms of figuration. Subsequent rhetoricians . . . are in confused disagreement as to its function . . . but there is a general sense that it is a kind of meta-trope, or figure of linkage between figures, and that there will be one or more unstated middle terms which are leapt over, or alluded to, by the figure. A synchronic treatment of metalepsis—a trope of a trope, as it were—might merely be a *catachresis*, or thoroughly mixed metaphor. But in a highly allusive situation, in which an image or fable is being presented as a revision of an earlier one, the diachrony is inescapable.[62]

Hollander gives a simple and revealing example of a suppressed middle term in John Milton's "blind mouths," a complex trope in Milton's Lycidas, where "a metaphoric *blind* operates on a synecdochic *mouths*, with a metalepsis across the unstated term, *preachers*."[63] Numerous historical examples of metalepsis involve a single word that implies a string of associated meanings. For example, Henry Peacham, in *The Garden of Eloquence* (1593), writes that Virgil's "ears of corn" signify harvests, by harvests, summers, and by summers, years.[64] Hollander glosses this by commenting that in English we may hear a substitution of "ears" for "years." He goes on to say that the substitution of a like-sounding word for an expected one is commonplace in modern poetry. In this context, Hollander cites John Ashbery: "the mooring of starting out, that day so long ago," where "mooring" substitutes for the expected "morning."[65] *The Mooring of Starting Out* would later become the title of the collected first five books of Ashbery's poetry, published in 1997. The opposition/apposition of mooring ↔ starting out, like laying anchor ↔ setting sail, opposes and apposes stasis and momentum, but mooring ↔ starting out also includes an ever-early mooring that tethers starting out. The turning of mooring ↔ morning might be conceived as a dialectic that well-explains Bloom's turning of the trope of metalepsis.

As we have noted, metalepsis crowns Bloom's rhythm of tropes. In so doing, Bloom makes most central an aspect of metalepsis that was negligible in earlier characterizations of the trope, a sense of diachronic reversal. In *A Map of Misreading*, Bloom develops an extended example of metalepsis in Book I of John Milton's *Paradise Lost*, including Milton's metalepsis on "the fiction of the leaves."[66] In his final book, *Take Arms Against a Sea of Troubles*, Bloom returns to Milton's "fiction of the leaves," a trope with precursors in Isaiah, Homer, Virgil, and Dante.[67]

Isaiah prophesizes:

And all the heaven shall be dissolved . . . and all their host
shall fall down, as the leaf falleth off the vine, and as a falling
fig from a fig tree.[68]

Homer's use of the trope reflects the human condition, our mortality:

Like leaves on trees the race of men is found,
Now green in youth, now withering on the ground;[69]

Virgil transforms the image, building on Homer, but now in ghastly afterlife.

Thick as leaves in autumn strow the woods,
Or fowls, by winter forced, forsake the floods,

Character, Canon, and Poetic Influence | 103

> And wing their hasty flight to happier lands;
> Such, and so thick, the shivering army stands,
> And press for passage with extended hands.
> Now these, now those, the surly boatman bore:
> The rest he drove to distance from the shore.[70]

And Dante expands upon Virgil, inflecting the prior image with Catholic meaning.

> Charon the demon, with the eyes of glede,
> Beckoning to them, collects them all together,
> Beats with his oars whoever lags behind.
> As in the autumn-time the leaves fall off,
> First one and then another, till the branch
> Unto the earth surrenders all its spoils;
> In similar wise the evil seed of Adam
> Throw themselves from that margin one by one,
> At signals, as a bird unto its lure.[71]

Milton transumes the trope as Satan rallies his troops of fallen angels. The fallen Lucifer uses his massive spear as walking cane as he walks along the burning shore.

> Of that inflamèd sea, he stood and called
> His legions, angel forms, who lay entranced
> Thick as autumnal leaves that strew the brooks
> In Vallombrosa, where the Etrurian shades
> High overarched imbower . . .[72]

Here is Bloom's gloss:

> Homer accepts what must be. Virgil acquiesces with sorrowful splendor, in his vision of those who stretch forth their hands out of love for the further shore. Dante is grim; the evil seed of Adam goes down with the falling leaves. John Milton remembers when he stood in the woods at Vallombrosa, before his blindness, and saw the leaves of autumn strewing the brooks. His metonymy of shades for words [sic] puns on Virgil's and Dante's images of the shades that gather for Charon the boatman. Transumptively Milton carries Dante and Virgil back to

> their beginnings in Homer. The forerunners become belated, and Milton joins himself to Isaiah. The leaves come down from the trees, the generations of men die, only because a third of the heavenly host came falling down.[73]

An unfortunate typo, I assume, obscures the sentence "His metonymy of shades for words puns on Virgil's and Dante's images of the shades that gather for Charon the boatman." It should read "shades for woods," where "Etrurian shades" refers trebly to the Tuscan woods, their shady bowers, and the ghostly, charred remnants of the fallen angels. Vallombrosa is literally "valley of shades." In itself, the multiple meanings of the word "shades" exemplify earlier descriptions of metalepsis. But for Bloom, and presumably Milton, much more is at stake.

The final sentence in the passage quoted by Bloom, "the generations of men die, only because a third of the heavenly host came falling down," places Milton's imagery as antecedent to Homer's: the fallen angels, in particular Lucifer, become Satan, are the precipitant of human mortality, a concomitant of expulsion from the Garden of Eden.

In *The Breaking of the Vessels*, Bloom extends his reflections on "the fiction of the leaves," tracing a "transumptive chain" through Coleridge, Shelley, Whitman, Stevens, and Beckett.[74] Bloom's last words on transumption are in his final book, *Take Arms Against a Sea of Troubles*, as I've already noted, parts of which were written just days before his passing. "I want now to go beyond my previous understanding of transumption. A trope that revises earlier figurations so as to make them seem belated, and itself as possessing priority, is no longer a synchronic phenomenon but takes us into the realm of diachronic rhetoric. Such a rhetoric remains to be fully formulated."[75] Bloom's corporeal passing was imminent; do I go too far in saying that our very lives are a diachronic trope? To turn from one state into another, troping that language and music have in common, is also the concomitant of our very being, a process of becoming that includes coming into and out of existence.

Musical Metalepsis

Rhetorical figures, including transumption, were widely used to describe musical procedures as early as the late fifteenth century and continuing through the baroque period, with occasional resuscitations into our own time.[76] Evidently, the earliest application of metalepsis to music is in Joachim Burmeister, *Musica Poetica* (1606). The Burmeister example is nicely studied in John Hollander's *The Figure of Echo*. Earlier in his study, Hollander's chapter "Echoic Scheme" examines how *echoic figures* are deployed in literature, in distinction from *echoic tropes*: the former mimic literal echo, the latter transformative, functioning either as metaphor or metalepsis. In discussing Burmeister's musical example, Hollander notes that it is a version of *transumptive scheme* rather than *transumptive trope*. As Hollander admits, Burmeister's prose is hard to sort out. "Metalepsis . . . that manner of fugue in which two melodies are transumed from here to there in Harmony and converted into fugue." (*Metalepsis . . . est talis habitus Fugae, in duo Melodiae in Harmonia hinc inde transsumuntur et in fugam vertuntur.*)[77] Luckily for us, Burmeister cites a motet by Orlando di Lasso, *De ore prudentus*, as "the most splendid example of this (*exemplum luculentissum*)."[78] The score is available online and can clarify what I can convey in prose.[79]

The Lasso motet, in five voices, is divided into two principal sections, each terminated by a melisma on the word "Alleluja" that leads into a cadence. The second principal section is subdivided, roughly into halves. A less definitive articulation, halfway through the second half, is once again led into by a melismatic "Alleluja," only here the melisma overlaps with the entry of new text and the opening of the second half of the second part. Our concern here is only with the opening ten measures.

The text for the entire first section is the same as the title of the motet: *De ore prudentis procedit mel* ("From the mouth of the wise honey comes forth"). The five voices are labeled, from lowest to highest, *bassus*, *quintus*, *tenor*, *altus*, and *cantus*. The *cantus* is the first voice to enter, singing "*De ore prudentis procedit mel*" over a five-measure span, with a half-bar rest separating *De ore prudentis* from *procedit mel*. The setting is syllabic, each syllable set by one note, except for the second syllable in *pru-den-tis*, which is expanded by an ornamental *gruppetto*. The second voice to enter is the *altus*, which mimics the first, delayed by a half measure and down a perfect fifth. The imitation at the lower fifth is exact up until the second syllable of *pru-den-tis*, where the *altus* omits the musical turn and proceeds directly on to the next portion of the text, *procedit mel*, punning on the word "*procedit*," now singing the words before the *cantus*, so that *dux* (leading voice) and *comes* (that which follows) have reversed positions, the leader becoming the follower, and instead of the *altus* imitating the *cantus* at the fifth below, the *cantus* imitates the *altus* at the fifth above. The reversal of leader and follower curiously parallels the temporal reversal in Bloom's use of metalepsis. As the *fuga* continues, we hear *procedit mel* in imitative counterpoint spun through all of the voices except for the *tenor*, the last voice to enter, singing the entire sentence "*De ore prudentis procedit mel.*" The sweetness of the imitative counterpoint is a lovely example of word painting, commonplace in the music of this period, here perfectly apposite to *procedit mel*. Unfortunately, Burmeister's prose, at least so far as I can understand, does not make clear where he considers the transumption to be. Is it in the reversal of *dux* and *comes* heard in the *cantus* and *altus*, or is the transumption in the truncation of the text, omitting "*De ore prudentis*," in the echoic transformations of *procedit mel*, where *procedit mel* is understood to allude to the first (omitted) part of the text, *De ore prudentis*? Or does the transumption include both aspects? Arguably, given that one of the meanings of transumption is the suppression or omission of a term (Hollander's example was "blind mouths"), the musical transumption in *De ore prudentis* is twofold: the omission of the ornamentation of *pru-**den**-tis* in the *altus*, and the omission of the first three words in the flowing forth of honey, *procedit mel*. This twofold omission does not explicitly address the reversal of *dux* and *comes*.

Thinking of the Lassus as an example of metalepsis in this way (omitting the reversal of leader and follower) reduces the musical version of the trope to a repetition that omits some part of the original. That doesn't seem like a very satisfactory way of defining musical metalepsis, although the technique is commonplace in musical composition.

As we have noted, a key aspect of Bloom's concept of rhetorical metalepsis is that in addition to transforming a trope over time, the later poet achieves figurative anteriority to the one who came before. Perhaps my musical imagination is inadequate to the task, but I find this principle impossible to imagine in musical terms. I cannot hear Johann Sebastian Bach, or some aspects of his fugues, as antecedent to Dieterich Buxtehude, his teacher. I cannot hear Beethoven, or some aspect of his works, as antecedent to Haydn. I cannot hear Jimi Hendrix as antecedent to Blind Lemon Jefferson. In each case, the later musician arguably overshadows the precursor, but temporal antecedence doesn't seem to be a convincing way to understand musical relationships. On the other hand, instances where a later musician overshadows a precursor are easily found. J. S. Bach certainly overshadows Buxtehude, as does Louis Armstrong overshadow King Oliver, as does Bessie Smith overshadow Ma Rainey. (Some readers might not agree with my evaluations; if so, choose your own examples.)

Instances such as these might make a better case as musical metalepses. But Bloom's examples are interesting because the strong poet (Milton, for example) overcomes, figuratively places himself before, an earlier strong poet (Homer or Isaiah). While I wouldn't say that Beethoven places Bach in the shadows, I do hear the fugue in late Beethoven as escaping Bach's shadow. Beethoven reimagines what a fugue might be, and he makes that reimagination necessary to his own musical rhetoric, just as Bach's fugues are necessary to his musical rhetoric. We're nibbling at the edges of what musical metalepsis might entail.

With the example of Beethoven's fugues in mind, we might say that the locus for musical metalepsis could be found in a radical transformation of a musical genre, one already strongly presented and then strongly reconceived. The final chapter of my 2007 monograph, *Schoenberg's Musical Imagination*, titled "The String Trio: metaleptic Schoenberg," explores just this approach toward musical metalepsis.[80] Schoenberg's trio is a late work, written after a near-death experience. I allow myself the luxury of quoting myself at length.

> The image of death locked in embrace with life takes on various forms in various cultures. Chief among them is what we call "the dance of death." For the musical imagination coming of age in turn-of-the-century Vienna, the waltz is synecdoche for dance. The waltz had taken many turns by the time that Schoenberg's life, in incarnate bodily form, was soon to close. This is to say that the image had been troped, and so turned into another, several times over. In Schoenberg's Trio, that troping continues. The troping of a trope is metalepsis; it is the centrality of Schoenberg's re-imagining of the waltz that gives this chapter its title.
>
> To make sense of all this, I fabricate a short story about the history of the dance from the First Viennese until the Trio. The story is simplistic history, but useful nonetheless. In the Classical style the dance movement had generally been a place devoid of the kinds of longing, struggle, and questioning that might be dramatically expressed in other movements. Even in Haydn's scherzo, there is no real *Angst*, no real yearning. The Classical dance is a most *heimlich* movement. Beethoven's scherzi up the ante. At times the metric and formal displacements suggest more than a playful joke. Later in the nineteenth

century, anxiety within the dance intensifies, and in some works the dance becomes a macabre affair. By the generation of Mahler, and most emphatically in Mahler's symphonies, the dance has become *unheimlich*, an ironic mockery of what it once was. The third movement of Mahler's Second Symphony or the third movement of his Seventh Symphony provide vivid examples. The dance as signifying *horror* takes its place within the semiotic code for the Second Viennese School, the waltz in Berg's *Wozzeck* being a prime example.

The role of the waltz in Schoenberg's music could easily be the topic of another chapter. Some remarkable examples include Tove's first song in *Gurrelieder* ("Sterne jubeln"), the grotesque Mahlerian parody of "Ach du lieber Augustin" in the Second String Quartet, the "Valse de Chopin" in *Pierrot Lunaire*, the "Orgie der Trunkenheit" in the Golden Calf scene of *Moses und Aron* (Act II, beginning m. 605), and the waltz parody in the first movement of the Violin Concerto (beginning at m. 93). In all of these passages, with the exception of Tove's song (and even here there are foreshadowings of the tragedy to come) the waltz is used as an *unheimlich* parody of what it once was.

With Schoenberg's Trio, however, another turn of the spiral is complete, for the dance has once again become *heimlich*, even as it takes on its most *unheimlich* role of all. Death has been stripped of its macabre mask and has become peace.[81]

In addition to reimagining the genre of the waltz, the Trio reimagines Schoenberg's own reception of the waltz, as in its previous manifestations, and it also reimagines Schoenberg's approach to twelve-tone technique and the musical rhetoric to which it gives rise. With an example of this sort, we approach an adequate musical representation of metalepsis.

At the risk of overly repeating myself, I once again emphasize that a key aspect of metalepsis is its function as a diachronic trope. While the other principal tropes—metaphor, irony, and metonymy—are synchronic, at least in their normal usages, metalepsis, at least as we have applied the term, requires change over time. We might expand this aspect of metalepsis toward a wide range of musical applications.

One of our most basic ways in perceiving or understanding musical flow is through recognizing the transformations of musical events/

characters as they change over time. This principle is analogous to the diachronic aspect of rhetorical metalepsis. Things get tricky in determining just what that object/event/character *is*. It's tricky because there are many ways to define a musical object, and each event/object so defined may be understood in multiple, complementary or opposed, ways. Compounding this already complex problem, there is a seductive tendency to fall into synchronicity, with a focus on instantiations rather than transformations. So, for example, we might liken an instance of a musical motive, one that transforms over time, to a photograph of a person. The photo's image captures a moment in time, but an adequate understanding of the person entails a moving picture, spanning birth to death. Moreover, an adequate picture of a person must involve their relations to those who came before, foremothers and forefathers, and to those who come after, children, both literal and figurative. An instantiation of a musical motive is analogous. To reduce the motive to a single manifestation is to misrepresent what it is, for *what it is* entails what it was and what it will become.

This same principle can be applied toward understanding relations among composers, genres, and so forth, always focusing on the transformation that allows one instantiation to transform into another. In sum, only with a diachronic understanding of musical elements, performance traditions, or compositional practices can we approach an adequate idea of musical transumption. In addition, musical transumption entails a radical reimagining of just what those elements, traditions, and practices entail: Beethoven reimagining what a symphony or string quartet might be; Jimi Hendrix reimagining the sonic possibilities of the electric guitar and its place within a tradition of blues-derived singing and playing; Louis Armstrong reimagining trumpet and voice placed within a musical ensemble so that a new musical form, jazz, might emerge; the Beatles reimagining British music hall traditions as they intersect with American rock and roll. When that reimagining is vivid and compelling enough so that the shadow of what came before is reversed, so that precursor's light is eclipsed, overshadowed, by the light of what comes chronologically later, only then do we approach an adequate idea of musical metalepsis. When that eclipse is intergenerational, or between radically different traditions, or both, then we approach a way of measuring the place of a musical work or musical performance within a canon of works or performances.[82]

Part II

A theory of music is a theory of life in that the experiential flow of living is a concomitant of the experiential flow of music as is the experiential flow of music a concomitant of the experiential flow of life. Scholars may debate whether music is a branch of bio-chemistry or bio-chemistry is a branch of music. Scholars of religion may place both, music and bio-chemistry into the sphere of religious studies. Good cooks may insist that all three, music, bio-chemistry, and religious studies, are subsumed under the heading of food understood as life sustaining.

—Unattributed note on an index card

7

Phrase as Musical Event, Wave as Musical Metaphor, and the Silence of Musical Space

Musical Phrase, Musical Interval

Events occur in phases, phases of the moon, phases of life's passing. A phase is a stage in a developmental process. When Shakespeare's Jacques says "all the world's a stage," he equates us humans with actors on a theatrical stage, playing scene after scene until the final scene brings "mere oblivion, sans teeth, sans eyes, sans taste, sans everything." Jacques's theatrical stage puns upon stage as phase, where the actor's phrases mimic life's phases. The means through which Jacques propounds his melancholic philosophy are the words of the poet, gathered into the syntactic units of phrases. We speak, sing, quarrel, and praise through phrases. We might even say that the phases of language and music are expressed through their phrases. Both phase and phrase unfold in time.

The word *phrase* has multiple meanings when applied to music. In most instances, a musical phrase indicates a syntactic unit terminated by a cadence, where cadence indicates closure roughly analogous either to the period at the end of a sentence or to a semicolon where we find a significant articulation embedded in a larger unit, in language, the sentence. We might say that a cadence concludes a musical thought, action, event, or that it demarcates a musical object. In some usages, a musical phrase indicates a smaller division, roughly analogous to a comma in language or a group of words clustered together, as in a prepositional phrase. When an instrumentalist or singer speaks of musical phrasing, the shaping of both small and larger spans is taken into account. Like most music theorists and historians, I avoid using the term *phrase* in this latter sense, preferring the term *subphrase* or *motive* to indicate smaller units that together comprise a musical phrase concluded by a cadence.[1]

Musical phrase shapes, often called *phrase rhythms*, are extremely variable in the ways they are formed and extended, and there is a formidable literature devoted to categorizing their various prototypes. We need not go into the fine points of musical phrase formation here. Suffice it to say that in most cases the ability to recognize a musical phrase as such does not require a sophisticated musical education. In most cases, an attentive listener or performer, with or without formal training in music theory, will intuitively recognize musical phrasing. I know this was the case for myself. In my formative years as a musician, I recognized musical phrases long before I had a technical vocabulary with which to name or categorize them. In the pragmatics of teaching tonal music, my advice to students confronting complex musical structures was always to begin by locating the cadences, the places at which musical phrases are concluded. Once we recognize phrase rhythms, we can work outward toward understanding more expansive zones, combinations of interrelated phrases that comprise larger spans of music, or we can work inward, understanding how smaller units combine to form the phrases that contain them. In this sense, too, the musical phrase is like the linguistic sentence. Just as sentences combine to form paragraphs, musical phrases can combine to form thematic areas or other larger spans of musical thought. And just as a complex sentence can be subdivided into subordinate phrases and clauses, a musical phrase can be subdivided into its generating constituents.

Like *phrase*, the word *interval* applied to music can take on various meanings. Outside of music, an interval usually denotes a temporal span, as in "after an interval, the concert resumed." Walter Pater memorably uses the word "interval" to denote our span of life. "We have an interval, and then our place knows us no more. Some spend this interval in listlessness, some in high passions, the wisest, at least among "the children of this world," in art and song. For our one chance lies in expanding that interval, in getting as many pulsations as possible into the given time."[2] In most musical usages (though not all), interval denotes a measurable distance between two pitches, where, apart from before and after, temporality (e.g., lapsed time between the onset or ending of notes) is not taken into account. We might say that in its most common usage, musical interval measures distance traversed (where a unison comprises a distance of zero) rather than time elapsed (including the option of simultaneity). We will return to the idea of musical interval as a measure of time in due course. First, however, it will be useful to consider the more common usage, distance traversed.[3]

A twofold division of consonant and dissonant intervals, the latter requiring "resolution" into a consonant interval, is useful in many different musical practices. In Western music theory, consonant intervals are further divided into "perfect" and "imperfect." Here the terms correlate with their meanings in grammar, where imperfection denotes an action still ongoing and perfection denotes an action completed: I am eating the cake versus I ate the cake. In the musical practices to which they pertain, perfect intervals are suitable for the conclusion of a phrase, while imperfect (or dissonant) intervals require that the phrase continue. This same nomenclature, perfect and imperfect, is applied to cadences; full closure is obtained through a *perfect cadence* (like the sentence-ending period in language), while partial closure is obtained through an *imperfect cadence* (more or less like a semicolon or a strongly articulated comma).

The theoretical writings of Arnold Schoenberg (1874–1951), with examples principally drawn from the late eighteenth century through the nineteenth century, divided musical phrases into two principal types, the *period* and the *sentence*.[4] Schoenberg's nomenclature has been widely adopted in the scholarly literature, and I follow it here. The *period* comprises two symmetrical parts, an antecedent phrase, usually terminated by an imperfect or half cadence, and a consequent phrase, terminated in its simplest form by a perfect or full cadence. A children's song provides a familiar example: "Mary had a little lamb, little lamb, little lamb [half cadence]; Mary had a little lamb, whose fleece was white as snow [full cadence]." The half cadence is a significant pause, but it leaves you, as it were, up in the air. The opening of Mozart's Piano Sonata KV 331 provides the most commonly cited example of a musical period in the classical style. A musical *sentence* opens with a short idea, its reiteration with or without modification, followed by a continuation of variable duration, terminated by a cadence. We hear a variant of this phrase type in the children's song "Three Blind Mice": "Three blind mice, three blind mice (in this case, two iterations combining to form the first idea), see how they run, see how they run (two iterations combining to form the modified reiteration of the first idea), they all ran after the farmer's wife, who cut off their tails with a carving knife, did you ever see such a sight in your life, as three blind mice? (an extended continuation, closing with a cadence). The opening of the Overture to Mozart's *Le Nozze di Figaro* provides a well-known example from the classical period, as does the opening of Beethoven's Fifth Symphony.

While the categories of musical sentence and period are extremely useful in understanding musical phrases throughout the "common-practice period" of Europe and the United States, roughly from the mid-eighteenth through the early twentieth centuries, and much else since then, including a wide range of popular and folk music, sentence and period are not adequate toward understanding phrase shapes in other periods and other places. In contrast, we find a much more flexible idea if we understand musical *phrase* as any musical thought, event, characteristic, or object that reaches a conclusion, a sense of completion that temporarily or terminally brings the ongoing musical event to a halt. With this in mind, we can define the technical means by which cadence is achieved in ways more inclusive than the cadential formulas coming out of European practices.

Yet even cadence as defining musical phrase has its limits in that cadence implies conclusion, as we said before, a grammatical perfection wherein a thought or action or event is completed. Not all music imagines such completions. Before considering poetry or music that denies closure, perfection in the grammatic sense, I would like to give some thought to the ways that meter impacts the ways we come to hear musical phrases and poetic forms. Later, we will return to consider the relations between poetic meter and musical meter more fully. Here our concern will be limited to the interactions of musical meter and musical phrasing. Toward that end, consideration of alternative meanings for the word *cadence* will prove a good starting point.

Apart from its meaning in musical syntax, cadence has a range of meanings associated with regular divisions of time. The first definition of cadence in the *Oxford English Dictionary* is taken from Samuel Johnson's dictionary: "The flow of verses or periods." OED's second definition is "The measure or beat of music, dancing, or any rhythmical movement e.g., of marching." OED also lists a rare but interesting use of cadence as a transitive verb: "To put into cadence, to compose metrically." Meter is a strong determinant of how we hear music, and musical phrases specifically. Music suitable for dancing, I assume, would always have had a sense of measured time. Notated meter evolved in Europe as early as the time of Pérotin (d. ca. 1238), and Western art music has since then been conceived predominantly through a kind of temporal grid, the various evolving and changing concepts of musical meter.[5]

What all musical meters have in common is a sense of regular pulse, where tempo controls the rate of that pulse. Poetic meter, in accentual syllabic languages (like English, German, Italian), indicates regular patterns of accented and non-accented syllables. In pure syllabic languages (like modern French and Japanese), accent depends on context, and poetic meter measures the number of syllables rather than accentual patterns. What all modern poetic meters have in common is a regular patterning of the syllabic constituents of language. And though poetic meter does not control evenly placed pulses in the same sense as musical meter, poetic meter can nevertheless be thought of as a kind of temporal grid superimposed on or generated by the music of poetry. The ancient poetry that I know of, both Hebrew and Greek, was chanted. And so the metrics of that poetry, however conceived, were one and the same with the metric of that music.

David Lewin's treatment of generalized musical intervals, though not explicitly concerned with meter, can shed some light on our concepts of measured time, the underlying prerequisite for musical meter. We recall that Lewin, in *Generalized Musical Intervals and Transformations*, formulated two broad approaches toward conceptualizing music, intervallic and transformational.

> We tend to imagine ourselves in the position of *observers* when we theorize about musical space; the space is "out there," away from our dancing bodies or singing voices.
>
> "The interval from s to t" is thereby conceived as modeling a relation of *extension*, observed in that space external to ourselves; we "see" it out there just as we see distances between the holes in a flute, or points along a stretched string. The reader may recall our touching on these matters . . . where we pointed out how the historical development of harmonic theory has depended on such a projection of our intuitions into a geometric space outside our bodies, that is, the "line" of the stretched string, a space to which we can relate as detached observers.
>
> In contrast, the transformational model is much less Cartesian.[6]

Lewin was extremely careful in his use of language. He doesn't say that the transformational approach is *not* Cartesian, but rather that it is *much less* Cartesian. The move away from a Cartesian understanding that Lewin emphasizes, "projection of our intuitions into a geometric space outside our bodies," has two aspects: first, "a geometric space," plotted on a Cartesian grid by implication, and, second, the objectification "outside our bodies." Lewin's solution to the objectification of "outside our bodies" is his transformational approach, as musical events (now not objectified) morph into other events. But transformation in itself does not get rid of the "out there" problem. I can watch the chrysalis morph into a butterfly while objectifying the whole process. To get rid of the problem of music being "out there," we need to accept either a deep subjectivity, something like Levinas asserts, or a middle-voiced experience; indeed, I have asserted that Levinas's deep subjectivity and middle voice are virtually the same. In any case, phenomenology's solution to the problem is middle voiced. However, the first problem, that of a geometric grid, is of a different nature. Metered poetry or music either places events/objects (words, sounds) into an a priori temporal grid, or the events/objects generate that grid.[7] Whether meter is perceived as generated inside-out (more in line with a transformational approach) or superimposed outside-in (in Lewin, an intervallic approach), metrically conceived poems and music have a temporal grid built into their structured objects/events. Whether metered poetry and music are perceived as objective, subjective, or middle voiced, the time grid is necessarily part of the experience.

Of course, meter antedates Descartes. Meter's bases are presumably organic in origin. Heartbeat and respiration are human metrics, as is the measured footfall of a walking cadence. The question arises, is an internal metric intrinsic to all things, from subatomic to cosmic? Does all the world go tick-toc in infinitely varied ways? Let's set that mind boggler aside and set our sights a bit lower, asking how we experience time passing. Here I can say with assurance that many experiences in life have a flow that eludes or denies metric expression.

Yesterday was a good day for the roses in my backyard. The buds had opened to a vivid yellow flowering; the color saturation and folded nestings of petal on petal, so beautiful in roses, had reached a peak. Today the color will have lost some of its vividness; the folded petals will begin to droop. In a few days the roses will shrivel and the petals will fall. My experience of the organic flow of the roses, from emergent bud to emergent flower to an emergent withering, is temporal but not metric. To be sure, I could have precisely timed the events—bud appears at time X and lasts until X+n, flower appears at X+m and lasts until X+m', withered petals manifest at X+q and are gone by X+q'—placing them into a metric, but my experience of the roses not only does not depend on meter—it's off the grid. Placing the roses' bloom into a metric falsifies my experience of gradual transformation by imposing measured steps onto the flow of an emerging process experienced without discrete building blocks.

The models for musical phrase that we have considered so far are all imagined on a temporal grid. The balance of antecedent and consequent depend on it, the measured reiteration of the opening in a musical sentence, likewise. As we have said, so long as music is metered, hearing through a temporal grid, regularly measured intervals of time, is not only appropriate but necessary. An analogous observation can be made about metered poetry. However, if there is no regulating meter intrinsic to the music, then a superimposed metric, from "out there," like a clock that measures elapsed time on a CD player, runs counter to the fluidity of the musical experience.

Wave as Musical Metaphor

Sidestepping the complex biological mechanism through which we perceive sound, we can say that from the perspective of physics, sound is the fluctuation of air, the familiar waves depicted visually on an oscilloscope. In physics, waves are objective phenomena, measurable flows of energy, with each wave defining its own metric, visible as the measurable, linear curves on an oscilloscope. We can also think of waves figuratively, where flow and energy are metaphors. In thinking about American politics, I waver between hope and despair. My wavering emotions are purely figurative. A Wikipedia article tells me that "new wave" music emerged out of punk rock. The clever label, "new wave," applied to music combines literal (new combinations of sound waves) and figurative meanings (where the music is like a new wave in fashion where torn denims supplant tailored trousers).

We have considered at some length the idea of liminal time-space, deriving our vocabulary and inspiration from Angus Fletcher and others. The idea of *waves* as a metaphor for the energized, variable flow of poetic imagery, sound, and syntax is another of Fletcher's terms that is suggestive toward understanding analogous, variable flows of energy and gesture in music. Escaping the regularity of poetic meters, Walt Whitman's oceanic waves imagined a new way of shaping poetry's song. "Whitman developed a theory of poetry and of its imaginative partner, democracy, precisely by recurring to the paradigm of wave-motion. Waves of change will permit the poem and the nation to become a unity arising from a diversity, exactly as the aggregates of environment compose a composite unity, according to a pragmatic rather than Platonic resolution between the One and the Many."[8]

Whitman was born in Huntington, Long Island. His family later moved to Brooklyn, on the western tip of the island, and still later Whitman moved to Manhattan, an island as well. Surrounded by the sea, and traveling between Long Island and Manhattan by ferry, Whitman grew up with the Atlantic Ocean and the Long Island Sound as everyday presences.

> Late in life Whitman told his friend Horace Traubel that his work was a part of Ocean. Whitman was never a literalist of natural forces, yet he knew from nature the shaping of the turns of verse. Characterizing the "rhythmic patternings of long and short lines, aligned, variously interjected, refrained, extended, receding," John Hollander reminds us that the analogy is just that: speaking of his *Leaves* as Ocean, Whitman says to Traubel "its verses are liquid, billowy waves, ever rising and falling, perhaps wild with storm, always moving, always alike in their nature as rolling waves, but hardly any two exactly alike in size or measure, never having the sense of something finished and fixed, always suggesting something beyond."[9]

Through writing in variable waves, Whitman imagines a new way of creating poetic form. The variable lines of *free verse* in twentieth-century poetics can be traced back to Whitman's waves. Marianne Moore, A. R. Ammons, John Ashbery, and more poets than I can name are Whitman's children in this regard. When I heard Amanda Gorman reciting "The Hill We Climb" at Joe Biden's inauguration, I recognized the rhythms of Whitman's poetics as inflected by the African American accents of rap.

Wave understood as the force and momentum of energized flow, literal or metaphoric, needs to be complemented by that which opposes flow, a resistance or impedance that is overcome or overwhelmed. In music, in poetry, as in all aspects of nature, motion cannot be understood apart from its opposite, rest. Energized flow resists rest, just as rest resists motion. Force and counter-force, the rolling of the wave, the breaking of the wave impeded. From the gentlest ripples in a pond to the horrific force of a tsunami, we perceive the power of a wave through its setting into motion that which just before had been at rest. A massive oceanic wave moves a massive weight of water, overwhelming all in its path. Being overwhelmed, literally to be turned upside down, is a watery metaphor, like a wave that capsizes a ship, but also like a wind that bends, then snaps a mainmast so that what was topmost plunges down. Wind too is wave, air instead of water. And, like the massive oceanic wave, wind of sufficient force overwhelms all in its path. Breath is wave and sound is wave, and sound in music and poetry sets being into motion. And the power and flow of that motion are measured by that which it moves. The metaphor of motion is alive in the music and poetry that move me. If that power is sufficient, whether through air set into motion or imagined in silence, no matter, I am overwhelmed.

Stillness, the slowing or stopping of flow, can be energy spent, or it can be restive, like a horse impatient and unmanageable in restraint. I read that "impede," from the Latin *impedire*, literally entails shackling of the feet. Restraint impedes flow, just as flow overcomes impedance. The power of a massive waterfall is impedance suddenly, precipitously absent. The breaking of a wave on a massive rock is impedance suddenly, precipitously present. Just so, waves in music, whether riverine or oceanic, can burst forth, all of a sudden, impedance removed; or inversely, musical flow, suddenly impeded, breaks, so that flow is dispersed into a white foam of sound, to dissipate until the next wave comes along. In biblical imagery, God's breath, *ruach ha-kodesh* (the holy breath), sets the universe into motion. It is the biblical poet's imagery of the first wave. Musical works begin with their first waves.

Wave as metaphor for energized flow can be applied to both metered and non-metric music, but the metaphor works especially well in musical practices that are fashioned without regular meter, both ancient and contemporary. And, unlike phrases concluded by cadences, waves, at least as Whitman conceived them, have the quality of "never having the sense of something finished and fixed, always suggesting something beyond." Moreover, the relation of sound to silence takes on a different meaning depending on whether we perceive in a metered or non-metered time-space. Metered silence can do many things, including creating a sense of expectation or giving a space for reflection. Still, silence in a measured time-space has a different sense than silence that is felt as an unfathomable void out of which sound emerges. Meter walks us through the silence, though the steps are felt rather than heard, or rather they are heard in the imaginative inner ear, not through their manifestation in audible waves moving through the air. I suppose that astronomers in their mappings of the universe must superimpose some sort of grid (a dynamic, non-rectilinear grid, post-Einstein) on the vastness of space. But the mystery of outer space, the silent, dark container and conveyor of all that there is, resists metric description. In my experience, lack of meter heightens a sense of sound emerging out of silence, whereas metered time-space attenuates that sense.

Brian Ferneyhough, considered by many, including myself, as one of the most gifted composers of our moment, opens his 1984 essay "*Il Tempo della Figura*" by quoting a passage from John Ashbery, "Self-portrait in a convex mirror." The passage uses the metaphor of a wave breaking upon the rocks, a metaphor that Ferneyhough finds suggestive for his understanding of musical flow.[10] I want to carefully consider some aspects of Ferneyhough's essay, but it will be useful first to consider the wave metaphor in Ashbery's poetry.

Wave forms, in the sense of irregular flow and open-endedness as first developed by Whitman, are pervasive in Ashbery's poetry. As might be expected, wave imagery per se, the evocation of oceanic or riverine flow, or the explicit metaphoric use of wave motion as in wavering emotions, is not common in Ashbery. His poem "A Wave," the final poem in a book of poems by the same name, is a striking case in point. Aside from the title, the word *wave* is found only once in the entire twenty-two-page poem. Even if I take into account images that imply literal waves without literally saying "wave," I find only three additional instances. I quote all of the apposite passages below.

> As with rocks at low tide, a mixed surface is revealed,
> More detritus. Still, it is better this way
> Than to have to live through a sequence of events acknowledged
> In advance in order to get a primitive statement.
> . . .
> The covenant we entered
> Bears down on us, some are ensnared, and the right way,
> It turns out, is the one that goes straight through the house
> And out the back. By so many systems
> As we are involved in, by just so many
> Are we set free on an ocean of language that comes to be
> Part of us, as though we would ever get away.

. . .
Moments as clear as water
Splashing on a rock in the sun . . .
. . .
And as the luckless describe love in glowing terms to strangers
In taverns, and the seemingly blessed may be unaware of
    having lost it,
So always there is a small remnant
Whose lives are congruent with their souls
And who afterwards know no mystery in it,
The cimmerian moment in which all lives, all destinies
And incompleted destinies were swamped
As though by a giant wave that picks itself up
Out of a calm sea and retreats again into nowhere
Once its damage is done.[11]

In the first cited passage, beginning with "As with rocks at low tide," the ebb tide reveals the "detritus" of our lives. The wave that brought the detritus near the shore is gone, and we can only know what it brought after it is gone. We will find a similar sentiment in the passage that Ferneyhough cites from Ashbery's "Self-Portrait in a Convex Mirror." Ashbery tells us that "it is better this way" than to be directed by "a sequence of events acknowledged in advance." The "primitive statement" has no previously defined concepts. It is emergent, and only known after the wave that brings it into being has subsided. The form is formed only after it is gone.

Along analogous lines (although absent wave imagery), Richard E. Goodkin begins "Zeno's Paradox: Mallarmé, Valéry, and the Symbolist 'Movement'" by quoting a paragraph from Paul Valéry's "Existence du Symbolisme."[12] Valéry's article, written in 1936, observes that the term "Symbolism" is a term that was applied only in retrospect, denoting a movement that had begun fifty years previously in 1886, a term not applied to the movement as it emerged. Goodkin subsequently goes on to say, "It is only the passage of time which, by showing what the past was 'leading' to, shows what it 'was' but did not know it until it was no longer."[13] Also kindred is Hegel's famous phrase "the owl of Minerva flies at dusk," where Minerva, signifying wisdom, arrives only after the happenings of the day are over.

Wave imagery is deep-seated in the second passage excised from Ashbery's poem. The "ocean of language that comes to be part of us" is forever unsettled in its ebb and flow. Ashbery will often contradict something he has just said, an exaggeration of the same quality in Emerson and Whitman. Here he hints toward self-contradiction with "as though we would *ever* get away," so easily misheard as the more normative "as though we would *never* get away." We recall John Hollander's observation concerning "the mooring of starting out," where *mooring* is easily misheard as *morning*. "By so many systems . . . are we set free on an ocean of language . . . as though we would ever get away." Earlier in the passage, foreshadowing "ever get away," we read that "the right way, it turns out, is the one that goes straight through the house and out back." Presumably, the house we go through and out the back door is the prison house of language (to borrow Fredric Jameson's phrase), where "some are ensnared."

"Moments as clear as water / Splashing on the rocks" returns to imagery similar to the earlier "rocks at low tide." The wave is finally named as such in the final passage that I cite. The passage is yet another variant on the first image, there life's detritus, here our swamped destinies and incomplete destinies. The giant wave picks itself up out of a calm sea and retreats again into nowhere once its damage is done. Converted to music, the "nowhere" that the wave "retreats again into" is silence.

Ashbery's "Self-Portrait in a Convex Mirror" is an ekphrastic poem on steroids. The global topic of the poem is a self-portrait painted by Francesco Parmigianino (1503–1540).

> Vasari says, "Francesco one day set himself
> To take his own portrait, looking at himself for that purpose
> In a convex mirror . . .
> . . .
> . . . he set himself
> With great art to copy all that he saw in the glass."[14]

Seventeen pages long, the poem veers back and forth from descriptions of the painting, remarkable in themselves, to reflections on a world of emotions, ideas, and images, all imagined as contained in, or suggested by, the image on the convex globe. Wave as metaphor recurs intermittently throughout the poem. I cite the apposite passages below. (Images of Parmigianino's painting are easily found on the internet. I highly recommend reading the poem with the image in mind.)

> As Parmigianino did it, the right hand
> Bigger than the head, thrust at the viewer

    And swerving easily away, as though to protect
    What it advertises. . . .
    . . .
    Lively and intact in a recurring wave
    Of arrival . . .
    . . .
    Finally reversed in the accumulating mirror.
    They seemed strange because we couldn't actually see them.
    And we realize this only at the point where they lapse
    Like a wave breaking on a rock, giving up
    Its shape in a gesture which expresses that shape.
    . . .
    But what is this universe the porch of
    As it veers in and out, back and forth,
    Refusing to surround us and still the only
    Thing we can see? . . .
    . . .
    . . . To be serious only about sex
    Is perhaps one way, but the sands are hissing
    As they approach the beginning of the big slide
    Into what happened . . .[15]

"As Parmigianino did it . . ." opens the poem, with the ambiguity of beckoning or waving away as the artist's left hand, distorted by the convex mirror, fills the lower quarter of the globe, "thrust at the viewer / And swerving easily away." Ashbery, either mistakenly or deceptively, says "right hand," forgetting, or letting us forget for the moment, that we are seeing a mirror image. This is the first hint of flood and ebb. A bit later the image is reinforced as "a recurring wave of arrival."

The four-line passage that Ferneyhough cites in "*Il Tempo della Figura*," beginning with "They seemed strange because we couldn't see them," is embedded in the longer passage that begins "What should be the vacuum of a dream / Becomes continually replete as the source of dreams." "The vacuum of a dream" is nothingness, like the *Ein Sof* of Kabbalah from which all emerges, like silence out of which sound emerges. This vacuum "becomes continually replete," continually filling near the point of bursting; it is "the source of dreams." And this source of dreams "Is being tapped, so that this one dream / May wax, flourish like a cabbage rose, / Defying sumptuary laws . . ." Wikipedia tells me that the cabbage rose, also named *rosa x centifolia* (hundred leaved rose), is a hybrid developed by Dutch breeders between the seventeenth and nineteenth centuries, and possibly earlier. "Flourish like a cabbage rose" transfers a figurative meaning of flourish (to thrive) onto a literal meaning (to bloom). Sumptuary laws arose in Italy as early as the twelfth century, taxing luxury items.[16] This extravagant dream-flowering defies such laws. But then we awake "in what / Has now become a slum." The bubble pops and the dream of riches becomes a dilapidated neighborhood where people live in poverty: another variant on the empty vacuum becoming replete, here reversing the order.

Ashbery continues by quoting the art historian Sydney Freedberg, as he had quoted Giorgio Varsari earlier. "Realism in this portrait / No longer produces an objective truth, but a *bizarria* . . . / However its distortion does not create / A feeling of disharmony . . . . The forms retain / A strong measure of ideal beauty." I have just inserted a period after "ideal beauty," but Ashbery uses a comma. Instead of allowing closure to the quote, Ashbery continues in his own words, "because / Fed by our dreams, so inconsequential until one day / We notice the hole they left." Is the hole they left the slum we awake to, or is it another void, not the vacuum that becomes continually replete as the source of dreams, or is it that very vacuum that once again might become replete? The word "they" ("the hole they left"), if I read the sentence correctly, refers back to "forms." The forms are fed by our dreams and they leave a hole, a space that cannot be filled, or is yet to be filled. The words "their" and "they" in the following three sentences also refer back to forms fed by dreams, not dreams per se (*pace* Ferneyhough).

> Now their importance
> If not their meaning is plain. They were to nourish
> A dream that includes them all, as they are
> Finally reversed in the accumulating mirror.
> They seemed strange because we couldn't actually see them.

The forms we cannot see are fed by dreams that in turn nourish a dream that includes them all. "Reversed in the accumulating mirror. / They seemed strange because we couldn't actually see them." We couldn't actually see them, the dream-fed forms that nourish a more inclusive dream, because the convex mirror distorts. And we couldn't actually see them because they are *ideal forms*, Platonic ideas, presumably informing Parmigianino's forms, antecedent to the necessarily distorted manifestations that are available to us.

This brings us to the four lines that Brian Ferneyhough quotes at the opening of "*Il tempo della figura.*"

> They seemed strange because we couldn't actually see them.
> And we realize this only at the point where they lapse
> Like a wave breaking on a rock, giving up
> Its shape in a gesture which expresses that shape.

Analogous to the passage in "A Wave" where we recognize remaining detritus only after the wave is gone, here the strange forms are realized "only at the point where they lapse / Like a wave breaking on a rock, giving up / Its shape in a gesture which expresses that shape." The two lines that follow recall Freedberg's description of ideal forms that inform the distorted images: "The forms retain / A strong measure of ideal beauty."

> The forms retain a strong measure of ideal beauty
> As they forage in secret on our idea of distortion.

The word "forage," echoing form, resumes the metaphor of feeding ("fed by our dreams, . . . to nourish a dream"), but to forage also can mean to gather and destroy as one goes, "like a wave . . . giving up its shape in a gesture which expresses that shape."

Later in the poem, Ashbery asks, "But what is this universe the porch of / As it veers in and out, back and forth / Refusing to surround us and still the only / Thing we can see?" Here we have a further development of the poem's initial image, the hand "Bigger than the head, thrust at the viewer / And swerving easily away." The universe of the convex globe is all that we can see. As "porch" it is extension of some main structure, which remains like the ideal forms outside of view. And later yet we read that "no previous day would have been like this." "That the present looked the same to everybody" is a confusion that "drains away as one / Is always cresting into one's present." We recall and amplify Merleau-Ponty's "we are the sudden upsurge of time." A. R. Ammons beautifully expresses a similar sentiment in his poem "Zero and Then Some":

> . . . there is
> an ongoing we nearly cheapen by being its
> specific crest, but humbly we know too it
> bore us and will support us into whatever
> rest remains: . . .[17]

The final wave metaphor in "Self-Portrait" is yet another wave, one that drains away confusion. Ashbery tells us that our habits confuse issues. "To be serious only about sex / Is perhaps one way . . ." Is he kidding us? ". . . but the sands are hissing / As they approach the beginning of the big slide / Into what happened. . . ." "What had happened" is yet another variant of the detritus that Ashbery had imagined in "A Wave."

Brian Ferneyhough's Figura

Having considered Ashbery's waves, we can now turn to their adaptation in *Il Tempo della Figura*. I would characterize the term *figura* (sometimes spelled *figure*) as idiosyncratically developed by Ferneyhough as a way of naming the musical impetus that gives rise to what we have called a *wave*. We will return to this idea of figure, but let's first consider Ferneyhough's observations about Ashbery's breaking wave.

In the ramp-up to his discussion of Ashbery's image, Ferneyhough contrasts the idea of musical objects as "morphologically discrete, self-consistently affective" with "those same objects considered as free-floating mobile structural radicals possessing the potential to unfold and reproduce themselves in independently meaningful linear trajectories." The distinction is close to our differentiation of musical object and musical event, where "object" can be abstracted and manipulated and event flows out of a previous event and into a subsequent one, although "radicals" might better denote the constituents of an event. Ferneyhough's stated interest is to develop and distinguish "concepts of *musical energy* and *lines of force*" that interrelate the two perspectives (morphologically discrete objects, free-floating mobile radicals).[18]

Having made the distinction between discrete objects and free-floating radicals, Ferneyhough then turns to an appraisal of the breaking wave where a subsequent distinction between musical *energy* and musical *force* is clarified.

> Returning to the Ashbery citation from the beginning: two main ideas seem to be inextricably entwined in those few lines. Firstly, the view that the present constitutes itself only as *sensed absence*; secondly, that our "life-line" to reality might perhaps be interpreted as a special form of *motion*. What, after all, is "expression" but a sort of passage from one state

to another, in which neither the presumptive beginning and end points are primary, but rather the "no longer" and "not yet" whose *impressum* they bear. In this context, the image of the wave refers both to some natural, unformed undertow of creative potential, shaping events according to whatever form of dynamic law, and to the fleetingly insubstantial moment of perception, born along the crest of the wave as an unrepeatable trace of being. The energy entrapped in the wave (which *is*, in a sense, the wave) being ejected into concrete form by the unyielding resistance of the rock, is instrumental in effecting the transition from the physical to the configurational, thereby becoming invested, as action, with symbolic stature. Force, as the liberation of entrapped energy, finds its counterpart in an energy definable as the application of force to a resistant object. The intersection of these trajectories in the musical discourse is the locus of the present, which is thus weighted, at any given juncture, by a unique balance of tensions, a unique "fingerprint." Thus, musical force and musical energy are not identical. Energy is invested in concrete musical objects to the extent that they are capable of rendering forces acting upon them visible. Lines of force arise in the space between objects—not space as a temporal lacuna, atopia, but at that moment of conceptual differentiation in which identity is born—and take as their vehicular object the connective impetus established in the act of moving from one discrete musical event to another.[19]

The idea of *sensed absence* is one we have already noticed in Ashbery's wave imagery, "the big slide into what happened." The senses of "no longer" and "not yet," respectively, place us after the wave has broken, and while riding the wave that will break in some future, as yet unknown. That "reality might perhaps be interpreted as a special form of *motion*" is a lovely formulation of the diachrony we have recurrently encountered. The *"impressum"* or imprint of what is "no longer" is like the gradual erosion of the rock that seems unyielding to the sea. The imprint on "not yet" is just as strong, though as yet unrealized. The nexus of images and metaphors that follow edge up to a metaphorical description of the mechanics of Ferneyhough's *figura*: "The energy entrapped in the wave . . . the unyielding resistance of the rock . . . the application of force to a resistant object . . . Energy is invested in concrete musical objects to the extent that they are capable of rendering forces acting upon them visible." The active forces remain invisible, "They seemed strange because we couldn't actually see them," but they render visible, which is to say audible, their impact on "concrete musical objects." Without mentioning the word *figura*, Ferneyhough has described the workings of figure as he will further develop the term.

Il Tempo della Figura, in a sense an aesthetic manifesto, begins with a critique of what might apply to neoclassicism, neo-Romanticism, or postmodernity in general.

> Ripping such units [the elements of music] out of the contexts which gave them being leads to a fatal debilitation of their expressive powers at the same time that their integration into new montage forms demands precisely this unimpaired semantic impact in order to support and bring out the envisaged innovatory impact of their juxtaposition. Denuded of their auratic mantles, such isolated elements present themselves, more often than not, as references to anterior worlds of sensibility rather than as their symbolic re-evocation.[20]

Ferneyhough borrows the term *auratic* from Walter Benjamin as it is used in "The Work of Art in the Age of Mechanical Reproduction."[21] Benjamin's sense of *aura* in works of art is concerned with presence: "presence in time and space, its unique existence at the place where it happens to be."[22] The synoptic concern of Benjamin's article is that the aura of art, its sense of presence, is easily lost in the age of mechanical reproduction. Suggestively, Benjamin also applies aura to natural objects, where he finds the "unique phenomenon of a distance" irrespective of physical distance or proximity.[23] We might translate Benjamin's auratic *distance* as an otherness, correlating aura with Levinas's mystery of the other, an idea that we have applied to one's relationship with the musical score or the musical performance. Ferneyhough anticipates this very idea near the end of his article, where he posits a conjunction of aura with his idea of figure: "The idea of figure seen as a constructive and purposive reformulation of the gesture should clear the path for aura, the visionary idea of a work entering into conversation with the listener *as though it were another aware subject*."[24] *As though it were another aware subject*: we recall our augmentation of Levinas's idea of responsibility to the other; that a musical work or musical performance is not an object, but rather a human utterance.

So what is this mysterious *figure*; how does it work? Here is Ferneyhough's first pass toward a definition. "The *figure* is proposed as an element of musical signification composed entirely of details defined by their contextual disposition rather than their innate, stylistically defined referential capacity. The synchronic is replaced by diachronic successivity as the central mode of 'reading' musical states."[25] The attribution of diachrony to figure is crucial, and the idea resonates nicely with thought we have already observed in scholars as distinctive as Levinas and Bloom. Near the end of the article, we read: "The search for a fixed definition of the term 'figure' is, in my view, an enterprise of doubtful utility. It will I hope, have emerged from the above considerations that a figure does not exist in material terms, in its own autonomous right; rather it represents a way of perceiving, categorizing and mobilizing concrete gestural configurations, whatever the purpose of these latter might be."[26] A series of musical examples within the article clarifies what remains vague apart from them (ibid., 38–39). The examples, for simplicity's sake, are given in rhythmic notation, without designated pitch, dynamics, or orchestration. Of course, nothing is simple in the imagination of Brian Ferneyhough. In the first example, five dyadic rhythms move through a durational series of 7:1, 3:1, 2:1, 3:2, 1:1 so that the second duration in each dyad relates respectively to the first as $1/7$, $1/3$, $1/2$, $2/3$, $1/1$, giving rise to a process of diminishing differences between the long and short, until in the final iteration we have equality. The *figure* is not the "concrete gestural configurations," but rather the process that informs them, a diminishing difference in duration first-to-second and so on as we move through the series. Although the likelihood of our hearing the ratios per se is slim to none, the process of gradually moving from extreme differentiation of long-short toward equality of the paired durations is very audible. Each successive example further develops this process, adding increasing complexity to the design, rendering the possibility of hearing the underlying process more and more difficult to perceive, but adding richness and complexity to the resulting musical expression.[27]

We might say that Ferneyhough's *figure* is a metaphor for the dynamics of metaphoric waves. As metaphor for metaphor, *figure* approaches metalepsis. I find compelling the idea that musical objects are energized to the extent that they are capable of rendering forces acting upon them *audible*. Using another metaphor, we can say defined motion transforms musical objects into the constituents of events. To conflate Lewin's idea of transformational functions with Ferneyhough's idea of figure would do violence to both ideas, but to overlook their deeper relations would be a mistake. Both ideas are liminal, and both are manifest (heard) only in their resultants, as not as objects, but as musical events perceived and reperceived in the flow of a musical wave.

The Silence of Caesura

In the CD liner notes for a recording of his composition *Infinito Nero*, Salvatore Sciarrino is quoted as saying "Silence is not empty, it gives birth to sound. Not only in music."[28] Brian Ferneyhough, writing about his Second String Quartet, locates silence as central to the work. "This piece is about silence—not so much literal silence (although this, too, is an obvious feature of the opening section) but rather that deliberate *absence* at the center of musical experience which exists in order that the listening subject may encounter itself there."[29] Having moved from musical phrase and its sense of conclusion to wave or poetic/musical gesture informed by dynamic force, we now move on to a consideration of what silence might come to mean in these larger contexts.

John Hollander's *Rhyme's Reason* is replete with clever self-referential verses that embody the verse forms and sonic constituents of poetry that they describe. His description of *caesura* and rhymed *couplets* is found in the same six-lined verse.

> Here's a *caesura*: see what it can do.
> (And here's a gentler one, whose pause, more slight,
> Waves its two hands, and makes what's left sound right.)[30]

The initial caesura calls attention to itself. It is a present absence, a break that halts ongoing motion, like suddenly slamming on the breaks of a moving automobile. Having stopped, momentarily, we look back to "see what it can do," like noting an avoided collision after having slammed on the breaks (no avoided collision here, just a line broken in two). The accentual pattern of cae-**su**-ra, weak-strong-weak, adds to the effect of leaving us up in air; all of the other terminal words are accented, single syllables: point . . . joint . . . two . . . do . . . slight . . . right. Music too can have screeching halts, sudden moments of silence that suspend ongoing motion, that we can reflect on as motion continues. The gentler caesura, whose pause is "more slight," is as connective as it is separative.

It is more like the pause that separates antecedent from consequent in a musical period. It makes what's left (punning on the twin meaning of what came before—to the left—and what remains), sound right (punning on the twin meaning of what comes afterward—to the right—and what's correct), bringing the partial statement into a cohesive whole.

(In addition to exemplifying what a caesura can do, the verse also contains splendid examples of enjambment and the double-meanings inherent in strong enjambments. As the first line terminates, "makes a point" is equivalent to "makes an observation" or "points out." As we move into the second line, "which hinges on its bending," the meaning of "point" changes into a Euclidian point, as in a point in a line. John Hollander gave us an insightful discussion of enjambment in the fifth chapter of his book *Vision and Resonance: Two Senses of Poetic Form*.[31] There he writes, "Much of what happens in strong or hard enjambments, then, forces a reinterpretation of the position of the syntactic cut at the line break, based upon the *contre-rejet*."[32] *Contre-rejet*, literally opposed-rejection, gives us a term evidently not available in English. It entails a reinterpretation of the line that came before. So far as I know, this aspect of setting poetry to music has not been adequately addressed in the scholarly literature.)

We normally think of poetic caesuras as mid-line, as in Hollander's "Here's a *caesura*: see what it can do." Transferred to music, this is kindred to abruptly breaking off the expected continuation of a melody, what in classical rhetoric is called an *abruptio*. Giuseppe Verdi was a master of this technique. The orchestral introduction to the drinking song (*Brindisi*) in the first act of *La Traviata* provides a memorable example. The orchestral melody is immediately repeated with words sung by Alfredo, the young man who falls in love with Violetta, a courtesan, the "fallen one" referred to in the opera's title, *la Traviata*. In Alfredo's version, instead of the breaking off that abruptly ends the orchestral version, we reach a melodic conclusion. The melody divides into two phrases, with the second phrase leading to a more definitive conclusion than the first (both phrases end on the tonic harmony, but the first has the fifth in the melody whereas the melodic second phrase ends more definitively with the tonic, a *perfect authentic cadence*). Here are Alfredo's words sung immediately after the orchestral introduction.

> *Libiamo, libiamo ne' lieti calici,*
> *che la bellezza infiora;* [Authentic Cadence]
> *E la fuggevol, fuggevol ora*

s'inenbrii a voluttà. [Perfect Authentic Cadence]
(Drink from the cheerful chalice,
which bring loveliness to flower;
And inebriate with pleasure,
the fleeting, fleeting hour.)

Whereas Alfredo's tune brings the second phrase to conclusion with the word *voluttà* (intense, sensual pleasure), the orchestral introduction ends abruptly on the penultimate note. If the orchestral version had had the text included, it would entail breaking off *volut*—without its final syllable—*tà*. Instead, we are left, figuratively, up in the air. A full bar's rest, with a fermata (a pause that momentarily suspends metric counting) stands in lieu of the resolving tonic and, as it were, the consummation of pleasure. In the opera, we learn early on that Violetta has consumption. Prior to the drinking song, the very opening to the opera foreshadows the music we will hear at the very end, as Violetta perishes. The caesura that breaks off the orchestral introduction to the drinking song might easily be interpreted as the halting, stumbling of intoxication. But the master Verdi more subtly foreshadows a love that will not be consummated.

The Beatles use a similar effect three times in *Abbey Road*. There, in each case, the abruption comes near or at the place where the song might have concluded. The song "I Want You (She's So Heavy)" ends with a circular progression that is repeated over and over until it is cut off abruptly, midstream, without conclusion. As though no final resolution were possible, the sexual longing of the song's "I want you" concludes without conclusion. The following song, "Because the world is round it turns me on . . . love is old, love is new . . ." also ends abruptly, without closure. The turning of the world, love old and new, is presumably ongoing, after the tape is cut. The final *abruptio* of *Abbey Road* cuts off the little codetta to the album, "Her Majesty is a very nice girl but she doesn't have a lot to say . . . someday I'm gonna make her mine, someday I'm gonna make her mine . . ." After the final words, we hear a single note in the guitar that insinuates, at least to me, that a third iteration of "someday I'm gonna make her mine" is about to begin, even though Paul McCartney has achieved a perfect authentic cadence. This kind of celebration of the cadence, reiterating a perfection already achieved, is common in Mozart, and it might have happened here. Instead, the tape is cut. Although far-fetched, the final silence can be interpreted as being symbolic of the Beatles' imminent breakup, where the abrupt end of the musical album signals the end of an era in popular music. Somewhere, the philosopher Richard Rorty observes that most philosophical arguments do not reach resolution, but rather the topic is changed. Grace Schulman, in her poem "God Speaks," makes a similar observation: "Worlds are never finished, only abandoned."[33] The poem begins "Before the hour I cried, 'Let there be light!' / I tossed out some three hundred early versions. / Revisions help." The poem's comic ending combines abruption and closure: ". . . the Babylonians / have many gods. Always I work alone."

More subtle pauses in poetry can be either internal to a line, like Hollander's "And here's a gentler one, whose pause, more slight," or at the end of a line with or without syntactic closure. In music, such pauses translate into more subtle rests, like taking a breath. In musical settings, a very common pattern is for a poetic couplet to comprise a single phrase, with a lesser articulation midway. The song "Summertime" from *Porgy and Bess* (music by George Gershwin, lyrics by DuBose Heyward) provides a clear example. The musical pauses flow naturally along with the lyric's syntax, and the music breathes in a way similar to the way we might breathe in reading the verse as a poem. Soft caesuras are heard internal to each line of verse. So, summertime—and the living is easy / fish are jumping—and the cotton is high / Oh, your daddy's rich—and your ma is good-lookin' / so hush little baby—don't you cry.

Or, to choose a well-known song of Franz Schubert setting a poem by Heinrich Heine, "Am Meer":

Das Meer erglänzte weit hinaus
im letzen Abenscheine; [half cadence, short rest]
wir sassen am einsamen Fischerhaus,
wir sassan stumm und alleine. [full cadence, longer rest]
(The sea glistened far in the distance
In the last evening's glow;
We sat in the lonely fisherman's house
We sat silent and alone.)

Placed into Schubert's musical setting, the first couplet forms an antecedent phrase closed by a half cadence and a short (eighth-note) rest in the vocal part. The second couplet forms a complementary consequent phrase leading to a full cadence and a longer rest, and this in turn leads into new musical figuration that sets up the second stanza of the poem (not given above). This type of musical silence, rests that articulate basic syntactic units in music with or without words, is fundamental to many types of music. The shorter rests give a place for a breath; the longer rests allow space for reflection on the thought or image just concluded or a space of anticipation toward what is yet to come.

Emerging out of Silence, Fading into Silence

Some musical openings seem designed to bring our attention to the silence that precedes any sound, just as some musical endings are designed to slowly fade into silence. Leo Treitler has written about opening strategies in Beethoven's symphonies.

> The Ninth Symphony is a difficult work to begin in performance.
> Of course the beginning is always a crucial moment for the way in which the listener settles into a piece, for it must achieve a reversal from silence to music, and with that a radical shift of worlds for the listener's consciousness. Beethoven followed different strategies in the symphonies. In the Sixth and Eighth there is an immediate engagement with a strong melody in *tempo allegro*. In the Third and Fifth there is a call to attention, wiping away the silence and announcing an event of importance. In the Fourth and Seventh a need is created for the beginning first, a deliberate disorientation for the listener that requires the beginning as a restoration of balance. The engagement is psychologically more complicated. The opening of the Ninth Symphony seems like that at first, but it turns out not a be.
> Its beginning is difficult because the first sounds must be just a shade louder than silence. The silence is not broken, it is gradually replaced by sound. The listener is not drawn into the piece, he is surrounded by it as the orchestra fills and expands its space.[34]

The remarkable opening of the Ninth Symphony is well captured in Treitler's prose. Instead of the big bang that opens the Third, here is a slow gathering, a quiet emergence out of the nothingness that precedes. Instead of a sudden event that disrupts silence, seemingly opposed to silence, we experience gradual coming-into-being whose unfathomable seed is silence itself. The sense of being "surrounded by it as the orchestra fills and expands its space" places ourselves inside the musical environment that grows around us. I cannot say that Beethoven initiates the idea of sound growing out of silence in music, but it is clear that the Ninth Symphony is a landmark work in this and many other respects.

Two of Gustav Mahler's symphonies strike me as responding in particular to this aspect of Beethoven's Ninth: Mahler's First and Ninth. Like Beethoven, Mahler was marvelously gifted at creating a sense of expansive space. Mahler opens his First Symphony with an extended A pedal tone, supported by the low basses and reaching into extremely high overtones in the violins, all *pianississimo*. The effect is of a great expanse, emergent out of silence, a near-void waiting to be filled. Mahler's sustained A♮ pays homage to Beethoven's sustained A-E fifth, the first sound in his Ninth, but with a difference. Whereas Beethoven will gradually expand space, Mahler initiates his First Symphony with a space that has immediately opened the full orchestral gamut. Both composers create a sense of emergence out of silence; however, in Mahler it is the vastness of an empty space waiting to be filled rather than an environment that gradually expands and so creates space. Whereas the first linear motive in Beethoven's symphony is a descending pattern, E-A, then A-E, played sotto voce in the first violins, Mahler's first linear idea is reduced to the second half of Beethoven's, the descending A-E. But where Beethoven's motive is a single line, Mahler's is doubled at the octave, double octave, and triple octave in the woodwinds. Still inside the full gamut space of the pedal, the emergent linear idea also expresses height and depth, a vastness of space. Young Gustav Mahler attempts a metaleptic transformation of Beethoven's trope. And he does rather well. Both composers mimic natural processes. Mahler makes this explicit, writing into the score the indication "*Wie ein Naturlaut*" ("like a sound of nature" or "as if spoken by nature").

Like Beethoven's Ninth and Mahler's First, Mahler's Ninth begins with the note A. And like the other two symphonies, the A will eventually be clarified as dominant to D, D minor in Beethoven, D major in both Mahler symphonies. And like the earlier works, Mahler's Ninth begins with a soft dynamic, marked *pianissimo* in the cellos. The opening of Mahler's Ninth, however, engages with silence in a different way. The initiatory A pedal is intermittent, being handed off from the cellos to the French horn as fragments of the work's motives, each surrounded by silence, gradually emerge and gradually coalesce into melody. While the initial effect of coming out of silence is somewhat attenuated, the fragments that will combine as generative of all that follows seem to float on a sea of silence, emerging and then returning to the palpable absence that surrounds them. By the time the tonic definitively appears in measure 16, full coalescence is achieved. And even before that, in measure 7, we hear a well-formed melody as fragments, still separated by silence, combine to form an extended linear flow. While the process of coming-into-being is not as extended as in the earlier works, one senses something new here. Among the next generation of composers, Anton Webern will be particularly apt in further developing this sense of silence as the bed on which sounds rest, where broken fragments emerge and become resubmerged in silence.

This newfound sense of silence (actually ancient in various traditions of non-Western music) is heightened when no metric is perceivable. Instead of marching along, or dancing along, the music floats or is propelled through its silent medium. It is here that our metaphor of waves takes on its most cogency. I want to hold off on a discussion of this aspect of Western music post-Webern as well as in non-Western practices and instead, for now, turn to another phenomenon, instances where music fades into silence.

Fading to silence is quite common in pop music from the 1960s and following decades; in fact, my term for this practice, one that I've used for decades, is "the Motown fadeout." The effect is made in the studio rather than in live performance. Its general meaning is clear and principally, though not exclusively, erotic: whatever we're doing, let's do it on and on, far into the night. William Weir has written an article on this topic: "A Little Bit Softer Now, a Little Bit Softer Now . . . The sad, gradual decline of the fade-out in popular music."[35] According the Weir, "among the year-end top ten songs for 1985, there's not one cold ending . . . The year-end top ten lists for 2011, 2012, and 2013 yield a total of one fade-out, Robin Thicke's purposely retro 'Blurred Lines.'" As Weir's article continues, he cites the work of David Huron, a music theorist who has contributed distinguished work on cognitive aspects of music.

> David Huron, of the School of Music and Center for Cognitive and Brain Sciences at Ohio State University, has struck upon a different interpretation. "With a fade-out, music manages to delay closure indefinitely," he writes in *Sweet Anticipation: Music and the Psychology of Expectation*. "The 'stop' gesture is replaced by a gesture toward the 'infinite.'" And Huron's notion has some empirical support. Researchers at the music

lab of Hanover University of Music in Germany recently had music students tap along to the beat of different versions of the same song. One ended with a fade-out, another with a cold ending. Listening to the cold ending, they stopped tapping an average of 1.4 seconds *before* the song's end. Listening to the fade-out, though, their tapping continued 1.04 seconds *after* the song's end. This suggests that the fade-out allows a song to live on beyond its physical self; the listener senses that it never truly ends.

Wier's article is entertaining and informative, well worth reading for anyone inquisitive about fade-outs in popular music.

Corinna da Fonseca-Wollheim, music critic for *The New York Times*, composed an article titled "How Silence Makes the Music: A brief, incomplete, very quiet guide to the history of music's negative spaces."[36] Fonseca-Wollheim's article deals principally, though not exclusively, with Western classical music. Like Wier's treatment of popular music, Fonseca-Wollheim's article is entertaining and informative. Discussing a wide range of musical silences, the article mentions two examples of Romantic symphonies that recede into silence: Tchaikovsky's Sixth Symphony and Brahms's Third Symphony. Both of these instances are worth thinking about in more detail, and I give them more expansive consideration in what follows.

Tchaikovsky begins the penultimate movement of the Sixth with an *Allegro molto vivace*, a sampling of the Russian master at his frothy, scampering best. Later, the movement turns into a theme that, as it gains momentum, becomes a triumphant march, a march that sounds valedictory, that might have been suitable for the final scene of *Return of the Jedi* (except for the omission of the Star Wars leitmotivs). The movement ends with a rousing bang, an ending conclusive enough, in the recorded live performance that I watched on YouTube yesterday, to convince at least some members of the audience that the piece was over, time for applause. But the temptation to applaud has come too soon. The finale that follows, to my mind, sounds like an epilogue to a piece whose initial (proper?) ending is rejected.

Marked *Adagio lamentoso*, the finale's overall affect strikes me as passionate in both senses of the word: ardent and suffering. As we approach the end of the finale, huge orchestral swells, reaching a dynamic of *fortississimo*, compose out Tchaikovsky's heartthrob theme. Upward sweeps of scalar motion reach their peak and then fall in throbbing descents, again and again. Are we dying or just plumb tuckered out? However one interprets the end of this lament, the waves of emotion (do I overuse the metaphor?) subside, and the register lowers as the dynamic level softens to a final *pianississississimo*, fading into nothingness. Here the fade to silence evokes a sense of expiring, the universal blank.

The fade-out in Brahms's Third Symphony is conceptually more complex, and I'd like to consider it through several approaches, the first being rhetorical. In classical rhetoric we find the term *epanalepsis*: when the opening sentence, clause, or word is repeated at the end. Here's a little ditty whose author shall remain anonymous.

> First thing in the morning
> I brush my teeth,
> Take a shower,
> Have a coffee,
> First thing in the morning.

I think of epanalepsis as a variant on the more general term *chiasmus*. In *Rhyme's Reason*, John Hollander composes multiple self-referential examples, of which I give three.

> Resounding syllables
> In simple nouns.
> Echoing adjectives,
> And nouns resounding.
> Imagined mirrors mirror imagining.[37]

In the first chiasmus, *resounding* and *nouns* share the same vowel sound, poetic assonance. *Syllables* and *simple* share the same consonant sound, alliteration. The chiasmus is formed by their exchange of place: <u>Resound-ing syllables</u> /<u>simple nouns</u>. The second chiasmus puns on the word resounding as echo (re-sounding); the chiasmus *echoing . . . resounding* embeds the assonance of the previous couplet in its second line (*nouns resounding*). The third chiasmus comes close to a palindrome, changing the plural noun *mirrors* into the verb *mirror* and the verb *imagined* into the gerund (verb as noun) of *imagining*.

In his prose poem "Instructions to the Landscaper," Hollander provides a beautiful example of what epanalepsis can do in concept rather than poetic technique. Here is the second of seven instructions: "At the entrance, one must be made to pass through a representation of the whole Garden, but so placed that it is only while leaving it all, deliciously wearied by the walking in the heats and shades, that one sees the entrance again in the new light of what it had always stood for—as to have given a point to exiting."[38] The entrance to and exit from the garden's maze is one and the same, and yet having walked through the garden gives the entrance-become-exit new meaning because of all we've experienced in between. Although without using the term, we have already come across one example of musical epanalepsis: the children's song "Three Blind Mice." After all the chasing and cutting, the song returns to its opening "three blind mice."

Scott Burnham recognizes a sense of grace and renewal in Mozart's adaptations of this technique. Writing about the Andante of Mozart's G-major Piano Concerto, K. 453, he observes, "The returning first theme triggers a welcome flush of recognition, not just because it is familiar but because it is fresh all over again: its freshness is restored precisely in the way it gathers and reflects the music that has ensued, the way it sounds now as a consequence as well as cause."[39] The technique of musical epanalepsis is commonplace in Brahms as it was in his precursor in this respect, Schubert. Schubert uses epanalepsis in many of his songs, and just as in Hollander's instruction to the landscaper, the repetition at the close is filled with meaning through what the song has expressed in between. Brahms, in many movements, uses the same technique, sometimes with a literal or near literal repetition at the end, and sometimes with wisps of melody reminding us of how we began. The technique is especially prevalent in first movements, where the opening melody returns at the very end. Brahms uses just this technique in the first movement of his Third Symphony, closing the movement with the motto that had opened it. The first movement finished, the work of the motto is seemingly completed, but the ending of the final movement tells us otherwise. At the very end of the finale, Brahms brings back the motto that had opened the first movement, but now, as we fade into silence, the motto is transformed and embedded in the texture, so much so that it is easily missed. We will consider the opening motto and its final manifestation more carefully in a moment, but let's first take a second approach toward understanding Brahms's adaptation of epanalepsis and fade-into-silence in the Third Symphony.

We recall Thomas Weiskel's discussion of Wordsworth's "spots of time," privileged moments of experience that shape later events, where the "efficacious spirit . . . lurks," as though it were some subterranean force hidden from conscious thought. The advent of the motto that opens the first movement of Brahms Third might be likened to Wordsworth's efficacious spirit. The motto returns literally or almost literally twice in the movement, first where it might be expected, at the recapitulation of the sonata-form exposition, and second, as we've already noted, at the end of the movement. However, genetic traces of the motto are ubiquitous throughout the first movement, both in small-scale manifestations, as in melodic fragments, and in large-scale implications, as in generating key areas, local tonics that are eventually subsumed into the overriding key of F major. As we move through the second and third movements on into the finale, the traces of the opening are attenuated, having receded into deep structure. Part of the profile of the opening motto is its wavering between F major and F minor. With the last first-movement statement of the motto, we settle into a resolving F major, but without the prototypical perfect cadence, where tonic closure is preceded by an emphatic dominant chord. This is a hint, a very subtle one, that the work of the motto is not yet done.

This instability of key that we noticed at the outset of the first movement is heightened in the finale, which opens by prolonging the dominant of F minor in search for its tonic. That tonic is not realized, and we move through a number of key areas before finally reaching a tonic F, not F minor, but F major, 281 measures into a movement of 309 measures in total. Moreover, by the time tonic arrives, the home key we've been searching for all along, the music has already begun its dissolution, what Schoenberg would have called its *liquidation*. This process continues on into the quiet ending, and it is as we approach that ending that the final manifestation of the opening motto appears, like a revenant emerging out of the wavering figuration that works to dissolve the last remnants of the theme that opened the finale. Brahms tells us that our revels now have ended, have faded into air, into thin air.

Our final approach toward understanding the fade-out to silence in Brahms's Third will bring us back to Ferneyhough's concept of *figure* as the force that's only manifest as it impacts on musical objects, the behind-the-scenes dynamics of musical flow and transformation. However we conceptualize the force behind the opening bars of the symphony, the overall trajectory is of a force not fully spent until the closing bars of the finale. Recall that we characterized "Il Tempo della Figura," as an aesthetic manifesto, placing Ferneyhough's development of *figure* within a system of musical values. His fairly explicit discontent with the aesthetics of neoclassicism, neo-Romanticism, and postmodernity makes that clear. Ferneyhough's aesthetic doesn't come from nowhere. As profoundly as he transformed the stuff of music, it is clear that he comes out of the tradition, reaching backward in time, that includes the Second Viennese (Schoenberg, Berg, and Webern), Brahms, Schubert, and Beethoven. Of these precursors, only Schoenberg wrote extensively about music. Among Schoenberg's terms for musical processes, the one that comes closest to Ferneyhough's concept of figure is *Grundgestalt* (literally grounding-shape, typically translated as "basic shape"). Schoenberg posited that each musical composition has a unique *Grundgestalt*, the dual source for expansion and cohesion, the idea for a musical composition that is fully manifest only as the musical composition itself. A Schoenbergian analysis of Brahms's Third would entail tracing the force of the *Grundgestalt* as it plays out over time. If we read Schoenberg with Ferneyhough in mind, we might amend Schoenberg's descriptor to refer to force rather than object or shape. In this sense, the fade to nothingness at the end of Brahms Third is the dissipation of a force that has been expended.

In the next generation after Brahms, fade-into-silence becomes nearly normative in the Second Viennese School. Arnold Schoenberg uses the technique with great effect in his great tone poem *Pelleas und Melisande*; in his dream piece, *Die glückliche Hand*; and perhaps most astonishingly in his hallucinatory *Erwartung*, where the effect seems to mimic all being swallowed into a black hole. Alban Berg ends his *Lyric Suite* with a repeated, fading, wavering third (between D♭ and F) and with instructions that annotate the score, *morendo* (dying) and *"bis zum völligen Verlöschen"* (until completely extinguished). Berg's *Violinkonzert* also ends with a dying out, reminiscent of the ending of Brahms Third Symphony only in that the work ends with the same figuration as its opening. Berg's celebrated opera *Wozzeck* is yet another example of the technique of dying out. Anton Webern is particularly associated with his uses of silence, and fading-to-silence is among the techniques that comprise his musical language, especially in his middle period, post-tonal and pre-twelve-tone. Examples abound in Webern's *Five Pieces for String Quartet*, Op. 5; *Six Pieces for Orchestra*, Op. 6; and *Six Bagatelles for String Quartet*, Op. 9.

Gustav Mahler, of a generation in between Brahms and the Second Viennese, was an early champion of Schoenberg's music, and a composer particularly revered by Schoenberg, Berg, and Webern. We find a stunning development of fade-to-silence in *Der Abschied* (The Farewell) the final song of Mahler's *Das Lied von der Erde* (The Song of the Earth). The texts for *Das Lied von der Erde* are all taken from Hans Bethge, *Die chinesische Flöte*, a collection of free translations of Chinese poetry. The poetry incorporated into *Der Abschied* begins with a depiction of sunset and the augmenting evening shadows. The moon floats like a silver barque in the blue lake of heaven, a soft wind blows in the dark spruces, the rippling of a brook sings euphoniously in the dark, flowers waver, pale in the twilight, and the earth breathes, filled with peace and sleep. Mahler tone-paints all of these images with transformations of a single motive, a simple wavering between two notes. (It is quite possible that Mahler's wavering motive is the inspiration for the wavering at the end of Berg's Lyric Suite.) The notes and the interval between the notes, in both senses of the term, intervallic space and time, vary with each poetic image, now more compressed, now dilating, as though mimicking breathing itself. This wavering motive will continue, intermittently, until the music finally dies out. As we approach the second large-scale section of the song, the wavering motive now depicting the wavering shadows in the spruce trees (Rehearsal 22), a new poetic idea emerges as the singer awaits her "friend" in anticipation of a final farewell, *Lebewohl* in the German. Whether or not the "friend" is an actual person might be questioned. I tend to think not, and instead read the awaited friend as a personification of death.

Another simple motive emerges out of a wavering D-C near the opening of the second large section of the movement (Rehearsal 24), an expansive, lyrical outpouring, D-C, C-B♭. First heard in the violins, without voice, Mahler marks this point in the score, *pp aber mit innigster Empfindung* (very softly but with most heartfelt feeling). When the alto resumes singing, this new motive is given words, the first three in a longer sentence: *Ich sehne mich, o Freund, and deiner Seite / Die Schönheit dieses Abends zu geniessen.* (I long, oh friend, to enjoy the beauty of this evening at your side.) Later, toward the very end of the song, this motive of longing is transposed to the tonic key, comprising a descent to the tonic C (E-D, D-C), and given its final words: *Ewig, ewig* (forever, forever). The German word *Ewigkeit* translates into English as eternity. The longed-for friend is transformed into the longed-for step into eternity. The paired *ewig, ewig*, each time descending to C, is heard three times. Then there are another three iterations of a single statement of *ewig*, each time breaking off the motive by giving only its first half, E-D, without resolution to tonic. The song ends without a perfect cadence, A♮ suspended over a C major chord. Mahler's final indication in the score, along with the marking *ppp*, is *gänzlich ersterbend*—completely dying away. In Mahler's extraordinary transformations of the wavering motive, including its development into the *ewig* motive, the composer subsumes all of the natural imagery in the poem, including the life-force of the one who sings yearning for her friend and yearning for peace, into a single idea manifest in many, many ways. All of our metaphors, wave, figure, metalepsis, and middle voice, come together in Mahler's *Abschied*.

8

Metric, Ametric, Fractured Meter, and a Sea of Silence

Metric Poetry, Metric Music

In its musical usages, meter has two coefficients, regular pulse and regular groupings of pulses.[1] The pulse stream can be accelerated or slowed down in a smooth transition or changed abruptly by change of tempo. Groupings can be modified locally by syncopation and in larger spans by changes of meter. Neither pulse stream nor groupings need be uniform for us to perceive meter; we need just enough consistency of pulse/grouping to recognize variables as such within an overall, recursive temporal grid.

In contrast to metered music, metered poetry shows great variation in terms of evenly pulsed time. There are some poems where a sense of underlying regular pulse is built into the use of poetic meter, and others where regularity of pulse would place a straitjacket on the poem, destroying its music, syntax, and imagistic flow. And then there are poems that slide in and out of rhythmic regularity.

Children's nursery rhymes are generally designed with a regular underlying pulse in mind. Written in *pure accentual* meter, the common pulse coincides with accented syllables.[2] In "Little Miss Muffet," the first, second, fourth, and fifth lines have two accents each, while the third and sixth lines have three plus a punctuation mark, semicolon then period. (Bold letters indicate accented syllables.)

Little Miss **Muff**et
Sat on a **tuff**et,
Eating her **curds** and **whey**;

Along came a spider,
Who sat down beside her,
And frightened Miss Muffet away.

As I read "Miss Muffet," time pulses are regular. I can tap out time with metronomic precision as I read. Even the semicolon and period are measured, one beat each in my performance: 1—2 / 1—2, / 1—2—3—(4); 1—2, / 1—2, / 1—2—3—(4). But such an analysis, rudimentary as it is, objectifies my experience. Advocating for a middle-voiced reading, we switch from a quantitative perception (counting beats) to a qualitative experience, the easy, even flow of the words.

When nursery rhymes are set to music, the regularity of flow remains: think of the children's song "Mary Had a Little Lamb." Regularly paced, four-square pulses set each and every subphrase: Mary had a little lamb / little lamb, little lamb / Mary had a little lamb / whose fleece was white as snow. And as with my reading of Miss Muffet, the punctuating period takes a final fourth beat after "white as snow."

When meter, uniformly present over time, suggests a uniform underlying pulse, the poem runs the danger of musical tedium, a singsong quality that can too easily sound like parody. When accomplished poets adopt a highly regular meter, they find ways to use the regular flow to their advantage. Here is the opening of Henry Wadsworth Longfellow's Introduction to "The Song of Hiawatha."

Should you ask me, whence these stories?
Whence these legends and traditions,
With the odor of the forest,
With the dew and damp of meadows,
With the curling smoke of wigwams,
With the rushing of great rivers,
With their frequent repetitions,
And their wild reverberations,
As of thunder in the mountains?[3]

The meter is strongly presented trochaic tetrameter (four feet of strong-weak accentuation): doesn't waver, no exceptions, keeps on going, as it used to. But Longfellow is able to energize each line so that it drives to its end and makes us expect more. The heaping up of "with," opening five of the nine lines, adds to the momentum that mimics the rushing of great waters, frequent repetitions, wild reverberations, as of thunder in the mountains. The rhetorical technique, anaphora, is one that will energize many of Walt Whitman's variable waves. The recurrent sound of trochaic feet is also mimetic, evocative of the crashing of waves, rushing rivers, reverberating thunder.

Just so, a gifted composer or performer can energize highly regular rhythms, avoiding tedium by creating forward momentum. Seemingly from a different universe, Otis Redding's "Dock of the Bay" makes an interesting comparison to Longfellow's introduction to "The Song of Hiawatha." Written in 1967, Redding's song became a posthumous hit shortly after a plane crash ended Redding's life at the age of twenty-six. The recording is easily available online. In contrast to Longfellow's unvaried trochaic meter, Redding's lines use variable prosody. However, like Longfellow, Redding uses an abundance of trochaic feet to begin his lines of verse: sitting, watching, watching, sitting, wasting. Each of these words is a present participle, indicating an ongoing event, a proliferation of that function, which we also hear in Longfellow's curling and rushing. When lines begin without a strong accent, they are set as a musical upbeat (anacrusis is the technical term), landing solidly on the accented word: I'll be *sitting*, then I *watch*. The recording features the sound of ocean waves breaking on shore as a sonic background to the song's opening, setting the scene and hinting toward the metaphor of time's wastings. As Whitman recognized, ocean waves are not metronomic. I don't know whether or not Redding thought of the juxtaposition of metered time (in the music) and unmetered time (in the watery waves) or if someone in production added the effect, but there is a separation or opposition of the two types of time, a self-alienation of sorts, where "this loneliness won't leave me alone."

In the classical repertory of Western art music, regular, recurrent divisions of time are common in dance and dance-like movements. "*La donne è mobile*," a familiar tune from Giuseppe Verdi's *Rigoletto*, can serve as an example. The melody, in 3/8 meter, is parsed into regular groups of eight bars, subdivided into ((2 + 2) + (2 + 2)). Once again, in quantifying the measure groupings, I objectify the musical space. By adding numeric values to the hypermeter, we similarly objectify the music. But experiencing the music (normally) does not require such objectification. As with our nursery rhyme, middle-voiced listening feels this regularity as qualitative; it doesn't count the measures projecting the music into objectified space. Instead, figuratively, we can simply ride the waves. By this way of experiencing the music, the pulsing and grouping are not objectified. Neither are they simply internalized. They are middle voiced, a mutuality of out there and in here, as we participate in riding the crests of these sound waves, simultaneously metaphorical and literal. This is not to dismiss the relevance of objectifying analysis, which can be extremely valuable in alerting the listener to properties of the music. But it is to say that if a middle-voiced hearing is desired, objectifying quantization should give way to a qualitative hearing, without the overlay of quantified metrics.

Like the orchestral introduction to the *brindisi* in *La Traviata*, the orchestral introduction to "*La donne è mobile*" breaks off just before completion; in lieu of the closing bar we have silence and, notated by a fermata, a temporary stopping of pulsed time. Apart from a single-bar anacrusis that sets the song into motion, once the vocal part of the song is underway, the only exceptions to the regular flow are terminal phrases that dilate time. To objectify: at the end of each of four cycles of (4+4), the terminal phrase is extended to six bars.

La donna è mobile is sung by the libertine Duke of Mantua: "Woman is inconstant, like a feather in the wind, changing in tone and in thought."[4] The final three words are repeated (*e di pensier* in the Italian) with misogynistic force, as the single extended phrase emphasizes their impact. (The hyper-metric patterning for the whole first half of the song is as follows: ((1) + (4+4) + (4+4) + (4+4) + (4+6)) + ((4+4) + (4+4) + (4+4) + (4+6)).) The second half of the song begins by repeating the orchestral introduction, complete with caesura, and then the pattern continues as before, without the single-bar anacrusis, the only other change being a longer extension at the very end. The libretto fits precisely into this temporal scheme with each four-bar unit containing four accented syllables. Thus, there is a mutuality of flow, verse and hyper-meter in concord. The only hint of rhythmic irregularity, not likely to be noticed in performance, is the irregular scansion of the first two words in Italian. Normally, *La donna è mobile* ("Woman is inconstant") would receive an accent on the first syllable of *donna*, whereas Verdi places the stress on the downbeat, *La*. This misplaced accent helps to propel the energy forward, flowing through *donna* on the way to *mobile*. The $^3/_8$ downbeats, one to the bar, and the groupings of bars, principally by fours, are clearly audible throughout, even on a first hearing.

Our examples of meter, poetic and musical, have so far involved regular groupings, maintained more or less throughout. Metric verse, metric music, and metric music coupled with verse can also slide in and out of a clearly embodied meter with its regular, recurrent sense of underlying pulse. Try placing a metronomic pulsed regularity onto the opening quatrain of Shakespeare's 73rd Sonnet:

> That time of year thou mayst in me behold
> When yellow leaves, or none, or few, do hang
> Upon those boughs which shake against the cold,
> Bare ruined choirs where late the sweet birds sang.

In the opening line, the meter's accentual pattern (iambic pentameter) emerges out of the sounds of words and their syntactic groupings. Imagining a regular underlying pulse, if softened a bit, does no harm. By the second line, the preestablished pulse is out of sync with the words. "Yellow" breaks the pattern of iambs that are coincident with two words (that time, of year, thou mayst, in me) or within one word (behold). And then there are the commas (yellow leaves, or none, or few), breaking the flow into smaller units, giving time for the consideration and reconsideration of yellow leaves (or none, or few). If there is to be a pause at the end of line two, it need be a subtle one. The syntactic unit crosses the line "do hang / upon those boughs." A soft enjambment wraps the end of line two onto the whole of line three, a palpable shaking as we disrupt the pentametric groups. For me, the comma after "cold" is of a longer duration than the previous three: a space needed to set off the apposition "Bare ruined choirs," landing hard on "bare," "ruin-ed" and "choirs"; the hard c of "cold" echoing "choirs," as s in "choirs" points toward further development in "sweet birds sang," while reflecting back to "boughs which shake."

Poetic meter more often than not exists within an irregular flow of time. Of course, it is the performative aspect of reading poetry that brings this out. In this sense, learning to read a poem is kindred to learning how to shape a musical phrase; indeed, the poetic phrase *is* a musical phrase. In musical practices involving meter, regularity of pulse streams varies greatly. Marches will have a steady pulsed flow, as will most dance forms, many types of folk music, and virtually all popular music. As in Shakespeare's sonnet, composers working within a metric frame will often establish and then disrupt regular groupings, so that irregularities are perceived as such. In such cases we hear the temporal grid being tugged and pulled like taffy, or dilated and compressed like experiential time (as opposed to the unwavering tick-toc of clock time).

In our example from Verdi's *Rigoletto*, we noted that the only exceptions to metric and hyper-metric regularity were in those phrases where groups of four measures were extended to six and in those places where a fermata momentarily disrupted the ongoing pulse-stream. These two techniques are part of a host of ways that composers and performers can alter regular groupings of metric flow in music, listeners participating in the experience. Acceleration of pulse (typically marked as *accelerando*) and deceleration of pulse (*rallentando* or *ritardando*) are commonplace ways of altering the flow of pulse, and composers have used myriad ways to expand or extend (or more rarely truncate) the groupings of musical phrases.[5]

In classical repertory, both Mozart and Beethoven show wonderful elasticity of phrase shapes, a practice inherited by Brahms with his rich complexity of musical phrase shapes. In the early twentieth century, Maurice Ravel often shapes phrase rhythms with such elasticity and grace that the voice seems to float, the notated meter coming in and out of perceptibility. Ravel's exquisite *Trois Poèmes de Stéphane Mallarmé* is remarkable in this sense, and many others. In teaching "music and text" for nearly thirty years, there were pieces that I grew tired of after a few iterations and others that were rich enough to engage me year after year. Once I settled into including Ravel's settings of Mallarmé in the syllabus, they were there to stay. I returned to Ravel's set year after year, the music slowly revealing the depths of its splendors so that every time I returned to the work it seemed as fresh as it was in my earliest hearings. There are many aspects of the work that combine to make it extraordinary; among them are the shapings of musical phrases, coincident with the musical shapings of Mallarmé's poetry.

Rubato, subtle rhythmic shadings of give and take, is commonplace in many musical practices. Gifted singers often use rubato intuitively, subtly anticipating a beat or falling slightly behind the underlying pulse. These subtle shadings of rhythm often make the difference between a compelling performance and one that falls flat in its too mechanical precision. Rubato can be built into a performance practice, so that notated rhythm implies a performed rhythm slightly or even significantly different from what is literally on the page. In jazz traditions, two equally notated eighth notes are performed with the first of the pair slightly elongated and the second slightly shortened. I recall hearing a lecture given by Jason Stanyek on "swing" in Brazilian dance rhythms (*suinge barsileiro*). Stanyek spoke of a Brazilian percussion player who had to slightly adjust the rhythmic units, making them more metronomic, when the music was transplanted into a Los Angeles recording studio. When I hear performances of Viennese classical music recorded early in the twentieth century, I hear a sense of rubato that is lost in our current age. In an analogous way, the rhythms of Italian opera are lost when the musicians, conservatory trained and highly competent, are nonetheless not native to the Italianate tradition. Similar observations might be made about any musical practice that is transplanted outside its native home.

Syncopation is another common way to disrupt groupings, where the expected placement of accent is displaced. George and Ira Gershwin's "I've Got Rhythm" comically plays with syncopation, as the vocal line is constant in its emphasis of "off-beats." Try singing the song with the words I've, got, and rhythm falling on the downbeats. Terrible, isn't it! In the world of nineteenth-century classical music, Brahms was especially adept at using syncopation. He will sometimes use extended displacement so that the perceived meter is at odds with that which is notated, the extended syncopation only perceivable at its outset or at the point of realignment with notated rhythm. Large stretches of the first movement of Brahms's Third Symphony work like this (see, for example, mm. 51–70, the entire section leading up to the repeat of the exposition). Another favorite device of Brahms is the hemiola, where groups of three, e.g., 3 + 3, are divided into groups of two, 2 + 2 + 2. Translated into the terms of poetic feet, the shift is from dactyls to trochees.

Leonard Bernstein, who would have known the Brahmsian technique well, used the same technique, alternating more quickly than Brahms would have, in setting Stephen Sondheim's lyrics to the song "America" from *West Side Story*: "I like to be in America! O.K. by me in America!" (a quick, even pulsed 1—2—3, 1—2—3 / 1—2, 1—2, 1—2, / 1—2—3, 1—2—3 / 1—2, 1—2, 1—2). As before, quantitative analysis gives way to qualitative experience.

Ametric, Fractured Metric

I make a distinction between music that is conceived without an underlying, regular pulse-stream, whether notated or not, and music where the pulsing and groupings of meter are so destabilized that no metric flow can be heard. I call music in the first instance *ametric*, conceptualizing the second type as *fractured meter*. Free verse in poetry, as I experience it, can sometimes be analogous to ametric music and sometimes seem more like what I've termed fractured meter.

A wide range of musical practices are ametric. Martin R. L. Clayton, in his 1996 article "Free Rhythm: Ethnomusicology and the Study of

Music without Meter," cites research that identifies about seventy genres worldwide.

> Free rhythm recitation of religious texts is a feature common to the Christian, Jewish, Islamic, Hindu, Buddhist and Shinto traditions . . . In art music, we must consider both vocal and instrumental forms right across the Arab and Arab-influenced world . . . We must also consider the related Indian *alap*, some traditions of Chinese *qin* playing and Japanese solo *shakuhachi* music, and recitative sections of various opera styles, particularly in China.
> . . .
> There exists a wide variety not only in the context and function of free rhythm genres but also in their rhythmic style and form. They range (in some cases within a single genre) from those apparently without pulse of any kind to those with a clear pulse but no higher level periodicity.[6]

Clayton goes on to point out that text, speech rhythms, and poetic meter influence rhythm in many musical practices that are ametrical, but that by no means is this a hard-fast rule. He proposes a "common-sense definition of 'free rhythm.'" "*The rhythm of music without pulse-based periodic organization*—in other words, free rhythm may or may not have a simple pulse, but where this pulse is organized periodically, free rhythm cannot be said to exist."[7] Periodicity, Clayton's preferred term, is identical to what I've called regular, recurrent grouping. His free rhythm with a regular but aperiodic pulse fits into neither of my two types, ametric or fractured metric, although fragments of various durations that embody a regular pulse often occur within what I am calling fractured metric. Igor Stravinsky famously uses this technique within *The Rite of Spring*. Regularly pulsed fragments are salient in some of Anton Webern's music, where they take on an uncanny quality. In *Schoenberg's Musical Imagination*, I called these regularly pulsed fragments *time shards*.[8] Often surrounded by silence, and embedded in textures without any sense of regular pulse, time shards are reminiscent of how time used to go, a Newtonian clockwork placed within a post-Einsteinian universe. Whereas the regular pulsing of metered music anchors emergent sound within an ongoing time frame (more or less like subdivisions of clock time), time shards float in and out of musical time-space, untethered from a sense of metric.

Implicit in what we've observed about metered music is the anchoring of sound patterns in a prevailing temporal grid where both sound and silence are measured and grouped. In cases where a fermata temporarily suspends pulse-groups, the silence is perceived as a pause. Music without meter can be anchored pitch-wise, as in modal chanting in the West or as in the *alap* in Indian classical music based on ragas. Or it can be free-floating in both aspects, as in some of Webern's compositions, with regard to temporal units and with regard to pitch.

The neumes, graphic indications for sound-shapes that eventually evolved into Western notation, were ametric in origin. *Mensural notation*, emerging in the late thirteenth century, allowed composers to notate relative durations and eventually to contrapuntally juxtapose what in modern notation would be different meters.[9] By the late fifteenth century, composers such as Josquin des Prez and Johnannes Ockeghem were composing contrapuntal prolation canons, where different rates of musical unfolding were presented simultaneously. We might liken the flow of time sustained by the workings of musical meter as a single perspective on how time goes by. A polyphony of clocks, each distinctive and each interlocked within the whole, gives a God-like multi-perspective understanding of how time goes by. Jumping ahead six hundred years or so, we find analogous techniques in much of the music of Elliott Carter, considered by some the most distinguished American composer to date (others might hotly contest this judgment in that aesthetic judgments are always dependent on one's aesthetic values). In Carter, the God-perspective gives way to an intersubjective space. Like his remote musical ancestors, contrapuntally juxtaposed voices with different rates of unfolding are fundamental to Carter's musical language. We've stumbled onto a remarkable example of musical transumption.

After a millennium where metered music dominated wide-ranging musical practices, Western composers in the twentieth century once again became interested in ametric musical spaces and toward that end developed a variety of approaches toward notating ametric music. Some of Luciano Berio's music is remarkable in this regard. His *Laborintus II*, with its text by Edoardo Sanguineti (heavily borrowing fragments from Dante and others), moves through a full spectrum of modes of temporal organization: ametric, fractured metric, and fully metric. Among its multiple meanings, *Laborintus II* is an exploration of how time goes, not one way, but many ways.

While ametric musics are probably as old as music itself, what I'm calling fractured meter developed out of metric practices, using the relative rhythmic precision of metric notation, but breaking it into fragments that run counter to the regular pulsing and groupings of metered music. The opening of Igor Stravinsky's *Petroushka* (1911), while notated in ¾, places its musical gestures so that any perception of meter is tenuous and intermittent at best. The effect is further complicated by short interjected musical fragments that project meters that contradict the ongoing temporal frame. Subsequently, quick shifts of meter add to the metric confusion as the musical texture thickens.

Whereas Stravinsky's innovations strike me as hard-edged variants on syncopation, some of Schoenberg's music and much of Webern's more fully realizes what I call fractured meter. At the age of seventy-six as I write, I can look back on a good number of decades working at and in varied contexts of music making and music scholarship, another kind of music making. A major part of my career as scholar and teacher was dedicated to the music of Arnold Schoenberg. While it saddened me, and still does, that Schoenberg's music hasn't been able to reach, emotionally move, and intellectually engage a more expansive audience, I was really never puzzled by this. There are intrinsic cognitive difficulties in Schoenberg's music that are not easily overcome by performers or by most audiences whose contact with music is casual. By contrast, I have been puzzled that Webern's exquisite miniatures have solicited a resistance that matches audience discomfort—hostility might be a better word—so typically targeted at Schoenberg. Not that Webern lacks complexity of musical design, but if complexity of design were a determining factor, neither Bach nor Brahms would have ever achieved a significant audience.

As in the case most famously with Beethoven, we can divide Webern's music into three periods: Wagner-influenced romantic music composed prior to his studies with Schoenberg; free "atonal" music primarily composed between 1909 and 1914; and the twelve-tone music composed after World War I, until his death in 1945.[10]

It is the music Webern composed between 1909 and 1914 that will concern me here. Examples include *Five Movements for String Quartet*, Op. 5, *Six Pieces for Orchestra*, Op. 6, and *Six Bagatelles for String Quartet*, Op. 9.

Early on in this study, we made a distinction between creation as emergent versus creation as constructive. Webern's twelve-tone music strikes me as remarkable, musically fascinating *constructions*. In contrast, the music composed between 1909 and 1914 has an almost mystical quality of emergence out of silence and disappearance back into silence. Julian Johnson, in *Webern and the Transformation of Nature*, provides us with invaluable glimpses into a kind of pantheism that informs Webern's oracular music. The Alpine Mountains of Webern's youth, on into his maturity, were of particular importance to the composer. Like Mahler, Webern drew spiritual inspiration from nature. "There are extensive pen-portraits of Mahler's life in his summer resorts, a life apparently divided between intense compositional work in his famous *Häuschen* and a round of swimming, rowing, cycling and, above all, walking in the mountains. But while Mahler was a keen mountain walker, Webern was more accurately a mountaineer."[11] Johnson quotes a letter that Webern had written to friends in 1930 (italics in the original): "A week ago I was at Dachstein. The day of the ascent there was bad weather, rain and fog, but nevertheless it was beautiful. The *diffused light* on the glacier was quite remarkable . . . Just a few paces in front of you snow and fog *blended together into a completely undifferentiated screen.* You had no idea whether you were going up or down hill. A most favorable opportunity to contract snow-blindness! *But wonderful, like floating in space.*"[12] Webern's spirituality was profoundly influenced by the writings of the Swedish mystic Emmanuel Swedenborg. In a kind of Platonism, or Neoplatonism, Swedenborg propounded "correspondences" between all things in nature and their divine sources. In 1920, Webern had written to Alban Berg, remarking the prevalence of such correspondences in Mahler's music. The letter continues, "For me the world is grasped at the root of correspondences. The impression, which something in nature exerts over me, I grasp in the spiritual. And thus you understand my frenzy for mountain streams—clear right to the bottom—the scent of flowers—the tenderness of alpine flowers—those forms of the trees 'up there,' that rain, and so on."[13] Musical evanescence is a quality that Schoenberg and Webern share, a quality arguably more evident (perhaps just more obvious) in Webern's practice. All music is fleeting: a sound is here and then it's gone. But when musical sounds, the "notes," coalesce into larger events, then the quality of evanescence is balanced with a sense of ongoing cohesion. In Webern's music, what we might perceive as a musical event might last only couple of seconds in clock time, or even less. One often senses that these evanescent events are synecdochic in that they are parts of a large whole submerged in the silence that surrounds them.

 The fourth movement of Webern's *Six Bagatelles for String Quartet* will serve as an example. Recordings are readily available on YouTube and elsewhere. The movement, with a duration of slightly less than a minute, is the second longest in the set. Although notated in a meter of ⅜ (with the fourth measure shortened to $^2/_8$), meter seen on the page is not aurally perceptible, nor is it meant to be perceptible. Nearly every musical event is regularly pulsed in and of itself, but the pulsing in each voice of the quartet is distinct from the others that overlap but never coincide with it. Here, the flow of time is unanchored, and these bits of time-flow seem to float, appearing and disappearing into timelessness. Curious as it may seem, Webern's aesthetic was profoundly influenced by Gustav Mahler. As Julian Johnson points out, Mahler was second only to Schoenberg in his influences on Webern's compositions.[14] In his symphonies, Mahler presented listeners with an entire world. Webern's musical worlds give us glimpses into eternity emerging out of silence.

Emergence from a Sea of Silence in Voice and Image

John Hollander's poem "Making Nothing Happen" opens with an epigraph from W. H. Auden, "Poetry makes nothing happen." Here is a fragment of the poem that follows.

> Before there could be nothing, there were too,
> Too many somethings . . .
> . . .
> She said, *Let there be night*, and there was night,
> . . .
> Setting its engines of denial stirring;
> . . .
> Nothing had, finally, happened. In future, then,
> Something would never be the same again.[15]

In Hollander's storytelling, nothing comes out of a prior something, a something that will never be the same. The "she" who complements the Hebrew Bible's God's "Let there be light" with "Let there be night" might be a female aspect of that same God, or Lilith, primordial she-demon and Adam's first wife in Jewish mystical writings, or a gnostic God contrary and opposed to the Hebrew God, or she may be the muse of poetry and music, Calliope, mother of Orpheus, or she may be Mnemosyne, mother of all the muses. Or she may be a composite of them all. In any case, Hollander's poem changes the meaning of making nothing happen from lack of import and efficacy to plenum of import and efficacy, where nothing changes everything.

The Yiddish playwright S. Ansky imagines a counter-image, where Hollander's something and nothing are replaced by sound and silence, and where silence is a "dreadful terror" created before the inception of sound.

> The third Hell is Dumah (Grave).
> In an icy, lifeless silence,
> In a gray, unstirring stillness,
> Which was made before the birth of
> Any sound in God's creation,
> Dreadful terror lies in wait,
> Lurking like a beast of prey.[16]

Ansky's silence is a negative space, a hell that lurks like a beast of prey, a desolation prior to the birth of sound. The story that I tell myself about sound and silence in music and poetry merges aspects from both poets, but rids itself of any necessary negative connotation. Like Hollander, silence/nothingness as I perceive it is an engendering force, a kind of presence rather than an absence. However, his Miltonian "engines of denial stirring" implies negation, whereas my sea of silence is without negative or positive attribution. Like Ansky, silence/nothingness as I imagine it is primordial, the stuff out of which sound/something emerges. Unlike Ansky, silence for me is not necessarily a "dreadful terror" that lies in wait. Silence, like darkness, can be frightening; it can also be soothing, a primordial state of rest, a blankness that underlies and surrounds our very being, very much as Prospero posits, "We are such stuff as dreams are made on, and our little life is rounded with a sleep."

Whatever silence might be taken to mean, I hear an intensified sense of sound emerging out of and disappearing back into a timeless silence in some non-Western music, Japanese shakuhachi music and Japanese vocal chanting accompanied by biwa being clear examples. Whether it comes out of an increased awareness of non-Western music or out of the impact of Webern's music (or others in the Western traditions) on later composers, much Western art music from the latter part of the twentieth century on into the present has this same quality. Music that seems to emerge and recede into a sea of silence finds common ground among composers as diverse as Morton Feldman, Brian Ferneyhough, and James Dillon. In

Dillon's music in particular the effect summons up images of the vast reaches of space in our ever-expanding cosmos. But before we approach some of that music, I'd like to further consider the role that silence or emptiness can play in literature.

We touched on this sense of sound emerging out of silence in our discussion of Walt Whitman's waves. Here is a fragment from the 1855 edition of what later would be named "Song of Myself." The ellipses are in the original.[17]

> Urge and urge and urge,
> Always the procreant urge of the world.
> Out of the dimness opposite equals advance . . . . Always
> substance and increase,
> Always a knit of identity . . . . always distinction . . . .
> always a breed of life.
> To elaborate is no avail . . . . Learned and unlearned feel
> that it is so.

Ellipses are placed throughout the untitled poem of 1855. They function like intensified caesurae. The poem falters, stops, and starts, and the fragments of song-speech seem part of one great tapestry woven together by the "stitches" of silence. Later in the poem, answering the child's question "What is the grass?" the poet answers with a series of suppositions, the first of which is "I guess it must be the flag of my disposition, out of hopeful green stuff woven."

As Whitman revised the poem over subsequent editions, the ellipses vanish. Here is the analogous passage from "Song of Myself" as in the edition of 1891–1892.[18]

> Urge and urge and urge,
> Always the procreant urge of the world.
> Out of the dimness opposite equals advance, always
> substance and increase, always sex,
> Always a knit of identity, always distinction, always a breed
> of life.
> To elaborate is no avail, learned and unlearned feel
> that it is so.

I'm happy to have both editions. In many places the filling in of the ellipses adds splendor to the poem. But something is lost as well, the silent "stitches" of time and space. It would be far-fetched to trace a causal relation between Whitman's silences of 1855 and Webern's silences of 1909, but the effect is kindred.

One doesn't have to look too far to find a biblical source of sound coming out of silence. In the beginning God says let there be light and there was light. Two things emerge simultaneously, light out of darkness and voice out of silence. My ability to read in Hebrew is quite limited, but it doesn't take advanced training to recognize the laconic power of biblical Hebrew.

The Hebrew Bible rarely depicts imagery. In his often-cited essay "Odysseus' Scar," Erich Auerbach contrasts the abundance of visual imagery in Homer's epics with the reticence of biblical writings. Referring to the story in Genesis 22, God's command that Abraham sacrifice his son Isaac, Auerbach writes:

> The King James version translates the opening as follows (Genesis, 22:1): "And it came to pass after these things, that God did tempt Abraham, and said to him, Abraham! and he said, Behold, here I am." Even this opening startles us when we come to it from Homer. Where are the two speakers? We are not told. The reader, however, knows that they are not normally to be found together on one place on earth, that one of them, God, in order to speak to Abraham, must come from somewhere, must enter the earthly realm from some unknown heights or depths. Whence does he come, whence does he call to Abraham? We are not told.[19]

We don't have visual descriptions of the matriarchs and patriarchs. We are told what they said, not what they looked like. Voices that emerge out of surrounding silence are a salient aspect of many biblical stories, perhaps none more so than the story where God commands Abraham to sacrifice his son Isaac. English cannot match the laconic quality of biblical Hebrew. Everett Fox's remarkable translation probably comes as close as an English rendition can be. Here is the opening of Genesis 22 in Fox's translation.[20]

> Now after these events it was
> that God tested Avraham
> and said to him:
> Avraham!
> He said:

> Here I am.
> He said:
> Pray take your son,
> your only-one,
> whom you love,
> Yitzhak,
> and go-you-forth.

And here is Fox's translation of Genesis 22:7 on into the beginning of the next verse.

> Yitzhak said to Avraham his father; he said:
> Father!
> He said:
> Here I am, my son.
> He said:
> Here are the fire and the wood,
> but where is the lamb for the offering-up?
> Avraham said:
> God will see-for-himself to the lamb for the offering-up,
> my son.
> Thus the two of them went together.[21]

And on into verse 10 through 12:

> And Avraham stretched out his hand,
> he took the knife to slay his son.
> But YHWH's messenger called to him from heaven
> and said:
> Avraham! Avraham!
> He said:
> Here I am.
> He said:
> Do not stretch out your hand against the lad,
> do not do anything to him!
> For now I know
> that you are in awe of God—
> you have not withheld your son, your only-one, from me.

We recall our extended discussion of הנני (*hineni*) and its centrality in Levinas's ethics. Here we find *hineni* in Abraham's initial response to God, Isaac's response to Abraham, and once again in Abraham's subsequent response to God. In all the utterances in this mysterious encounter with divinity, the words seem etched in a silent darkness that surrounds them. Even the few visual images—"Here are the fire and the wood / but where is the lamb . . ."—seem to emerge out of a surrounding darkness, as in a dream. The strangest of strange connections, an invisible filament, connects the cords of Isaac's binding, to the emergence out of darkness that I hear in Anton Webern, in Morton Feldman, in James Dillon.

∽

Personal Excursus

Any of us who have been deeply touched by art have had peak experiences, be it with a poem, a musical performance, a painting, an experience in theater, or whatever. Two or three years ago, immersed in a period of reading the Hebrew scriptures daily, I had a profound experience of the darkness and silence that surround the biblical passage that we are discussing. Never before (or since) had the passage had that kind of impact. Maybe a decade or so earlier, I had a similar encounter with Whitman's "Song of Myself," a poem that I had been reading since my teen years. Somewhere Harold Bloom writes that Whitman, the poet of the body, was remarkable in how much of his poetry seems disembodied. That sense of a disembodied floating from image to image over the whole of the poem struck me with force that I had never felt before or since. Over the years, I have had similar experiences with music and theater. These moments of excellence seem to come and go as they will. A lifetime of immersion prepares us, but when they come, they come as a gift.

∽

Morton Feldman was a composer who found a deep affinity with the abstract expressionist painters of his generation, Mark Rothko among them. Rothko committed suicide in 1970, having completed the paintings and his architectural design for the Rothko Chapel in Houston, Texas. A year later, Feldman was commissioned to compose a piece in memoriam for his friend, to be performed in the space that the painter had created.[22]

Jeremy Sigler, in "The Kabbalah of Rothko," beautifully describes the sense of darkness and light in Rothko's chapel.[23]

> It's as if the room is a nocturne—a forest with moonlight filtering through its canopy. Even by day, the paintings provide the quiet solitude and mystery of night. The dark presence of the canvases seems to articulate light itself and allow one to commune with the chapel's radiance. Dark as they may be, their geometric forms, alternating between translucence and opacity, create a milky luminescence and a compelling spectrum of tones and temperatures.
>
> . . .
>
> The venerable art historian Dore Aston once compared Rothko's used of light to the radiance of the *Zohar*, the principal text of Kabbalah. And I happen to think she was dead-on.

Much to the point of our ongoing discussion of silence and sound, Sigler also provides keen insights into the chapel's acoustics and Rothko's sensitive appreciation of "pockets of silence."

> There was also something distinct about the chapel's acoustics. Sound was very important to Rothko, and he referenced it throughout his career in a variety of ways. Once, he rejected the idea that his paintings were a language, calling them instead a form of speech. Much has been written about the silence that seems to ricochet off the paintings (negative speech, if you will). Rothko once said, "Silence is so accurate." In a famously brief talk he once gave at Yale University, he described his work as a search for "pockets of silence."

I can't be sure what Rothko meant in distinguishing "language" from "speech," but my guess is that the distinction was kindred to Levinas's where language totalizes, while speech is active, augmenting ourselves through its openness to the other. Also in his essay, Sigler quotes a 1983 oral-history interview with the poet Stanley Kunitz, a close friend of Rothko's. Kunitz had characterized Rothko as "the last Rabbi of Western art." Here is Sigler quoting Kunitz: "It made him feel very good. I meant that there was in him a rather magisterial authority, a sense of transcendence as well, a feeling in him that he belonged to the line of the prophets rather than to the line of great craftsmen."[24] To place Kunitz's characterization into context, we need to reflect on the education that Rothko received as a child in Europe and how that education impacted on the painter in his maturity. Here I rely on Annie Cohen-Solal, *Mark Rothko: Toward the Light in the Chapel*.[25] Marcus Rotkovitch, later to become Mark Rothko, was born in September 1903 in what is now part of Latvia, where his father was a local pharmacist. As was typical of successful bourgeois Jewish families, Rotkovitch's older siblings were given a secular education. Jews were never fully secure in that part of the world; however, just months before Marcus's birth, there was a particularly bloody pogrom not far from his birthplace. Antisemitism was on the rise, and during 1905–1906 there was a rash of massacres in the region. In defiant reaction, Marcus's father decided to give his youngest child a more traditional Talmudic education.[26] In this respect, Rothko's life experience is a negative image of that of Emmanuel Levinas. Levinas, we recall, was given a secular education as a youth, turning to Talmudic thought only after the Holocaust. In contrast, Rothko turned away from traditional rabbinical studies after his family moved to the United States. What Kunitz recognized was that although the trappings of traditional Judaism had been left behind, a deeper spirituality informed what we might call Rothko's ethics of painting.

In her biography of Rothko, Cohen-Solal discusses a significant 1954 showing of Rothko's work at the Art Institute of Chicago.[27] The showing had been facilitated by the art historian and curator Katherine Kuh. Rothko, always sensitive to the manner in which his art was displayed, wrote to Kuh in September of that year. "I also hang the largest pictures so that they must be first encountered at close quarters so that the first experience is to be within the picture."[28] Roy Edwards, Rothko's assistant during the period when the Chapel paintings were done, echoes this sentiment in "Mark Rothko: A Personal Reflection." "The space must be something that one can enter into, after all. The pictures are doorways to the unknown."[29] "To be within the painting" is as valuable an insight into Rothko's art as I can imagine. The sentiment also captures my sense of a vital musical experience: to be within the music.

Morton Feldman's "Rothko Chapel" can be heard as a wonderful translation of Rothko's painterly aesthetics into musical substance. There can be no doubt that Feldman was a composer who responded particularly to the work of painters in his milieux. However, it is the echoes of his musical precursors that I hear as vivid presences in the music. Although

I haven't seen references to the Second Viennese in commentaries on "Rothko Chapel," I hear vivid echoes of the voices of Schoenberg and Webern throughout. Feldman seems to have had mixed feelings toward Webern and, so far as I have seen in his prose writings, only strong negative feelings toward Schoenberg. This might explain why scholars of Feldman's music are reluctant to attribute Second Viennese influences to Feldman. There may be other influences that I have overlooked, Varese in particular, but I hear Second Viennese influences that the composer goes out of his way to disavow.

Perhaps most salient are the Webern-derived silences that surround each sound-gesture. The use of *ostinati* that float unanchored to a tonic also find their antecedents in Webern (and Schoenberg, to a lesser degree), including the *Bagatelles for String Quartet* that we discussed earlier. The lyrical fragments, principally in the viola, are sometimes reminiscent of Webern as well, although the lyrical lines often exhibit a simplicity, a plain-spoken quality, that is more American in flavor than we would find in the Viennese. The choral music (all without words), so important in creating the mysterious textures that are essential to the work, are to my ear direct descendants of Schoenberg's choral writing. I think especially of the opening scene of Schoenberg's opera *Moses und Aron*. There the chorus is identified as "the voice from the thornbush," emerging from a divine source. Feldman's choral writing has this oracular quality. The long-sustained choral episode about two-thirds of the way through the piece (mm. 211–42) strikes me as being derived from another source, the orchestral writing in the third of Schoenberg's *Five Orchestral Pieces*, Op. 16. Schoenberg originally gave his movement the title *Farben* ("Colors") and then later changed to the more descriptive *Sommermorgen an einem See* ("Summer morning by a lake"). In Schoenberg, the orchestral texture, almost hallucinatory, summons up the lake's mysterious depth, its waves gently lapping on the shore. In Feldman, the choral texture, without words, parallels the mysterious, silent depths that viewers perceive in Rothko's paintings. Readers who know Feldman's attitude toward Schoenberg, disparaging to say the least, might find it strange that some of the most striking moments in Feldman's piece are Schoenbergian. Talk about the anxiety of influence.

In my experience, some composers more so than others have an extraordinary sense of orchestral or vocal resonance as it interacts with an acoustic space. Schubert's string quartets strike me this way, as do Mahler's orchestrations. The acoustic resonance of Feldman's astounding choral harmonies belongs to this company. As we approach the end of "Rothko Chapel," a solo viola plays a "Hebraic" melody (so attributed by the composer) that Feldman had composed as a teenager. The advent of diatonic simplicity near the end of the work brings us back to a world antecedent to that which we've been inhabiting, a memory of time before this time, all this accompanied by an ongoing vibraphone ostinato, ticking off time going nowhere. The uncanny choral harmonies return, with the vibraphone ostinato still ongoing as the piece finally drifts into its final silence. If my surmise is correct, Feldman's in memoriam remembers not only his lost friend, but also an entire world that was lost in the Holocaust. The close of Feldman's work recognizes the Jewish spiritual roots that Rothko and Feldman had in common, deeply resisted, and, more deeply yet, affirmed.

We turn to another composer, raised in another tradition, who shows some affinities with Feldman nonetheless. James Dillon, born in Glasgow, Scotland, in 1950, was raised as a Catholic. We can count Dillon among the rarest of musical composers in that he is principally an autodidact. Dillon's background and his practice defy easy categorization. As Dillon matured, his early Catholicism was transformed into a wide-ranging catholicism, forging his own musical personality out of many different traditions, religious, philosophical, painterly, and of course musical.

Two sonic sources that have left their traces throughout Dillon's work reach back to his young days in Scotland: first and foremost, the ringing of bells. For a time an altar boy, young James Dillon experienced the ringing of bells as part of religious experience in the church of his youth. Bells have notoriously complex harmonics, a resonance that can be uncanny to the ears of a sensitive young person (before the devastations of aging take away our ability to hear the high overtones). Bell ringing and imitations of bell ringing, for example, in his writing for piano, remain a salient aspect of Dillon's compositional language. More importantly, a sensitivity to the acoustic properties of sound, its resonance, deeply inform Dillon's approach to composition. A second trace from Dillon's youth is heard in his propensity toward drone tones, a vestige of the incessant drone of bagpipes, self-defining of Dillon's Irish-Scottish heritage. Although drones and their kindred pedal tones (sustained tones, usually in the bass) are far less pervasive in their impact on mature Dillon, they are significant in some works, including *The Gates*, a work from 2016 that will concern us here.

I am not fond of the term "myth" and have used the word "stories" purposely to avoid the "I know better-than-thou" tone of *myth*. And so

I use the word hesitantly in saying that Dillon is fascinated by a wide range of myth-making; we might better call it storytelling. The word "mysticism," although I have used it in this study, is another word that gives me pause. It's hard to find a substitute word for the heightened sensibility of religious visionaries, poets, musicians, painters, and others who take us out of the mundane into a sense of altered time and space. In some contexts, the word *visionaries* is a suitable term, as in Harold Bloom's early study of British Romanticism, *The Visionary Company*. Still, metaphoric vision is ocular at its source, barely appropriate for a poet and even less so for a musician. The Hebrew word נביא (*navi*), and its English equivalent *prophet*, one who speaks by divine inspiration, come closer to what we need, and yet the word prophet has its own baggage. So, with those caveats in mind, I say that Dillon is particularly attracted to a wide-range of myth-making visionaries and that most of his compositions are musical embodiments of that visionary company. To show the range of Dillon's interest in this regard, I offer this selection of his titles (a good number more might have fit the bill).

> *Dillug-Kefitsah* for solo piano (1976): the title is adapted from Gershom Scholem's account of the Kabbalist Abraham Abulafia's method of jumping or skipping from one conception to another, using free association as a way of meditation.
> *Parjana-vata* for solo cello (1981): the Sanskrit title is taken from Vedic hymns personifying wind and rain.
> helle Nacht for orchestra (1986–1987): based on German mystical writing from eleventh century Jacob Boehme to Rainer Maria Rilke; the title derives from Hölderlin's translation of Sophocles *Antigone* at the moment of Antigone's burial alive.
> *ignis noster* for orchestra (1991–1992): the title, "our fire," is adapted from medieval alchemy, reaching back to pre-Socratic concepts of fire as in Heraclitus and Parmenides.
> *The Book of Elements* for solo piano (1997–2002): the five elements are air (or wind), water, earth/crystal, fire, and void; taken from ancient Greek, Celtic, and Chinese myth.
> *Philomela* an opera (2004): drawing on ancient Greek sources.
> *Stabat Mater dolorosa* cantata for 12 voices, chamber ensemble, and electronics (2014): the central poem concerning Mary's sorrow at the foot of the cross is attributed to the 13th c.

Franciscan friar Jacopone da Todi; the work also uses fragments from Julia Kristeva, Rainer Maria Rilke, John Donne, and Pablo Picasso.

Pharmakeia for sixteen players (2017–2020): In three movements: *Temenos,* from Sumerian *temen* (a sacred space), origin of Latin *templum*; *Strophe,* from Greek "turn, bend, or twist"; *Circe,* goddess of sorcery (*Pharmakeia*), the magic of transmutation, illusion, and necromancy.

Circe (2017): drawing on Greek myth of the sorceress, extended to the magical powers of music

Another crucial aspect of Dillon's work as a composer is his sensitivity to the sensuality of sound. In conversation, he often refers to the "grittiness" of sound (the rolled r and the hard t's of "grittiness" heightened by Dillon's Scottish accent), not just the pitches played, but also the sound of the bow on the string. I recall at some point having a conversation with Dillon concerning the thirteenth-century philosopher and theologian Duns Scotus. Scotus's concept of *haecceity*, the irreducible individuation of each being, an irreducible "thisness," might well apply to Dillon's concept of musical sound. So, for example, even the seemingly innocent reduction of sound to pitch bleaches out all of the other attributes that are concomitants of pitch: timbre (harmonic resonance), dynamics, surrounding environment, and so forth. It is because of this that Dillon's pedagogy is averse to the more typical division of the study of composition into separable elements: primarily harmony, rhythm, and orchestration. For Dillon, one doesn't compose first and orchestrate later. We have seen how the uniqueness (and unfathomable mystery) of each individual was central to Levinas's ethics. We might find an analogous musical ethics in Dillon.

The Gates (2016) is composed for large orchestra and string quartet. The recording of the world premier is posted on YouTube. I also highly recommend the excellently produced video of this performance, available online at SWR Web Concerts: Donaueschinger Musiktage 2016: Eröffnungskonzert. The orchestra, seventy-eight players in all, includes piano, celeste, and harp, as well as four percussion players using a wide range of bell and bell-like sounds. Here is Dillon's program note as in the published score.[30]

>**Gate** [from Old Norse *gat*]; Opening, passage, a means of entrance or exit.
>(Oxford English Dictionary)

> A single line, measured, drawn with precision marks, divides, separates and at the same time creates a liminal space; across this line erect, the "gate" marks a boundary, the point where the one territory stops and another begins; to "pass through" traces a transition.
>
> Here it is the "fermata" or "pause" a suspended time interval defines a boundary, opens into, and cuts off areas of musical activity, areas patterned by greater or lesser intensity. The movement between "string quartet" and "orchestra" is confronted by silence.
>
> Any musical work exists on the edge between the heard and the unheard, between the measures, between the worldly and the spiritual, that axis, the pole or centre, which contains its own periphery. We may speak of an "edgy" work or an "edgy" performance, where the pressure of what is bounded defines certain limits.
>
> Like the Japanese *Torii* the gate or often a series of gates to a Shinto temple, marks the entrance to a sacred space. To enter through the gate is to "*en'trance*," to put into "trance," to delight; the gate as "exit" is to enable *departure*.
>
> The ancient Egyptian *Pylon* was the monumental gate to a temple, associated with a place of birth and recreation.

"A single line" is either imaginary or a mark on a score ("drawn with precision") that divides and separates, noting or notating a liminal space. It is a space that we pass through, where one territory stops and another begins, as in a region of music with its characteristic types of flow and figuration, affects and shadings, scope and duration. Over the course of the work, fourteen fermatas articulate fifteen "areas of musical activity," some fairly consistent in their characteristics, some erratic or volatile, some of greater duration, some more quickly traveled through. The limina are the places where movement "is confronted with silence." Dillon's note here is potentially confusing. I take it to mean that the totality of movement, between *concerto* (string quartet) and *tutti* (orchestra), is silence-confronted—not that silence is in between the two constituents of the larger ensemble.

The "edge between the heard and the unheard" is another kind of liminal space, one that we've thought about intermittently throughout this study. In Lewin's phenomenology and in Lewin's transformational theory, emergent meaning (or function) as the sonic event (anticipated, heard, recollected) is cast into new light by what proceeds. In this sense, the musical event/object is not a stable, unchanging occurrence or entity but rather something that takes on changing, even contradictory meanings over time. The "heard" is the sonic event; the "unheard" is the imaginative flow of perceptions that it engenders. Of course, the paradox is precisely in that hearing entails hearing the unheard *through* the heard. Dillon's *gates* are more inclusive than the region-defining fermatas; they are limina that traverse "the worldly and the spiritual." The "axis, pole or centre" is a part of a dynamic system, analogous to an axis of rotation that implies the circle or sphere (or the spiral of a galaxy), and so "contains its own periphery." An edgy work or performance, Dillon tells us, presses up against the periphery, "where the pressure of what is bounded defines certain limits," the circle, sphere, or galaxy.

Noriko Kawai, Dillon's life partner, a remarkable pianist who has so beautifully performed so many of Dillon's works, is the daughter of a Shinto priest. And so the mention of Japanese *Torii* is anchored in life experience; they mark "the entrance into a sacred space." In this context, I want to recall our earlier discussion of Angus Fletcher's threefold, labyrinth-threshold-temple. Quoting what we noted before: "Roughly speaking, we may say that the labyrinth is the archetypal space of historical time, while the temple (as its name suggests) is the home of the timeless. The liminal crossover between these two 'spaces' marks the moment of prophetic vision in which the poet sees life from the joint perspective of passing and immutability."[31] In pre-Socratic philosophy, Heraclitus conceptualized the universe as ever-changing flux, while Parmenides argued that passing time is an illusion. In Dillon's *ignis noster*, the composer plays with fire, imagining a transformational alchemy that somehow contains them both. Dillon's limina are thresholds between passing time and timeless eternity, where music emerges out of a sea of silence, where nothing and everything meet at threshold's edge. Dillon closes his prefatory note with a reference to the ancient Egyptian *Pylon*, "monumental gate to a temple, associated with a place of birth and recreation."

I queried James Dillon about *The Gates* as the new year 2022 had just begun. His response, in part, was: "Thresholds, borders, boundaries as both entrances and barriers have always attracted me and occasionally this is directly reflected in the title of a work (*Crossing Over, Le rivage*)."

Another locus of crossings, literal and figurative, is the bridge, and another meaning of *pylon* designates the towers that anchor suspension bridges. The great poet of the bridge is Hart Crane, who envisioned the Brooklyn Bridge as both harp and altar. In Crane's "*To* Brooklyn Bridge," we find the lines "O harp and altar, of the fury fused . . . vaulting the sea . . . And of the curveship lend a myth to God."[32] Crane's neologism "curveship" adds yet another metaphor to harp and altar, the bridge "vaulting the sea." Religious imagery, Kabbalistic and otherwise, contains both ascents into divine realms and descents where the divine is brought into our common sphere. Here divinity is brought down to "lend a myth to God." As with any significant composer, Dillon's music cannot be pigeonholed into any one single concern. Yet so many of his works "of the curveship lend a myth to God."

Dillon's musical language is very much his own. Yet, as would be the case with any significant work of music, there are precursors whose voices echo throughout. Going backward through time, I principally hear three Western composers whose trace is heard in *The Gates*, all of whom are transmuted through Dillon's alchemy: Ligeti, Mahler, Beethoven. In addition, I surmise that non-Western cyclic music, such as the *tala* in Indian classical music or the rhythmic cycles of Balinese Gamelan music, inform aspects of *The Gates*.

The musical precursor most pervasively evident in *The Gates* is György Ligeti, especially Ligeti's String Quartet, No. 2 (1968), and the Chamber Concerto (1969–1970). In both of these works, Ligeti extensively develops a technique that he named *micropolyphony*.[33] Ligeti's technique contrapuntally combines swiftly moving voices (instruments), often in canon, but always with similar figuration, to create orchestral textures. In contrast to traditional polyphony, the individual voices in micropolyphony are not audible as such; instead we hear the resultant textures that arise out of their combinations. In *The Gates* Dillon develops analogous techniques, more extreme in their technical virtuosity, and mostly reserved for the string quartet. As Dillon composed *The Gates*, he surely had the Arditti String Quartet in mind. Irving Arditti formed the quartet in 1980, and although the personnel have changed over time, the quartet has remained preeminent in the performance of new music in Europe and internationally. Their technical ability is unsurpassed. Seemingly, if the composer can imagine it, they can play it. In contradistinction to Ligeti's technique, Dillon's micropolyphony usually involves cyclic patterning, often used in conjunction with rapidly moving swells, *crescendi* and *diminuendi*, that create a doppler-like effect, a sense of the sound objects/events moving toward and away from the listener. As I've mentioned, Dillon's cyclic patterns are reminiscent of non-Western practices, though, as with everything in this music, such patterning is redefined in its new contexts.

Ligeti sometimes juxtaposes his micropolyphonic textures, with their rapidly flowing constituents, against expansive, prolonged chords of varying harmonic complexity. Dillon uses this technique as well, but here the precursors strike me more as Mahler and Beethoven. We have considered how Mahler's First Symphony opens with the effect of a great expanse, emerging out of silence, a near-void waiting to be filled. Dillon too creates a sense of great expanse, a sense of cosmos that he has in common with Mahler and Mahler's precursor, the first movement of Beethoven's Ninth Symphony.

Instead of beginning with a pedal tone as in Beethoven's Ninth Symphony or Mahler's First Symphony, *The Gates* begins with an explosive energy flow, the xylophone morphing into the micropolyphony of the string quartet. A massive D pedal gradually emerges, enveloping the quartet's busy flow and continuing to be sustained and augmented as the micropolyphony eventually dissipates. At one point, near the end of the first region, we hear the oboe playing a near quote from the opening of Beethoven's Fourth Symphony. Later in *The Gates* the use of distanced chimes, Dillon's beloved bells, is reminiscent of the ways Mahler uses distanced brass. But all of these presences are ghostly presences, Dillon edging up to a memory of what we've known before, transformed into what we now perceive.

The Gates drifts in and out of metric space, paradoxically never really seeming anchored in the metric even when it is strongly insinuated through recurrent cycles. As is common in Dillon's orchestral compositions, the music summons up images of vast stretches of space, a time ongoing yet somehow standing still, a mystical time. Waves of sound are defined by color, pulsation, mass, and variable forms of musical energy emerging from surrounding silences and when spent receding again into nothingness.

Sound and silence are opposed. Approaching oppositional tension in *The Gates* from another perspective, we might speak in terms of *cosmos* and *chaos*.[34] Some musical events endure over time, either through cyclic reiterations or through long-sustained chords, like the pedal tones in Beethoven and Mahler. Other events are evanescent in the extreme, gone as soon as apprehended. There is also the slow unfolding of coming into being or its opposite, a slow decay or breaking apart. The synoptic textures of the music depend on these oppositions.

Dillon's music still awaits an adequate response from music theorists. To my mind, we simply do not yet have the technical language to properly address this music. Luckily, the ear outraces the conceptualizing mind. The fallings, driftings, explosions, contractions are all part of the musical universe that we step into in Dillon's music.

Black Fire, White Fire, Darkness and Light

In considering depictions of darkness and light, we might tend first to think of music's sibling arts, painting, photography, and cinematography. Stagecraft too is expert in creating lighting effects, and when music is staged, as in opera and musical theater, lighting effects can be a powerful part of the experience. But music without staging can also depict light in remarkable ways. Arnold Schoenberg, no doubt influenced by the staged lighting effects in Richard Wagner's operas, was a master of creating depictions of changing light. I think of *Gurrelieder*, whose expansive orchestral opening depicts the lengthening shadows of twilight, and whose majestic close depicts the overwhelming onrush of a new dawn. And then there's Schoenberg's extraordinary string sextet, *Verklärte Nacht*, with its spellbinding depiction of transfiguring moonlight. And, of course, there's *Pierrot Lunaire*, where moonlight cascades down, intoxicating Pierrot with the wine that one drinks through the eyes.

I suspect that my reader can fill in many other examples of light, starlight, moonlight, twilight, and glaring sunlight through its musical settings. Close to the time of the writing of this book, I find Chaya Czernowin's *The Fabrication of Light* (2019–2020) to be a remarkable extension and transformation of that aspect of musical traditions that depicts the play of darkness and light through musical means alone. Composed for seventeen players, Czernowin's expansive piece gives the sonic impression of comprising a much larger ensemble. The listener's imagination is co-creator as the composer fabricates her wonderfully wrought variations on the theme, "Let there be light."

To close this discussion of sound and silence transformed into darkness and light, I return to Talmudic and Kabbalistic writings and their images of *black fire* and *white fire*. *Midrash Tanchuma*, named after the Talmudic sage Tanchuma, comprises commentary on the five books of the Torah, composed c. 500–c. 800 CE. The commentary on *Bereshit* (Genesis in English bibles) asks, "How was the Torah written?" and then says, "It was written with letters of black fire on a surface of white fire."[35] The image of black fire on white fire becomes a recurrent image in Jewish mysticism, summoning a wide variety of interpretations. Here is part of Moshe Idel's observations in *Absorbing Perfections* regarding that imagery.

> Contemplating the Torah will, accordingly, involve more than a study of certain sacred contents, more than the disclosure of an ideal *modus vivendi*; it will include, at least partially, a divine self-revelation. Thus the white fire will stand for the divine substance of the Torah, the black one for the letters.
>
> Semiotically, only the black dimension operates as a meaningful signifier because it alone imparts content to the readers. Mystically, however, the white fire involves a higher status which, though semantically meaningless, directly reflects the divine body rather than God's intention as articulated in the Torah . . . The implicit preference for the white and amorphous fire may represent a tendency to be immersed into a more contemplative and direct approach to the divine, which will regard the letters, namely the limited content of the revealed religion, as a lower and mediated relation to the beyond.[36]

In thinking of sound as emerging out of a sea of silence, it is as though we have reversed the Talmudic and Kabbalistic imagery: sounds of white fire emerge out of a substratum of black fire, where light and voice are co-determinates.

9

Smooth Space, Striated Space
Nomadic Space, Agrarian Space

Two Types of Musical Time-Space

In *Music Today*, Pierre Boulez distinguished between two principal types of musical space, *striated* and *smooth*.[1] Boulez's twofold space is kindred to the spatial/conceptual bifurcation that Gilles Deleuze makes in *Difference and Repetition*, *agrarian* and *nomadic* space (also denoted respectively by *logos* and *nomos*).[2] In *A Thousand Plateaus*, Deleuze, along with his co-author Félix Guattari, greatly expand their treatment of the two spaces. Here they adopt Boulez's terminology, striated and smooth, using it interchangeably with Deleuze's terms, logos and nomos, and nomadic/agrarian modified into nomadic/sedentary. The authors also explore an expanded range of conceptual schema and associated practices, each shedding light on different aspects of the two spatial and temporal modes.[3] I turn to these three discussions to further augment our understanding of metric and ametric spaces.

Boulez begins his discussion of the two spaces by considering the concept of "continuum." "The continuum is *manifested* by the possibility of *partitioning* space according to certain laws; the dialectic between continuity and discontinuity thus involves the concept of partition; I will go so far as to say that continuum *is* this possibility, for it contains both the continuous and the discontinuous."[4] We might say that for Boulez, the world is digital rather than analogue; the perception of analogue (smooth space) occurs when the deviations among partitions are so minute that they can no longer be perceived as such. Limiting his descriptions to pitch at the outset, Boulez addresses the perception of intervals between pitches in light of his distinction.

> The finer partition becomes . . . the more it will tend toward continuity . . . Frequency space may undergo two sorts of partition: the one, defined by a standard measure, will be regularly repeatable, the other, imprecise, or more exactly, undetermined, will occur freely and irregularly. Temperament—the choice of a standard measure—will be an invaluable aid in estimating an interval; in short, it will "*striate*" the surface, the musical space . . . in the opposite cases, where partition can be effected at will, the ear will lose all landmarks and all absolute cognizance of intervals; this is comparable to the eye's inability to estimate distances on a perfectly smooth space.[5]

As we shall see, Deleuze and Guattari, while coinciding with some aspects of Boulez's bifurcated space/time as smooth and striated, modify Boulez's metaphor of a perfectly smooth space (which we might whimsically liken to the world as an infinitely expanded bowling alley). For Deleuze/Guattari, an ever-varying landscape can be conceptualized as *smooth*, so long as it is not partitioned, or so long as it is so variously partitioned that no unifying metric can be applied.

Boulez makes two further distinctions, both nested in striated space: *straight space*, where the partitions ("modules") are fixed, and *curved space*, where the partitions are variable. In contrast, smooth space has undefined partitions, no module, and what Boulez calls (without clarification) "statistical distribution of frequencies."[6] (Neither Boulez, nor Deleuze/Guattari as they subsequently develop the terms, give a specific musical example of "statistical distribution," but it seems clear that they are referring to what became known as *sound clouds*, stochastically generated sound masses found especially in the music of Iannis Xenakis but also associated with György Ligeti and others. We will return to further consideration of such statistical distribution later in this study.) Applying the same ideas to time, Boulez distinguishes *pulsed time* from *amorphous time*, where amorphous time is comparable to a smooth surface and pulsed time to a striated surface.[7] "Pulsation is for striated time what temperament is for striated space; it has been shown that, depending on whether partition is fixed or variable, defined space will be regular or irregular; similarly, that the pulsation of striated time will be regular or irregular, but systematic."[8] Analogous to straight space and curved space, *straight* or *regular time* will have a consistent module, regular partitioning, while *curved* or *irregular time* will have variable partitions.[9] Striated and smooth time/space can be variously combined, as Boulez says, through alternation or superimposition. Boulez calls this interactive space/time *non-homogeneous*.[10] We can think of this heterogeneity in terms of a dialectical opposition between striated and smooth time/space. More so than pure smooth or pure striated, I find the interaction of the two time/spaces to be particularly suggestive in thinking about music's making. We will return to this idea after further consultation with Boulez, Deleuze, and Guattari.

Boulez makes another useful distinction in considering time as directional or non-directional, further saying that striated time that is static (non-directional) is suggestive of smooth time; similarly, smooth time that is directional is suggestive of striated time.[11] We can clarify by providing an example of each. In Debussy's music, there are passages, often based on whole tone configurations, where a sense of directed motion gives way to a sense of drift. Even though time is parsed into regular pulses, the effect is smooth, as though the tic-toc of passing time is suspended. The *alap* in Indian classical music, the first section of a raga, performed without a regular underlying pulse, might serve as an example of the opposite effect: tension and release with regard to the underlying drone suggest modules, partitions of time, that we associate with striated time.

Boulez closes his discussion of striated and smooth with a consideration of timbre and amplitude, the former normally discontinuous (akin to striated space) and the later continuous (akin to smooth). Both of these aspects of music can be developed toward approaching the opposed time/space, timbrel transformation approaching smooth space, amplitude approaching striated space. I will provide a simple example of each. Debussy's "Prelude to 'The Afternoon of a Faun,'" a work whose opening we will consider in some detail in due course, begins, famously, with a solo for the flute, alone. The flute's first phrase ends with a decrescendo that dovetails with the same pitch being sustained by the oboe. This happens again, with the second iteration of the flute's melody, once again dovetailed by the oboe, which this time continues the melodic flow. The effect is a smooth transformation of the flute's timbre into that of the oboe. As an example of amplitude approaching striated space, I might choose the terraced dynamics of the baroque period. I find an even more compelling example in some of Anton Webern's music, where sudden shifts in dynamics create the sense of sudden shifts of distance and presence, these perhaps a development of Mahler's effects of sudden distancing and presence.

I would add a single observation to Boulez's thoughtful analysis: habituated to conceptualizing in striated space as we have become, Boulez does not entertain the idea that a radically smooth space would make no distinctions between space and time, let alone frequency, amplitude, and timbre. He seems to take these divisions for granted, as though the conceptual/emotional space-time is composed a priori of separate elements, like ingredients in a recipe. That's a rather big assumption. Take our experience of time, for example. The concept of time is empty apart from the events (amorphous or well-delineated, directed or static) that let us perceive passing time. Events in music comprise a melding of elements (pitch, timbre, amplitude, etc.), separable analytically but inseparably fused in music's makings. The problem with what we might call striated knowing is reflected in music pedagogy, where the student learns "harmony" separately from orchestration, with rhythm, the temporal embodiment of harmony, scarcely noted, separate and apart from the harmony all but abstracted from its temporal flow.

∽

Winter is a good time for daily walks in the part of Arizona where I've retired. Walking exemplifies a dialectic between smooth and striated. My steps, left-right-left-right, in fairly even pacing, divide motion into equivalencies, the metric of a walking cadence. The landscape unfurls smoothly, things close by move from ahead of me to behind me; things in further distance giving the optical illusion of moving contra-wise to the things closer to me, left to right inverting to right to left. I can attend to my measured footfall, or I can attend to the passing landscape, or I can attend to a polyphony of measured and unmeasured, pacing and flow. The measured and unmeasured polyphony of natural sounds adds to another dimension to the visual and bodily aspects of walking. This time of year, I hear the regular-irregularities of the mocking birds, and the polyphony of doves, nearer and further in the distance.

∽

In *Difference and Repetition*, apparently not yet cognizant of Boulez's distinction of smooth and striated, Deleuze formulates a similar division of space.

> We must first of all distinguish a type of matter of dividing up the distributed . . . A distribution of this type proceeds by fixed and proportional determinations which may be assimilated to "properties" or limited territories within representation. The agrarian question may well have been very important for this organization as the faculty which distinguishes parts ("on the one hand and on the other hand"). Even among the gods, each has his own domain, his category, his attributes, and all distribute limits and lots to mortals in accordance with destiny. Then there is a completely different distribution which must be called nomadic, a nomad *nomos*, without property, enclosure or measure. Here, there is no longer a division of that which is distributed but rather a division among those who distribute *themselves* in an open space—a space which is unlimited, or at least without precise limits.[12]

In that Deleuze's formulation was initially made (evidently) without knowledge of Boulez's, it is fascinating to recognize an underlying parallel in their metaphors, striated and agrarian. *Stria* is borrowed from the Latin cognate denoting the furrows of agricultural or agrarian space. We can extend these etymological connections by recognizing that the word *verse*, a concomitant of metered poetry, also derives from a Latin word denoting furrow, where *vertō* (to turn around) denotes the turning of the plow, the completing one furrow (verse) to begin another.

Deleuze adds another aspect to nomadic space that I find particularly useful in thinking about time-space in music and literature, the idea of leaping over boundaries. "Such a distribution is demonic rather than divine, since it is a peculiarity of demons to operate in the intervals between the gods' fields of action, as it is to leap over the barriers or the enclosures, thereby confounding the boundaries between properties."[13] Angus Fletcher describes a nearly antithetical view of demonic space in *Allegory: The Theory of a Symbolic Mode*.[14] In Fletcher's description, the divisions among demons are fixed, each associated with a particular function (on this in particular, see page 45). As such, demon (and daemon, beneficent spirits) share in the hierarchical, striated space as conceptualized by Deleuze. In contrast, Fletcher comes very close to Deleuze's idea of demonic in his article "Allegory without Ideas."[15] There he invokes a metaphorical wall that stands between the fable and its interpreted meaning. "Personifications, typical faces and masks of the mode, are ideas that are treated as if demonic agents . . . In theory, these are the figures of action who should be able to slide through the hermeneutic wall or fly over it, from the story to the *significatio* and back again."[16]

Generalized into agrarian and nomadic space, Boulez's striated and smooth, the distinction begins to approximate the ancient Greek division of Apollonian and Dionysian, a conceptual division appropriated and further developed by Friedrich Nietzsche. Leo Bersani, in *The Culture of Redemption*, describes the opposition of Apollonian and Dionysian in terms not very different from Deleuze's two spaces. "In contrast to 'primordial unity,' associated with Dionysus—a unity in which the boundaries between individuals as well as between humanity and nature have been erased or, more exactly, have not yet been drawn—there is Apollo, 'the glorious divine image of the *principium individuationis,*' which 'knows but one law . . . the delimiting of boundaries of the individual.'"[17] The delimitation of boundaries, a hallmark of agrarian space, is likewise a concomitant of Apollonian space. Conversely, the primordial unity of Dionysian space is like undivided nomadic space. In contrast, the principle of individuation in Deleuze shifts (paradoxically?) onto nomadic space; the regularities of agrarian space induce equivalencies that are opposed to the Apollonian ideal. While there are parallels, there are also distinctions, and Deleuze's emphasis on the divisions and distributions of space, literal and metaphorical, adds new and important aspects to the ancient division.

As I have mentioned, the concepts of striated and smooth space are more deeply explored in the Deleuze/Guattari collaboration, *A Thousand Plateaus*. Part of the difficulty in assessing and adopting descriptions of smooth and striated space in *A Thousand Plateaus* is that the book is most fundamentally a political manifesto. As such, it is filled with the fervor of the revolutionary left of the 1960s. Within those contexts, striated space is broadly associated with "royal science" and the powers of the state, while smooth space is broadly associated with subversive elements. Although Levinas is not mentioned in *A Thousand Plateaus,* as in Levinas's writings, the book shows a deep distrust of the state's totalizing power, a distrust that is evident throughout.[18] Rereading the book in 2022, against the background of a revolutionary fervor among neofascists, brings a distaste for much of its rhetoric, at least for me. Fully aware that its ideas were not meant to be separated from their political message, I do just that. It's not that I am not sympathetic to the claims of those who are oppressed by the state or its corporate proxies (although who is the proxy for whom is debatable), but it is not my aim to foment revolution, left or right.

One of the ideas about smooth space in *A Thousand Plateaus* that I find particularly resonant in musical and poetic contexts is its descriptions in terms of fluid motion. We earlier on developed the idea of *waves* citing Whitman and Ashbery, Fletcher and Ferneyhough. Deleuze/Guattari take pains to distinguish the rhythm of waves from measured, cadenced movement. "However, rhythm is never the same as measure . . . There is indeed such a thing as measured, cadenced rhythm, relating to the coursing of a river between its banks or to the form of a striated space; but there is also a rhythm without measure, which relates to the upswell of a flow, in other words, to the manner in which a fluid occupies a smooth space."[19] The claim that smooth space is unmeasured space will find many different instantiations throughout *A Thousand Plateaus*. We recall a different but related distinction, quantified objectification versus a middle-voiced participation in musical flow, where quantification in itself is a concomitant of objectification, as though the music (or poem) is "out there." Deleuze/Guattari hit upon a similar concern in making a distinction between two types of science or scientific procedures, one consisting in reproduction and the other in following the course of a flow.

> Reproducing implies the permanence of a fixed point of *view* that is external to what is reproduced: watching the flow from the bank. But following is something different from reproduction. Not better, just different. One is obliged to follow when one is in search of the "singularities" of a matter, or rather of a material, and not out to discover a form . . . when one ceases to contemplate the course of a laminar flow in a determinate direction, to be carried away by a vortical flow; when one engages in a continuous variation of variables, instead of abstracting constants from them, etc.[20]

In this formulation, reproduction involves taking a point of view external to that being reproduced, whereas following intends no such external perspective. Laminar flow is at a consistent, regular rate. Vortical flow denotes turbulence. My only misgiving about the distinction of reproducing versus following is that "following" may be misconstrued as passive. In contrast, following along is active, or better yet, middle voiced. Follow me?

Along similar lines, Deleuze and Guattari distinguish "royal science" from "nomadic science." The former entails a *hylomorphic* model, where nature is understood in terms of matter and form, whereas nomadic science attends to content and expression.

> Thus matter, in nomad science, is never . . . homogenized matter, but is essentially laden with singularities (which constitute a form of content). And neither is expression formal; it is inseparable from pertinent traits (which constitute a matter of expression).
>
> . . .
>
> An invariable form for variables, a variable matter of the invariant: such is the foundation of the hylomorphic schema. . . . [In] nomadic science the relevant distinction is material-forces rather than matter-form. Here, it is not exactly a question of extracting constants from variables, but of placing variables themselves in a state of continuous variation.[21]

In saying that nomadic science is never homogenized matter, Deleuze and Guattari make a distinction that differs from Boulez's characterization where both smooth and striated space are homogenous, whereas the mixture of the two is considered *non-homogeneous*. In contrast, Deleuze/Guattari emphasize the variability of unmeasured flow outside of a metric, where only by placing a metric onto time/space do we denote equivalences, and hence assert homogeneity. In the sentence cited below, Deleuze/Guattari use the same term as Boulez, smooth, but with the distinction I have just mentioned. "Smooth space is precisely the space of the smallest deviation: therefore it has no homogeneity, except between infinitely proximate points, and the linking of proximities is effected independently of any determined path."[22] If I read Deleuze/Guattari correctly, "the linking of proximities . . . independent of any determined path" approximates the rhetorical trope of metonymy, at least when that trope is taken to mean association by contiguity.

As with Boulez, the smooth and striated spaces of Deleuze/Guattari exist in mixtures. The philosophers describe a dynamic relationship between the two modes of understanding and experiencing time and space. ". . . we must remind ourselves that the two spaces in fact exist only in mixture:

smooth space is constantly being translated, transversed into a striated space; striated space is constantly being reversed, returned to a smooth space."[23] Having gathered a sense of how the two proto-spaces can be variously conceptualized, as well as how they function as interactive forces or mutually affective modes of perception, we can now turn to literature and music specifically with such mixture in mind.

Fabric as Metaphor: Patchwork and Weaving; the Errant Thread

Fabric and the making of fabric by sewing, weaving, spinning, and pressing, give rise to a cluster of metaphors for living experience, each of which may be applied to music. Fiction, as we have seen, is an active making, like the shaping of clay or the kneading of bread. Earlier on we considered the story in Genesis 2 where God is the Divine worker with clay who instead of making pots shapes the first of mankind. We also noted that by this way of imagining, the human made in God's image is *homo faber*. *Faber* is the etymological ancestor of *fabric*, and fiction and fabrication are close cousins.

Walt Whitman, in "Song of Myself," answers the child's query "what is the grass" at first by saying "I do not know what it is any more than he." But he then ventures a guess or several guesses: "I guess it must be the flag of my disposition, out of hopeful green stuff woven. Or I guess it is the handkerchief of the Lord, A scented gift and remembrancer designedly dropped." We might imagine "out of hopeful green stuff woven" as an appropriate subtitle for the entirety of *Leaves of Grass*.

In the story of Philomela, as told by Ovid, Philomela is brutally raped by Tereus who then cuts out her tongue so that she cannot speak of what has happened to her. In Charles Martin's translation, "Upon her loom, she hangs a Thracian web and starts to weave threads of deep purple on a white background, depicting the crime."[24] The warp and woof of Philomela's bitter experience become embodied metaphor as realized in the tapestry that tells her tale, out of bitter stuff woven.

Walter Pater, in the Conclusion to his essay *The Renaissance*, writes of the evanescence of experience, where each moment is "gone while we try to apprehend it, of which it may ever be more truly said that it has ceased to be than that it is." We have seen the same idea expressed through the metaphor of wave as developed by Ashbery and Ferneyhough. Pater then goes on, shifting metaphors: "It is with this movement, with the passage and dissolution of impression, images, sensations, that analysis leave off—that continual vanishing away, that strange, perpetual weaving and unweaving of ourselves."[25]

Deleuze and Guattari develop a number of fabric-derived metaphors for time and space. We turn to them now, first considering the pressed fabric felt. The Wikipedia article on textile *felt* describes the process of condensing and pressing fibers together. Historically associated with nomadic tribes, felt, because of its texture and history, becomes one of the many metaphors for nomadic or smooth space in *A Thousand Plateaus*.[26] In the short section devoted to musical time-space, Deleuze/Guattari draw upon Boulez's discussion in *Music Today*, describing what we might think of as parallel to the pressed fibers of felt. "When there is no module, the distribution of frequencies is without break; it is 'statistical,' however small the segment of space may be; it still has two aspects, however, depending on whether the distribution is equal (non-directed smooth space), or more or less rare or dense (directed smooth space)."[27]

As previously noted, "statistical" evidently refers to "sound clouds," musical time-spaces generated by stochastic processes, where ranges of probability determine pitch, timbre, rhythmic distribution, and other constituents of musical events. I'm not sure why equal distribution is characterized as non-directed, while variants in density are characterized as directed. Directed music gravitates toward some goal, usually a combination of pitch and temporal placement, even if that goal is vaguely defined. (In tonal music, cadences provide the goal, temporally placed to close a musical phrase, while resolving harmonically and/or melodically to a stabilizing "perfection.") Or, alternatively, directed music denotes an intervallic space measured from some point to another point, forward or back in time, ascending or descending in motion. The density of a texture, sparse or rarified in its musical fabric, is largely independent of whether or not the texture is directed, although an extremely dense, variegated texture would tend to blot out any tendency toward goal orientation. Such a texture would be the musical analogue to the pressed fibers of felt. On the other hand, a musical texture, otherwise non-directed, might gradually thicken or gradually become more sparse. In such a case, we will hear directed motion (toward sparsity, toward density), even though the constituents of the texture, at any given moment, are not directed. We find a vivid example of the gradual drift toward sparsity in Ligeti's

Poème Symphonique for 100 metronomes (1962). The "ensemble" in *Poème Symphonique* is composed of 100 mechanical metronomes, wound and set to different speeds. The piece begins with all 100 metronomes ticking, with a resultant thick texture where the individual rates of ticking are not perceptible. As the metronomes wind down, the texture gradually thins out. Eventually, as the piece approaches its end, the polyphony of different click-rates begins to be perceptible. In this instance we find a slow, directed motion toward sparsity, where sufficient sparsity reveals a striated space embedded in what had been smooth.

While the pressed fibers of felt can be a clever metaphor for some kinds of musical textures, its use is limited, and, moreover, as metaphor I do not find it particularly revealing. For example, in the Ligeti piece we've just considered, an attenuating rainstorm would be a more apposite metaphor. Deleuze/Guattari discuss two other fabrics and their metaphorical extensions that I find far more useful in thinking about music: patchwork quilts and woven textures. To these I add a third, the metaphor of an errant thread. (In thinking of an errant thread, I am cognizant of the errant knight of Ariosto, Spenser, and others. The errant knight, both male and female, can appear unexpectedly, like the later American image of the cavalry coming to the rescue.)

Patchwork, as in free-form quilting, displays the heterogeneity that Deleuze/Guattari associate with nomadic space. The authors contrast this with the warp and woof of weaving, an example of striated space. In the quilt, each patch, within its own boundaries, is a woven space. The additive process, connecting patch to patch in free form, creates a more encompassing nomadic space. The patches are not equivalent in size, shape, or color; in short, there is no overall metric. The authors do not consider geometric quilts where the varied sizes and patterns of the patches form an overall regularity of quilt-rhythm; here the discontinuities and irregularities of texture combine to form a more encompassing regularity of flow.

Quilt and weave provide interesting metaphors for the fabric of narrative space in literature as well as its analogues in music. For example, it is often the case that each chapter within a novel explores a unified locale, time continuum, and network of characters, human or otherwise. Chapters can be linked, continuing locale, time, and characters; or they can abruptly shift to different locales, times, and characters. A unified narrative, with continuities of character, time, and place, will share the characteristics of a woven space; a narrative built on discontinuities of character, time, and place will be more like a patchwork quilt. A novel that is built on discontinuities of narrative, chapter to chapter, will usually tie all together in a larger narrative design, more like a geometric quilt.

To follow a thread is a common metaphor in narrative as well as in discourse more generally. It sometimes happens that a narrative thread (a local continuity) will disappear for an extended period, only to abruptly reemerge, breaking into a locale, time, and set of character relations that are discontinuous with the time and place of their earlier presence. Especially at the juncture of irruption, the errant thread violates that ongoing continuity of time and place. The errant thread may remain an alien presence, a strange misfit in its new environment, or it may be woven into the ongoing texture, converting nomadic space into settled space.

All of these possibilities apply to musical narrative as well as to literature. Within the worlds of classical music (I wish there were a better term for this amazingly diverse and long-lived repertory), the expanded musical narratives of the nineteenth century provide many examples. We might think of an opera composed of varied songs and varied combinations of singers as analogous to a patchwork quilt: each aria, duet, or larger ensemble is woven of interrelated stuff, while all the patches (arias, duets, ensemble pieces) combine to form the larger quilt of the whole. Analogues to a more geometric quilt is found is song forms with an ABA structure (as in the da capo aria), in minuets with their contrasting middle section (called the *trio* but not to be confused with trios comprising an ensemble of three), as well as in more complex palindromic forms (as in some of Béla Bartók's compositions). The metaphor of an errant thread is apposite in music in surprisingly varied ways. Beethoven, most famously in the final movement of his Ninth Symphony, brings back fragmentary recollections of the earlier three movements. It would have seemed that the work of these movements was completed and that they do not belong here at the outset of the finale. And they don't, for the baritone soloist rejects them, *Nicht diese Töne!* The three moments, fragments of three movements from the past, are like an errant thread breaking into the faltering weave at the outset of the finale. An inquisitive listener can find analogous examples in Wagner, Brahms, Debussy, Mahler, Schoenberg, and numerous others. For one example, I turn once again to Verdi's *Rigoletto*.

We have noted the regularities of pulse and groupings in Verdi's *La donna è mobile*. As such, the aria provides a clear example of striated space. A fragment of the song returns near the end of the opera; readers who know the work will recall this vividly. In the terms we have been developing, the fragment is an errant thread. A selective synopsis of the plot will clarify. At minimum, we need to take five characters into account: the Duke of Mantua, I will call him Mantua; Rigoletto the court jester; Gilda, Rigoletto's daughter; Sparafucile, an assassin; and Maddalena, Sparafucile's sister, a prostitute. Mantua is a debaucher, capable of murdering those he betrays. Rigoletto, at the outset of the opera, in his role as jester, is complicit with Mantua, mocking those whom Mantua has betrayed. Rigoletto is cursed by a doomed man, and he carries this burden until the tragic end of the opera. Later, Rigoletto's daughter Gilda is abducted, with Rigoletto's unwitting help. Rigoletto assumes (wrongly as it turns out) that the abduction was arranged by Mantua. Gilda returns safely, but Rigoletto, now remorseful for his past allegiance to Mantua, plots revenge. To this end, he hires Sparafucile. Sparafucile lures Mantua into his tavern under the guise of arranging an assignation with his sister, Maddalena. Rigoletto, who is with his daughter Gilda, sees this unfolding, and tells her to disguise herself as a man and proceed to Verona, where father and daughter will be reunited. It is while waiting for Maddalena that Mantua sings his song *"La donna è mobile."* After spending some time with the Duke, Maddalena pleads for his life. Sparafucile is willing but only if a substitute is found. With the implausibility, yet dramatic power that is typical of nineteenth-century Italian opera, Gilda has returned to the tavern and has heard the discussion. In the impetuosity of the moment, Gilda decides to sacrifice herself (this is an opera, after all). She is murdered and placed into a sack, as had been prearranged for the disposal of Mantua's body. Rigoletto picks up the sack and while carrying it to the river for disposal overhears Mantua, in the distance, singing a fragment from his earlier song, *"La donna è mobile."* Rigoletto opens the sack to find his dying daughter. The curse has been fulfilled. Dead men don't sing, and the tavern song doesn't belong here. While we the audience know better, from Rigoletto's perspective, the voice and song tear into the ongoing fabric of the plot, turning triumph to despair. In terms of our metaphor, it is an errant thread: it doesn't belong here. The moment that Rigoletto hears the song, leading to the opening of the sack and the realization that the body is Gilda's and not Mantua's, exemplifies a remarkable pairing of *anagnorisis* and *peripeteia* (realization and turn of fortune). Verdi's *Othello* (and Shakespeare's play on which it is based) provides another striking example.[28]

Demonic Leaping over Boundaries

We recall Deleuze's contrast of gods who divide space among them and demons who leap over boundaries, violate enclosures. Demonic spirits, as we normally think of them, are evil spirits, devils and the like. But the term is derived from Ancient Greek, δαίμων (*daímōn*), where it denotes a beneficent spirit. As such, respelled as *daemon*, this is the spirit that Harold Bloom surmises as allowing authors to surmount their own limitations. Here, the pertinent characteristic is of an agent who disrespects boundaries, who will appear where it will, without invitation, and without advance warning.

Kindred to our imagined errant thread, but placing greater emphasis on demarcated sections and agency, this aspect of nomadic space is very suggestive in musical contexts. There is a long tradition of dividing musical time-space into structural blocks. In popular music, we make a distinction between chorus and verse, each section with its characteristic content. In strophic songs, each subsequent strophe repeats the music from before, but with new words. Sonata forms provide a richer field in that their structural blocks form a hierarchy of greater and lesser divisions. We divide sonata forms most basically into exposition, development, and recapitulation. Finer divisions include thematic areas, transitions, developmental episodes, retransitions, and coda space. Finer yet would be phrases terminated by cadences. And getting even closer to the granular level, phrases are divided into their constituent motives, all the way down to individual sonorities. The approach is very hierarchical, parallel to dividing the earth into continents, continents into countries, countries into regions (provinces in Canada, states in the United States), regions into smaller regions (counties or parishes in the United States), on down to individual plots of land, which may be subdivided further into front yard, back yard, and so forth.

Converted into Deleuzian terms, such concepts of musical form (or geographical/political space) are quintessentially agrarian: the space of the sonata (like the earth) is subdivided into smaller sections, each with its own boundaries and characteristics, and these subspaces enter into hierarchical relationships, all subsumed under the unifying form of the sonata.[29]

When a musical idea, an event recalled or reemergent, wanders through divisions of time-space, violating the ongoing integral unity of that space, its workings are kindred to the demonic aspects of nomadic space, leaping over boundaries, appearing where they will. The *Fate* motive in Claude Debussy's *Pelléas et Mélisande* works this way, an agent that appears and disappears through the work. The *Fate* motive in Arnold Schoenberg's tone poem *Pelleas und Melisande* works similarly.[30]

Theodor Adorno, in *Mahler: A Musical Physiognomy*, recognizes a kindred technique in the symphonies of Gustav Mahler, manifest as early as the composer's First Symphony. Adorno discusses a fanfare, heard faintly "as if from behind the curtain that it vainly seeks to penetrate."[31] "Then, at the height of the movement, six measures before the return of the tonic D, the fanfare explodes in the trumpets, horns, and high woodwinds, quite out of scale with the orchestra's previous sound or even the preceding crescendo. It is not so much that this crescendo has reached a climax as that the music has expanded with a physical jolt. *The rupture originates from beyond the music's intrinsic movement, intervening from the outside.*"[32] Adorno subsequently names this rupture as a *Durchbruch* (breakthrough), a place from another world that breaks into and disrupts the ongoing fabric. If we make a distinction between daemonic (salutary or benign) and demonic (destructive, evil), the idyllic spaces of *Durchbruch* fall on the daemonic side of the ledger. Adorno also discusses the dark side of demonic space. In a very suggestive passage discussing breakthroughs comprising "a vortex of terror," Adorno invokes Jewish mysticism.

> Sometimes the characters of the outbreak and gloom become one in a tone of panic wildness . . . the power of the musical stream, its whirling into a vortex of terror, is potentiated above all in the development of the Third . . . The outbreak, from the place it has escaped from, appears as savage: the anti-civilization impulse as musical character. Such moments evoke the doctrine of Jewish mysticism that interprets evil and destructiveness as scattered manifestations of the dismembered divine power; all in all, the Mahlerian traits to which the cliché of pantheistic belief has been crudely applied are more likely to originate in a subterranean mystical stratum than in portentous monistic natural religion.[33]

Adorno's "vortex of terror" correlates with the "vortical flow" in nomadic fluid dynamics as described by Deleuze/Guattari. Adorno's "dismembered divine power" sounds more like Dionysian *sparagmos* than Jewish mysticism, but there are depictions of demonic agency in kabbalah that approximate the vortex of terror that Adorno describes. I do not know for sure, but I surmise that Adorno is referring to the kabbalistic idea of קליפות (*qelippot*). Arthur Green, in *A Guide to the Zohar,* discusses the Castilian Kabbalist Isaac of Soria (ca. 1225–1285), who envisioned a realm of evil, *Sitra Aḥara* ("the Other Side"). There *qelippot*, translated literally as "shells," become the vehicle for demonic forces. "The image of the shell, surrounding and protecting the inner content of a particular divine constellation, was part of the older kabbalistic legacy. But in the Zohar these shells take on the frightening countenance of actively demonic forces. The names of these *qelippot*—'stormy wind,' 'huge cloud,' 'flashing fire,' and 'radiance'—were derived from the blustery configuration envisioned by Ezekiel as surrounding the Divine Chariot."[34] The *qelippot* later become a significant aspect of Isaac Luria's kabbalah in sixteenth-century Safed. Gershom Scholem discusses *qelippot* (there transliterated as *kelippoth*) in that context in *On the Kabbalah and Its Symbolism*.[35] This, or other writings of Scholem, the first great modern scholar of kabbalah, were most likely the source for Adorno. This scholarship, originally published in German, was not available to Mahler's generation. There is no indication that Mahler had the linguistic skills to study the original texts, though it is possible that he was aware of some kabbalistic ideas from less scholarly sources.

While I agree with Adorno that Mahler massively repressed his Yiddish roots, as Adorno puts it, his music spoke with an accent, yet it seems highly doubtful that Mahler, even a Mahler who repressed his creative sources, would have had specific knowledge of this rather esoteric aspect of kabbalah. Yet some knowledge of such matters is not outside the realm of possibility. On the other hand, the idea of an overpowering force irrupting into the quotidian world from without would have had vivid resonance for any Jew of Mahler's generation, as well as for the generation that followed, the generation of the Holocaust. Every pogrom of Judaism's long diaspora would have instantiated such an overpowering force. Transferred into American sensibilities, African Americans might well recognize the sudden force of a lynching mob or the burning of an entire community.

In jazz and popular music, most of the dialectical variables between striated and smooth space occur between the rhythm section (usually drums and bass or sampled rhythms), which have a regular flow, and the soloist or singer who will come in and out of coincidence with that flow. Subtle inflections of regular pulse and groupings are an important part of the singer's craft, and that is true of "classical singing" as well as in the pop realms. (In this regard, listen to the rhythmic freedom with which Enrico

Caruso interprets the rhythmic notation of Verdi or Puccini, or for that matter any of the Italian opera composers in his repertory.) In addition to subtleties of rhythmic placement, singers and soloists, particularly in pop realms, subtly inflect pitch and timbre.

The irruption of a nomadic element into the ongoing flow is found less often in popular music, but examples can be found nonetheless. The Beatles tune "All You Need Is Love" is a case in point. Mark Spicer's "Strategic Intertextuality in Three of John Lennon's Late Beatles Songs" provides an analytic interpretation of the song.[36] The song opens with *La Marseillaise*, scored for brass. This alone is discontinuous with the song that follows. As we enter into the closing vamp ("love is all you need" repeated into a fade-out), we hear fragments of a J. S. Bach two-part invention (scored for piccolo trumpet, and so adding another nomadic layer where the two-part invention recalls Bach's Second Brandenburg Concerto), Glenn Miller's swing band hit "In the Mood," the British folk tune "Greensleeves," and Lennon/McCartney's earlier tune "She Loves You." For Spicer, this is an example of *bricolage*, a technique applied to the other songs discussed in the article as well.[37] Written for a television "spectacular" linking twenty-four countries by satellite, the first-ever attempt at a worldwide broadcast, the international sources of the quoted music were appropriate to the situation.[38] Nonetheless, they are readily perceived as alien to the ongoing texture of the song, superimposed from a time/space extrinsic from the striated space intrinsic to the song. Returning to our textile metaphors, we might say that "In the Mood" and the others introduce counter-weaves, patchwork superimposed on the principal weave of the song.

In a footnote, Spicer mentions Luciano Berio's *Sinfonia* (1968) as another example of musical bricolage.[39] The celebrated third movement of Berio's *Sinfonia* is a complex affair, a collage of Berio's music along with various fragments of texts including fragments from Samuel Beckett's *The Unnamable*, all superimposed on a sound-matrix derived from the Scherzo of Mahler's Second Symphony. The Mahler symphony movement is based, in turn, on an earlier song by Mahler, set to a text from the collection *Des Knaben Wunderhorn* (Youth's Magic Horn), where St. Anthony preaches to the fish. The Mahler song, and the symphony movement based on the song, emphasize a fluidity that may be heard, depending on the listener, as mocking simple faith, or as confirming that faith. The Mahlerian matrix provides the subterranean stream along which Berio's movement flows. Mahler's stream emerges and resubmerges repeatedly over the course of the movement. In addition, as the movement progresses, multiple fragments from the classical repertory waft in and out of the texture. As the movement progresses, fragments from Beckett memorably assert, over and over, "don't stop, keep on going." For me, as listener, it is as though the fusion (or confusion) of Mahler/Berio gives rise to quickly evanescent memories of the larger tradition that informed Mahler and informs Berio. The fragments are fleeting memories of that tradition, and the mantra from Beckett implores its continuation. Bricolage is a metaphor of construction, an assessment of how something is built. In contrast, the metaphors of nomadic space indicate a way of inhabiting that space. Bricolage objectifies, while nomadic space is amenable to the kind of middle-voiced expression we have been exploring throughout this study. While bricolage is useful as a formal designator, I find the metaphors of nomadic space to be more suggestive. Berio has taken the Mahlerian *Durchbruch* and reformulated its nomadic violations of time and space to form the singular expression of *Sinfonia*.

Cluster as Singular-Plural

In considering the cluster of names associate with the two types of time-space, I have not even mentioned the most celebrated division developed by Deleuze and Guattari: rhizomes and taproots. (They elevate rhizomes, while grudgingly granting taproots their place in the sun. Ask any gardener and they will tell you that both are necessary to the well-tended garden.) Moreover, while mentioning fluidity and hence waves as an aspect of nomadic space, I have not developed the division favored in physics, the particle and the wave. These and more metaphors might be fruitful in thinking about music, but rather than individual metaphors, it is the cluster of names and manifestations associated with each type, *as cluster*, that I want to consider further in closing this section.

We can begin by noting that the cluster of names and exemplifications associated with each type is not hierarchical; we might say that the distribution of subtypes within both nomadic and agrarian time/space is itself nomadic. The cluster including nomadic-smooth-demonic-fluid-non-hierarchical can be designated by any of its names, either depending on the particular situation, or by bringing multiple perspectives to any given situation. The same can be said about the cluster including agrarian-striated-delimited-settled-hierarchical. To be sure, once space is divided into stria, we can then induce hierarchies; we gave the example of sonata forms, as well as the divisions of continents-countries-provinces/counties-towns-individual plots, where each smaller division is subsumed under a larger division. The hierarchies in the military or in the Roman Catholic Church might provide analogous divisions and rankings. Yet in our primary cluster (agrarian-striated-delimited-settled-hierarchical) no term need be given priority over the others. In a similar way, while space-time might subsume both agrarian and nomadic modes (and their affiliates), neither mode need be considered as more encompassing or as being of a higher rank than the other.

I have intermittently drawn on kabbalistic thought for parallels to modes of musical perception and do so once again in thinking about the clustering of aspects subsumed under the bifurcated division of time-space in Deleuze/Guattari. The distribution of the ten sefirot can be considered as hierarchical with *Keter*, the crown, at the top. To be sure, the unformed, unfathomable source of all there is is imagined as inherent in this singular source of all being and becoming. Moreover, the ten sefirot can be understood as a linear development, the first engendering the second, and so forth until the divine circuit of the ten is completed. This top-down conception would be hierarchical, and hence a variant on Deleuze's agrarian space. But the sefirot are also imagined as an interactive circuit, with each attribute mutually conditioning and being conditioned by its interactions with the others. We might say that divine time includes the all-at-once, and that understanding the sefirot as unfolding in time does not take this quality of all-at-once into account. Conceptualized this way, the sefirot are an interactive cluster rather than a hierarchical state. The idea of an interactive cluster then extends to each individual sefirah.

Arthur Green, in *Ehyeh: A Kabbalah for Tomorrow*, discusses the sefirot in precisely these terms.

> Each of the ten *sefirot* is described by a host of symbolic terms, and it is the links created among these symbols that make Kabbalah such a profound and powerful tool for contemplative expansion of the mind. To follow the path of the kabbalists is to learn this language and to enter into the world of associative thinking that it inspires.
>
> . . .
>
> For this purpose, it is most useful to think of the *sefirot* not as some sort of cosmic "entities," but as *clusters of symbolic*

> *associations*, the mention of any of which (whether in daily life, in speech, or in a text) automatically brings to mind all the others as well. For this purpose, the conventional names of the *sefirot* (*keter, hokhmah, binah*, etc.) have no particular importance; they are simply one more layer in the complex network of associated symbols.[40]

Green goes on to discuss the cluster of names and associations that are concomitants of *binah* and its various affiliations with the other sefirot.[41] *Binah*'s cluster of associations by analogy extends into everyday human interactions with places (palace, temple, Eden), persons (mother, spouse), modes of cognition (reflection, understanding), and more encompassing nature (quarry, spring, source).

Moving away from the images of kabbalah to the conventions of everyday speech, we can consider how each singularity invites (and requires) multiple perspectives on its individuality. Among my personal attributes are son to my parents, spouse to my wife, father to my children, nephew to aunts and uncles, uncle to my nieces and nephews, student to my teachers, teacher to my students, and on and on.

Just so, a musical event, a singularity, invites a multiplicity of names, associations, and perspectives. This holds true if we are thinking about some moment in a piece of music (or literature) or if we are thinking about a musical composition as a whole, whether it be a song or some larger-scale composition, a symphony, ballet, and so forth. Each vital interpreter (performer, scholar, listener, reader) brings their own cluster of shapings, associations, and the like. Each singularity is a multiplicity as well.[42]

10

What Repetition Can Do

Time's Arrows

Repetition at the Outset: Say Again?

Rodgers and Hammerstein's song "Oh, What a Beautiful Morning" from *Oklahoma* begins with a repeated line, "There's a bright golden haze in the meadow." Curly McLain's eyes wander across the meadow as he observes the bright golden haze of morning. His voice confirms, affirms what his eyes see. And then he says it again, well, sings it again, this time descending to the tonic note (although the harmony, the relative minor, disallows tonal closure—after all, there's more to say). After this introductory verse, the music confirms the musical tonic, bringing us into the principal topic and affect of the song, "Oh what a beautiful morning."

The initial reiteration is a reaffirmation, as though Curly is settling into the hazy morning. We see a beautiful vista and stop for just a moment to better take it all in. There is a psychological realism here. This despite the whimsy of measuring the height of corn through comparison with the height of an elephant's eye, elephants being presumably nonexistent in the corn fields of Oklahoma. I speculate, irresponsibly and without any evidence whatsoever (it's done all the time), that the brilliant Oscar Hammerstein had at some point visited the Bronx Zoo. That's where the elephants of his childhood lived; mine too. But I digress. My topic is repetition (not elephants) and the many, many different things that repetition can do, in music and in her sibling art poetry.

∾

I spent twenty-eight years of my life in Minnesota, where corn fields are abundant. Through all those years, Hammerstein's lyrics came to mind each time I drove past a corn field. The corn *was* as high as an elephant's eye. And Hammerstein made it so.

∾

One of the many ways that repetition can be used at the outset of a song (or at the outset of a more extended musical composition) is by way of affirmation, a settling in that brings us into a musical/poetic time and place. In such cases, we might imagine the reiteration as bringing an objective space inward, correlating observation and emotional/cognitive response, bridging outer and inner to achieve a middle voice. Or we might reverse the process to discover an inward reckoning projected outward. In either case, the iteration is conditioned, modified, and augmented by the reiteration.

I find an extraordinary development of a related but distinctive use of repetition at the outset of Claude Debussy's "Prélude à l'Après-midi d'un faune." Whereas in the Rodgers and Hammerstein song the repetition is a settling into the beautiful morning and a solidifying of the singer's emotional response, Debussy's opening repetitions achieve a sense of coming-into-presence as memory, emotion, and atmosphere gradually (and only partially) clarify and take hold.

Debussy's tone poem *translates* the words, images, emotions, and sounds of Stéphane Mallarmé's poem "L'Après-midi d'un faune" into wordless music. Though tone poems, musical compositions inspired by literary works, were common in the late nineteenth and early twentieth centuries, I cannot bring to mind another work of the Prelude's stature that reimagines a poem of equivalent stature. Both Mallarmé's poem and Debussy's tone poem are pinnacles of their respective art forms, and though neither *needs* the other (that is to say that I can learn to read the poem without knowing the music and learn to hear the music without knowing the poem) each powerfully augments our understanding of the other. I find a somewhat analogous case in Arnold Schoenberg's "Verklärte Nacht," at least so far as knowing the Richard Dehmel's poem augments our understanding of Schoenberg's tone poem. Like Debussy's Prelude, Schoenberg's string sextet is a masterpiece of the first rank. However, the parallel only goes that far. The Dehmel poem, I surmise, would be known only by specialists were it not for Schoenberg's composition. Schoenberg takes a mediocre poem and turns it into an extraordinary work of music. Debussy takes a landmark poem and turns it into a landmark composition.

To reduce Mallarmé's poem to a narrative is egregiously insufficient. The music of the words, the elusive images, the play of light and shadow, the heat of the afternoon sun versus the coolness of the morning shade, the groping toward what happened (or was it only dreamt), the sense of erotic longing, the sublimation of eros into music/poetry, and the resonances of earlier myth and storytelling are all integral to the poem.[1]

Although the tone poem is a careful translation of the poem into musical terms, the opening strategies of poem and prelude couldn't be more different. Mallarmé opens his poem with a proclamation, then a recollection "so clear," which quickly moves to self-doubt. Here are the opening lines, along with Henry Weinfield's translation.

> Ces nymphs, je les veux perpétuer.
>
> Si clair,
>
> Leur incarnat léger, qu'il voltige dans l'air
> Assoupi de sommeils touffus.
>
> Aimai-je un rêve?

> These nymphs that I would perpetuate:
> so clear
> And light, their carnation, that it floats in the air
> Heavy with leafy slumbers.
> Did I love a dream?[2]

In contrast, the Prelude opens with what I have called a gradual coming-into-presence. Part of that presence is atmospheric, the sultry heat of the afternoon and an accompanying languor that tempers the faun's reflections. And part of that coming-into-presence is a groping toward recapturing a sense of what had happened, as though recapturing the memory could fulfill the faun's erotic longing. In the poem, the faun recalls (uncertain of reality or dream) raping or attempting to rape two nymphs whom he happened upon as they slept, their arms intertwined in the dark foliage. This recollection gradually and intermittently gets filled in with details as the poem progresses. It is this sense of emerging atmosphere, emotion, and eros that Debussy so beautifully captures in the opening three musical phrases of his Prelude.

Having established the faun's first, partial recollections of the rape, Mallarmé gives us a sense of the atmosphere, the sultry afternoon that conditions the faun's mood. Mallarmé's faun then refers to a flute that he has fashioned out of a reed found by the water's edge. Here are lines 14 through 22 of the poem, followed by Weinfield's translation.

> . . . par l'immobile et lasse pâmoison
> Suffoquant de chaleurs le matin frais s'il lutte,
> Ne murmure point d'eau que ne verse ma flûte
> Au bosquet arrosé d'accords; et le seul vent
> Hors des deux tuyaux prompt à s'exhaler avant
> Qu'il disperse le son dans un pluie aride,
> C'est, à l'horizon pas remué une ride,
> Le visible et serein souffle artificial
> De l'inspiration, qui regagne le ciel.

> . . . through the motionless and weary swoon
> Of stifling heat that suffocates the morning,
> Save from my flute, no waters murmuring
> In harmony flow out into the groves;
> And the only wind on the horizon no ripple moves,
> Exhaled from my twin pipes and swift to drain
> The melody in arid drifts of rain,
> In the visible, serene and fictive air
> Of inspiration rising as if in prayer.

In Debussy's orchestration the faun's reed flute becomes a modern flute, and later an oboe, then clarinet (double reed, single reed) as well. The work opens, famously, with the flute alone playing a chromatic line descending and then ascending a tritone.[3] The faun's musical figure is repeated immediately, the first of an extraordinary wealth of repetitions that stay fresh in their ever-changing atmospheres.

As the second chromatic gesture ends, the flute's rhythms broaden, incorporating two gestures with a related contour: C♯ up to D♯, ascending to G♯ down to E, then G♯ up to B, ascending to C♯ down to A♯. Symbolically, we can designate the related contours, as <+ (+) –>, a dyadic ascent, reaching upward to a dyadic descent. This rising and falling might be interpreted as breathing, sighing, or as mimicking recollected tumescence and detumescence. As the first musical sentence continues to unfold, this breathing, sighing, eros move into the French horns where the diffused sound creates a distancing effect, an echoing that fuses remembering and misremembering. The horn's figure, E-F, B♭-A♭, has the same contour as the close of the flute's melody, now broadened through wider pitch intervals and expanded through a dilated temporal span. In a final iteration, the E-F returns, this time ascending E-F-F♯ as D♮ arrives in the bass and the sentence concludes, overlapping with the initiation of a second sentence.

The close of the first sentence, coincident with the opening of the second sentence, feels like a point of arrival, but not a cadence, hence not a point of conclusion. The cadence will arrive only as the third phrase ends.

The second musical sentence begins with the flute playing exactly as before, only now accompanied by shimmering chords in the strings. The isolated flute has been placed into an atmosphere; the shimmering evocative of heat refraction. This time, the close of the flute's melody is handed off to the oboe, and later the clarinet, other "pipes" in Debussy's pastoral coloration.

The third musical phrase, this time a musical period (divided symmetrically into antecedent and consequent), expands and extends the flute's melody with florid figuration so that the first iteration takes up five bars, fully half of the ten-measure period. As in the second sentence, the flute is placed in an atmosphere, this time with more motion/emotion, a wavering figure that will return later in the piece during its erotic climax. The second half of the larger phrase, the consequent of the musical period, brings back the initial gesture in the flute leading into new elaboration, and finally into the first cadence of the piece (to the dominant of the eventual tonic).

The journey from poem to tone poem to dance was completed when Vaslav Nijinsky choreographed Debussy's music for Ballets Russe in 1912. A version of the dance posted on YouTube, the Bolshoi Ballet with Nikolay Tsiskaridze as the faun, nicely complements my own understanding of the music's opening phrases.[4] The curtain rises only after the flute's first solo; we find the faun supine, eyes closed. He begins to awaken and stir only with the second phrase, stretching more pronouncedly during the third and final phrase of the work's opening. This beautifully captures the sense of coming-into-presence that I have described, the first iteration of the faun's melody as liminal, a coming into consciousness, not actually played but only imagined in half-sleep.

We move from a consideration of Debussy's piece to more general thoughts about repetition, noting that a poor speaker repeats haphazardly while a gifted speaker repeats strategically. Poets and composers have refined repetition into high art. The functions, affects, and cognitive complexities of poetic and musical repetition are bewilderingly various. And while the scholars of literature have given extensive consideration to the many roles that repetition can take on, musical scholarship has given minimal consideration to the myriad ways repetition takes on meaning. At least, this has been my experience. The question is not just to notice that measures x to z repeat material from measures a to c, which we do all the time; the question is what are x to z doing there and how do they in their context impact the way we think about a to c.

Even if we limit our consideration to literal repetition alone, further limiting that to repetition that happens as a piece begins, we find endless varieties of settling in emotionally and cognitively, coming-into-presence through emergent perceptions (taking inward and projecting outward), triggering an impetus that energizes a wave, signifying some mysterious potential to be realized over the course of the piece, or merely announcing *hineni, hineni,* "here I am, here I am!"

Poetry can range from being highly reiterative, as in much of Gertrude Stein's poetry and prose, to a constant transformational flow, as in the longer poems of A. R. Ammons and John Ashbery. Music has an analogous range, from the highly reiterative works of Steve Reich, or the equally reiterative rhythms of many dance forms, to the constant and quicksilver transformations of Milton Babbitt or Brian Ferneyhough.

In *Feeling and Form*, the philosopher Susanne Langer characterizes "the great dramatic forms" in terms of *comic rhythm* and *tragic rhythm*. Langer's concept of comedy and tragedy is not equivalent to "funny" and "sad." Comic rhythms are repetitive or cyclic, like a theme and variations. Tragic rhythms are unilinear. Their trajectory can happen only once. And so a comic rhythm might entail great sorrow, the incessant return of the repressed, while a tragic rhythm might entail a life well lived. "Destiny in the guise of Fortune is the fabric of comedy; it is developed by comic action, which is the upset and recovery of the protagonist's equilibrium, his contest with the world and his triumph by wit, luck, personal power, or even humorous, or ironical, or philosophical acceptance of mischance."[5] Here Langer's characterization of comic rhythm lists various modes of *triumph* over misfortune. Later in the book (334), Dante's *Commedia* is among her examples of comic rhythm, so designated because of its never-ending cycles. Classical rhetoric would have named the *Commedia* as such because at the end of Dante's journey all are reconciled to Divine justice. But Langer emphasizes the great poem's cyclic patterns, most proper to the *Inferno* and *Paradiso*, and in contrast to the more-or-less linear ascent in *Purgatorio*. The rhythms of despair. like the rhythms of eros, are "comic" in that comic rhythms are repetitive, eluding final resolution. (A different but related sense of Dante's *Commedia* is developed by Wye Allanbrook in *The Secular Commedia* (31–32). There, Allanbrook links the range of characters in Dante's *Commedia* to the range of characters in opera buffa while also emphasizing the happy endings of both Dante's poem and opera buffa.)

Langer contrasts repetitive comic rhythms with the singular events of tragic rhythms.

> As comedy presents the vital rhythm of self-preservation, tragedy exhibits that of self-consummation.
>
> . . .
>
> But creatures who are destined, sooner or later, to die . . . hold the balance of life only precariously, in the frame of a total movement that is quite different; the movement from birth to death. Unlike the simple metabolic process, the deathward advance of their individual lives has a series of stations that are not repeated; growth, maturity, decline. That is the tragic rhythm.[6]

TV situation comedies can go on and on, episode after episode, with each episode variations on a theme. There cannot be a sequel to Hamlet, Othello, or Romeo and Juliet.

Camille Paglia, in *Sexual Personae*, puts a different slant on related topics, bringing gender and sexuality into the discussion. Paglia's gendered, binary essentialism is likely to rub many of today's readers the wrong way. She means to be provocative, perhaps with unintended consequences.

> Female tragic protagonists are rare. Tragedy is a male paradigm of rise and fall, a graph in which dramatic and sexual climax are in shadowy analogy.
>
> . . .
>
> Tragedy plays a male game, a game it invented to snatch victory from the jaws of defeat. It is not flawed choice, flawed action, or even death itself which is the ultimate human dilemma. . . . the chthonian drama that has no climax but only an endless round, cycle upon cycle. . . . Tragedy's inhospitality to woman springs from nature's inhospitality to man.[7]

> Nature's cycles are woman's cycles.[8]
>
> The western idea of history as a propulsive movement into the future, a progressive of Providential design climaxing in the revelation of a Second Coming, is a male formulation. No woman, I submit, could have coined such an idea, since it is a strategy of evasion of woman's own cyclic nature, in which man dreads being caught. Evolutionary or apocalyptic history is a male wish list with a happy ending, a phallic peak.
>
> Woman does not dream of transcendental or historical escape from natural cycle, since she *is* that cycle. Her sexual maturity means marriage to the moon, waxing and waning in lunar phases. Moon, month, menses: same word, same world.[9]

While I would dispute that evolutionary history necessarily has a happy ending, or phallic peak (though theories of inception do *begin* with a big bang), Paglia's gendering of unilinear versus cyclic has indubitable historical resonance; we need go no further than *father time* and *mother nature*.

Brought into the realm of poetry and music, I think of a dialectic between what Paglia genders as male and female and what Langer characterizes as tragic and comic. Poems and musical works can be understood as having a dynamic relation between that which returns, exactly or transformed, and that which goes on, either to conclusion or to dissipation without sense of closure.

Life is that way too. I wake up each morning and go to sleep each night. I celebrate and mourn dates that are recurrent, like anniversaries and *Yahrzeit*. The seasons end and they return, spring training being the paramount reminder of such return for baseball lovers such as myself. And all the while, I grow older, approaching the day marked differently in my own calendar of life, the day when I will be no more, except in memory, and that too eventually will fade into nothingness.

Gilles Deleuze: Difference and Repetition

For an extended philosophical treatment of repetition, I return to Gilles Deleuze's book of 1968, *Différence et repetition*.[10] In the author's preface, Deleuze says that he wants to develop a concept of "difference without negation" along with a concept of repetition "in which a 'differential' is disguised and displaced . . . independent of the negative and liberated from the identical."[11] "Difference without negation" is presumably an anti-Hegel stance, whereas in Hegelian dialectic each idea or event spawns its opposite.

I paraphrase Deleuze's twofold proposal as simultaneously entailing difference as "not 'not that'" *and* repetition as "not identical." If I read this aright (always difficult to say with an author as elusive as Deleuze), then the attitude toward difference and repetition is transformational. X transformed into Y (e.g., the girl named Rose become the woman named Rose) exemplifies "not 'not that'" (Rose = Rose) while "not identical" (girl ≠ woman).

As he continues, Deleuze distinguishes repetition from generalization: "Repetition is not generality . . . Generality presents two major orders: the qualitative order of resemblances and the quantitative order of equivalences."[12] So, for example, we generalize in saying that lemons (generally) resemble one another, and that 2 + 2 = 4. Deleuze continues, "The exchange or substitution of particulars defines our conduct in relation to generality." When a recipe calls for one lemon, it does not specify a particular, unique lemon.

In contrast, "Repetition as a conduct and as a point of view concerns non-exchangeable and non-substitutable singularities."[13] Deleuze goes on rather enigmatically (as is often the case), "exchange is the criterion of generality, theft and gift are those of repetition." Presumably the point is that exchange implies equivalence (e.g., this much money for this many lemons), while gift and theft imply specificity (I stole *this* lemon and gave it to *you*).

> To repeat is to behave in a certain manner, but in relation to something unique or singular which has no equal or equivalent . . . This is the apparent paradox of festivals: they repeat an "unrepeatable." They do not add a second and third time to the first, but carry the first to the "nth" power . . . as Péguy says, it is not Federation Day that commemorates or represents the fall of the Bastille, but the fall of the Bastille which celebrates and repeats in advance all the Federation Days . . . [14]

As I had previously paraphrased Deleuze's understanding of difference and repetition as *transformational*, I can add that it is also *generative*; repetition emerges out of the singularity that engenders it. This forward, progressive sense of repetition will be a constant in Deleuze's way of understanding repetition; while I find the generative and transformational aspects of conceiving repetition as so conceived to ring true, I also find that Deleuze's single-minded insistence on forward progression to be counterintuitive to reflective or reminiscent aspects of repetition that I hear in music and poetry. We will return to this concern shortly.

For me the most striking aspect of Deleuze's consideration of difference and repetition centers around what we might call the engendering principle in organic growth, where the organism self transforms while repeating selfhood. In that music and poetry mimic organic growth, may even be considered as instantiations of organic growth, the same principles apply. Deleuze describes repetition in this sense as disguised or covered. "Repetition must be understood in the pronominal. We must find the Self of repetition, the singularity within that which repeats . . . ."[15] In this context, Deleuze goes on to distinguish two types of repetition:

> The two repetitions are not independent. One is the singular subject, the interiority and the heart of the other, the depths of the other. The other is only the external envelope, the abstract effect . . .
> However, we wished to show the coexistence of these instances in every repetitive structure, to show how repetition shows identical elements which necessarily refer back to a latent subject which repeats itself through these elements, forming an "other" repetition at the heart of the first . . . The material sense results from this other, as if secreted by a shell.[16]

Paul Ricoeur develops a similar idea in *Oneself as Another*. There he posits a dialectical relationship between self as *idem* (identical) and self as *ipse* (self-same, but capable of changing over time).[17]

As already noted, Deleuzian repetition is transformational and generative. The hidden or disguised force behind organic difference maintains the same (the applicable pronoun remains unchanged), a hidden repetition underlying manifest change. This underlying force is "as if secreted by a shell." This disguised principle of repetition is pretty close to, if not identical with, Ferneyhough's idea of *figure*, there restricted to musical thought by analogy with a wave, here broadened to subsume transformation in nature. We can say that art mimics nature, or better yet, we can say that one of the myriad ways that the forces of nature are manifest and augmented is through art. We recall that figure (or *figura*) as Ferneyhough develops the term refers to an underlying generative dynamic that manifests in change.

In that context, Ferneyhough distinguished force from energy. Here is part of a passage from *Il Tempo della Figura* that I cited earlier. "Energy is invested in concrete musical objects to the extent that they are capable of rendering forces acting upon them visible. Lines of force arise in the space between objects—not space as a temporal lacuna, atopia, but at that moment of conceptual differentiation in which identity is born—and take as their vehicular object the connective impetus established in the act of moving from one discrete musical event to another."[18] Ferneyhough's distinction between *energy* (manifest in concrete musical objects) and *force* (the space between objects through which emergent identity is born) is roughly equivalent to Deleuze's distinction between his two types of repetition: repetition that is visible or audible versus an underlying repetition that engenders the visible and audible.

The Deleuzian idea of repetition has interesting implications for understanding repetition in music and poetry. On one extreme of a spectrum, we can have manifest repetition that, aside from temporal placement, is identical to that which precedes it, as in "I will say this again and again, I will say this again and again." Even here, the second iteration might involve subtle change, not in words but in inflection: "I will *say this* again and again, I *will* say this again and again." On the other extreme of the spectrum, all the words are changed, but there is an underlying continuity in gesture: "I will say this again and again, repeating myself as I go along." We might go so far as to say that each lyric poem has an underlying force, disguised *and* revealed through the variables of trope, music, semantics, and affect that are apparent in the poem.

In music, as in poetry, there is a wide spectrum of types of repetition, from the extremes of non-literal repetition in Ferneyhough, to the extremes of literal repetition in Steve Reich or Brazilian dance rhythms.

༄

Within the world of "classical music" composition, scholarship, performance, and critical response, practitioners often take sides. If they admire the aesthetic of Steve Reich or John Adams (two very different composers, both pigeonholed as minimalists), they dismiss the music of Brian Ferneyhough or Milton Babbitt (two very different composers, both pigeonholed as maximalists). I think that while we must grant that music that constantly and radically transforms generally presents a greater cognitive challenge, just in terms of keeping track of where we are in relation to where we've been, we must also recognize that excellence in music takes many forms. I see no reason to disparage the excellence of Steve Reich because I recognize the excellence of Brian Ferneyhough, and vice versa. My experience is that some critics (and listeners) quickly disparage what they cannot understand, instead of realizing that it is their lack of capacity or dedication (or simply available time) that causes a deficit in evaluative criteria. I'm fine with someone saying, "I don't have the time or will to grapple with the complexities of Brian Ferneyhough's music," but that is not the same as saying, with an air of objective observation, "If I can't hear it, it's all noise." That's stupidity and arrogance.

∽

Repetition plays a significant and varied role in Freudian theory, some aspects of which are discussed by Deleuze. Of particular interest is Deleuze's discussion of Freud's *death instinct*. Freud's late work reduced the various psychological drives to two fundamental types: Eros and Thanatos, the latter named after the Greek personification of death. As Freud understands it, Thanatos manifests as a psychological drive to return to pre-organic form; in contrast, the life-force, Eros, opposes this instinctual return to the elements. Here is Deleuze commenting on Freud's death instinct as generative of repetition.

> Death has nothing to do with a material model. On the contrary, death instinct may be understood in relation to masks and costumes. Repetition is that which disguises itself in constituting itself, that which constitutes itself only by disguising itself.
> . . .
> I do not repeat because I repress. I repress because I repeat, I forget experiences only in the mode of repetition . . . Eros and Thanatos are distinguished in that Eros must be repeated, can be lived only through repetition, whereas Thanatos (as transcendental principle) is that which gives repetition to Eros, that which submits Eros to repetition.[19]

Presumably "Thanatos . . . gives repetition to Eros" through its opposition, an opposition requiring a response that is manifest in the infinite varieties of repetition. Eros, so-considered, is a defense against death. Seen in this light, heard in this way, repetition as manifest in music and poetry is a variety of the life-drive, a defense against death. We will return to this larger sense of eros as this book nears its conclusion.

We might well argue that such an all-encompassing idea of repetition becomes worthless: if it's everywhere, repetition cannot be a useful differentiator. Yet the idea that repetition need not be exact or literal can be extremely useful in understanding music and poetry. Questioning what changes, and what remains the same, along with wherefore and how so, should be central to any thought about these sibling arts.

We have considered Deleuze's concept of repetition as "first to the nth power," as essentially generative. Along these lines, Deleuze opposes repetition to generalities of habit as well as to the particularities of memory or reminiscence.[20] As becomes clearer later in the book, Deleuze's reasons for this counterintuitive denial of habit and reminiscence as instances of repetition have to do with the correlation of his idiosyncratic concept of repetition with his ideas of *passive synthesis* and *active synthesis*. He posits a passive synthesis that connects past to future via the present. Our experience of duration is a resultant of this passive synthesis (he cites Hume in this context). Supported by passive synthesis, active synthesis is concomitant with memory and understanding.[21] Later, Deleuze names passive synthesis *Habitus* and active synthesis *Eros-Mnemosyne*, the latter referring to the Greek muse of memory.[22] Hence, for Deleuze, habit and reminiscence are respectively products of passive and active synthesis, and distinct from his concept of repetition per se. My own sense of repetition is Janus-faced. Deleuze's sense of repetition as generative and transformational usefully corrects the tendency to think in terms of "I repeat what I said before," as a default, while ignoring (even to the point of making its grammatically difficult to say) "what I say, I will say," or more precisely "what I say, (becomes) what I say." In this battle of generative versus reflective, I refuse to take sides, because I need both. I want it both ways. In the arts as in life, what we call repetition is Janus-faced. As I understand it, time's arrows run both ways, and in the mystical middle of before and after lies an eternal now.

In what may strike my reader as a far-fetched analogy, I turn to Jewish commentary on the name of God, Arthur Green as in אהיה *Eyeh: A Kabbalah for Tomorrow.*

> The name Y-H-W-H should not be translated as "God" or "Lord," but rather as "Is-Was-Will Be." It is not really a noun at all, but a verb artificially arrested in motion and made to

> serve as it were a noun. A noun that is really a verb is one you can never hold too tightly. As soon as you think you've "got it," that you understand God as some clearly defined "entity," that noun slips away and becomes a verb again.[23]

We recall Bloom's discussion of Emerson as American prophet, where he quotes Henry James Sr: "Try to grasp the American prophet and Proteus slips away."[24] In the case of repetition, we do have a verbal form, *to repeat*. This transformational and generative repeating as it operates in literature, music, theater, and dance is, was, and will be. This is not to equate repetition with God, but to realize that the temporal qualities we attribute to divinity are qualities of human expression and human experience inherent in the art that we make.

I circle back to John Hollander's "Instructions to the Landscaper" where the entrance to the garden is also its exit, representing the whole garden as we enter, seen again as we exit, so "that one sees the entrance again in the new light of what it had always stood for." Janus-faced repetition, simultaneously recollecting and furthering motion and emotion, lies at the seat of our greatest joys and deepest sorrows. Embracing all of our tomorrows and all of our yesterdays, time's vectors run both ways. The tortured soul of Shakespeare's Macbeth understood this.

> Tomorrow, and tomorrow, and tomorrow,
> Creeps in this petty pace from day to day,
> To the last syllable of recorded time;
> And all our yesterdays have lighted fools
> The way to dusty death.[25]

Unlike Macbeth, who seemingly has no sense of humor, Hamlet never loses his sense of humor, although it has become a mocking humor, more bitter than sweet.

> Alas, poor Yorick! I knew him, Horatio. A fellow of infinite jest, of most excellent fancy. He hath borne me on his back a thousand times. And now how abhorred in my imagination it is! My gorge rises at it. Here hung those lips that I have kiss'd I know not how oft. Where be your gibes now? Your gambols? your songs? Your flashes of merriment that were wont to set the table on a roar? Not one now, to mock your own

grinning? Quite chap-fall'n? Now get you to my lady's chamber, and tell her, let her paint an inch thick, to this favour she must come. Make her laugh at that.[26]

Somewhere Harold Bloom posits that Yorick was the one unsullied love of Hamlet's life. This catalogue of repetitions is summoned up in the graveyard where Hamlet's other love, Ophelia, is soon to be interred. It posits a termination of repetition in death. But even here, the merriment, now abhorred, returns. Hamlet's love for Ophelia is sullied either by Hamlet's madness, a mounting suspicion that has become pathological, or by Hamlet's prodigious death-drive that infects those around him in its overwhelming force. Such is the power of repetition.

No poet, not even Dante, has the emotional and cognitive range of Shakespeare. In particular, humor, so basic to human health, is rarely part of Dante's *Commedia*, while it is sprinkled graciously throughout Shakespeare, even in his tragedies. Even so, from the eternal rounds of the *Inferno* to and through the eternal dance of *Paradiso*, Dante's *Divine Comedy* might well be the greatest study of repetition that we have had.

Temporal Vectors

We will distinguish three basic ways that we experience the flow of time in literature, theater, and music: future oriented, past oriented, and as now-time. I think of these as *temporal vectors*, metaphoric forces that condition our cognitive and emotional lives. Simply put, thought and emotion might reflect on passed events, anticipate future events, or be immersed in some present time, without thought of past or future. These three temporal vectors are not mutually exclusive. I can think of the past while fearing or happily anticipating the future. I can be immersed in a now-time (erotic or ecstatic) that envelopes a depth of then-times, past or future or both. Repetition, through literal reiteration, or modified reiteration, or through the continuity of a deeper, hidden force, can be understood to be generative of all three vectors as well as their mixtures.

In literature, past, future, or present orientation is built into the syntax of language. When music is wed to words, verbal syntax provides temporal orientation. Although in sophisticated music the sense of the music can contradict the sense of the words, when this happens the irony involved normally does not impact temporal orientation but rather cognitive and emotional response. And while it would be foolish to say that temporal orientation is a simple matter when language is involved, such matters are far more complicated in music without words.

In instrumental music, there are instances where temporal orientation is fairly clear. The outset of an energized musical sentence, as in the opening of Beethoven's Fifth Symphony, drives toward the cadence. Its principal temporal flow is future oriented, and repetition is in service of that drive. In contrast, when a musical idea returns in the space of a coda or as we near the end of a musical composition, repetition serves as recollection. Transitional space, that which connects one theme area to another, can combine future and past orientations, remembering where we've just been, anticipating where we are heading.[27] Temporal orientation along with emotional response is not a matter of a toggle switched off/on indicating future/past or happy/sad, but a matter of shading, we might say ratios of mixture, as in a variable recipe: ⅛–½ cup honey to ½–¾ tablespoon salt, depending on how sweet or savory you want the dish. We can think of a temporal spectrum, where a remote past-perfect lies at one extreme and an equally remote future-imperfect lies at the other, and where both termini are asymptotic: either extreme can approached but never actually be reached. Each event is either weighted in one direction or another, predominantly future or past in its orientation, or placed in the middle of the scale, hovering in a now-time that will always have traces of past and future.

My thoughts return to David Lewin. Within *Generalized Musical Intervals and Transformations* Lewin develops a graphic system comprising nodes and arrows. The nodes contain musical events, usually ranging from a single note to a motif of three or more notes. The arrows connect the nodes, showing how one node of musical content morphs into another through some defined transformation. In generating his graphs, Lewin adopts a convention whereby time progresses left to right on the page, so that an arrow pointing to the right moves from earlier to later. Left to right arrows are predominant in Lewin's graphs, but he also allows for right to left arrows.[28]

While Lewin's right to left arrows imply a relation of later to earlier, rather than earlier to later, their functions, as Lewin describes them, focus on inverse relations rather than temporal orientation. For example, an ascending C major triad can be depicted as containing the network C → E, E → G, and C → G, respectively comprising the intervals (in semitones) of +4, +3, and +7. A mirror image, for example a descending F minor triad, becomes A♭ ← C, F ← A♭, and F ← C, respectively −4, −3, and

−7. While temporal orientation might be implied in the direction of the arrows, thinking forward and back in time is not emphasized in Lewin's commentaries; rather it is the reciprocals of + and −, right and left, that are brought out by the analysis.[29]

Temporal orientation becomes central in Lewin's article "Music Theory, Phenomenology, and Modes of Perception," which we recall was written immediately on the completion of *Generalized Intervals and Transformations*. There, Lewin imagines a moving cursor placed at a continuing now-time, each moment of which reevaluates the implications of what has preceded as well as what is now anticipated. Lewin's examples involve a relatively short span of time, and, to my knowledge, he didn't develop the model as it might apply over larger spans of music. One easy fix for this would entail moving the imaginary cursor by larger units of time, for example, considering an entire melody as a temporal unit to be compared with other similarly understood temporal units. In that each moment (or dilated moment) can confirm or negate the anticipations of a previous moment, we might extrapolate a sense of how a particular moment is weighted, emphasizing the past through reevaluation or continuing into the future through affirming (and thus not necessarily reconsidering) the anticipations of the past. Since quantitative analysis necessarily objectifies, the phenomenological sense of such moments, the "weight" of their temporal orientation, would be qualitative rather than quantitative, matching the qualities of retrospection, anticipation, and immersion in a now-time that we experience more generally.

As I imagine further developing Lewin's phenomenological model, retrospective re-hearing would have to include not just the immediate past, but also remote pasts. We recall our discussion of William Wordsworth's "spots of time," an "efficacious spirit" that lurks as though it were some subterranean force hidden from conscious thought. We also recall Freudian *Nachträglichkeit*, a traumatic experience only recognized as such in retrospection. Wordsworth's conception of spots of time emphasizes their forward trajectory in time, symbolically →. Freud's conception of *Nachträglichkeit* emphasizes retrospection, symbolically ←. Along the lines we have been exploring, we can say that each concept is weighted differently, but that both entail a Janus-faced arrow, ↔. To recall an event, seemingly forgotten, while realizing that it is the secreted source of what we've now become, is a mode of repetition revealed through multivalent temporal vectors reaching into a remote past, remembered or misremembered in the present, and having deep implications for the future.

Another aspect of what we might call the phenomenology of temporal perception of music, literature, and theater takes into consideration the effect of multiple hearings, readings, and seeings, which of course, as with all that we are considering, will vary from person to person. Familiarity with a work that unfolds over time tells us where it is going. Knowing the play *Hamlet* entails knowing the tragic fate of Ophelia even before she is introduced in the action of the play that we are attending or reading. Knowing Beethoven's Ninth Symphony entails knowing that vocal soloists and a chorus will join the orchestra in the final movement, and that the first three movements will be recollected in fragments, and then seemingly rejected "*Nicht diese Töne!*" A theory that doesn't take multiple hearings into account is simply inadequate, if not disingenuous. Multiple hearings not only clarify what we might have heard the first time through were our cognitive abilities up to it; they also radically alter our perceptions of past, present, and future.

Emergence, One More Time

Repetition, especially as Deleuze conceptualizes it, is a concomitant of emergence, creation as coming out of itself as we have considered earlier in this study. Intimately connected with the experience of something emerging out of itself is the question of how it is that some musical compositions, like some poems or novels, bear multiple hearings or readings, always keeping fresh, even over a lifetime of experience, while others are spent after one or two hearings or readings. Put another way, how is it that some works sustain a sense of tension even though we know very well where they are going in the end because we've heard or read them before. We have considered the relationship of Hamlet and Ophelia. An even more vivid example from Shakespeare is *Romeo and Juliet*: the likelihood that someone watching the play doesn't know how it will end approaches zero. And even if that were the case, Shakespeare tells us in the prologue to the play "of their death-marked love." And yet, at least in a good production or an attentive reading, the play stays fresh, and we are moved time and again.

How is it that some plays, novels, and music maintain or even intensify their dramatic force after multiple readings or hearings? Moreover, how is it that the strongest works invite or even require multiple readings or hearings for their dramatic impact to be most deeply appreciated? I first formulated these questions to myself soon after finishing graduate school, wondering if scholarship addressed my concerns. I brought my question to David Lewin, who suggested that I ask John Hollander (whose work I didn't yet know at the time). I wrote to Hollander, and he replied in a terse postcard, those being the days before the internet. Hollander told me to read Proust's *À la recherche du temps perdu*. I took quite a few years, decades in fact, before I was able to complete that task, and yet I was not perceptive enough to find Proust's answer to my question. Is it merely the case of a memory evoking madeleine, a taste, texture, faintly perceived aroma, that brings past into present, a repetition that enlightens and vivifies? I remember posing the question at some point, at least a decade after my initial queries, to my then colleague Dominick Argento, a gifted composer who loved to hate much of the music I cared about, though we found common ground in Mozart. Argento's response was that music is just like food: if it tastes good then you want to eat more. I silently thought this analogous to sex: if it feels good, you want to do it again. There is more than a grain of truth in Argento's claim, but I don't find the analogy quite satisfying. After all, a mystery novel might be a page-turner, fully engaging the reader, and yet after the mystery is solved, and we know "who did it," there is little incentive to read it again: it tastes good, but once is enough.

A couple of more satisfying explanations occur. First, in a well-wrought drama, novel, or musical composition, emergence entails surprising situations, events that we didn't see coming. In drama and dramatic music, we sense how things could have been otherwise. In a work that sustains multiple hearings or readings, rather than being dissipated, this sense of contingency is heightened with successive readings, seeings, hearings. Thus, while surprise is attenuated, the junctures of contingency, moments that point toward roads not taken, are intensified with deeper familiarity. These junctures of contingency entail rich temporal vectors, blends of "as now" and "as then," past and future. Watching or reading *Romeo and Juliet* for the nth time, it is these moments of contingency that are augmented in their potency. The same principle is involved in rehearings of music dramatically conceived.

Second, in a complex poem or musical composition, the richness or oddness of thought cannot be taken in in a single reading or hearing. Connections that elude initial readings or hearings become vivid through repeated experiences of the work. The work coheres in new ways that can only emerge with familiarity. The perceptions of temporal vectors emerge as networks of association emerge and as we gain a stronger sense of how temporal units coalesce and dissolve over time, modifying and augmenting our perceptions and emotional response to the flow of temporal orientations. Perhaps, after all, it is this sense that Hollander alluded to in *À la recherche du temps perdu*.

Augmenting the purview of the time-space of any given work, we might ask how our sense of temporal orientation might impact on our sense of families of works and artistic lineages. The very word *lineage* implies a chronological successive of works and creators, but these metaphoric left to right arrows are no more adequate in thinking of traditions then they are in thinking of other aspects of temporal orientation.

I ask my reader to indulge me in imagining hearing the first movement of Mozart's string quartet K. 421 as sounding like Brahms's hearing of Schubert superimposed on Mozart's sensibilities. How can this be? A linear chronology would entail Mozart (1756–1791) influencing certain aspects of Schubert (1797–1828), who in turn influenced certain aspects of Brahms (1833–1897). Any reasonable music historian might agree. But in our imagined hearing (one based on personal experience), it is experientially otherwise. Again, how can this be? Perhaps Michael's dyslexia has kicked in. Or perhaps the habits (limited as they are) of reading Yiddish, right to left, have warped my sense of before and after. Or perhaps there is another explanation. My hearing only makes sense if, more than characteristic of Mozart, per se, more than characteristic of Mozartean elements in Schubert, it is Brahms, specifically Schubert-informed Brahms, that I hear in the Mozart.

I spent a considerable portion of my career in musical scholarship immersed in the works of Arnold Schoenberg. While I vividly hear the influences of Brahms and Wagner (the latter more so in the early work, the former all through Schoenberg's oeuvre), hearing Schoenberg also influences the way I hear Brahms. The impact of Schoenberg in Brian Ferneyhough's music is profound, but Ferneyhough's music also makes me hear Schoenberg in new ways. The temporal reversals that we considered in Bloom's concept of metalepsis participate in these complexities of temporal orientation, metaphoric energy flows (Ashbery's waves) we've named temporal vectors.

11

The Horizontal and the Vertical
Worldly and Spiritual

Our word *horizontal* is derived from its ancient Greek cognate, which entailed marking or separating boundaries. The horizon is a bounding circle, a delimitation of space. *Vertical* derives from the Latin *vertex*, "highest point," originally denoting a whirling column, a whirlpool (from *vertere*, to turn). As such, the twin terms horizontal/vertical are coincident with metaphors Deleuze/Guattari develop in *Difference and Repetition* and *A Thousand Plateaus*. The making and marking of boundaries is a concomitant of agrarian or striated space. The turbulence of the vortex (also derived from *vertere*), in contrast to laminar states of steady flow, is one of the many metaphors describing nomadic space. Yet while there is significant overlap with the metaphors of smooth and striated space, the horizontal and the vertical provide yet another lens basic to human experience, including the ways we experience the arts, music being no exception. Moreover, as we shall see, the transformation of the horizontal into the vertical provides us with a principal metaphor for understanding religious experience, the experience of prophets, mystics, but also everyday people who have less intense but nonetheless significant experiences of something beyond the boundaries of everyday visual and conceptual horizons. Not all composers, performers, and listeners experience music as spiritual. But most, if not all, religions incorporate singing or chanting into their practices. Prayer itself is a kind of poetry that moves from the horizontal to the vertical.

Keeping the root meanings in mind, whirling column and bounded circle, a host of associations jumps up immediately. Let's think of verticality in terms of whirlwind or whirlpool first. In both whirlpool and whirlwind, respectively spiraling turbulences of water and air, overwhelming force pulls surrounding material, water, air, and whatever is caught up in them into their vortices/vertices. Both transform the horizontal into the vertical, one downward, into the whirlpool, one upward, into the whirlwind.

In the verticality of the geocentric natural world, we have tornadoes, hurricanes, cyclones, and whirlpools; in the larger expanses of the cosmos, forces of planetary revolution and rotation, the equilibria of spinning about vertical axes, the whirl of galaxies, the vortex of black holes. *Vertigo*, induced by dizzying heights or physical affliction, is likewise derived from the root, *vertere*.

Vertex and vortex, being pulled up into the whirlwind or down into the whirlpool, are instantiations taken from nature, paralleled in the twin directions of vertical thought: upward and downward. Both aspects are found in biblical imagery. In Exodus, "The Lord went before them in a pillar of cloud by day, to guide them along the way, and in a pillar of fire by night, to give them light."[1] We imagine the Israelites gazing upward. The pillars of cloud and fire mysteriously descend and magnificently pull us upward toward their ineffable source. The prophet Elijah goes up to heaven in a whirlwind, reaching downward, pulling upward.[2] The prophet Ezekiel's great vision comes to him out of a whirlwind: "And I looked, and, behold, a whirlwind came out of the north, a great cloud, and a fire infolding itself."[3] In the King James version of the Bible, the Lord answers Job out of the whirlwind.[4] The biblical proverbs say "and calamity arrives like a whirlwind."[5] We find a striking development of whirling in Sufi mysticism where whirling Dervishes bridge heaven and earth, aspiring to divine love.

The downward descent of the vortex finds some remarkable examples in secular literature as well (assuming we make a distinction between sacred and secular). In Homer's *Odyssey*, Charybdis is the personification of a deadly whirlpool. Of course, *between Scylla and Charybdis* has become proverbial. In *Paradise Lost*, Lucifer become Satan experiences a vertiginous descent into a "wild abyss / the womb of nature and perhaps her grave."[6] Harold Bloom, in his 1970 book on William Butler Yeats, identifies William Blake's idea of vortex as the source for Yeats's "double gyre." In Blake, the vortex can be doubly understood either from our fallen perspective as the "labyrinth of the natural world" or from visionary consciousness as that which opens into a higher reality, a whirlpool at the center of every object of perception. In Yeats, the double gyre gives rise to a cyclic movement where subjectivity (the source of creativity for Yeats) and objectivity constantly interpenetrate.[7] In Herman Melville's *Moby-Dick,* arguably the single most powerful example of American myth making, a whirlpool takes the Pequod down into the sea, with only Ishmael surviving to tell the tale. Moving to popular culture, the most memorable whirlwind, at least for me, is Dorothy's ascent to the land of Oz.

There is no solid line separating physical manifestations of vortex and vertex from their metaphorical extensions, and any of the examples we have noted of physical whirlwinds or whirlpools can be understood as having a metaphoric meaning generated from the physical manifestation. The turning about, spinning within the vertical, is kindred to the unsettled meanings that arise from rhetorical tropes, also turnings, where the boundaries of literal meaning are constantly undone.

We sleep on the horizontal but dream in the vertical. Returning to scripture, we note what is perhaps the most famous invocation of verticality in the Bible, Jacob's dream. "And he dreamed, and behold a ladder set up on the earth, and the top of it reached to heaven: and behold the angels of God ascending and descending on it. And, behold, the LORD stood beside him, and said: 'I am the LORD, the God of Abraham thy father, and the God of Isaac.'"[8] Ascent to the heavens above, and descent from the heavens bringing the divine down to earth, is arguably the chief metaphor of all Abrahamic religions. The verticality of mystical experience is an intensified aspect of a more pervasive orientation. In secular language we rise to an occasion or we fall down on our way.

From the vertical we pivot to the horizontal. The pivot from horizontal to vertical is an everyday affair for bird watchers. A flock of geese flies overhead, emerging from one horizon and disappearing into another. We seamlessly shift from horizontal to vertical and back again. Analogously, the turbulent whirlpool is dependent on the smoother surface that feeds into it. In a similar way, a horizon of expanse feeds into the black hole.

The horizon as boundary that encircles becomes as fundamental a metaphor for experience as we can conceive. As anyone who has experienced the view from a mountaintop or an airplane window will recognize, we expand our horizons by ascending on the vertical. The horizon as boundary marker can dilate and contract as we zoom in and out on the vertical, be it metaphorical or otherwise. Think for a moment of musical boundaries; the single note expands to the small cell or motif within which it is a constituent. The motive expands to the phrase, the phrase to a musical theme, on and on toward the expanses of multi-movement musical forms, and the even more expansive musical traditions and lineages that give rise to them.

Like the metaphors of nomadic and agrarian time and space, the terms vertical and horizontal suggest associative clusters of cognitive and emotional experience, worldly and spiritual. And, as with nomadic and agrarian space, it is the interaction of horizontal and vertical that is most suggestive in thinking about music and the other arts, in getting at how we experience music, and in finding ways to augment that experience.

Clifford Geertz's celebrated distinction between *thin* and *thick description* as applied to cultural anthropology is suggestive as an analogue to the metaphoric extensions of horizontal and vertical.[9] For our purposes, I imagine an object found in an archeological dig, say a bowl. A thin description of the bowl might be limited to a description of its shape, color, and material. This might entail a scientific description of its constituents and/or an aesthetic description of proportions and the like. A thicker description might include the technology and aesthetic values involved in the bowl's making, leading to a description of the social division of labor entailed in that making. Thicker yet, a description would consider the place of the bowl in daily life, how it was used, including the foods that the bowl might have contained. And thicker yet, the description of the bowl would correlate with the production of food, whether by hunting and gathering or agrarian, and the human relationships involved in those enterprises. And finally, the thickening description would address the role that the bowl might have played in the spiritual, religious life of the community to which it belonged.

We closed our earlier discussion of Merleau-Ponty's phenomenology noting that his poetic "we are the sudden upsurge of time" implies a gathering of the horizontal into a verticality. Scattered through Merleau-Ponty's working notes for his posthumous publication *The Visible and the Invisible*, we find references to a *vertical* conception of the world and of thought. As I understand his distinction between vertical and horizontal, the vertical is a unified field perceived all at once, whereas the horizontal is divided into constituents, spread out over time. I find the clearest presentation of this idea in the paragraph quoted below. "Just as it is necessary to restore the *vertical* visible world, so also there is a *vertical* view of the mind, according to which it is not made of a multitude of memories, images, judgments, it is one sole movement that one can coin out in judgments, in memories, but that holds them in one sole cluster as a spontaneous *word* contains a whole becoming, as *one sole grasp* of the hand contains a whole chunk of space."[10] Adapting this understanding to my example of the bowl in thicker description, we can say that elements of that description, for example, modes of production or of hunting, gathering, or farming, are spread out over the horizontal, while my deepening understanding of the bowl as artifact (the thickness of my description) instantiates a vertical experience.

Experiential metaphors of height and depth participate in the vertical. Experiential metaphors of breadth and expanse participate in the horizontal. Along these lines, when we speak of a deep thinker, or the depths of despair, or the heights of human achievement, we are thinking in vertical terms. When we speak of breadth of knowledge, or its opposite, spreading oneself thin, we speak along the horizontal. Yet, following Merleau-Ponty, when breadth of knowledge leads to a singular grasp, holding our experience in "one sole cluster," then the horizontal tilts toward the vertical. In literature, narrative space tends toward the horizontal as it unfolds over time. Yet, again following Merleau-Ponty, we can say that to the degree that we grasp the narrative as a whole, we move from horizontal to vertical thought. Lyric poetry, poetry that revolves around a single emotion or emotionally fraught event, tends toward the vertical. Poets, such as Paul Celan or Giuseppe Ungaretti, who infuse even single words with cognitive and emotional resonance, bring heightened vertical experience into being.

Along similar lines, music that summons up multiple associations, fusing diverse times and places into our experience of this time and place, is experienced as vertical. When performers or scholars or listeners get to know a musical composition "inside and out," the horizontal experience of time flow merges with the kind of singular grasp that Merleau-Ponty describes.

By this way of thinking, any experience that involves cognitive and emotional depth tends toward the vertical. But musical acoustics embody another aspect of verticality in the ways a sounding body generates its overtones, guaranteeing that each moment of musical time/space necessarily involves the interaction of vertically induced sonorities as they interact with horizontally generated flow. To be sure, music can produce semblances of downward spiral, for example, by "falling" through a downward circle of fifths, or through spirals of descent more generally. But the "natural" properties of sound metaphorically reach upward toward higher and higher partials. (The metaphor "higher" has become so natural that we have trouble describing the phenomenon without it.) While it would be too reductive to attribute the spiritual dimensions of music to its acoustic properties alone, the inherent verticality of sound must be factored in when thinking of music's merging of "body and soul."

At another point in *The Visible and the Invisible*, Merleau-Ponty writes suggestively (and enigmatically) about "vertical Being" and the relations between body and soul. "The unicity of the visible world, and, by encroachment, the invisible world, such as it presents itself in the rediscovery of the vertical Being, is the solution of the problem of the 'relations between the soul and the body.'"[11] The "mind-body" problem had been a central concern of philosophy since the dawn of enlightenment thought, most famously in Descartes. In formulating or reformulating the query into terms of body and soul, Merleau-Ponty chooses words that evoke questions of religious experience. It is this aspect of phenomenological inquiry that becomes the central concern of Anthony J. Steinbock in *Phenomenology and Mysticism: The Verticality of Religious Experience*.

Early on in *Phenomenology and Mysticism*, Steinbock observes that "The central issue in phenomenology is neither the subject or the object, but *givenness*."[12] Distinguishing two modes of givenness, Steinbock opposes the experience of *presentation* (implicitly horizontal) and *vertical* experiences in the spheres of religion, morality, and ecology. For Steinbock, *presentation* is the principal mode of experience as described in philosophical phenomenology. "The constitution of both simple and categorial objects, the foreground/background of the phenomenal field—all this belongs to the province of *presentation* and is governed by its systematic laws and interconnections. There is nothing intrinsically problematic or illegitimate about this order of givenness. However, the difficulty has been and continues to be the "presentation" is assumed to be the *only* mode of givenness."[13] In contrast,

> Modes of givenness are "vertical" in the sense that they take us *beyond* ourselves. These modes of vertical givenness are testimony to the radical presence of "absolutes" *within* the field of human experience.
>
> By "absolute" I mean a presence that is so unique that it can be predicated neither of singularity nor plurality. "Absolute" in this sense is not synonymous with "universal." There are three main spheres of absolute experience: the religious which

pertains to the vertical experience of the Holy; the moral, which pertains to the vertical experience of the other person; and the ecological, which pertains to the vertical experience of the Earth as aesthetic ground.[14]

First, it is important to notice that Steinbock's understanding of verticality emphasizes augmentation of one's self in that vertical experience takes us *beyond* ourselves. Although Steinbock, limiting his discussion to the first of his three spheres, religious experience, does not consider the verticality of art as modes that "take us *beyond* ourselves," in what follows that is precisely the aspect of art that I intend to explore. But I get ahead of myself.

Steinbock's rather mysterious characterization of *absolute*, neither singular nor plural and not synonymous with "universal," is clarified later in the book.

> The relation to the Holy through which I am given to myself charges me with a kind of "ought." This "ought" comes to me, comes to me "alone" such that it can neither be exchanged for another "ought" nor transferred to another person. It is given independently of my explicit knowledge of it and before I could choose it for myself.
>
> . . . Here is one place where we find the "universal" and the "absolute" parting ways. The good-in-itself is necessary, binding, decisive, and in this sense, absolute.
>
> . . .
>
> The good-in-itself-for-me, grasped as my vocation, is one moment of personal individuation that individuates me as *unique*.[15]

Rather than emphasizing a universal "golden rule," this characterization of "ought" is a calling unique to each individual, indeed it is the principal force toward individuation, that which makes each individual distinct. We might say that the golden rule asserts universality, whereas the good-in-itself-for-me is personal. Once again, I recall Hillel's threefold saying: "If I am not for myself, who will be for me? If I am only for myself, what am I? If not now, when?" In light of Steinbock's descriptions, we can paraphrase Hillel's first query as regarding the personal *ought*; his second query as recognizing that this personal *ought* is necessarily interpersonal, opening the individual's responsibility to the other; and his third query as indicating the necessity of acting upon this two-pronged imperative. All of this echoes what we have found in Levinas.

While the *ought* is individuating, its vectors of influence are interpersonal. My personal imperative involves my relationships with others. The individuating aspect of the *ought*, here orienting the self toward the Holy, is highly concordant with the values I have placed on the uniqueness of authentic musical voices (the voices of the composer, the performer, and of the listener who silently sings along). As such, musical experience (or experience of any of the arts) edges toward spiritual experience. Indeed, for many they are one in the same.

Focusing on verticality in the religious sphere, Steinbock explores the writings of three mystics, collectively representing the three Abrahamic religions, Judaism, Christianity, and Islam: Rabbi Dov Baer, "the Mitteler," (1773–1827), St. Teresa of Avila (1515–1582), and Rūzbinān Baqlī (1128–1209). Watery imagery dominates St. Teresa's experiences, becoming one of her chief metaphors for divine grace. Successive images of drawing water from a well, being aided by a water wheel, irrigating by way of a stream or river, and finally, and most high, rain from the heavens signify ascending stages of divine love.[16] For Rūzbinān Baqlī, the chief metaphor is *unveiling*, where successive stages of spiritual development entail both visual and auditory beauty.[17] Dov Baer's descriptions separate stages of *natural ecstasy*, where human effort is a concomitant, and stages of *divine ecstasy*, gifts of divine grace. The descriptions of *natural* and *divine ecstasy* both emphasize imagery based on hearing and singing. Stages of natural ecstasy include *hearing-from-afar* augmented to a hearing where one is absorbed and engrossed in contemplation of the divine. In the third of five stages of divine ecstasy, "the heart spontaneously 'sings for joy unto the living God.'"[18]

Love is the characteristic that all three mystics emphasize. "In each case, loving is a dynamic orientation toward this "other" such that the latter's intrinsic value is not exhausted in the loving; rather, as allowing it to unfold of itself, it is open toward infinity such that this "other" toward which loving is directed realizes the highest possible quality; the deepest value peculiar to its own being."[19] Again, the sentiments involved are almost identical to those we find in Levinas. Steinbock subsequently develops the term *idolatry* as self-limiting while spiritual love is self-augmenting. In that context, Steinbock considers the Hebrew word הנני (*hineni*), "an immediate, absolute, unconditional readiness to serve. This is what we understand as genuine self-love and is compatible with the disposition of humility."[20] As we have seen, it is this same term that more than any other sums up Levinas's understanding of our obligation to one another, that which opens our experience to the divine.

One more aspect of Steinbock's presentation of vertical spiritual experience that we've already mentioned needs to be emphasized in our context: at least within the Abrahamic traditions, the verticality of experience is interpersonal. Early on in his book, Steinbock says that the "mystical tradition," as he uses the expression, is "a special genre of inter-Personal experiences."[21] This interpersonal aspect of religious verticality is emphasized throughout the book, love being chief among its expressions. (Steinbock's spelling, inter-Personal, presumably reflects the idea that the love expressed, even when applied toward other persons, is ultimately understood as a love of God.)

Once again, Steinbock's ideas are concordant with those we have explored in musical contexts. We have said that the composition, performance, and audition of music is an interpersonal experience. When I sit at the keyboard and play a movement by Mozart, Mozart speaks (or sings) to me, or rather, we two collaborate in singing together. For me, this generalizes into any vital musical experience. Like poetry, and like the other arts, by this way of thinking, music is not composed of objects. It is composed of individuated interpersonal utterances that give rise to individuated interpersonal experiences.

The vertical, rising or falling, gathers the horizontal; it is our road to the spiritual. We have characterized music as embodied. Paradoxically, music also signifies, perhaps more than any other art, disembodied spirit. For the ancient Hebrews, God's *ruach,* (breath, spirit, wind) sweeps over the waters as He says, "Let there be light." To speak or to sing places air in motion. Music moves the air around me, and imagined music imagines that breath that moves what is not yet into being. There is a dynamic, interactive circuit between music as embodied and music as disembodied, where the health of the body is coefficient with the health of the spirit.

Work Songs: Physical Health and Mental Health

"Hark ye, does thou not ever sing working about a coffin? The Titans, they say, hummed snatches when chipping out the craters for volcanoes; and the grave-digger in the play sings, spade in hand. Dost thou never?"

> "Sing sir? Do I sing? Oh, I'm indifferent enough, sir, for that; but the reason why the grave-digger made music must have been because there was none in his spade, sir. But the caulking mallet is full of it. Hark to it."
>
> —Herman Melville, *Moby-Dick*, chapter 127

The gravedigger in the play who sings, spade in hand, is the one who unearths the skull identified as Yorick's. He is the one who will shortly inter Ophelia. He sings while he works, and his singing as well as his intermittent conversation with Hamlet reveals a certain kind of wisdom, let's call it the wisdom of a gravedigger. That the caulking mallet is full of song is part of the wisdom of the carpenter who prepares the coffin designed for Queequeg, the coffin, as fate would have it, that saves Ishmael's life.

We have seen that the biblical understanding of wisdom entailed not just the kind of wisdom that we find in the psalms and proverbs, but also wisdom of the hands, which is a bodily wisdom. Stanley Moss's poem "The Carpenter" is a parable about Jesus, here given his Hebrew name "Yeshua." In the poem Yeshua is a youth, learning the trade of his "earthly father's shop." In the poem, Moss captures a sense of the wisdom of the hands that merges with a spiritual knowing. We recall the story of Enoch as cobbler for whom sewing the sole to the upper leather becomes an image of the spiritual healing of the world.

> To the boy the workbench with its candle seemed
> an altar, the tools its offerings. That boy
> could speak the languages of Babel. "Bevel"
> he learned refers to an angle not cut-square.
> At first he heard *angle* as *angel*.
> He heard "take the angel directly from the work,
> the only precaution being that
> both stock and tongue be held tight to the work."[22]

Playing on the Hebrew pronunciation of the name "Bavel," Moss slides into "bevel," the angled-angled cuts of the workshop, cuts so that "both stock and tongue be held tight."[23]

In times past, workers with wisdom of the hands often accompanied their work with song. The amazing variety of work songs is nicely studied by Ted Gioia in his book *Work Songs*.[24] The book's nineteen chapters divide work songs into categories based on the types of work that they accompanied. Yet, as Gioia emphasizes throughout, the functions of these songs cannot be reduced to utility. Some enhanced work, some were diversions, and some simply made the intolerable tolerable. In the chapter titled "The Hunter," Gioia discusses songs that are talismanic, summoning protective or propitiatory forces, we might say magic, and songs that are celebratory, recounting a successful hunt. In agricultural settings such as the Southern slave plantations in America, work songs were adapted to the different tasks associated with various crops. In a similar way, the rhythmic patterns of some sea shanties were suited to certain tasks, rowing, hauling anchor, and the like. "Among the Ewe, the word *lo* means both 'to weave' and 'to sing,' which indicates a long-associated history between the two activities in Africa. Even today, an attractive metaphor is provided in the concept of weaving a song or spinning tale, and possibly suggests an intrinsic similarity between making cloth and making music . . . Almost three thousand years ago, Homer described Circe singing at the loom."[25] Gioia's observations resonate well with the metaphors of weaving, quilting, the production of felt, and the idea of an errant thread that we have previously explored.

A worker might relate to his or her tools in ways similar to the ways a musician relates to his or her musical instrument. "In a postindustrial age, when most workers measure their productivity in clicks and bytes, we inevitably forget the erstwhile intimacy between manual laborers and their tools. The carpenter's hammer, the lumberjack's axe, the sailor's knife, even the writer's trusty typewriter (now all but obsolete): these may possess a simple utilitarian function. But for their user, they are something more. . . . It may not be going too far to claim that the hammer is the quintessential percussion instrument of the work song."[26] As already noted, in numerous places, Gioia discusses the aspects of work songs that go beyond utilitarian function. His observations about chain gangs' songs are particularly revealing.

> As with workers on the outside, convicts relied on music to alleviate the drudgery of their labor and coordinate the effort of the individual with the rest of the group . . . These songs must also have helped to protect the individuals who sang them. As Bruce Jackson has explained: "They kept a man from being singled out for a whipping because he worked too slowly. The songs kept all together, so no one could be beaten to death for mere weakness."[27]

Work songs in most societies are things of the past. At best (or worst, depending on your point of view), piped-in music substitutes for self-made music. "We have come a long way from such times. Not only have we lost singing at work, but simply listening to songs *about* work is difficult for most people unless the tone is sufficiently infused with bitterness, irony, or ridicule."[28]

Personal Excursus

My Dad, Jacob, was one of those persons who had wisdom of the hands. His training as a tailor in Europe was interrupted by World War I and then the Russian Revolution. He used to say, "I got as far as the vest," pronouncing "vest" as "west" with no pun intended. Coming to America as a teenager, he worked for an uncle as a carpenter and became quite skilled in that craft. Dad would swing the hammer with such grace that you didn't notice the power engendered by that grace, except in seeing the three-inch nails driven into the wood through three strokes. If you watched him long enough, you'd see that once in while Dad would bend the nail. Invariably when this happened the Yiddish curse "a choleria" would escape from his lips. A musician with instrument acquires a similar power through grace. They learn to leave behind their versions of "a choleria" in the practice room. Having developed a love of music while a child in Europe, Jacob was later a musician in US Army bands, first as a clarinetist and later, after losing his teeth, as a percussion player. And later yet he became trained as a photographer, attending the Army War College, then in Washington, DC, and managing the photo lab at Fort Knox, Kentucky, during World War II. When I knew him, as an older dad, he did the family sewing, carpentry, and in a dark room, complete with plumbing and urinal, hidden behind a false wall of his making, he did the wizardry that photography entailed prior to the digital age. In all these things, Dad sang as he worked. The songs were a variety of pop tunes from the 1920s and 1930s, Yiddish songs, Hebrew prayers, and odds and ends that he had picked up along the way. Dad sang while he worked. Work song, in many cultures, was until recently a commonplace. Now, with earbuds and cell phones, that practice, so far as I can tell, is mostly gone. I personally don't use earbuds, at least not yet, yet I'm sure they bring delight to many. Perhaps I'm simply nostalgic, but the loss of work song seems to me to be a great one.

Grace

Grace, a word recurrent throughout this study, has a range of meanings wonderfully apt toward describing so many aspects of music. Grace is elegance and poise, the quintessential attribute of dance, and music as dance. Grace is a prayer of thankfulness, and God's grace is given irrespective of merit. Grace combines power with ease, so that to do our work with equanimity and grace is chief among our blessings.

Scott Burnham, in *Mozart's Grace*, writes about the "feeling of floating gently and effortlessly down to the appointed resolution" in the falling fifths typical of Mozart's retransitions (the passages leading to the recapitulation in sonata forms).

> This type of harmonic sequence performs work without seeming to work: the local passing of one dominant relation to another, the often beautifully wrought textures that Mozart puts into play at just these moments, all conspire to take us off the tracks of time, precisely at musical time's biggest juncture. Or, better, the sequence has the effect of divorcing time's progress from human effort—it seems to run by itself, apart from, and regardless of, our interventions. The effect is of otherworldly calm, as though to quiet the noise of local time, so that we can hear the passing of global time.[29]
>
> . . .
>
> Mozart's graceful landings transform thematic renewal into an act of grace. Here Schiller's *Anmut*, grace as beauty in motion, rises to a higher orbit and becomes *Gnade*, the dispensation of grace. Here at the most consequential fulcrum of the entire form, the heavy structural downbeat lands light as a feather; the inevitable becomes the miraculous. Return is staged not as an act of resolution, not as a thing willed—but as a thing granted. Form as *Gnade*, then as gift: the great thematic redoubling of sonata form is performed not as an enactment of convention but as a miracle of renewal.[30]

To perform work without seeming to work is a variation on many of the themes we have been concerned with intermittently throughout this book: Heidegger's *Gelassenheit*, the daemon from Socrates, through Emerson, to Harold Bloom, and the effects of God-given grace as described by the mystics in Steinbock's account. Performance artists of any stripe as well as their audiences will recognize those special moments when a performance, in theater or music or dance, turns magical; when the theater or concert hall seems indeed to become an altered space; when experience is heightened beyond the norms of appreciation or enthusiasm or even wonder. Such moments may be described as an influx of grace. There are many ways to experience the influx of grace; music is surely among them.

I opened this book arguing that music is among our necessary fictions, among the ways we tell stories about ourselves. This book has been meant to be a celebration of music's ways of telling stories. Yet authors have also attributed a dark side to music making, what we might call a falling from grace. In his article "The Singing Birds," Amnon Shiloah cites the work of an anonymous medieval Arabic author.

> The prophet David used to sing his psalms with 70 different melodies or modes with which he charmed birds and beasts. Upon hearing his chanting, some people died under the powerful effect of his sounds, the water stopped flowing and the wind began to dance. Iblis (the devil) witnessing the effect of David's chanting, invented types of instruments which are still in use among people. Nevertheless, those who listen to the instruments as an act of faith, like the Sufis, are in the right.[31]

From Plato to Levinas and beyond, philosophers and religious leaders have cautioned about the intoxicating, seductive power of music. Shiloah's anonymous author goes so far as to attribute the invention of musical instruments to the devil, but then goes on to say that "those who listen to the instruments as an act of faith, are in the right." Whether celebratory or cautionary, it is the power of music as life-shaping that has been recognized in every tradition that I know of. My own concern in what we might call an ethics of music focuses less on the dangers of music as the road to perdition than on the trivialization of music, where it becomes background static rather than a focused bodily *and* spiritual experience, an experience that gathers the experiential horizon into intensified moments, vertices of vertical ascent, as well as vortices that plunge us into the darker regions of human experience.

I return to Amnon Shiloah for another citation, this from the Sufi master Majd al-dīn Aḥmad ibn Muḥammad al-Ṭūsī al-Ghazālī (d. 1121) on the symbolic meaning of music and dance in Sufi ritual.

> The tambourine is a reference to the cycle of existing . . . a reference to the descent of divine inspiration from the innermost arcana upon general existence to bring forth the things . . . from the interior to the exterior . . . And the voice of the singer is a reference to the divine life which comes down . . . The flute is a reference to the light of Allah (Exalted is He!) penetrating the reed of man's essence . . . And the dancing is a reference to the circling of the spirit round the cycle of existing things.[32]

Music, as the "divine life which comes down," takes on many guises. No book, no listener, can touch on them all. When divine life comes, seemingly of its own accord, we are granted grace.

Eros

In our previous discussions of experiential time, we developed the term *temporal vector*; we suggested that energized flows of temporal orientation exist within a spectrum with a remote past-perfect at one extreme and an equally remote future-imperfect at the other, where both termini are asymptotic, where either extreme can be approached but never actually reached. In the middle sits now-time, a dilated moment infused with traces of the past and future. Our metaphors of vertical and horizontal experience posited that vertical experience gathers the horizontal into vortex or vertex; mystical experience is a heightened awareness of this now-time, this gathering into the vertical. The time-space of eros can also be experienced as a now-time, and, as with other instances of now-time, it bears traces of past and future. Indeed, we might say that the now-time of heightened eros is suffused with all-time, past-present-future focused on a concentrated now.

Bob Dylan's song *Lay Lady Lay* has a verse that sings "Why wait any longer for the one you love, when he's standing in front of you." The song is found on Dylan's album of 1969, *Nashville Skyline*, Dylan's full-fledged step into "country music." As with the other idioms of American popular music, love songs have always been among the staples of what was once called "country and western."

There's an immediacy in Dylan's lyrics, suggesting something like seize the moment, but promising something that expands that moment. Whether or not that promise might be fulfilled might be questioned. Eros can be dangerous, its promises tenuous or even deceitful. Country songs are full of broken promises. But this song doesn't feel that way, at least to me. The song, in telling us that there's no need to wait for the world to begin, implies that paradise, the world as at was at its beginning, is here now, at hand, if only we could recognize it as such. Dylan's lyrics are reminiscent of a parable by Franz Kafka that begins as follows: "The expulsion from Paradise is in its main significance eternal: Consequently the expulsion from Paradise is final and life in this world irrevocable, but the eternal nature of the occurrence (or, temporally expressed, the eternal recapitulation of the occurrence) makes it nevertheless possible that not only could we live continuously in Paradise, but that we are continuously there in actual fact, no matter whether we know it here or not."[33] Another of Kafka's parables tells of a door, a threshold that cannot be crossed, although it was made only for you. We might imagine eros as a threshold, fulfilled only in the crossing. If only we can recognize and realize our potential opening of the door when we see it.

And then there's Dylan's "have your cake and eat it too," reversing a common cliché into its opposite, where the lyrics verge on silliness. Eros can be deadly serious (there are not too many chuckles in Wagner's *Tristan und Isolde*), but here it is lighthearted, leavened while being likened to a self-replenishing dessert. Like so many of the terms we have considered, eros doesn't mean just one thing; erotic space comprises a cluster of meanings, including opposed terms such as sorrow and joy.

Desire and longing, both associated with eros, are generally weighted toward the future, although either can be past-oriented; bitterness and remorse, also associated with eros, are generally weighted toward the past, a paradise lost, but a future-orientation is also possible. Famously, Sappho, at the inception of erotic poetry (which was also music, though we've lost the tune), described eros as γλŭκŭπῑκρον (*glukupikron*), sweet-bitter, reversed into bittersweet in normative English.[34] Sappho's term posits change over time, sweet then bitter.

Time, in all its aspects, is shaped by rhythm. The rhythms of dance, music, and poetry manifestly share this quality with all else that unfolds through the ebb and flow of time. Eros too has its characteristic rhythms of ebb and flow. In the storytelling of ancient Greece, Orpheus, more so than any other, personifies and embodies music. His story has given rise to a wealth of poems and music, enough to fill a capacious library shelf devoted to that topic alone. The story of Orpheus and Eurydice remains one of mankind's the most poignant fictions of love lost; it is a story retold generation after generation, each telling building on the echoes of prior tellings. James Merrill added to those tellings with his sonnet *Orfeo*. Here is its final couplet.

> Her loss within his music's rise and fall
> Having become perpetual.[35]

In the sonnet, as is so often the case, poetic rhythm is to a large extent concomitant with the flow of poetic feet, the rise and fall of sound and syntax. In Merrill's closing couplet, the iambic pentameter of the penultimate line gives way to the mixed meter of the final line, trochee then iamb into the soft double iamb of perpetual, softly echoing "fall," while ending the line one foot short, so that echo continues into silence, the no-more that perpetually swallows sound. The single trochee, "having," disrupts the iambic flow, as it hovers indeterminately between continuous past (as in having had . . .) and continuous future (an indeterminate becoming that is perpetual). Her loss, which is his loss, becomes transposed, implanted inside, or transformed into music's rise and fall. It has become music's throbbing sensuality, music's alternating hope and despair; it has become the musical analogue to *glukupikron*, sweet, then bitter.

Shakespeare's sonnets, in large part comprising a varied and extended contemplation of the vicissitudes of eros, all end with poetic closure. Merrill's sonnet feels open-ended, breaking off with the echoic-perpetual of music's rise and fall, as generations on generations retell, re-embody Orpheus's story. Shakespeare is the greater poet; comparisons with him are unfair. But Merrill, at least in this non-ending, better captures the sense of eros as open ended, as encoded in music's rise and fall.

Manifest in music's rise and fall, eros is a pervasive, even essential, aspect of music making. Eros, as understood by Freud and many others, is more than sexual desire: Eros is the life-drive opposed in majesty only by Thanatos, the death-drive. In this more inclusive sense, basic to our very being, music cannot but manifest both drives. In its peak experiences, the vortexes and vortices of musical life, music is co-creator of our most vital sense of self. Music as Eros is music as life-force. Thanatos is there too, for we have recognized how fading to silence, at least in one of its guises, expresses the death-drive, as so remarkably instantiated in *Der Abschied*, the closing song of Mahler's *Das Lied von der Erde*.

If we expand the meaning of eros beyond its sexual connotations, even beyond its Freudian sense as the life-force opposed to the death-drive, we might characterize eros as a spiritual quest for wholeness. This is how Socrates characterizes eros in the *Symposium*, and it is in part how Friedrich Hölderlin understood eros, naming eros "Diotima" after the woman whom Socrates identifies as the one who taught him the nature of love.

Plato's *Symposium* contains speeches by six different characters on the nature of eros. The final speech is that of Socrates, and his recounting of Diotima's teachings on eros is embedded within. R. E. Allen's commentary on the dialogue notes that "Diotima will treat the intercourse of man and woman as a divine thing, an immortal element in the mortal living creature."[36] We have found kindred understanding of sexual intercourse in Kabbalah. "Eros belongs to that class of terms that have their meaning 'toward' (πρoς τι) something else. If so, then Eros lacks what it loves and desires to possess it . . . Eros as Eros cannot exist as satisfied, for when it is satisfied it ceases to exist. When it is, its object is not; when its object is, it is not. In this respect, love is like death."[37] Eros aims at immortality through procreation as well as through other creative acts such as the writing of poetry, law giving, and education; the immortality achieved however is not real, and so Eros is in this respect "frustrated and vain"; however, there is a higher stage "in which the lover ascends as by a ladder from bodily beauty, through spiritual and intellectual beauties, to the contemplation of Beauty itself, and there, if anywhere, becomes immortal."[38] Eros, intermediate between gods and men, is a daemon (δαιμων), a tutelary spirit guide, sometimes denoted by the word genius as well as its German cognate, *Genius*.[39]

In the music of the twentieth century, we find a remarkable instance of eros so understood in Luigi Nono's string quartet *Fragmente-Stille, an Diotima*. The name of Nono's quartet, *Fragmente-Stille, an Diotima*, is worth thinking about in some detail. We will do so, one word at a time.

Fragmente translates from the German into the English word *fragments*. The fragment—where some piece points toward a greater whole—is central to Romantic aesthetics. Sometimes the fragment is part of a ruin, a vestige of something once whole, of which we can get some sense, if only a glimmering, by contemplating the what remains. In every case, the Romantic fragment points beyond its own boundaries. If the fragment is verbal, it points to words that are not said, and perhaps cannot be said. If the fragment is musical, the music that is heard points to unheard music that is its source or its goal or both. In some sense, every utterance, musical or otherwise, is a fragment, part of a more encompassing language, culture, worldview.

The fragments alluded to in Nono's title include fifty-three fragments from Hölderlin's poetry that are embedded in the score, but they also include the fragmentary nature of the music. As the textual fragments point toward larger texts within which they are embedded, so the music points beyond its sounding events into a world of things not yet heard, perhaps not yet hearable.

The instructions at the beginning of the score seem to be somewhat self-contradictory. On the one hand, they indicate that the words, never to be spoken during a performance, should under no circumstances be taken as indicating a program. On the other hand, Nono indicates that "the players should 'sing' [the words] inwardly."

By including text (beyond indications for affect or tempo) within the score of a string quartet, not to be spoken or sung, Beethoven is Nono's historical precursor. Beethoven famously inserts music and text at the outset of the final movement of his last string quartet: *Der schwer gefasste Entschluss: Muss es sein? Es muss sein! Es muss sein!* (The resolution reached with difficulty: Must it be? It must be! It must be!). Beethoven's inserted text and melody are derived from a comic song he had composed concerning payment for a concert season.[40] In the context of this last work from a gravely ill composer, Beethoven's text takes on existential meaning, its comic sense receding to the background but leaving its trace. Unless the audience has a score, or program notes that include the text, in both cases, Beethoven and Nono, the text remains unheard, except indirectly from the ways it might inform a performance. In Nono's quartet, the words, here explicitly sung inwardly by the performers, are scattered throughout the score. The texts are inaudible, and unless the listener is following along with a score, they are also invisible.

The score includes a catalog prepared by Nono showing the derivation of each textual fragment, naming the poem and line from which it is derived.[41] Surely the text fragments are meant to point to their contexts within the poems, just as the poems, at least in many cases, point to something ineffable, beyond what can be said. Nono's enigmatic music is composed of many short fragments (tying musical expression in with the embedded verbal fragments) emerging from and returning to silence. Like so much in Schoenberg and Webern, Nono's principal musical precursors, the music too points to something ineffable and unreachable, beyond the sounding tones.

In my book *Schoenberg's Musical Imagination*, I used the word *imperfection* to characterize the open-ended quality of Schoenberg's post-tonal musical language. We have seen that musical "perfection" implies closure, completion, a final state of being, similar to its meaning in grammar. It may be useful to recall some observations I made in naming music among our necessary fictions.

> The *inevitability* of the closing tonic in Bach brings us to our final resting place. It is essential to his worldview. It expresses his religious faith and his sense of the order of the cosmos. The *inescapability* of the final tonic in Schubert is essential to *his* worldview, a very different world from that Bach once knew. Schubert's tonic often expresses tragically that which cannot be avoided. The *unattainability* of a closing tonic for post-tonal Schoenberg is expressive of his worldview, where ending in perfection can no longer express an honest fiction.

Nono's string quartet participates in Schoenberg's worldview, where ending in perfection can no longer express an honest fiction.

The word *Stille* in Nono's title translates from the German to a cluster of English words, *quiet, stillness, silence; calm, tranquility, peace, repose*. As we have noted, Nono's fragmentary musical gestures are surrounded by silence. We have spent considerable time thinking about such silences. Among our ruminations we drew parallels between silence surrounding sound and the white space that surrounds words of poetry, white fire surrounding black fire in the Jewish mystical tradition. In our thoughts about music emerging out of silence, we have suggested reversing the image, so that the white light of sound emerges out of the blackness of silence.

Our thoughts on silence and sound dovetail with our thoughts concerning liminal time and space, thresholds of in-between. Such thresholds are central to Hölderlin's poetry, as they are to Nono's music. Hölderlin scholar and translator Richard Sieburth discusses this aspect in the poet's commentary to his translation of *Oedipus* and *Antigone* (1804).

> Hölderlin compares the highest moment of tragic emotion (he uses the French term *transport*) to the role of caesura in prosody: both define a space in between, an "antirhythmic suspension" of temporal progression, an interval of silence in which the "pure Word" may appear . . . The fragile exchange between mortals and gods, however, is forever threatened by man's restless reach beyond his rightful bounds. "No action, no thought can reach the extent of your desire," writes Hölderlin in an early draft of *Hyperion*.[42]

To borrow Heidegger's terminology, the space in between that lets the "pure Word" appear is an unanticipated *Lichtung*, a clearing that opens a space. "Man's restless reach beyond his rightful bounds" is equivalent to a Promethean quest. Music and poetry as a Promethean quest are a commonplace in Romantic thought.[43] The model for creativity we have developed, drawing on seeing/knowing/hearing-through, as instantiated in Kabbalah's depiction of the sefirot, opposes this conception and suggests that instead of stealing fire from the gods, we think of human creativity as a participation in ongoing creation, consonant with God, not opposed.

Fragmente–Stille: the dash between *Fragmente* and *Stille* in Nono's title is enigmatic, as is the work itself. The poet Emily Dickinson comes to mind; her prolific use of dashes often creates syntactic ambiguity and multiplicity of meaning. For Nono, the dash likely expresses a dialectical opposition, where the opposition is natural, necessary, and productive. The musical fragments are assertive and active principles of creative making while the surrounding *Stille*—stillness, silence, tranquility, peace, and repose—is both their source and their receptor. The dash between *Fragmente* and *Stille* is both opposition and connection.

an Diotima can be translated as "to Diotima," or as "about Diotima." The name "Diotima," as we have noted, is derived from Plato's *Symposium*, where Socrates identifies Diotima as the woman "who instructed me in the things of love."[44] *An Diotima* is the title of several poems by Hölderlin, one of which is referred to by a fragment embedded in Nono's score. *Diotima* (without the preposition *an*) is the title of numerous poems by

Hölderlin, including a longer poem of 120 lines that is represented by fragments fourteen times in Nono's score; Diotima is also a character in Hölderlin's unfinished novel *Hyperion*, represented by three fragments in Nono's score, and Diotima is the name that Hölderlin gave to Susette Gontard, the love of his life, a relationship that ended tragically for both the poet and his beloved.[45] Diotima, the name for Hölderlin's beloved and for his muse, is also among the names that the poet uses to refer to an unattainable ideal, what we might characterize as a spiritual quest for wholeness. This spiritual quest includes both the high ecstasies and the deep agonies of our human condition.

Within Nono's string quartet, the note D♮ plays a major structural and expressive role. D♮ is the final sonority of the piece, although that sonority does not suggest perfection in the sense that a final cadence would in tonal music. Within the traditions of tonal music, a world where closure through perfection was still imaginable, the keys of D major and D minor had played an outsized role: Beethoven's Ninth Symphony as well as Mahler's First and Ninth Symphonies provide examples we have discussed, and there are many, many more. The prevalence of D as a key center takes on "extra-musical" meaning (which is really "intra-musical" meaning), as composers later in the tradition point toward their precursors through the use of key. Mahler pointing toward Beethoven is a case in point. But the prevalence of D is also based on acoustics. The string instruments form the core of the classical orchestra, the basic timbre and texture that is augmented but not supplanted by the winds and percussion. Open strings, those not stopped by player's left hand, are the most resonant, their overtones the most vibrant. The open strings on a violin are tuned to G, A, D, E, tones that are maximized in the key of D.[46] If we take the resonance of a vibrating string to connote an open-endedness, a verticality built into musical sounds, D is the perfect embodiment of imperfection! Given the preeminent role of D in Nono's string quartet, it is not far-fetched to think of the second part of the title, *an Diotima*, as implying, in part, "toward D."

The chief transformation of Diotima from Plato to Hölderlin is in that Hölderlin's Diotima signifies eros itself. Hölderlin's Diotima is both daemon as tutelary deity *and* signifier of the unattainable and ineffable, that which we desire. Just as Plato's eros belongs to that class of terms that have their meaning in pointing toward something else, that something else being something never achievable, so Nono's music and the text fragments embedded within point toward an ideal that cannot possibly be achieved.

Most musicians will be familiar with the feeling that the performance of a work that one aspires toward always remains just beyond any that have been realized. Among canonical composers, performances of Brahms often strike me this way. There is something in his music that always remains beyond the horizon, just out of view, which is to say just out of hearing. Nono's *an Diotima* makes this idea programmatic within a work that paradoxically denies having a program.

Eros is bodily and eros is spiritual. We have considered Peter Cole's poem "The Reluctant Kabbalist's Sonnet," and Harold Bloom's citation of Moshe Idel's *Kabbalah and Eros,* evoking the kabbalistic tradition where marital intercourse is regarded as redemptive, "both of individuals and of the cosmos." The eros of music too can be redemptive, healing in every sense of the word.

As we have noted, Sappho characterized eros as sweet, then bitter. I can think of no more powerful examples of this aspect of eros than Shakespeare's tragedies *Romeo and Juliet* and *Othello*. Both plays have inspired multiple musical settings. In my experience, none surpasses Verdi's *Otello*. In the first act, Verdi composes a magnificent love theme, portraying the mutual love of Othello and Desdemona beyond words, even Shakespeare's words, so brilliantly adapted by Arrigo Boito, Verdi's librettist. In the last scene, this same music returns; that which was sweet has truly become bitter.

Erotic love can also be thunderstruck, sudden and overwhelming. Anne Carson translates one of Sappho's fragments:

> Eros shook my
> mind like a mountain wind falling on oak trees.[47]

Such is the love of Pelléas for Mélisande in Maurice Maeterlinck's play and in Claude Debussy's opera. And such is the love of Rodolfo for Mimi in Giacomo Puccini's *La bohème*. And love can also take its time, ripening and maturing slowly, augmenting over time as it does in the best of marriages. Rabbi Akiva famously called the *Song of Songs* the most ardent expression of erotic longing, "the holy of holies," in the Hebrew Bible. "For the whole world is not as worthy as the day on which the Song of Songs was given to Israel; for all the writings are holy but the Song of Songs is the holy of holies."[48] The second verse of the poem might be paraphrased as "you can't hurry love." Here is the second verse, lines 5–7, in Robert Alter's translation:

> Stay me up with raisin-cakes,
> cushion me with quinces
> for I am in a swoon of love.
> His left hand beneath my head,
> his right hand embracing me.
> I make you swear, O daughters of Jerusalem
> by the deer or the gazelles of the field,
> that you shall not rouse nor stir love
> until it pleases.[49]

We have seen how canonical art resonates through generation after generation. Sappho's sweet then bitter through Shakespeare and beyond, Sappho's wind fallen on oaks, as thunderstruck love in Debussy and Puccini; in the middle 1960s, no musical group dominated popular music more than Diana Ross and the Supremes. "That you shall not rouse nor stir love until it pleases" resonates in their song "You Can't Hurry Love." It still resonates today.

My longtime friend Susan McClary is preeminent among musicologists of her generation, especially for her studies of sexuality and subjectivity in musical works of the seventeenth century. Her book *Conventional Wisdom* includes extended discussion of Alessandro Stradella's oratorio *La Susanna*, based on the biblical story of Susanna and the Elders. I find McClary's comments about the fusion of sexuality and spirituality particularly apposite to our context.

> *La Susanna* also participates in several other areas of cultural representation, including one quite alien to us now: namely, the sacred erotic. To many of us today, religion and sexuality reside at opposite ends of the spectrum. But seventeenth-century artists often mapped these realms upon one another because of many factors—including the charismatic example of St. Teresa . . . If human desire is at its most fervent at moments of sexual transport, then the church wanted access to that experience, albeit harnessed and redefined as love for God.[50]

I don't think I do violence to McClary's observation by noting its cynical voice, where eros is "harnessed and redefined as love of God." I am hardly a kabbalist, but for me eros and spiritual longing are not opposed, although, as powerful forces, either can be abused toward in ways that are not healthy. Music does many things and can be heard in as many ways as there are listeners and music to be heard. Music as Sacred Eros is among them.

A Coda

In music, as we have noted, the coda space is often the space of recollection and reflection. And though the music remains ongoing, the temporal vector that predominates is no longer prospective, or even immersed in now-time, but rather is a final gathering up just before we close our journey, whether through some sense of resolution or through an expiration into silence.

As I promised at the outset, this has been a personal book, reflecting my very personal relationship with music and with the other disciplines that for me have become part of music, as music has been part of them. Once again, I recall Emerson's observation from "The American Scholar," with the hope that my reader has found that it rings true. "The deeper [the scholar] dives into his privatest, secretest presentiment, to his wonder he finds, this is the most acceptable, most public, and universally true. The people delight in it; the better part of every man feels, This is my music; this is myself." Our musings on imagery from Kabbalah have considered following and reflecting and, most importantly, seeing and hearing *through*, so that we become a middle-voiced participation in creation's emanations. Through Levinas, Bloom, Hollander, and others, we have considered the diachrony of transformation. And we have understood how the diachrony of music mimics and instantiates the diachrony of our lives; its flowing fictions part and parcel of our lives.

In Levinas's writings we have seen how the "saying" of the other breaks open the enclosed spaces of subjective totalization, how a proximity to the other, impossible to reduce to the same, augments our selves, indeed links the human to the divine. And we have suggested that Levinas's "saying" itself needs be augmented to include the nonverbal sayings and seeings, those fictions that make us more fully human.

Through Angus Fletcher, John Ashbery, and Brian Ferneyhough, we have explored the metaphor of waves, the carriers of music's ever-changing modes of flow. And we have seen how music's horizontal ebb and flow swirl upwardly or downwardly into vortices or vortexes and that these are constituents of the peaks and valleys of our cognitive, emotional, spiritual, and sexual lives, our transport in lieu of Jacob's ladder. We have considered the pulsing of our hearts and the cadence of our breathing as concomitants of the rhythmic pulses of music, neither cause nor effect but mutual. And we have considered how music is a taking in and a giving out, and that the intake and outflow of *ruach*—breath, spirit, wind—is that music that presses up against and then expands the very boundaries of our being. Neither object nor subject, we have considered music that we make as music that makes us in turn. And such is *Music's Making*.

Through Boulez and Deleuze we have explored principal divisions of time and space: that which divides, creating modules and hierarchies, called *agrarian* among its many names, and that which does not impose modules, hierarchies, or boundaries, called *nomadic* among its many names. And through Angus Fletcher and Harold Bloom we have explored another way of parsing time and space, the wanderings of the labyrinth, the timelessness of the temple, and the thresholds of liminal space. And through many voices, David Lewin and Harold Bloom included, we have explored how the interstices of liminal time and space dilate to include the uncanny, recognizing that the unheard matches and augments what's heard, and that silence and sound are sibling twins, mutual in giving sense to it all. And although the voices have been many, we have recognized each as singular. And that the scholar, or artist, or teacher who augments my singularity through my encounter with theirs is greatly beloved.

The show is over. The curtain closes. The lights dim, and the audience shuffles out of this theater of mind, this concert space of heard and unheard, to "the hum of thoughts evaded in the mind," as aspect of Wallace Steven's "supreme fiction." The words we've heard, the songs, the musings, echo in our inner ear, linger in our inward eye. A silence that gave forth sound envelopes that sound, reminds us once again that to make music is to fuse body and spirit. And that our health, bodily and spiritual, depends on it. And such is *Music's Making*.

Rabbi Akiva said, "Sing every day, sing every day."

Notes

Introduction

1. Even speaking this way is misleading, because if the cosmos is truly one, whence comes the perspective that can judge it so? Such questions trouble mystics of all traditions.

2. Carl Safina, *Becoming Wild: How Animal Cultures Raise Families, Create Beauty, and Achieve Peace*, 162. Elsewhere in the book, Safina describes research done on the male zebra finch, native to Australia. "Singing zebra finch males who have no audience show brain activity in the regions involved in vocal control, song learning, and self-monitoring. When a female is listening, though, the male's learning and monitoring activity stops . . . It's like the difference between practicing an instrument and playing music" (184–85). Thanks to Kelly Kinney Fine for recommending this book.

3. Roseanna Warren, from "Rosh Hashanah," *So Forth: Poems*, 27.

4. Grace Schulman, *Days of Wonder: New and Selected Poems* (Boston: Houghton Mifflin Company, 2002), 43.

5. "The American Scholar," in *Ralph Waldo Emerson: Essays and Lectures*, selected and annotated by Joel Porte (New York: Library of America, 1983), 64–65.

6. David Lewin, *Generalized Musical Intervals and Transformations* (New Haven: Yale University Press), 1987. Reissued with a foreword by Edward Gollin, Oxford University Press, 2007.

7. "Music Theory, Phenomenology, and Modes of Perception," *Music Perception: An Interdisciplinary Journal* 3, no. 4 (summer 1986): 327–392.

8. For a background and critique of Lewin's mathematical modeling, see Dmitri Tymoczko, "Generalizing Musical Intervals," *Journal of Music Theory* 53, no. 2 (2009): 227–54. Tymoczko's ongoing critique of Lewin's formalisms is found in his article "Rethinking Transformations," still in progress as of this writing. For a thoroughgoing application of Lewin's models, see Steven Rings, *Tonality and Transformation* (New York: Oxford University Press, 2011).

9. GMIT, 159.

10. Kevin Korsyn discusses Lewin's phenomenological model in *Decentering Music*, 166–75. There Korsyn characterizes Lewin's approach as "ironic," in that Lewin entertains multiple perspectives toward the identical musical objects. The characterization is not objectionable, but inadequate to be sure.

11. The song is "Morgengruss" from Schubert's song cycle *Die schöne Müllerin*, discussed on pages 343–57 of Lewin's article. Years prior to the phenomenology article, Lewin had written an extensive analysis of the song, viewed from multiple perspectives; this multifaceted analysis might be the most virtuosic display of analytic prowess ever attempted by this most virtuosic of analysts. The analysis was published posthumously, along with extensive commentary, in *David Lewin's Morgengruss: Text, Context, Commentary* (New York: Oxford University Press), 2015.

12. Lewin's essays in the area have been collected in *Studies in Music with Text* (New York: Oxford University Press, 2006).

Chapter 1

1. Online Etymology Dictionary, etymonline.com.

2. Wallace Stevens, "The Noble Rider and the Sound of Words," in *The Necessary Angel: Essays on Reality and the Imagination* (New York: Vintage Books, 1951), 31.

3. Wallace Stevens, *Opus Posthumous: Poems, Plays, Prose*, ed. Milton J. Bates (New York: Alfred A. Knopf, 1989), 189.

4. Ibid., 204.

5. Nelson Goodman, in *Languages of Art*, shows an acute awareness of this aspect of seeing. The following is taken from pages 7–8.

> The eye comes always ancient to its work, obsessed by its own past and by old and new insinuations of the ear, nose, tongue, fingers, heart, and brain. It functions not as an instrument self-powered and alone, but as a dutiful member of a complex and capricious organism. Not only how but what it sees is regulated by need and prejudice. It selects, rejects, organizes, discriminates, associates, classifies, analyzes, constructs. It does not so much mirror as take and make; and what it takes and makes it sees not bare, as items without attributes, but as things, as food, as people, as enemies, as stars, as weapons. Nothing is seen nakedly or naked.
>
> The myths of the innocent eye and of the absolute given are unholy accomplices.

6. The significant role of narrative fiction in contributing to our sense of self is explored by Paul Ricoeur in *Oneself as Another,* especially in the book's sixth chapter, "The Self and Narrative Identity" (140–68).

Chapter 2

1. All that follows is a paraphrase of Patrick Olivelle, *Upaniṣads* (Oxford: Oxford University Press, 2008), 13–14.

2. Ibid., 14.

3. This translation is taken from Everett Fox, *The Five Books of Moses* (New York: Schocken Books, 1995).

4. The Wikipedia article on Neoplatonism provides a good start for anyone wanting to do further reading on the topic.

5. John Rahn discusses the roots of Schenker's thought coming out of Jewish sources in his 2004 article "The Swerve and the Flow: Music's Relationship to Mathematics," *Perspectives of New Music* 42, no. 1 (winter 2004): 130–50. In a personal correspondence (July 17, 2023), Rahn emphasized that Schenker would have recognized only the Jewish derivations, without connection to Plato or Neoplatonism. He also quoted Schenker: "Only the Genius is connected with God, not the people," as describing the idea of a Tzaddik (a Yiddish sage), an idea not emerging out of Neoplatonism. Wayne Alpern did a presentation titled "Schenker's *Yiddishkeit*" at the joint meetings of the American Musicological Society and the Society for Music Theory in Milwaukee, Wisconsin, in 2014.

6. Radek Chlup discusses this aspect of Proclus's thought in *Proclus: An Introduction* (Cambridge: Cambridge University Press, 2012), 62–85, and elsewhere.

7. Paul Ricoeur, *Oneself as Another,* trans. Kathleen Blamey (Chicago: University of Chicago Press, 1992), 158.

8. John Hollander discusses *contre-rejet* in chapter 5 of *Vision and Resonance: Two Senses of Poetic Form,* 91–116. We discuss this technique further within Part II of *Music's Making* in the subsection titled "The Silence of Caesura."

9. Helen Vendler, *Dickinson: Selected Poems and Commentaries* (Cambridge: The Belknap Press of Harvard University Press, 2010), 157–60.

10. For an introduction to Kabbalistic symbolism and the *sefirot* in particular, see Gershom Scholem, *On the Kabbalah and Its Symbolism,* 35–37 and passim. Also highly recommended is Arthur Green, intro. to *The Zohar: Pritzker Edition,* xxxi–lxxxi. Arthur Green augments the work of his introduction to the Pritzker Edition in *A Guide to the Zohar* (Stanford: Stanford University Press, 2004).

11. *The Zohar: Pritzker Edition,* xi, xlvi.

12. *JPS Hebrew-English Tanakh,* 2nd ed. (Philadelphia: Jewish Publication Society, 1999), 187.

13. See, for example, the experiences of both R. Abraham Burukhim and R. Isaac Yehuda Yehiel Safrin cited in Moshe Idel, *Kabbalah: New Perspectives*, 80, 83.

14. M. H. Abrams considers "the mirror" along with "the lamp" as the two basic metaphors for understanding. *The Mirror and the Lamp*, passim.

15. Introduction to *The Zohar: Pritzker Edition*, xlvii–xlviii. Green expands his description of the sefirot in *A Guide to the Zohar* (Stanford: Stanford University Press, 2004), 28–59.

16. Martin Heidegger, *Country Path Conversations*, trans. Bret W. Davis (Bloomington: Indiana University Press, 2016), 105–31.

17. Ibid., 110.

18. Kevin Korsyn discusses *seeing through* and *hearing through*, observing that "aural experience includes something inaudible, a social frame that cannot be heard." See *Decentering Music: A Critique of Contemporary Musical Research* (New York: Oxford University Press, 2003), 35.

19. Peter Cole discusses this aspect of Ibn Gabirol in *The Poetry of Kabbalah: Mystical Verse from the Jewish Tradition* (New Haven: Yale University Press, 2014), 51–52.

20. *Kingdom's Crown*, IX, 11–19; from Peter Cole, *Dream of the Poem: Hebrew Poetry form Muslim and Christian Spain 950–1492* (Princeton: Princeton University Press, 2007), 101.

21. Scholem, *On the Kabbalah and Its Symbolism*, 132.

22. Benjamin Harshav provides striking examples in *The Meaning of Yiddish* (1990; repr., Stanford University Press, 1999).

23. Sholem Aleichem, *Tevye der milkhiker* (Warsaw: Ventigo Media, 2020), 25. My translation.

24. Ruth R. Wisse, *The Modern Jewish Canon: A Journey Through Language and Culture* (New York: The Free Press, 2000) includes an insightful discussion of Sholem Aleichem and his "comedy of endurance." Wisse writes eloquently on the character Tevye, including his propensity to quote (and misquote) biblical adages that are sprinkled through his dialogue. Benjamin Harshav, *The Meaning of Yiddish* (Stanford: Stanford University Press, 1990), also provides insight into Aleichem's Tevye and the incorporation of sayings derived from Hebrew scripture applied, often ironically, to the problems of everyday life (92–94).

25. I consider Mahler's embarrassment of being associated with Jewish culture, and Yiddish culture specifically, in Michael Cherlin, "The Embarrassments of Yiddish," in *Varieties of Musical Irony: From Mozart to Mahler* (Cambridge: Cambridge University Press, 2017), 241–51.

26. "Theodor Adorno, Mahler: A Musical Physiognomy," 32–33, cited in *Varieties of Musical Irony*, 225.

Chapter 3

1. Edging up close to what I am calling a middle-voiced approach, Kevin Korsyn uses the term *reflexivity*. In that context Korsyn cites Shoshana Felman on Jacques Lacan. "But the new Freudian mode of reflexivity precisely shifts, displaces, and unsettles the very boundaries between self and other, subverting by the same token the symmetry that founds their dichotomy, their clear-cut opposition to each other." *Decentering Music: A Critique of Contemporary Musical Research*, 89, citing Shoshana Felman, *Jacques Lacan and the Adventure of Insight* (Cambridge: Harvard University Press, 1987), 61.

2. John Llewelyn, *The Middle Voice of Ecological Conscience* (London: Palgrave Macmillan, 1991).

3. Llewelyn's book extends Levinas's responsibility to the other (another human) to include human responsibility to other creatures. My own adaptation of Levinas, although with a different focus, is in the same spirit.

4. John Llewelyn, *The Middle Voice of Ecological Conscience*, xi.

5. Dan Zahavi, *Husserl's Phenomenology* (Stanford: Stanford University Press, 2003).

6. Ibid., 29.

7. From "Syrinx," in Amy Clampett, *A Silence Opens* (Alfred A. Knopf, 1994), 3–4.

8. John Hollander, "The Art of Memory," *The New Republic*, September 19, 1994, 51–52.

9. Zahavi, *Husserl's Phenomenology*, 76.

10. Ibid., 199–20.

11. Ibid., 99. Matthew Rahaim, *Musicking Bodies: Gesture and Voice in Hindustani Music* (Middletown, CT: Wesleyan University Press, 2012) provides a fascinating study of embodiment in Hindustani music where hand gestures parallel singing.

12. Maurice Merleau-Ponty, *Phenomenology of Perception*, xiii. A more recent and comprehensive study integrating cognitive science, biology, embodiment, and historical phenomenology is Evan Thompson, *Mind in Life: Biology, Phenomenology, and the Sciences of Mind* (Cambridge: The Belknap Press of Harvard University Press, 2007).

13. Ibid., 137.
14. Ibid., 137.
15. Ibid., 153.
16. Ibid., 205.
17. Ibid., 366.
18. Ibid., 393.
19. Ibid., 452.

20. Don Ihde, *Listening and Voice: A Phenomenology of Sound* (Athens: Ohio University Press, 1976).

21. Ibid., 75.

22. Ibid., 153.

23. Ibid., 158–59.

24. Rahaim, *Musicking Bodies*, 35.

25. Bret W. Davis, *Heidegger and the Will: On the Way to Gelassenheit* (Evanston: Northwestern University Press, 2007), 20.

26. Martin Heidegger, *Being and Time: A Translation of "Sein und Zeit,"* trans. John Macquarrie and Edward Robinson (New York: Harper & Row, 1976), 51. Text in square brackets added.

27. Bret W. Davis provides a lucid and thoughtful study of both "willing" and *Gelassenheit* in his *Heidegger and the Will: On the Way to Gelassenheit* (Evanston, IL: Northwestern University Press, 2007).

28. Heidegger, *Country Path Conversations*, trans. Bret W. Davis (Bloomington: Indiana University Press, 2016).

29. Ibid., xiii.

30. Ibid., 70.

31. Ibid., 87.

Chapter 4

1. *Collected Works of Paul Valéry, Volume 14: Analects*, trans. Stuart Gilbert (Princeton, NJ: Princeton University Press, 1970), 211. My attention to Valéry's aphorism was first drawn by Emmanuel Levinas, who quotes Valéry's aphorism without giving its source (*Otherwise than Being*, Footnote 29, 189). Thanks to Peter Cole for steering me to the source in Valéry's writings.

2. *The Prophetic Moment*, 26–27.

3. *Colors of the Mind*, 124.

4. Ibid., 124.

5. Charles Wright, *Buffalo Yoga* (New York: Farrar, Straus and Giroux, 2004), 54.

6. *Colors of the Mind*, 168.

7. Harold Bloom quoting Ralph Waldo Emerson in *Poetics of Influence*, 313. The passage may be found in *Emerson: Essays and Lectures* (New York: Library of America, 1983), 271.

8. See, e.g., *Wallace Stevens: The Poems of Our Climate*, 2.

9. *Colors of the Mind*, 170.

10. *The Palm at the End of the Mind*, 307. The poem is cited and discussed in Harold Bloom, *The Daemon Knows: Literary Greatness and the American Sublime*, 374.

11. *The Anatomy of Influence*, 300.
12. Ibid., 300.
13. John Ashbery, *Quick Question: New Poems* (New York: Ecco, 2012), 1.
14. *Mozart's Grace* (Princeton, NJ: Princeton University Press, 2013), 5.
15. Ibid., 38–40.
16. Ibid., 97.
17. *Colors of the Mind*, 186.
18. Ibid., 186–87.
19. Thomas Weiskel, *The Romantic Sublime* (Baltimore: Johns Hopkins University Press, 2019, originally published in 1976), 165–204.
20. *The Romantic* Sublime, 168–69, quoting William Wordsworth, "Prelude," 12.208–23.
21. *The Romantic Sublime*, 169. Bracketed text added.
22. For an extended analysis of Schoenberg's tone poem, see *Schoenberg's Musical Imagination*, chapter 3, 68–154.
23. *The Romantic Sublime*, 181, citing Wordsworth, "Prelude," 12.297–301.
24. Ibid., 182, citing Wordsworth, "Prelude," 12.312–26.

Chapter 5

1. Ethan Kleinberg, *Emmanuel Levinas's Talmudic Turn* (Stanford: Stanford University Press, 2021). Citing the work of multiple other scholars, Kleinberg also provides a thoughtful critique of Levinas's work. See especially 129–30 and 140–44.
2. Ibid., 17–20.
3. Ibid., 24–25.
4. Ibid., 26.
5. Ibid., 62–65.
6. The Talmud, also known as the Oral Torah (although we have it in written form), comprises rabbinic commentary on Jewish scripture, principally the Mishnah, codified in the third century CE, and the Gemara, commentary on the Mishnah, compiled over the next several hundred years. The Lithuanian Talmudic tradition, with its origins in the exegetic methods of the Gaon of Vilna (1720–1797) and Hayyim (also spelled Chiam) of Volozhin (1749–1821), comprised an ongoing study and augmentation of thought based in Talmud, but was also cognizant of Western learning.
7. *Totality and Infinity*, 89.
8. Theodor Adorno shared Levinas's strong antipathy toward totalizing thought, and, like Levinas, Adorno was profoundly affected by the Holocaust. Daniel Chua, in his *Beethoven & Freedom*, cites a passage from Adorno's *Negative Dialectics*: "It is the question whether one can *live* after Auschwitz. This question has appeared to me, for example, in the recurring dreams which plague me, in

which I have the feeling that I am no longer really alive, but am just the emanation of a wish from some victim of Auschwitz." (The passage, from page 362 of *Negative Dialectics* is cited by Chua on page 108, footnote 4.) To my mind, Adorno's nightmare of the Holocaust tempers his dark vision of humanity in general and his writings on music in particular. I do not find this darkness of vision at the core of Levinas's thought. *Beethoven & Freedom* draws copiously from philosophical discourse, principally Immanuel Kant and Theodor Adorno. The last "movement" of Chua's three-movement book brings Levinas and others into the conversation, at least in part to overcome the impasses inherent in Adorno's rather bleak outlook with a humanizing alternative.

9. *Otherwise than Being, or Beyond Essence*, xlvii.

10. This is contradicted a few verses later in Exodus 33:20: "He said, 'you cannot see My face, for a man may not see Me and live" (Jewish Publication Society translation).

11. Edith Wyschogrod, "Emmanuel Levinas and Hillel's Questions," in *Postmodern Philsophy and Christian Thought* (Bloomington: Indiana University Press, 1999), 229–45; Ephraim Meir, "Judaism and Philosophy: Each Other's Other in Levinas," *Modern Judaism* 30, no. 3 (2010): 348–62; Hillary Putnam, "Levinas and Judaism," in *The Cambridge Companion to Levinas*, 33–62. See especially 37–39.

12. Catherine Chalier, "Levinas and the Talmud," trans. Annette Aronowicz, included in *The Cambridge Companion to Levinas*, 102.

13. Hillary Putnam provides an insightful discussion of הנני (*hineni*) and its central role in Levinas's thought in his essay "Levinas and Judaism" included in *The Cambridge Companion to Levinas*, 33–62. The distinguished French philosopher Paul Ricoeur makes strikingly similar observations in *Oneself as Another*.

> Self-constancy is for each person that manner of conducting himself or herself so that others can *count on* that person. Because someone is counting on me, I am *accountable for* my actions before another. The term "responsibility" unites both meanings: "counting on" and "being accountable for." It unites them, adding to them the idea of a *response* to the question "Where are you?" asked by another who needs me. This response is the following: "Here I am!" a response that is a statement of self-constancy. (*Oneself as Another*, trans. Kathleen Blamey, 165)

14. *Otherwise than Being*, 13.
15. Ibid., 114.
16. Ibid., 144–45.
17. *Totality and Infinity*, 39.
18. Ibid., 62.
19. Ibid., 66.
20. Ibid., 70.

21. Ibid., 180.
22. *The Cambridge Companion to Levinas*, 9.
23. *Totality and Infinity*, 119.
24. Ibid., 110.
25. Ibid., 163.
26. *Otherwise than Being*, 63.
27. Ibid., 73.
28. *Totality and Infinity*, 203.
29. *Otherwise than Being*, 40.
30. Ibid., endnote 29, 189.
31. *Totality and Infinity*, 58.
32. Paul Valéry, *Dialogues, Eupalinos, or the Architect*, 83.
33. Frederick von Schelling, *The Philosophy of Art* (Minneapolis: University of Minnesota Press, 1989), trans. By Douglas W. Stott, 165.
34. As the composer James Dillon points out, these are better just called techniques.
35. *Otherwise than Being*, 41.
36. Gerald L. Bruns, "The Concepts of Art and Poetry in Emmanuel Levinas's Writings," in *The Cambridge Companion to Levinas*, 216.
37. Ibid., 218.
38. Levinas, *Outside the Subject*, 147–48. I added the text in square brackets.
39. Levinas, *Difficult Freedom*, 3–10.
40. "Ethics and Spirit," 6–8.
41. *Nine Talmudic Readings*, 30–50.
42. Ibid., 42.
43. *Otherwise than Being*, 46–47.
44. Ibid., 40.
45. Ibid., 82.
46. Levinas broaches the topic of diachrony versus synchronicity as early as page 9 of *Otherwise than Being*.
47. Levinas, *Of God Who Comes to Mind*, 71.
48. *Otherwise than Being*, 71.
49. This enigmatic "hesitation" is further described in ibid., 155.
50. *The Cambridge Companion to Levinas*, "Levinas and Judaism," 56.
51. *Otherwise Than Being*, xxxix.
52. Ibid., 12–13.
53. "Levinas and Judaism," 57.

Chapter 6

1. Bloom, *The Anatomy of Influence: Literature as a Way of Life*, 8.
2. Ibid., 209.

3. Ibid., 210.

4. Ibid., 211. I have modified the spelling of "daimonic" in the passage to match Bloom's preferred spelling "daemonic."

5. Masha Gessen's *The Future is History: How Totalitarianism Reclaimed Russia* brilliantly moves between larger social and historical issues and individual persons whose living experience is conditioned by those factors. Gessen's ability to move back and forth between individual persons and large, looming historical situations reminds me of Leo Tolstoy's techniques as a novelist, in *War and Peace* in particular.

6. Bloom, *Ruin the Sacred Truths*, 4.

7. Bloom, *The Daemon Knows*, 3.

8. Bloom, *The Anatomy of Influence*, 212. Taken from "Self-Reliance," included in *Ralph Waldo Emerson: Essays and Lectures*, selected and annotated by Joel Porte (New York: Library of America, 1983), 268–69.

9. Bloom, *The Anatomy of Influence*, 213.

10. "The American Scholar," in Porte, *Ralph Waldo Emerson: Essays and Lectures*, 64–65.

11. Bloom, *Novelists and Novels: A Collection of Critical Essays* (Checkmark Books, 2007), 515–23.

12. Ibid., 515.

13. Bloom, *The Anatomy of Influence*, 326.

14. Bloom, *Shakespeare: The Invention of the Human*, xvii.

15. The quartet opens with a characteristic statement by the cello, followed by a very different, though complementary, idea in the first violin. The viola then begins a restatement of the cello's opening, differently inflected so that the cello's initial descent of five semitones (a perfect fourth in the terminology of tonal music) becomes a descent of six semitones in the viola (a tritone). Before the viola can continue, the second violin interrupts, playing a far-fetched transformation of the cello's opening statement, where the curve of the line is maintained, though barely recognizable. Only after this does the viola continue and complete its version of the cello's opening.

16. Kofi Agawu advocates for a semiotic approach in *Playing with Signs* (Princeton, NJ: Princeton University Press, 1991). Two notable books on music topics are Robert S. Hatten, *Interpreting Musical Gestures, Topics, and Tropes: Mozart, Beethoven, Schubert* (Bloomington: Indiana University Press, 2004), and Raymond Monelle, *The Musical Topic: Hunt, Military and Pastoral* (Bloomington: Indiana University Press, 2006).

17. Cited by Monelle, *The Musical Topic*, 3.

18. The best essay on this aspect of Don Giovanni that I know of is Daniel Heartz's "An Iconography of the Dances in the Ballroom Scene of Don Giovanni," in *Mozart's Operas* (Berkeley: University of California Press, 1990), 179–93.

Notes to Chapter 6 | 253

19. Wye Jamison Allanbrook, *The Secular Commedia: Comic Mimesis in Late Eighteenth-Century Music* (Berkeley: University of California Press, 2014). Thanks to Sumanth Gopinath for recommending this reading.

20. Ibid., 14. Text in square brackets added.

21. Ibid., 76. Text in square brackets added.

22. Bloom, *Possessed by Memory*, 90.

23. *A Map of Misreading*, 48, cited in *Harold Bloom: Towards Historical Rhetorics*, 50.

24. Peter de Bolla, *Harold Bloom: Towards Historical Rhetorics* (Oxon: Routledge, 1988), 74.

25. *Agon*, 18–19, cited in ibid., 74.

26. Italics added.

27. Francis Bacon, *The Essays: or Counsels of Civil and Moral* (New York: Barnes and Noble Books, 2005), 102.

28. *Country Path Conversations*, trans. Bret W. Davis, 105–6.

29. Bloom, *The Western Canon*, 3.

30. Ibid., 4.

31. Ibid., 10.

32. Ibid., 25–26.

33. "Schoenberg's Music for the Theater," in *The Great Tradition and Its Legacy: The Evolution of Dramatic and Musical Theater in Austria and Central Europe*, ed. Michael Cherlin, Halina Filipowicz, and Richard L. Rudolph (New York: Berghahn Books, 2003).

34. Bloom, *The Anatomy of Influence*, 326.

35. Kathleen Marie Higgins, *The Music between Us: Is Music a Universal Language?* (Chicago: University of Chicago Press, 2012), exhaustively and sympathetically explores music as a commonality among humans as well as some other species.

36. María Rosa Menocal, *Shards of Love: Exile and the Origins of the Lyric* (Durham, NC: Duke University Press, 1993), 24–25.

37. Ibid., 127, citing Gershom Scholem, *Origins of the Kabbalah*, 13–14. Italics in the original.

38. Ibid., 128–29, bracketed text added.

39. Paul Ricoeur insightfully discusses a range of "practices" in his *Oneself as Another*, 153–58.

40. *Possessed by Memory*, xix.

41. "The Reluctant Kabbalists Sonnet" by Peter Cole, from THE INVENTION OF INFLUENCE, copyright ©2014 by Peter Cole. Reprinted by permission of New Directions Publishing Corp.

42. Bloom, *Possessed by Memory*, 18–19, from Peter Cole, *The Invention of Influence*, 27.

43. Peter Cole, *The Poetry of Kabbalah: Mystical Verse from the Jewish Tradition* (New Haven: Yale University Press, 2012).

44. Bloom, *Possessed by Memory*, 14.

45. Ibid.

46. Personal correspondence, October 20, 2021.

47. Amnon Shiloah, "The Symbolism of Music in the Kabbalistic Tradition," *The World of Music* 20, no. 3 (1978).

48. Bloom, *Poetics of Influence*, 309–23.

49. Ibid., 313.

50. My description of the stem Niphal is taken from online access: uhg.readthedocs.io. Accessed November 1, 2021.

51. Bloom, *Take Arms Against a Sea of Troubles*, 7.

52. Ibid., 459.

53. Ibid., 491.

54. Ibid., 535.

55. Ibid., 565–67.

56. Bloom, *Kabbalah and Criticism*, 78.

57. Two noteworthy attempts to apply Bloom's ideas to music are Joseph N. Straus, *Remaking the Past: Musical Modernism and the Influence of Tonal Music* (Cambridge: Harvard University Press, 1990), and Kevin Korsyn, "Towards a New Poetics of Musical Influence," *Musical Analysis* 10, no. 2 (March–July 1991), 3–72.

58. Bloom, *The Anatomy of Influence*, 195.

59. David Lewin, "Music Theory, Phenomenology, and Modes of Perception," 381.

60. John Hollander, *The Figure of Echo*, 21.

61. Ibid., 65.

62. Ibid., 113–14.

63. Ibid., 136.

64. Ibid., 141.

65. Ibid.

66. Bloom, *Map of Misreading*, 130–39.

67. Bloom, *Take Arms*, 50–52. The phrase "fiction of the leaves" is taken from Wallace Stevens, "The Rock," part II, "The Poem as Icon."

68. Isaiah, KJV, 34:4, quoted in Bloom, *Take Arms*, 50–51.

69. Homer, *Iliad* 6, trans. Alexander Pope, quoted in Bloom, *Take Arms*, 51.

70. Virgil, *Aneid* 6, trans. John Dryden, quoted in Bloom, *Take Arms*, 51.

71. Dante, *Inferno* 3, trans. Henry Wadsworth Longfellow, quoted in Bloom, *Take Arms*, 51.

72. John Milton, *Paradise Lost*, book I, lines 300–4. Alluded to without direct quotation in Bloom, *Take Arms*, 52.

73. Bloom, *Take Arms*, 50–52.

74. Bloom, *The Breaking of the Vessels*, 95–107.

75. Bloom, *Take Arms*, 20.

76. Gregory G. Butler studies the applications of rhetorical figures to fugue in his "Fugue and Rhetoric," *Journal of Music Theory* 21, no. 1 (spring 1977). Butler's article includes the example from Joachim Burmeister (1564–1629). The same example is cited and interpreted more fully by John Hollander. For a general introduction to the historical uses of rhetorical figures to describe musical techniques, see "Rhetoric and Music," in *Grove Music Online*.

77. Hollander, *The Figure of Echo*, 143.

78. Ibid.

79. https://www.cpdl.org/wiki/images/2/28/Lassus_De_ore_prudentis.pdf.

80. Michael Cherlin, *Schoenberg's Musical Imagination*, 299–39.

81. Ibid., 330–31.

82. Only after having completed a full draft of *Music's Making*, did I become aware of Yoel Greenberg's book *How Sonata Forms: A Bottom-Up Approach Toward Musical Form* (Oxford University Press, 2022). In his study, Greenberg develops a diachronic approach toward the historical emergence of sonata forms through the confluence of separable elements found in sonata-form precursors. Greenberg's bottom-up approach toward musical form is somewhat at odds with the interactive top-down and bottom-up approach that generally I espouse toward understanding virtually any environment. I say "somewhat at odds" in that Greenberg although emphasizing a bottom-up approach is appreciative of the dynamic interactions of wholes and parts.

Chapter 7

1. Musical phrase shapes in the contexts of tonal music are studied in William Rothstein, *Phrase Rhythms in Tonal Music* (New York: Schirmer Books, 1989) and in William E. Caplin, *Classical Form: A Theory of Formal Functions. For the Instrumental Music of Haydn, Mozart, and Beethoven* (New York: Oxford University Press, 1998).

2. Walter Pater, from *The Renaissance: Studies in Art and Poetry*, included in *Selected Writings of Walter Pater*, ed. and intro. Harold Bloom (New York: Columbia University Press, 1974), 61.

3. In the first half of *Generalized Musical Intervals and Transformations*, David Lewin defines and formalizes a wide range of intervallic types, including both non-temporal and temporal aspects of the term. In the second half of *GMIT*, Lewin reconceptualizes directed intervals (from X to Y) as functional *transformations* (in transforming X into Y, X is reconceptualized as a function of Y). Lewin's very first example reconceptualizing interval into transformation is of a C major chord moving to an F major chord, where C major is transformed into the dominant of F (176). Interval as transformation involves temporality

(first this then that) but also change (through the temporal span, X changes into Y).

4. Arnold Schoenberg, *Fundamentals of Musical Composition*, ed. Gerald Strang and Leonard Stein (New York: St. Martin's Press, 1967), 3–81.

5. The *Harvard Dictionary of Music* has a useful introduction to the history of meter in Western art music. I consulted the 2nd edition, where the history of meter is found under the heading RHYTHM, section III (*Harvard Dictionary of Music*, 2nd ed., 730–31).

6. *Generalized Musical Intervals and Transformations*, 159.

7. Christopher F. Hasty, *Meter as Rhythm* (Oxford: Oxford University Press, 1997) gives numerous examples where musical meter is generated out of rhythm, rather than rhythm being subordinated to an overlay of meter. I find Hasty's approach appealing in that it allows meter to be emergent.

8. Angus Fletcher, *A New Theory for American Poetry: Democracy, the Environment, and the Future of Imagination*, 143.

9. *A New Theory for American Poetry*, 146, citing John Hollander, *The Work of Poetry* (New York: Columbia University Press, 1997), 183.

10. Brian Ferneyhough, *Collected Writings*, ed. James Boros and Richard Toop (London: Routledge, 1995).

11. Excerpted from "A Wave," in John Ashbery, *A Wave* (London: Penguin Books, 1985), 68–89.

12. Richard E. Goodkin, "Zeno's Paradox: Mallarmé, Valéry, and the Symbolist 'Movement,'" *Yale French Studies* no. 74 (1988): 133–56. The Valéry quote is on page 133.

13. Ibid., 134.

14. John Ashbery, *Self-Portrait in a Convex Mirror*, "Self-Portrait in a Convex Mirror, 68.

15. Ibid. The passages cited are found respectively on pages, 68 (twice), 73, 77, 78, and 81.

16. There is a Wikipedia article on the history of sumptuary laws, including their prevalence in Italy and elsewhere. Simon Schama discusses sumptuary laws during the Dutch seventeenth century in *The Embarrassment of Riches: An Interpretation of Dutch Culture in the Golden Age*, 186–87. Elsewhere in *The Embarrassment of Riches* Schama discusses the tulip craze (not cabbage rose) that impacted seventeenth-century Dutch economies to the point of creating great wealth as well as the loss of family fortunes. However, Dutch sumptuary laws were evidently not correlated with investments in tulips (or roses).

17. A. R. Ammons, *The Complete Poems of A. R. Ammons*, vol. 2, 60–61.

18. Brian Ferneyhough, *Collected Writings*, "Il Tempo della Figura," 34–35.

19. Ibid., 35.

20. Ibid., 34. Text in square brackets added.

21. Walter Benjamin, *Illuminations*, ed. and intro. Hannah Arendt, trans. Harry Zohn (New York: Schocken Books, 1969), 217–51.

22. Ibid., 220.

23. Ibid., 222.

24. "*Il Tempo della Figura*," 41. Italics in the original.

25. Ibid., 34.

26. Ibid., 41.

27. Readers interested in following the logic of Ferneyhough's extended example should refer to the essay. Ferneyhough's example, like his musical compositions, is of dizzying complexity. In what immediately follows, I render the processes of Ferneyhough's musical example into prose with as much lucidity as I can summon.

Example 2(a) places the original notated rhythms into a succession of changing meters, while holding the ratios internal to each dyad intact. Each dyad is assigned its own meter forming the sequence $\frac{2}{8}, \frac{5}{16}, \frac{3}{8}, \frac{2}{8}, \frac{1}{8}$. We can clarify the pattern by using the same denominator for each metric dyad: $\frac{4}{16}, \frac{5}{16}, \frac{6}{16}, \frac{4}{16}, \frac{2}{16}$ or 4:5:6:4:2. The process of incremental change in durations has taken on a new sense as the metric units systematically expand and then contract, while the durational ratios internal to each metric unit are as they were before. As the multi-tiered example continues, Ferneyhough creates two subsequent transformations by applying incremental augmentation and diminution to pulse configurations, always keeping the underlying durational ratios intact, but progressively moving them further and further away from immediate perceptibility. 2(b) continues to maintain the original dyadic ratios (7:1, 3:1, 2:1, 3:2, 1:1) but evenly subdivides each first half of the dyad respectively into 5-4-3-2-1 pulses, while each second half of the dyad is evenly divided respectively into 1-2-3-4-5 pulses. The example, once again maintaining the original underlying ratios, has superimposed a palindrome of diminishing and augmenting pulse configurations: 5:1, 4:2, 3:3, 2:4, 1:5. The final example, 2(c), as with the others, still maintains the original dyadic-durational ratios across the whole, but now the pattern of superimposed pulses suggests three-part patterns with equally pulsed subdivisions within each unit parsing into groups of 3-2-5, 3-2-5, 5-5-3. The original dyads are thus obscured, running across the grain of the subdivided configuration: 3-2-5, 3-2-5, 5-5-3 (where 3-2 pulses are in the ratio 7:1, 5,3 in the ratio 3:1, etc.). The five-pulsed unit that begins the final three-group integrates the original 3:2 into five equal pulses, 3+2. By this point, if not before, the original manifestation of the figure (durational ratios of 7:1, 3:1, 2:1, 3:2, 1:1) is so deeply embedded in the final configuration that it seems to have disappeared. Yet it is the hidden force that engenders the manifest music.

28. Salvatore Sciarrino speaking to Harry Vogt, trans. Christina Preiner. Notes to *Infinito Nero,* Kairos CD 0012022KAI.

258 | Notes to Chapter 8

29. Brian Ferneyhough, "Second String Quartet (1982)," *Collected Writings*, 117.

30. *Rhyme's Reason*, 11.

31. John Hollander, "'Sense Variously Drawn Out': On English Enjambment," in *Vision and Resonance: Two Senses of Poetic Form*, 91–116.

32. Ibid., 106.

33. Grace Schulman, *Days of Wonder: New and Selected Poems* (Boston: Houghton Mifflin, 2002), 117.

34. Leo Treitler, "History, Criticism, and Beethoven's Ninth Symphony," in *Music and the Historical Imagination*, 19.

35. William Weir, "A Little Bit Softer Now, a Little Bit Softer Now . . . The sad, gradual decline of the fade-out in popular music," September 12, 2014, https://slate.com/culture/2014/09/the-fade-out-in-pop-music-why-dont-modern-pop-songs-end-by-slowly-reducing-in-volume.html. Italics (*before, after*) added.

36. Corinna da Fonseca-Wollheim, "How Silence Makes the Music: A brief, incomplete, very quiet guide to the history of music's negative spaces," *New York Times*, October 2, 2019, https://www.nytimes.com/2019/10/02/arts/music/silence-classical-music.html.

37. John Hollander, *Rhyme's Reason*, 49.

38. John Hollander, *Harp Lake* (New York: Alfred A. Knopf, 1988), 18.

39. Scott Burnham, *Mozart's Grace*, 128.

Chapter 8

1. Musical meter parses passing time by placing events into a regularly pulsed hierarchy. So, for example, ¾ time groups pulse into groups of three with each quarter-note receiving a single pulse. *Hypermeter* groups metric units into larger hierarchies. So, for example, music in ¾ time, parsed into four-bar hypermeter, would be counted **1**-2-3/**2**-2-3/**3**-2-3/**4**-2-3/**1**-2-3, etc.

2. John Hollander describes four systems of verse in *Rhyme's Reason: A Guide to English Verse*: pure accentual (as in early Germanic poetry and nursery rhymes); accentual-syllabic (iambic, dactylic, etc.); pure syllabic (as in modern French and Japanese and some more recent English poetry); free verse (without regular patterns); quantitative verse (as in Greek poetry and, later on, Latin), 4–5.

3. Henry Wadsworth Longfellow, *Longfellow: Poems and Other Writings*, selected and annotated by J. D. McClatchy (New York: The Library of America, 2000), 141.

4. The libretto by Francesco Maria Piave was adapted from a play by Victor Hugo, *Le roi s'amuse*.

5. Paul McCartney's song "Yesterday" provides a well-known example. The song plays with irregular groupings in its seven-bar verse: (1) "Yesterday / (+2)

all my troubles seemed so far away / (+2) now it looks as though they're here to stay; oh / (+2) I believe in yesterday," parsing into (1+2+2+2), with the next verse entering "Suddenly."

6. Martin R. L. Clayton, "Free Rhythm: Ethnomusicology and the Study of Music without meter," *Bulletin of the School of Oriental and African Studies, University of London* 59, no. 2 (1996): 323–32. Thanks to Matthew Rahaim for this reference.

7. Ibid., 329.

8. *Schoenberg's Musical Imagination*, 173–229.

9. The Wikipedia article on mensural notation provides an excellent introduction to the topic.

10. Note on terminology: the term "atonal" has been widely adopted to describe the music of Schoenberg and his students as early as 1908 and continuing until the twelve-tone technique emerged after World War I. Schoenberg explicitly disliked the term and suggested pan-tonal instead. Some writers, myself included, use the word post-tonal. None of these terms does justice to the fleeting sense of momentary tonal centers in this music that interact with music that seems to float untethered to any sense of tonal centricity. In Schoenberg and Berg, less so in Webern, vestiges of tonality will fleetingly emerge in post-tonal contexts.

Some commentators confuse twelve-tone music with that labeled "atonal." The twelve-tone technique emerges after World War I, first in Schoenberg and then in his students Webern and Berg. In this music, an ordered series of the twelve pitch-classes (where for example C♮, D♭♭, and B♯ comprise one of the twelve pitch-classes) is composed ab initio to form the basis of the various transformations of the series (most basically transpositions, inversions, and retrogrades of both) that form the harmonies and melodies of the composition. Normally, it is the interaction of smaller units within the twelve-tone series that form the audible relationships among transformations of the "tone rows." I surmise that tonality is massively repressed in this music, hidden beneath the surface, at least in Schoenberg and Berg, though many music theorists might not agree on this last point.

11. Julian Johnson, *Webern and the Transformation of Nature*, 27.

12. Ibid., 30–31.

13. Ibid., 34.

14. Ibid., 40.

15. John Hollander, "Making Nothing Happen," from *Tesserae & Other Poems* (New York: Alfred A. Knopf, 1993), 6.

16. From Tony Kushner and Joachim Neugroschel, *Dybbuk and Other Tales of the Supernatural*, adapted and trans. S. Ansky (New York: Theatre Communications Group, 1998), 152.

17. *Walt Whitman: Complete Poetry and Collected Prose* (New York: Library of America, 1982), 28.

18. Ibid., 190.

19. Erich Auerbach, *Mimesis: The Representation of Reality in Western Literature,* "Odysseus' Scare," 8.

20. Everett Fox, *The Five Books of Moses,* 93.

21. Ibid., 94.

22. Background, a formal analysis of Feldman's "Rothko Chapel," as well as a description of the space of Rothko's chapel, can be found in Steven Johnson, "*Rothko Chapel* and Rothko's Chapel," *Perspectives of New Music* 32, no. 2 (summer 1994): 6–53.

23. Jeremy Sigler, "The Kabbalah of Rothko," https://tabletmag.com/sections/arts-letters/articles/the-kabbalh-of-rothko.

24. Sigler quoting Stanley Kunitz in a recording in the Archives of American Art at the Smithsonian Institution.

25. Annie Cohen-Solal, *Mark Rothko: Toward the Light in the Chapel* (New Haven: Yale University Press, 2015).

26. Ibid., 1–11.

27. Ibid., 138–40.

28. Ibid., 142.

29. Roy Edwards, cited in Annie Cohen-Solal, *Mark Rothko: Toward the Light in the Chapel,* 195.

30. James Dillon, *The Gates: for String Quartet and Orchestra* (Edition Peters, 2016).

31. Angus Fletcher, *Colors of Mind,* 124.

32. Hart Crane, from "*To* Brooklyn Bridge," *The Complete Poems of Hart Crane,* ed. Marc Simon, intro. Harold Bloom (New York: Liveright, 2001), 44.

33. The Wikipedia article provides a good introduction to the term, although the easiest way to get a sense of how *micropolyphony* works is simply to listen to Ligeti's music.

34. I discuss related dialectical oppositions in Arnold Schoenberg's music in *Schoenberg's Musical Imagination,* chapter 2.

35. *Midrash Tanchuma, Bereshit 1,* accessed online through Sefaria.org.

36. Moshe Idel, *Absorbing Perfections,* 49.

Chapter 9

1. Pierre Boulez, *Boulez on Music Today,* trans. Susan Bradshaw and Richard Rodney Bennett (London: Faber and Faber, 1971), 83–98. (Originally published in 1963 in both German and French editions.)

2. *Difference and Repetition,* 36–37. (Originally published as *Différence et Repetition,* Presses Universitaires de France, 1968.)

3. Gilles Deleuze and Felix Guattari, *A Thousand Plateaus* (Minneapolis: University of Minnesota Press, 1987), 474–500, and passim.
4. *Music Today*, 85 (italics as in the original).
5. Ibid.
6. Ibid., 87–88.
7. Ibid., 88–89.
8. Ibid., 91.
9. Ibid., 93.
10. Ibid., 88, 93.
11. Ibid., 94.
12. *Difference and Repetition*, 36.
13. Ibid., 37.
14. Angus Fletcher, *Allegory: The Theory of a Symbolic Mode* (Ithaca, NY: Cornell University Press, 1964), 25–69.
15. Angus Fletcher, "Allegory without Ideas," *boundary 2: an international journal of literature and culture* 33, no. 1 (February 2006): 77–98.
16. Ibid., 95.
17. Leo Bersani, *The Culture of Redemption* (Cambridge: Harvard University Press, 1990), 86–87. The internal quotes are from Nietzsche, *The Birth of Tragedy*.
18. Brian Massumi, in his translator's introduction, briefly chronicles the times in which Deleuze and Guattari came into maturity, including the civil unrest in May 1968 along with the rise of feminism and gay rights: *A Thousand Plateaus*, x–xi.
19. Ibid., 363–64.
20. Ibid., 372.
21. Ibid., 369.
22. Ibid., 371.
23. Ibid., 474.
24. Charles Martin, *Ovid Metamorphoses* (New York: W. W. Norton & Company, 2004), 214.
25. Pater, *Selected Writings of Walter Pater*, 60.
26. Ibid., 475–76.
27. Ibid., 478.
28. I discuss these terms and their musical applications in *Varieties of Musical Irony: From Mozart to Mahler* (Cambridge: Cambridge University Press, 2017), 64–76.
29. The two most significant studies of sonata form are Charles Rosen, *Sonata Forms*, rev. ed. (New York: W. W. Norton & Company, 1988), and James Hepokoski and Warren Darcy, *Elements of Sonata Theory: Norms, Types, and Deformations in the Late-Eighteen Century Sonata* (Oxford: Oxford University Press, 2006). As different as their respective approaches are, for both Rosen and Hepokoski/Darcey,

formal divisions (as in agrarian space) are fundamental. Hepokoski and Darcy also divide sonatas into paradigmatic types, another agrarian division. They also discuss *parageneric* spaces, introductions and codas, which they consider to be add-ons to the generic sonata forms. As such, parageneric spaces remain within the realm of agrarian space.

30. Both works are based on Maurice Maeterlinck's play of the same name. I discuss the idea of *Fate* operating in both works in previous publications; Schoenberg's tone poem in *Schoenberg's Musical Imagination*, 68–154; Debussy's opera in *Varieties of Musical Irony*, 65–76.

31. Theodore W. Adorno, *Mahler: A Musical Physiognomy* (Chicago: University of Chicago Press, 1992), 4.

32. Ibid., 4–5. I have added the italics.

33. Ibid., 51.

34. *A Guide to the Zohar*, 118.

35. Gershom Scholem, *On the Kabbalah and Its Symbolism* (New York: Schocken Books, 1965), 110–77.

36. Mark Spicer, "Strategic Intertextuality in Three of John Lennon's Late Beatles Songs," *Gamut: Online Journal of the Music Theory Society of the Mid-Atlantic* 2, no. 1 (2009): 347–75.

37. Spicer cites Jean-François Lyotard's definition of *bricolage*: "the multiple quotation of elements taken from earlier styles or periods, classical or modern." Ibid., 351.

38. Ibid., 354.

39. Ibid., 351.

40. *Ehyeh: A Kabbalah for Tomorrow*, 74–75.

41. Ibid., 75–77.

42. Jean-Luc Nancy provides us with a stimulating and expansive meditation on this idea applied to divinity in *Being Singular Plural*, trans. Robert D. Richardson and Anne E. O'Byrne (Stanford: Stanford University Press, 2000).

Chapter 10

1. In studying the poem, I have benefited from multiple sources including Robert Greer Cohn, *Toward the Poems of Mallarmé* (Berkeley: University of California Press, 1980), Henry Weinfield, *Stéphane Mallarmé: Collected Poems* (Berkeley: University of California Press, 1994), and Richard E. Goodkin, "Zeno's Paradox: Mallarmé, Valéry, and the Symbolist 'Movement,'" *Yale French Studies*, no. 74 (1988): 133–56.

2. Translation by Henry Weinfield, *Stéphane Mallarmé: Collected Poems*, 38.

3. In describing the shaping and reshapings of the music, I found that I could not avoid some technical terms. A reader with musical training will find all of these familiar. A reader without that background might find some of this

difficult to follow. For the latter, I recommend simply listening to the piece, as many times as necessary, plugging in the terminology as a way of describing what's heard. A second concern is that by reverting to the technical terms that describe musical events, there is an inadvertent tendency toward objectifying the music. While this is not problematic in itself, it does run counter to the middle-voiced approach that I espouse throughout this study. The solution, as always, is to integrate the objectifying language into an experience that allows the listener to merge with the music, so that it's no longer "out there." For me, all objectifying analysis of music (or any art) is always "on the way" toward an integration, not subjective, but middle voiced.

4. The Bolshoi Ballet version featuring Tsiskaridze as the faun, staged by Vatslav Nizhinsky, is found at https://youtu.be/V_LrFJsgmJc (the posting is mislabeled as Ballets Russe, which closed in 1929). My thanks to Peter Schmelz for translating the opening credits of the video for me.

5. Susanne K. Langer, *Feeling and Form* (New York: Charles Scribner's Sons, 1953), 331.

6. Ibid., 351.

7. Camille Paglia, *Sexual Personae* (New Haven: Yale University Press), 7.

8. Ibid., 9.

9. Ibid., 10.

10. Gilles Deleuze, *Difference and Repetition*, trans. Paul Patton (New York: Columbia University Press, 1994).

11. Ibid., xx.

12. Ibid., 1.

13. Ibid.

14. Ibid.

15. Ibid., 23.

16. Ibid., 24–25.

17. Paul Ricoeur, *Oneself as Another* (Chicago: University of Chicago Press, 1992), 2 and throughout.

18. *Il Tempo della Figura*, 35.

19. Deleuze, *Difference and Repetition*, 17–18.

20. Ibid., 7.

21. Ibid., 71–72.

22. Ibid., 108–9.

23. Arthur Green, *Eyeh: A Kabbalah for Tomorrow* (Woodstock, VT: Jewish Lights Publishing, 2003), 2.

24. Bloom, *The Anatomy of Influence*, 209.

25. *Macbeth*, act 5, scene 5.

26. *Hamlet*, act 5, scene 1.

27. Daniel Chua provides a fascinating example of just such a musical space in Beethoven's Third Symphony, the *Eroica*. In classical sonata forms, the return of the opening material is normally prepared by a prolonged dominant chord,

called the retransition, leading into the tonic of the recapitulation. In the *Eroica*, as we near the recapitulation, the work's opening motto, at the tonic level, is directly juxtaposed against the ongoing dominant sonority. Chua, provocatively, calls this an "echo," recalling the opening from afar. At the same time, the motto is anticipatory or proleptic, it summons up the recapitulation before the fact. *Beethoven & Freedom*, 85.

28. Lewin develops transformation graphs and networks over the second half of his book *Generalized Musical Intervals and Transformations*, 157–244. The node-arrow system (where a node holds musical content and an arrow denotes the transformation of the content of one node into another) is explained on pages 193–96.

29. An example from GMIT: Figure 10.19 in *Generalized Musical Intervals and Transformations* (239) exemplifies a more complex graph of similar general design. The graph is part of a larger analysis of Debussy's "Reflets dans l'eau." As might be expected, given the work's title, musical mirror images play a major role in the piece. Lewin's Figure 10.19 shows a network of transpositions and inversions of a three-note pattern embedded in the texture of m. 20, at the outset of the section labeled Quasi cadenza. As with my simplified example (C major and F minor triads), Lewin's node-arrow graphs reverse arrow direction, and change ascending intervals (+) into their inverses (-). Lewin's commentary here does not engage temporal orientation.

Chapter 11

1. Exodus, 13.21, translation of the Jewish Publication Society.
2. 2 Kings, 2.11.
3. Ezekiel, 1.4, KJV.
4. Job, 38.1. The Hebrew word translated as *whirlwind* in KJV is more literally "storm wind" or "tempest." The Jewish Publication Society translation uses "tempest." Robert Alter's translation preserves "whirlwind" from KJV, but adds a note saying that while "storm" is a more literal translation of the Hebrew, "the Voice from the Whirlwind" is so deeply embedded in the imagination of speakers of English after the King James Version that it seems wise not to tamper with it" (*The Wisdom Books: Job, Proverbs, and Ecclesiastes* [W. W. Norton & Company, 2010], 158).
5. Proverbs, 1:27, translation from the Jewish Publications Society, *Hebrew-English Tanakh*.
6. *Paradise Lost*, Book II, lines 910–1055.
7. Harold Bloom, *Yeats* (Oxford University Press, 1970), 222–23.
8. KJV, Genesis 28.12–19.
9. The Wikipedia article on Clifford Geertz gives basic background on thick description, including Geertz's sources.

10. Maurice Merleau-Ponty, *The Visible and the Invisible* (Northwestern University Press, 1968), 236.
11. Ibid., 233.
12. Anthony J. Steinbock, *Phenomenology and Mysticism: The Verticality of Religious Experience* (Indiana University Press, 2007), 2.
13. Ibid., 9.
14. Ibid., 14–15.
15. Ibid., 193–94.
16. Ibid., 53–54.
17. Ibid., 101, 108.
18. Ibid., 78, 80, 86.
19. Ibid., 159.
20. Ibid., 213.
21. Ibid., 24.
22. Stanley Moss, *Almost Complete Poems* (Seven Stories Press, 2016), 102.
23. In summoning angled cuts, Moss may be playing on Emily Dickinson's "tell all the truth but tell it slant."

Tell all the truth but tell it slant—
Success in Circuit lies
Too bright for our infirm Delight
The Truth's superb surprise
As Lightning to the Children eased
With explanation kind
The Truth must dazzle gradually
Or every man be blind—

(Helen Vendler supplies commentary on this poem in *Dickinson: Selected Poems and Commentary*, 431–33.) That "the truth must dazzle gradually" captures the emergent process, metaphorically from half-light to full light, that the revelations of poetry and music exemplify.

24. Ted Gioia, *Work Songs* (Duke University Press, 2006). Thanks to Sumanth Gopinath for recommending this reading.
25. Ibid., 80. An expansive treatment of Ewe music is found in V. Kofi Agawu, *African Rhythm: a Northern Ewe Perspective* (Cambridge University Press, 1995).
26. Gioia, *Work Songs*, 150, 155.
27. Ibid., 209.
28. Ibid., 249.
29. Scott Burnham, *Mozart's Grace*, 134.
30. Ibid., 142.
31. Amnon Shiloah, "The Singing Birds," in *Music and Its Virtues in Islamic and Judaic Writings* (London: Routledge, 2007), 85. Note: *Music and Its Virtues in Islamic and Judaic Writings* is a compilation of articles from different sources, in multiple languages. The book was evidently cut and pasted from those sources.

The pagination evidently reflects the original pagination of those sources; it is discontinuous as it jumps from source to source.

32. "Music and Religion in Islam," in *Music and Its Virtues in Islamic and Judaic Writings*, 151.

33. Franz Kafka, *Parables and Paradoxes: Bilingual Edition*, trans. Willa and Edwin Muir (Schocken Books, 1975), 29.

34. For an extended and engaging treatment of eros in antiquity see Anne Carson, *Eros: The Bittersweet*, originally published by Princeton University Press, 1986.

35. James Merrill, *Collected Poems*, 97.

36. Plato, *The Symposium*, trans. with comment by R. E. Allen (New Haven: Yale University Press), 18.

37. Ibid., 43.

38. Ibid., 47.

39. Ibid., 47–49 and 144–46.

40. Lewis Lockwood tells the story behind the inscription in exemplary fashion. *Beethoven: The Music and Life* (New York: W. W. Norton & Company, 2003), 479–83.

41. The score is published by Ricordi Milan, catalog number 133049. Nono's list omits five of the fifty-three fragments, presumably inadvertently.

42. Friedrich Hölderlin, *Hymns and Fragments by Friedrich Hölderlin*, trans. and intro. Richard Sieburth (Princeton: Princeton University Press, 1984), 17.

43. Daniel Chua considers this at length in his book *Beethoven & Freedom*, 19–23.

44. Plato, *The Symposium: The Dialogues of Plato, Volume 2*, trans. with commentary by R. E. Allen (New Haven: Yale University Press, 1991), 144.

45. David Constantine, *Hölderlin* (Oxford: Oxford University Press, 1988), 61–80.

46. The tonic triad is D-f♯-A, the dominant is A-c♯-E, the subdominant G-b-D.

47. Anne Carson, *If Not, Winter: Fragments of Sappho* (Vintage Books, 2002), 47.

48. *Mishnah Yadayim*, 3, trans. Joshua Kulp, accessed online through Sefaria.org.

49. Robert Alter, *Strong as Death is Love: The Song of Songs, Ruth, Esther, Jonah, Daniel: A translation with commentary* (New York: W. W. Norton & Co., 2015), 15.

50. *Conventional Wisdom*, 19.

Bibliography

Adorno, Theodor W. 1992. *Mahler: A Musical Physiognomy.* Translated by Edmund Jephcott. Chicago: University of Chicago Press.
Aleichem, Sholem. 2020. *Tevye der milkhiker.* Adam Wolański, series editor. Warsaw: Ventigo Media.
Allanbrook, Wye Jamison. 2014. *The Secular Commedia: Comic Mimesis in Late Eighteenth-Century Music.* Edited by Mary Ann Smart and Richard Taruskin. Berkeley: University of California Press.
Alter, Robert. 2010. *The Wisdom Books: Job, Proverbs, and Ecclesiastes.* New York: W. W. Norton & Company.
———. 2015. *Strong as Death is Love: The Song of Songs, Ruth, Ester, Jonah, Daniel.* New York: W. W. Norton & Company.
Ammons, Archie Randolph. 2017. *The Complete Poems of A. R. Ammons,* in two vols. Edited by Robert M. West; introduction by Helen Vendler. New York: W. W. Norton & Company.
Ashbery, John. 1975. *Self-Portrait in a Convex Mirror.* New York: Viking Press.
———. 1985. *A Wave.* New York: Penguin Books.
———. 1992. *Hotel Lautrémont.* New York: Alfred A. Knopf.
Auerbach, Erich. 1953. *Mimesis: The Representation of Reality in Western Literature.* Princeton: Princeton University Press.
Bacon, Francis. 2005. *The Essays: or Counsels of Civil and Moral.* New York: Barnes and Noble Books.
Bersani, Leo. 1990. *The Culture of Redemption.* Cambridge: Harvard University Press.
Bloom, Harold. 1970. *Yeats.* Oxford: Oxford University Press.
———. 1988. *Poetics of Influence: New and Selected Criticism.* Edited with an introduction by John Hollander. New Haven: Henry R. Schwab.
———. 1989. *Ruin the Sacred Truths: Poetry and Belief from the Bible to the Present.* Cambridge: Harvard University Press.
———. 1994. *The Western Canon: The Books and Schools of the Ages.* New York: Harcourt Brace & Company.

———. 1998. *Shakespeare: The Invention of the Human*. New York: Riverhead Books.

———. 2011. *The Anatomy of Influence: Literature as a Way of Life*. New Haven: Yale University Press.

———. 2015. *The Daemon Knows: Literary Greatness and the American Sublime*. New York: Spiegel & Grau.

———. 2019. *Possessed by Memory*. New York: Alfred A. Knopf.

———. 2020. *Take Arms Against a Sea of Troubles: The Power of the Reader's Mind over a Universe of Death*. New Haven: Yale University Press.

Boulez, Pierre. 1975. *Boulez on Music Today*. Translated by Susan Bradshaw and Richard Rodney Bennet. London: Faber and Faber.

Burnham, Scott. 2013. *Mozart's Grace*. Princeton: Princeton University Press.

Butler, Gregory G. 1977. "Fugue and Rhetoric." *Journal of Music Theory* 21, no. 1 (spring 1977).

Anne Carson. 1986. *Eros: The Bittersweet*. Princeton: Princeton University Press.

———. 2003. *If Not, Winter: Fragments of Sappho*. New York: Vintage Books.

Cherlin, Michael. 2003. "Schoenberg's Music for the Theater." In *The Great Tradition and Its Legacy: The Evolution of Dramatic and Musical Theater in Austria and Central Europe*, edited by Michael Cherlin, Halina Filipowicz, and Richard L. Rudolph. New York: Berghahn Books, 2003.

———. 2007. *Schoenberg's Musical Imagination*. Cambridge: Cambridge University Press.

———. 2017. *Varieties of Musical Irony: From Mozart to Mahler*. Cambridge: Cambridge University Press.

Chua, Daniel K. 2017. *Beethoven & Freedom*. New York: Oxford University Press.

Clampitt, Amy. 1994. *A Silence Opens*. New York: Alfred A. Knopf.

Clayton, Martin R. L. 1996. "Free Rhythm: Ethnomusicology and the Study of Music Without Metre." *Bulletin of the School of Oriental and African Studies, University of London* 59, no. 2: 323–32.

Cohen-Solal, Annie. 2015. *Mark Rothko: Toward the Light in the Chapel*. New Haven: Yale University Press.

Cohn, Robert Greer. 1980. *Toward the Poems of Mallarmé*. Berkeley: University of California Press.

Cole, Peter. 2007. *The Dream of the Poem: Hebrew Poetry form Muslim and Christian Spain 950–492*. Princeton: Princeton University Press.

———. 2012. *The Poetry of Kabbalah: Mystical Verse from the Jewish Tradition*. Co-edited and with an afterword by Aminadav Dykman. New Haven: Yale University Press.

———. 2014. *The Invention of Influence*. Introduction by Harold Bloom. New York: A New Directions Book.

Constantine, David. 1988. *Hölderlin*. Oxford: Oxford University Press.

Crane, Hart. 2001. *The Complete Poems of Hart Crane*. Edited by Marc Simon, with an introduction by Harold Bloom. New York: Liveright.
Davis, Bret W. 2007. *Heidegger and the Will: On the Way to Gelassenheit*. Evanston: Northwestern University Press.
de Bolla, Peter. 1988. *Harold Bloom: Towards Historical Rhetorics*. Oxon: Routledge.
Deleuze, Gilles. 1994. *Difference and Repetition*. Translated by Paul Patton. New York: Columbia University Press.
Deleuze, Gilles, and Félix Guattari. 1987. *A Thousand Plateaus: Capitalism and Schizophrenia*. Translation and forward by Brian Massumi. Minneapolis: University of Minnesota Press.
Emerson, Ralph Waldo. 1983. *Ralph Waldo Emerson: Essays & Lectures*. Selected and annotated by Joel Porte. New York: The Library of America.
Ferneyhough, Brian. 1995. *Collected Essays*. Edited by James Boros and Richard Toop. London: Routledge.
Fletcher, Angus. 1964. *Allegory: The Theory of a Symbolic Mode*. Ithaca: Cornell University Press.
———. 1971. *The Prophetic Moment*. Chicago: University of Chicago Press.
———. 1991. *Colors of Mind: Conjectures on Thinking in Literature*. Cambridge: Harvard University Press.
———. 2004. *A New Theory for American Poetry: Democracy, the Environment, and the Future of Imagination*. Cambridge: Harvard University Press.
———. 2006. "Allegory without Ideas." *boundary 2: an international journal of literature and culture* 33, no. 1 (February): 77–98.
Fonseca-Wollheim, Corinna da. 2019. "How Silence Makes the Music: A Brief, Incomplete, Very Quiet Guide to the History of Music's Negative Spaces." https://www.nytimes.com/2019/10/02/arts/music/silence-classical-music.html.
Fox, Everett. 1995. *The Five Books of Moses*. New York: Schocken Books.
Gessen, Masha. 2017. *The Future Is History: How Totalitarianism Reclaimed Russia*. New York: Riverhead Books.
Gioia, Ted. 2006. *Work Songs*. Durham: Duke University Press.
Goodkin, Richard E. 1988. "Zeno's Paradox: Mallarmé, Valéry, and the Symbolist 'Movement.'" *Yale French Studies* 74: 133–56.
Goodman, Nelson. 1976. *Languages of Art: An Approach to a Theory of Symbols*. Indianapolis: Hackett Publishing Company.
Green, Arthur. 2003. *Arthur Green, אהיה Eyeh: A Kabbalah for Tomorrow*. Jewish Lights Publishing.
———. 2004. *A Guide to the Zohar*. Stanford: Stanford University Press.
Harshav. Benjamin. 1999. *The Meaning of Yiddish*. Stanford: Stanford University Press.
Harshav, Benjamin, and Barbara Harshav. 2007. *American Yiddish Poetry: A Bilingual Anthology*. Stanford: Stanford University Press.

Heartz, Daniel. 1990. "An Iconography of the Dances in the Ballroom Scene of *Don Giovanni*." In *Mozart's Operas*. Berkeley: University of California Press.

Heidegger, Martin. 1976. *Being and Time: A Translation of "Sein und Zeit."* Translated by John Macquarrie and Edward Robinson. New York: Harper & Row.

———. 2016. *Country Path Conversations*. Translated by Bret W. Davis. Bloomington: Indiana University Press.

Hölderlin, Friedrich. 1984. *Hymns and Fragments by Friedrich Hölderlin*, translated and introduced by Richard Sieburth. Princeton: Princeton University Press.

Hollander, John. 1981. *The Figure of Echo: A Mode of Allusion in Milton and After*. Berkeley: University of California Press.

———. 1985. *Vision and Resonance: Two Senses of Poetic Form*. 2nd ed. New Haven: Yale University Press.

———. 1988. *Harp Lake*. New York: Alfred A. Knopf, 1988.

———. 1993. *Tesserae & Other Poems*. New York: Alfred A. Knopf.

———. 2000. *Rhyme's Reason: A Guide to English Verse*. 3rd edition. New Haven: Yale University Press.

Howe, Irving. 1987. *The Penguin Book of Modern Yiddish Verse*. Edited by Irving Howe, Ruth R. Wisse, and Khone Shmeruk. New York: Penguin Books.

Idel, Moshe. 1988. *Kabbalah: New Perspectives*. New Haven: Yale University Press.

———. 2002. *Absorbing Perfections: Kabbalah and Interpretation*. New Haven: Yale University Press.

Ihde, Don. 1976. *Listening and Voice: A Phenomenology of Sound*. Athens: Ohio University Press.

Johnson, Julian. 1999. *Webern and the Transformation of Nature*. Cambridge: Cambridge University Press.

Johnson, Steven. 1964. "*Rothko Chapel* and Rothko's Chapel," *Perspectives of New Music* 32, no. 2 (summer): 6–53.

Kafka, Franz. 1975. *Parables and Paradoxes: Bilingual Edition*. Translation by Willa and Edwin Muir. New York: Schocken Books.

Kleinberg, Ethan. 2021. *Emmanuel Levinas's Talmudic Turn*. Stanford: Stanford University Press.

Korsyn, Kevin. 2003. *Decentering Music: A Critique of Contemporary Musical Research*. Oxford: Oxford University Press.

Langer, Susanne. 1953. *Feeling and Form*. New York: Charles Scribner's Sons.

Llewelyn, John. 1991. *The Middle Voice of Ecological Conscience*. New York: Palgrave Macmillan.

Levinas, Emmanuel. 1969. *Totality and Infinity: An Essay on Interiority*. Translated by Alphonso Lingis. Pittsburgh: Duquesne University Press.

———. 1989. *The Levinas Reader*. Edited by Seán Hand. Cambridge, MA: Blackwell.

———. 1990a. *Difficult Freedom: Essays on Judaism*. Translated by Seán Hand. Baltimore: Johns Hopkins University Press.

———. 1990b. *Nine Talmudic Readings*. Translated and with an introduction by Annette Aronowicz. Bloomington: Indiana University Press.
———. 1994. *Outside the Subject*. Translated by Michael B. Smith. Stanford: Stanford University Press.
———. 1998a. *Otherwise Than Being, or Beyond Essence*. Translated by Alphonso Lingis. Pittsburgh: Duquesne University Press.
———. 1998b. *Of God Who Comes to Mind*. Translated by Bettina Bergo. Stanford: Stanford University Press.
———. 2002. *The Cambridge Companion to* Levinas. Cambridge: Cambridge University Press.
Lewin, David. 1986. "Music Theory, Phenomenology, and Modes of Perception." *Music Perception: An Interdisciplinary Journal* 3, no. 4 (summer): 327–92.
———. 1987. *Generalized Musical Intervals and Transformations*. New Haven: Yale University Press. Reissued with a forward by Edward Gollin, Oxford University Press, 2007.
———. 2006. *Studies in Music with Text*. Oxford: Oxford University Press.
Lockwood, Lewis. 2003. *Beethoven: The Music and Life*. New York: W. W. Norton & Company.
Longfellow, Henry Wadsworth. 2000. *Henry Wadsworth Longfellow: Poems and Other Writings*. Selected and annotated by J. D. McClatchy. New York: The Library of America.
Mallarmé, Stéphane. 1994. *Stéphane Mallarmé: Collected Poems*. Translated with a commentary by Henry Weinfield. Berkeley: University of California Press.
Matt, Daniel C. 2004. *The Zohar*. Vol. 1. Translation and commentary by Daniel C. Matt. Stanford: Stanford University Press.
McClary, Susan. 2000. *Conventional Wisdom: The Content of Musical Form*. Berkeley: University of California Press.
Meir, Ephraim. 2010. "Judaism and Philosophy: Each Other's Other in Levinas." *Modern Judaism* 30, no. 3: 348–62.
Merleau-Ponty, Maurice. 1968. *The Visible and the Invisible*. Evanston: Northwestern University Press.
———. 2012. *Phenomenology of Perception*. Translated by Donald A. Landes. London: Routledge.
Menocal, María Rosa. 1994. *Shards of Love: Exile and the Origins of the Lyric*. Durham: Duke University Press
Merrill, James. 2001. *Collected Poems*. Edited by J. D. McClatchy and Stephen Yenser. New York: Alfred A. Knopf.
Moss, Stanley. 2016. *Almost Complete Poems*. New York: Seven Stories Press.
Nadler, Steven, ed. 2014. *Spinoza and Medieval Jewish Philosophy*. Cambridge: Cambridge University Press.

Nancy, Jean-Luc. 2000. *Being Singular Plural*. Translated by Robert D. Richardson and Anne E. O'Byrne. Stanford: Stanford University Press.
Neugroschel, Joachim. 1998. *Dybbuk and Other Tales of the Supernatural*. Adapted and translated from S. Ansky by Tony Kushner and Joachim Neugroschel. New York: Theatre Communications Group.
Olivelle, Patrick. 2008. *Upanisads*. Oxford: Oxford University Press.
Paglia, Camille. 1990. *Sexual Personae: Art and Decadence from Nefertiti to Emily Dickinson*. New Haven: Yale University Press.
Pater, Walter. 1974. *Selected Writings of Walter Pater*. Edited with an introduction and notes by Harold Bloom. New York: Columbia University Press.
Plato. 1991. *The Symposium*. Translated with comment by R. E. Allen. New Haven: Yale University Press.
Rahaim, Matthew. 2012. *Musicking Bodies: Gesture and Voice in Hindustani Music*. Middletown: Wesleyan University Press.
Rahn, John. 2004. 2004. "The Swerve and the Flow: Music's Relationship to Mathematics." *Perspectives of New Music* 42, no. 1 (winter): 130–50.
Ricoeur, Paul. 1992. *Oneself as Another*. Chicago: University of Chicago Press.
Rings, Steven. 2011. *Tonality and Transformation*. Oxford: Oxford University Press.
Safina, Carl. 2020. *Becoming Wild: How Animal Cultures Raise Families, Create Beauty, and Achieve Peace*. New York: Picador, Henry Holt and Company.
Schama, Simon. 1988. *The Embarrassment of Riches: An Interpretation of Dutch Culture in the Golden Age*. Berkeley: University of California Press.
Schoenberg, Arnold. 1967. *Fundamentals of Musical Composition*. Edited by Gerald Strang and Leonard Stein. New York: St. Martin's Press.
Scholem, Gershom. 1969. *On the Kabbalah and Its Symbolism*. Translated by Ralph Manheim. New York: Schocken Books.
Schulman, Grace. 2002. *Days of Wonder: New and Selected Poems*. New York: Houghton Mifflin Company.
Shiloah, Amnon. 1978. "The Symbolism of Music in the Kabbalistic Tradition." *The World of Music* 20, no. 3.
———. 2007. *Music and Its Virtues in Islamic and Judaic Writings*. London: Routledge.
Jeremy Sigler, "The Kabbalah of Rothko." https://tabletmag.com/sections/arts-letters/articles/the-kabbalh-of-rothko.
Spicer, Mark. 2009. "Strategic Intertextuality in Three of John Lennon's Late Beatles Songs." *Gamut: Online Journal of the Music Theory Society of the Mid-Atlantic* 2: 347–76.
Stein, David E. Sulomm, managing ed. 1999. *JPS Hebrew-English Tanakh*. Philadelphia: Jewish Publication Society.
Steinbock, Anthony J. 2007. *Phenomenology and Mysticism: The Verticality of Religious Experience*. Bloomington: Indiana University Press.

Stevens, Wallace. 1951. *The Necessary Angel: Essays on Reality and the Imagination.* New York: Vintage Books.

———. 1971. *The Palm at the End of the Mind.* Edited by Holly Stevens. New York: Alfred A. Knopf.

———. 1989. *Opus Posthumous.* Edited by Milton J. Bates. New York: Alfred A. Knopf.

Treitler, Leo. *Music and the Historical Imagination.* 1989. Cambridge: Harvard University Press.

Tymoczko, Dmitri. 2009. "Generalizing Musical Intervals." *Journal of Music Theory* 53, no. 2: 227–54.

Valéry, Paul. 1070. *Collected Works of Paul Valéry, Volume 14: Analects.* Translated by Stuart Gilbert. Princeton: Princeton University Press.

———. 1977. *An Anthology.* Selected and introduced by James R. Lawler. Bollingen Series XLV. Princeton: Princeton University Press.

———. 1989. *Dialogues.* Edited by Jackson Mathews. Bollingen Series XLV. Princeton: Princeton University Press.

Vendler, Helen. 2010. *Dickinson: Selected Poems and Commentaries.* Cambridge: The Belknap Press of Harvard University Press.

Warren, Roseanna. 2020. *So Forth: Poems.* New York: W. W. Norton & Company.

Weir, William. 2014. "A Little Bit Softer Now, a Little Bit Softer Now . . . The Sad, Gradual Decline of the Fade-out in Popular Music." https://slate.com/culture/2014/09/the-fade-out-in-pop-music-why-dont-modern-pop-songs-end-by-slowly-reducing-in-volume.html.

Weiskel, Thomas. 2019. *The Romantic Sublime: Studies in the Structure and Psychology of Transcendence.* Baltimore: Johns Hopkins University Press.

White, Hayden. 2010. *The Fiction of Narrative: Essays on History, Literature, and Theory, 1957–2007.* Baltimore: Johns Hopkins University Press.

Whitman, Walt. 1961. *Leaves of Grass: Facsimile Edition of the 1860 Text,* with an introduction by Roy Harvey Pearce. Ithaca: Cornell University Press.

———. 1982. *Walt Whitman: Complete Poetry and Collected Prose.* Selected, with notes and chronology by Justin Kaplan. New York: The Library of America.

Wisse, Ruth R. 2000. *The Modern Jewish Canon: A Journey Through Language and Culture.* New York: The Free Press.

Wright, Charles. 2004. *Buffalo Yoga.* New York: Farrar, Straus, and Giroux.

Wyschogrod, Edith. 1999. "Emmanuel Levinas and Hillel's Questions." In *Postmodern Philosophy and Christian Thought,* edited by Merold Westphal, 229–45. Bloomington: Indiana University Press.

Yeats, William Butler. 1990. *The Collected Works of W. B. Yeats: The Poems.* New York: Macmillan Publishing Company.

Zahavi, Dan. 2003. *Husserl's Phenomenology.* Stanford: Stanford University Press.

Index

Abrams, M. H., 246
Abulafia, Avraham, 92–93
Adorno, Theodor, 24, 191–192, 246
Agawu, Kofi, 252
Agrarian Space, xxvi, 177–181, 190, 194–195, 217, 220, 242
Allanbrook, Wye, 76–77, 203, 253
Allen, R. E., 234, 266
Alpern, Wayne, 16, 245, 264
Alter, Robert, 239–240, 266
Ammons, Archie R., 120, 127, 202, 256
Ansky, S., 159, 259
Arditti, Irving, 172
Ashbery, John, xxv, 39, 46, 102, 120, 122–129, 183, 185, 202, 216, 241, 249, 256
Auden, W. H., 158
Auerbach, Erich, 161, 260

Babbitt, Milton, 2, 3, 202, 207
Bach, Johann Sabastian, 11, 32, 70, 79, 81, 106–107, 156, 193, 236, 238
Bacon, Francis, 82, 253
Baqlī, Rūzbinān, 224
Beatles, xxvi, 32, 35, 78, 86, 109, 134, 193, 262
Beckett, Samuel, 104, 193–194
Beethoven, Ludwig van, xxv, 16, 24, 31, 32, 41, 43, 46, 57, 70, 72, 79, 81, 84, 86, 87, 90, 107, 109, 116, 136–137, 143, 152, 156, 172–173, 188, 212, 214, 235, 249–250, 252, 255, 258
Benjamin, Walter, 130, 257
Berg, Alban, 2, 143, 157
Berio, Luciano, 155, 193–194
Bernstein, Leonard, 153
Bersani, Leo, 182, 261
Bloom, Harold, xxiii, xxiv, xxviii, 2, 38–39, 48, 55, 65–109, 131, 163, 168, 190, 210, 211, 216, 218, 230, 239, 241, 242
Boulez, Pierre, xxvi, 177–182, 184, 186, 242, 260
Brahms, Johannes, xiii, xxv, 24, 32, 40, 44, 46, 81, 86, 139, 140–143, 152, 153, 156, 188, 216, 239
Bṛhadāraṇyaka Upaniṣad, xxii, 13–14, 21, 27, 245
Bricolage, 193–194
Bruns, Gerald L., 57, 251
Buber, Martin, 62–63, 82
Burmeister, Joachim, 105–106, 255
Burnham, Scott, 39, 141, 229, 258, 265
Butler, Gregory G., 255

Caesura, xxv, 94, 132–135, 150, 160, 237, 245

Caplin, William E., 255
Carson, Anne, 240, 266
Carter, Elliott, 76, 81, 84, 155
Chalier, Catherine, 51, 250
Chlup, Radek, 245
Chopin, Frederick, 85
Chua, Daniel, 249–250, 263–264
Clampitt, Amy, 28–29, 268
Clayton, Martin R. L., 153–154, 259
Cluster (as singular-plural), xxvi, 185, 194–196, 220–221, 232, 236
Cohen-Solal, Annie, 165, 260
Cohn, Robert Greer, 262
Cole, Peter, xxviii, 22, 69, 92–94, 239, 246, 248, 253
Coltrane, John, xx, 41, 74, 86, 89
Constantine, David, 266
Contre-rejet, 17, 133, 245
Cortot, Alfred, 79, 85
Crane, Hart, 69, 95, 172, 260
Critchley, Simon, 53
Czernowin, Chaya, 174

Daemon, demon 181, 190–191
Dante Alighieri, 82, 102–104, 155, 202–203, 211, 254
Darcy, Warren, 261
Davis, Bret W., 35–36, 246
Davis, Miles, xx, 31, 86, 89
De Bolla, Peter, 79
Debussy, Claude, xxvi, xxvii, 42, 86, 179, 188, 191, 198–202, 239, 240, 262, 264
Dehmel, Richard, 198–199
Deleuze, Gilles, xix, xxvi, xxvii, 177–179, 181–184, 186–187, 191, 194–195, 204–209, 214, 217, 242, 261, 263
Derrida, Jacques, xxii, 26–27
Descartes, René, 3–4, 98, 117–118, 222
des Prez, Josquin, 155
Dickens, Charles, 74–75

Dickinson, Emily, 17, 70, 237, 245, 265
Dillon, James, xxv–xxvi, 81, 88, 159–160, 163, 167–174, 251, 260
Diotima, 234, 237–239
Durchbruch, 191, 194
Dylan, Bob, 78, 79, 85, 86, 231–232

Emergence, x, xix, xxi–xxii, 16–17, 22, 136–137, 156, 158–163, 214–215
Emerson, Ralph Waldo, vi, xix, 38, 70–73, 80, 94, 95, 124, 210, 230, 241, 243, 248, 252
Erdman, David V., 66
Eros, xxviii, 39, 93, 199–201, 203, 208–209, 231–241, 266
Errant thread, xxvi, 185, 187–190, 227

Faulkner, William, 10, 71
Feldman, Morton, 159, 163, 165–167, 260
Felt (fabric), xxvi, 186–187
Ferneyhough, Brian, xxv, 40, 46, 81, 122–123, 125–132, 142–143, 159, 183, 185, 202, 206–208, 216, 241, 256–258
Fiction (Music as), xvii, xxii, 9–12, 87, 185, 236, 241–242
Fletcher, Angus, xxiv, 37–38, 41–42, 66, 95, 100, 119, 171, 181–183, 241
Fonseca-Wollheim, Corinna da, 139, 258
Ford, Phil, ix–xiii, xvi, xxiii, xxix
Fox, Everett, 59, 161–162, 245, 260
Freud, Sigmund, xxiii, 40, 44–45, 66, 82–83, 95–96, 208, 213, 233–234, 247

Geertz, Clifford, xxvii, 220–221, 264
Gelassenheit, xxii, 34–35, 230, 248
Gershwin, George, 76, 89, 135, 153
Gessen, Masha, 71, 252

Gioia, Ted, xxviii, 226–228, 265
Goodkin, Richard E., 123, 256
Goodman, Nelson, xix, 244
Gopinath, Sumanth, 253, 265
Gould, Glenn, 79
Grace, 39, 57, 85, 141, 152, 224, 228, 229–231
Green, Arthur, xxvi, xxvii, 19–20, 192, 195–196, 209–210, 245, 246, 263
Guattari, Félix, xxvi, 177–179, 182–187, 191, 194–195, 217, 261

Hammerstein, Oscar, xxvii, 88, 89, 197–198
Hatten, Robert, 252
Hanslick, Eduard, 56–57
Harshav, Benjamin, 246
Heartz, Daniel, 252
Heidegger, Martin, xix, xxii, 21, 25, 27, 31, 34–36, 48, 50, 53–55, 80, 82, 95, 230, 237, 246, 248
Heine, Heinrich, 39, 135
Henderson, Joe, xx, 84
Hendrix, Jimi, 34, 79, 85, 86, 106, 109
Hepokoski, James, 261
Higgins, Kathleen Marie, 253
Hineni (here I am), 47, 51, 60, 163, 202, 224, 250
Hölderlin, Friedrich, 54, 168, 234–238, 266
Hollander, John, xxiii, xxiv, 28, 67–68, 100–102, 105–106, 120, 124, 132–133, 135, 140–141, 158–159, 210, 215–216, 241, 245, 247, 254, 255, 256, 258, 259
Homer, 28, 55, 81, 102–104, 107, 161, 218, 227, 254
Horizontal and Vertical, xxvii–xxviii, 30, 217–231, 241
Huron, David, 138
Husserl, Edmund, xix, xxii, 25, 26, 27–29, 31, 34, 48, 50, 54, 247

Ibn Gabirol, Shelomo, 22, 246
Idel, Moshe, 92–93, 175, 239, 246, 260
Ihde, Don, xxii, 31–32, 248
Irwin, John T., 69
Isaiah, 13, 102, 104, 107, 254

James, Henry, 70, 210
Johnson, Julian, 156–158, 259
Joyce, James, 10

Kabbalah, xviii, xxii, xxviii, 18–23, 27, 42, 69, 89–90, 92–94, 99, 125, 164, 191–192, 195–196, 209–210, 234, 237, 239, 241, 245, 246, 253, 254, 260, 262, 263
Kafka, Franz, xxiii, 40, 52, 232, 266
Keinehora, 98
Kleiber, Carlos, 97
Kleinberg, Ethan, 47–48, 249
Korsyn, Kevin, 244, 246, 247, 254
Kuh, Katherine, 165
Kunitz, Stanley, 164–165, 260

Lachenmann, Helmut, 40, 84
Langer, Susanne, xix, xxvii, 202–204, 263
Lasso (Lassus), Orlando di, 105–106
Lennon, John, 193, 262
Levinas, Emmanuel, xix, xxiii–xxiv, xxviii, 26, 29, 36, 47–63, 71, 72, 82, 93, 95, 100, 118, 130, 131, 163–165, 169, 182, 224–225, 230, 241, 247, 248, 249–251
Lewin, David Benjamin, xxi, xxiv, xxvii, 1–6, 16, 32, 36, 41, 53, 65, 68, 99–100, 117–118, 131–132, 171, 212–213, 215, 242, 243, 244, 254, 255, 264
Lichtung, 35, 237
Liminal, xxi, xxiii, 37–46, 56–57, 60–62, 91–96, 99, 119, 131–132, 170–171, 201, 236, 242

Llewelyn, John, 26, 247
Lockwood, Lewis, 266
Longfellow, Henry Wadsworth, 148–149, 254, 258
Lyotard, Jean-François, 262

Mahler, Gustav, xxii, xxv, xxvi, 24, 86, 108, 137, 143–145, 157–158, 166, 172–173, 180, 188, 191–194, 234, 238, 246, 262
Mallarmé, Stéphane, 123, 152, 198–200, 256, 262
Martin, Dean, 78
Massumi, Brian, 261
McClary, Susan, 240
Melville, Herman, 70, 219, 226
Menocal, María Rosa, 89–90, 253
Mensural notation, 155, 259
Merleau-Ponty, Maurice, xix, xxii, xxvii, 25, 29–31, 127, 220–222, 247, 265
Merrill, James, 233, 266
Metalepsis (transumption), xxiv, 36, 99–109, 131, 137, 145, 216
Meter, metric, xxiv–xxv, 116–119, 121–122, 147–158, 181, 233, 256, 257, 258, 259
Middle voice, xii, xix, xxi–xxii, xxix, 25–27, 29–30, 34, 49, 52, 62, 77, 94, 95, 118, 145, 148, 149–150, 183–184, 194, 198, 241, 247, 263, 270
Milton, John, 83, 101–104, 107, 159, 254
Moevs, Robert, 84
Monelle, Raymond, 76, 252
Montaigne, Michel de, 38
Morris, Robert, 3
Morrison, Toni, 10, 71, 73–74
Moss, Stanley, 226, 265
Musical Interval, xxiv, 3, 5, 76, 114–115, 117–118, 144, 170, 178, 186, 201, 212, 243, 255

Musical phrase, xxiv, xxv, 76, 113–116, 119, 121, 132, 133–135, 150–152, 179, 186, 190, 200–201, 220, 255
Mozart, Wolfgang Amadeus, 32, 39–40, 53, 67, 70, 75, 76, 81, 83–84, 86, 115, 116, 134, 141, 152, 215, 216, 225, 229, 249, 258, 265
Muwashshaḥāt, 89–90

Nachträglichkeit, 45, 213
Neoplatonism, xxii, 15–16, 23, 157, 245
Nijinsky, Vaslav, 201
Niphal, 94–95, 254
Nomadic Space, xxvi, 177, 181–182, 184, 186–188, 190–191, 193–195, 217, 220, 242
Nono, Luigi, 81, 90, 234–239, 266

Ockeghem, Johannes, 155
Olivelle, Patrick, 245
Orpheus, 158, 233

Paglia, Camille, xxvii, 203–204, 263
Parmigianino, Francesco, 124–126
Patchwork quilt, xxvi, 187–188, 193
Pater, Walter, 114, 185, 255, 261
Peacham, Henry, 102
Picker, Martin, 84
Plotinus, 15
Proclus, 15, 245
Proximity (in Levinas), xxiii–xxiv, 61–62, 93, 130, 241
Putnam, Hillary, 50, 62–63, 250

Qelippot, 192

Rabbi Akiva, vi, 239, 242
Rabbi Dov Baer ('the Mitteler"), 224
Rabbi Hillel, 23–24, 50–51, 72, 223, 250
Rahaim, Matthew, xxix, 32–33, 247, 248, 259

Rahn, John, 16, 245
Ratner, Leonard, 76
Redding, Otis, 32, 33, 86, 149
Repetition (in music, in poetry), xxvi, xxvii, 106, 141, 148–149, 197–215, 260, 261, 263
Richardson, Ralph, 78
Ricoeur, Paul, 16, 206, 245, 250, 253, 263
Rings, Steven, 243
Rorty, Richard, xix, 135
Rosen, Charles, 261
Rothko, Mark (Marcus Rotkovitch), xxv, 163–167, 260
Rothstein, William, 255
Rubato, xxv, 152
Rylance, Mark, 78–79

Safina, Carl, xv, 243
Sanguineti, Edoardo, 155
Schama, Simon, 256
Schenker, Heinrich, xxii, 15–16, 40, 245
Schmelz, Peter, 263
Schoenberg, Arnold, xviii, xxiii, xxv, xxvi, 1–2, 11, 24, 32, 40, 45, 68, 81, 83, 86, 107–108, 115, 142, 143, 154, 156–158, 166, 174, 188, 191, 198–199, 216, 236, 249, 253, 255, 256, 259, 260, 262
Scholem, Gershom, 22, 89–90, 168, 192, 245, 246, 253, 262
Schubert, Franz, 4, 11, 34, 39, 40, 43, 81, 135, 141, 143, 166, 216, 236, 244, 252
Schulman, Grace, xvi, 135, 243, 258
Sciarrino, Salvatore, 132, 257
Sefirot, xxii, xxvi, 18–21, 23, 92, 195–196, 237, 245, 246
Shakespeare, William, xx, xxvii, 10, 48, 71, 74–75, 77–78, 82–83, 113, 151, 189, 210–211, 214, 233, 239, 240, 252

Shelley, Percy Bysshe, 60, 70, 72, 85, 104
Shiloah, Amnon, 93, 230–231, 254, 265
Sholem Aleichem, 23–24, 246
Sieburth, Richard, 237, 266
Sigler, Jeremy, 164, 260
Silence, xxiv–xxv, xxvi, 28–29, 42, 57, 121–122, 124–125, 132–143, 150, 154–164, 166–167, 170–175, 233–234, 236–237, 241–242, 245, 247, 258
Smooth space, xxvi, 177–185, 186–187, 192, 194, 217
Sophocles, 83, 168
Spenser, Edmund, 35, 37, 42, 187
Spicer, Mark, 193, 262
Spots of time, 43–45, 141, 213
St. Teresa of Avila, 224
Stanyek, Jason, 152
Steinbock, Anthony, xxvii–xxviii, 222–225, 230, 265
Stevens, Wallace, 10, 38, 55, 56, 95, 104, 244, 248, 254
Straus, Joseph N., 254
Stravinsky, Igor, 32, 154, 156
Striated space, xxvi, 177–185, 187–189, 192–195, 217

Talmudic Judaism, 16, 47–48, 51, 59, 72, 165, 174–175, 249, 250, 251
Tchaikovsky, Pyotr Ilyich, 87, 139
Temporal vectors, xxvi, xxvii, 210, 211–213, 215–216
Tymoczko, Dmitri, 243
Transumption (metalepsis). *See* Metalepsis
Treitler, Leo, 136, 258
Trope, xxiii, xxiv, 42, 79–80, 97–108, 137, 184, 207, 219

Valéry, Paul, xxiii, 37, 55–57, 58, 61–62, 67, 87, 123, 248, 251, 256, 262
Vendler, Helen, 17, 245, 265

Verdi, Giuseppe, 75, 88, 133–134, 149–151, 188–189, 193, 239
Vertical. *See* Horizontal and vertical
Virgil (Publius Vergilius Maro), 102–104, 254

Wagner, Richard, 24, 32, 156, 174, 188, 216, 232
Wave (as musical metaphor), xxiv–xxv, 46, 119–132, 138, 140, 142–145, 149–150, 160, 166, 173, 183, 185, 194, 201, 202, 206, 216, 241, 256
Webern, Anton, xxv, 138, 143, 154–159, 161, 163, 166, 180, 236, 259
Weinfield, Henry, 199–200, 262
Weir, William, 138–139, 258
Weiskel, Thomas, 43–46, 141, 249

Western Canon, xxi, xxiv, 43, 63, 65, 80–91, 109, 239, 240, 253
Whitman, Walt, xxiv, xxv, 70, 104, 119–122, 124, 149, 160–161, 163, 183, 185, 259
Wilson, Paul, xxviii, 55
Wisse, Ruth R., 246
Wittgenstein, Ludwig, 83
Wordsworth, William, 43–46, 70, 141–142, 213, 249
Work Songs, 225–229
Wright, Charles, 37

Xenakis, Iannis, 57, 178

Yeats, William Butler, 218–219, 264

Zahavi, Dan, 27, 247